Cambridge Studies in Modern Political Economie
Editors
SUZANNE BERGER, ALBERT O. HIRSCHMAN, and CI

Political parties: organization and power

The "classical" scholars who wrote about political parties – Ostrogorsky, Michels, Weber, Duverger – conceived of them as being above all *organizations*, arguing that in order to understand and explain their activities and transformations, it was necessary to analyze their organizational core. This perspective was abandoned by later scholars, but in this innovative book, Angelo Panebianco takes it up again, and, with the benefit of recent advances in organizational studies, extends it to offer new insights into the functioning of political parties.

Making use of several different social scientific disciplinary traditions, Panebianco develops an original framework for the analysis of political parties. He formulates a wide-ranging theory of the "organizational development" of parties, paying particular attention to their internal power conflicts, on the basis of which he elaborates a general interpretive scheme for the analysis of party change. He also presents new hypotheses on the relations between parties and their environment, on bureaucratization, and on the role of ideology. He tests these theories through an historical comparative analysis of European political parties, re-examining their history in the light of his theoretical concerns.

As a fresh treatment of a central issue in political science, this distinctive and significant contribution to the theory of political parties will appeal widely to political scientists and sociologists, while its extensive and balanced discussion of other works on the subject, albeit in the context of its own argument, make it also a valuable resource for students.

Other books in this series

Suzanne Berger (editor): *Organizing interests in Western Europe: pluralism, corporatism, and the transformation of politics*

Charles F. Sabel: *Work and politics: the division of labor in industry*

Judith Chubb: *Patronage, power, and poverty in southern Italy: a tale of two cities*

Charles S. Maier (editor): *The changing boundaries of the political*

Political parties: organization and power

ANGELO PANEBIANCO
Professor of Comparative Politics, University of Bologna

TRANSLATED BY MARC SILVER

The right of the
University of Cambridge
to print and sell
all manner of books
was granted by
Henry VIII in 1534.
The University has printed
and published continuously
since 1584.

Cambridge University Press
Cambridge
New York   New Rochelle   Melbourne   Sydney

Published by the Press Syndicate of the University of Cambridge
The Pitt Building, Trumpington Street, Cambridge CB2 1RP
32 East 57th Street, New York, NY 10022, USA
10 Stamford Road, Oakleigh, Melbourne 3166, Australia

Originally published in Italian as *Modelli di partito: Organizzazione e potere nei partiti politici* by Il Mulino, Bologna, 1982, and © Società editrice il Mulino, Bologna, 1982

First published in English by Cambridge University Press, 1988
as *Political Parties: organization and power*.
English translation © Cambridge University Press, 1988

Printed in Great Britain by Billing & Sons Ltd, Worcester

British Library cataloguing in publication data
Panebianco, Angelo
   Political parties: organization and power.
   – (Cambridge studies in modern political economies).
   1. political parties
   I. Title II. Modelli di partito. *English*
   324.2   JF2051

Library of Congress cataloguing in publication data
Panebianco, Angelo.
   [Modelli di partito. English]
   Political parties: organization and power/Angelo Panebianco:
translated by Marc Silver.
   p. cm. – (Cambridge studies in modern political economies)
   Translation of Modelli di partito.
   Bibliography.
   ISBN 0 521 30627–2. ISBN 0 521 31401 1 (pbk.)
   1. political parties. 2. Politics. Practical. I. Title.
II. Series.
JF2051.P2613 1987
324–dc19   87–27724 CIP

ISBN 0 521 30627 2 hard covers
ISBN 0 521 31401 1 paperback

To my father and my mother

Contents

	page
Acknowledgements	x
Preface	xi

Part I Organizational order — 1

1 Organizational dilemmas — 3
Organizational dilemmas — 6
The articulation of ends — 15
A model of organizational evolution — 17

2 Power, incentives, participation — 21
Believers and careerists — 25
Incentives and unequal exchange — 30

3 Dominant coalition and organizational stability — 33
The dominant coalition — 37
Legitimacy — 40
Organizational stability — 42
Conclusion — 44

Part II Organizational development — 47

4 Institutionalization — 49
The genetic model — 50
Institutionalization — 53
Strong and weak institutions: two ideal types — 60
Genetic model and institutionalization: a typology — 63
Personal charisma: a deviant case — 65
Conclusion — 67

5 Oppositional parties (1) — 69
The German Social Democratic Party — 70
The French Communist Party — 78

viii   Contents

      The Italian Communist Party — 82
      Conclusions — 85

6 Oppositional parties (2) — 88
      The British Labour Party — 88
      The French section of the Workers' International — 95
      The Italian Socialist Party — 102
      Conclusion — 110

7 Governmental parties — 113
      The Christian-Democratic Union — 115
      The Italian Christian Democrats — 123
      The British Conservative Party — 130
      Conclusion — 141

8 Charismatic parties — 143
      The Union for the New Republic — 147
      The German National Socialist Party — 155
      Conclusion — 160

9 Organizational order: a typology — 163
      The organizational evolution of political parties — 164
      Dominant coalition conformation: cohesion and stability — 168
      The dominant coalition's own conformation: the map of organizational power (1) — 173
      The dominant coalition's own conformation: the map of organizational power (2) — 176
      Conclusion — 179

Part III Structural contingencies — 181

10 Size and organizational complexity — 183
      Party size — 185
      Size as independent variable — 186
      Size as a dependent variable — 190
      Organizational thresholds — 193
      The size of sub-units — 195
      Complexity and electoral control — 199
      Electoral systems — 202
      Conclusion — 203

11 Organization and environment — 204
      Environmental characteristics — 204
      Party environments: arenas — 207
      The electoral arena — 208
      Electoral and parliamentary arenas: interdependence — 214
      Opposition and competition: the politics of alliance — 217

		Contents	ix
12	Political and bureaucratic professionalism		220
	Political and bureaucratic professionalism		221
	Party bureaucracy: definitions		222
	Bureaucracy and political attitudes		226
	Experts and hidden professionals		229
	Bureaucratization and professionalism		231
	Executives and professionals: a classification		232

Part IV Organizational change — 237

13	Environmental challenges and elite circulation	239
	Evolutionism versus 'political development'	239
	Intentionality and non-intentionality	240
	Exogenous versus endogenous origins	242
	Change in political parties	243
	Extent of change: amalgamation and circulation	247
	Organizational change: some examples	250
	Bad Godesberg: the succession of ends	253
	The CDN: from electoral party to mass organization	257
	Conclusion	260
14	Parties and democracy: transformation and crisis	262
	Mass bureaucratic parties and electoral–professional parties	262
	Party crisis	267
	Changes in political cleavages	269
	Conclusion	273

Notes — 275
Index — 315

Acknowledgements

I am grateful to many colleagues for the important criticisms and suggestions they made concerning the individual chapters and the work as a whole. In particular, I would like to thank Carlo Carboni, Ugo Mancini, Arturo Parisi, Paolo Pombeni, Roberto Ruffilli, Stefano Zan and Peter Lange.

A special thanks goes to Gianfranco Pasquino for his critical comments and for his painstaking reading of the earlier drafts of the work.

I would finally like to thank the Ford Foundation which gave me the opportunity to carry out further research in the stimulating environment of Harvard University.

Preface

This book is not the result of empirical research even though in recent years I have been working in the field of political parties. It is instead a systematic effort to isolate, by means of interpretive tools pertaining to different disciplinary traditions, some of the basic factors explaining party politics.

The history of scientific research on parties at some point experienced a break, research took a different, partly new, direction. The "classical" authors, the founding fathers of studies in this specific field (from Ostrogorski to Weber, Michels and Duverger), dealt with political parties and their activities from the standpoint of their organizational "core." Their starting point was the idea of parties as organizations, to be studied in their organizational dynamics. The last thirty years, however, have seen a shift in the focus of political and sociological research on parties. Increasingly refined and precise techniques have been used, increasingly persuasive theories have thrown further light on the study of electoral dynamics, of the functioning of state institutions as influenced by parties, and of the relations between parties and social classes. As the systemic approach (in its broadest sense) became dominant amongst social scientists, party systems became more important than individual parties in the ranking of the scholars' interests. The understanding of political processes has thus gone a long way forward. However, something has been lost: namely the awareness that whatever else parties are and to whatever other solicitations they respond, they are above all organizations and that organizational analysis must therefore come before any other perspective. It is puzzling that all this occurred just as the study of complex organizations, starting more or less at the end of World War II, experienced a change in quality. A large number of organizations of all types have since been put to the empirical test; and a large number of models and quasi-theories have been proposed to explain the functioning and activity of organizations. Little innovation, however, has characterized the organizational theory of parties; it has remained ostensibly unchanged since the works of Michels and Duverger. But Michels and Duverger were quite aware of the organizational knowledge of their time: for example, Michels makes use, in his model, of a simplified version of Weber's theory of bureaucracy. Contemporary political scientists and sociologists concerned with political parties, when and if they take these aspects into consideration, often seem to ignore the results and developments of organizational disciplines.

This book can therefore be read as an attempt to bring back to center stage what has been stored in a dusty corner, forgotten by most researchers.

It is my conviction that the comparative theory of party systems has been very fruitful. But I'm just as convinced that the many hazy areas left by this theory can be clarified only if a serious return is made to the study of parties from the standpoint of their internal organizational dynamics.

In the theory of complex organizations, as in any other branch of social sciences, many approaches (as will be seen in the course of this book, and in particular in the first and third parts) contend for the field. My preference is for those theories and analyses that bring to the fore the dimension of *organizational power*, explaining the functioning and activities of organizations above all in terms of alliances and struggles for power amongst the different actors that comprise them. Organizations, and therefore even parties, have a series of characteristics imposed by "technical imperatives:" the need for a division of labor, for coordination between different offices, for specialization in relations with the external environment, etc. I will not leave aside the role of these factors. But the perspective I will adopt (first and foremost in the case of political parties) is one in which the dynamics of the struggle for power within an organization – be it a firm, a public administration, or a voluntary association – offer the key for understanding its functioning, as well as the changes it undergoes.

Organizations differ enormously from one another. But whatever their activities and whatever good or harm they do to mankind, each of them invariably also serves to guarantee, perpetuate, or increase the social power of those who control them i.e., of the elites that guide them:

Most important, however, organizations are tools for shaping the world as one wants it to be shaped. They provide the means for imposing one's definition of the proper affairs of men upon other men. The man who controls an organization has power that goes far beyond that of those that do not have any such control.[1]

The striving for or the defense of this power is an important component in the continual conflicts with "ALL" organizations, regardless of their category or type, and regardless of the functions they serve (or are supposed to serve) within the social system. In the realm of political relations, the emergence of a new organization can bring about a broadening of the boundaries of the political system, i.e. the entry of social groups which had previously been excluded from the benefits of participation. Invariably, however, this also brings about the rise of a new "power elite," one that will replace the pre-existing ruling classes or ally with them. The very organization that has consented to this rise to power will, from that moment on, be the principal instrument through which this new ruling class will defend its social power.

A perspective of this kind implies referring to Robert Michels' view of parties as instruments for the maintenance and the widening of power of some men over others, as well as to other theories of the neo-Machiavellian school, from Pareto's theory of elites, to Gaetano Mosca's theory of organizations as decisive instruments of domination of the minorities – the political classes – over the majorities. But the debt to neo-Machiavellian theories ends here. Michels' analyses have been an important starting point for this work. In the process of writing, however, I have adopted an approach which, if not an alternative to, is certainly far from that proposed by the author of *The Sociology of Political Parties*.

Modern organizational theory represents the domain from which I have largely drawn the analytical categories I find most suitable to the case of political parties. The core of this work, however (as is evidenced by the central chapters of this book), consists in an exercise in comparative history, in an attempt to apply a specific framework of organizational analysis to the examination of the formation of a certain number of European political parties. The underlying idea in this attempt was to reaffirm a fundamental intuition of classical sociology, in particular Weberian, concerning the importance of the founding moment of institutions. The way in which the cards are dealt out and the outcomes of the different rounds played out in the formative phase of an organization, continue in many ways to condition the life of the organization even decades afterwards. The organization will certainly undergo modifications and even profound changes in interacting throughout its entire life cycle with the continually changing environment. However, the crucial political choices made by its founding fathers, the first struggles for organizational control, and the way in which the organization was formed, will leave an indelible mark. Few aspects of an organization's functioning and current tensions appear comprehensible if not traced to its formative phase.

Attention to the historical dimension becomes, in this way, an integral part of the organizational analysis of parties. In this specific case, it has served as an important step in elaborating an organizational typology of parties which would stand as an alternative to those currently adopted in the literature. In this as in many other fields, it is worth considering the observation according to which

> major political transformations which occurred in the past may not repeat themselves in the present and future, and are very unlikely to repeat themselves in exactly the same way, but any theories which claim to encompass general processes of political transformation must be consistent with past experience, and ought to be checked carefully against that experience before gaining wide acceptance . . . we consider the historical experience to be more important than contemporary observation in the formulation or verification of some kinds of generalizations about large-scale political changes.[2]

A comparative-historical analysis always involves risks. To begin with, we are dealing with a type of investigation which must rely on indirect sources – historiographical works based on individual cases – and which is thus in large part at the mercy of data and interpretation furnished by the authors of these case studies.[3] Furthermore, to the extent to which one's research is based on a predetermined analytic picture, an investigation of this type will inevitably do an injustice to these historiographic interpretations (filtering them through different theoretical lenses) and to historiographic material in general. Comparative historical research almost always leaves historians (specialists in individual case studies) perplexed and unsatisfied. And this is virtually inevitable because the comparativist is more interested in the similarities and differences between different cases than in the problematic aspects of each of them. He can only be highly selective in his choice of historical literature, having to discard those aspects of the historiographic debate which are not compatible with his theoretical perspective. This inevitably carries other risks.

An ever-present risk is that of doing an overly superficial analysis of the different case studies. But the alternative is even riskier; in fear of doing an injustice to history, the researcher enters too far into the analysis of each case, and so loses sight of his goal: to isolate the similarities and differences between the various cases (which, in its turn, is possible only if the predetermined theoretical perspective is not abandoned in the process). It is for this reason that comparative analyses often oscillate between two poles: that of emphasizing similarities at the price of negating the particularity of each case, and that of investigating so thoroughly the specific and unrepeatable characteristics of each case that one case is simply juxtaposed with another without an effective comparison.

Finally another risk is related to the choice of historical case studies. What is excluded always counts just as much as what is included in determining theoretical results. The choice to utilize exclusively cases of Western European parties, in order to further historical control, has obviously contributed to the delimitation of the field of investigation. But behind this choice there is also a methodological rationale. For a number of very important differences notwithstanding, the affinities in the political modernization processes undergone by Western European countries with reference to (1) the formation of national "centers," (2) the mobilization of social groups, (3) the extension of rights of assembly, and (4) the "freezing" of political cultures,[4] assure a minimum base for comparison. As long as organizations set up complex relations of adaptation/domination with their environment, the existence of at least certain common environmental conditions becomes crucial.[5] This explains why I excluded the case of parties operating in political systems outside of Western Europe, as for example the one-party systems.[6] It is not that organizational analyses are not applicable to these cases (to give an example, we can find affinities between the modalities in the formation of the Russian Bolshevik party and that of various Western European parties). But since a one-party system impedes electoral competition, the country's state institutions are irreversibly altered and the resulting associative structures differ significantly from those in Western Europe.

Another important exclusion concerns American parties. My choice has been determined by distrust for the hasty comparisons in which researchers of parties often indulge. It is a recurrent theme in the literature that the distance that separates American political and social institutions from their European counterparts is greater than that which differentiates the institutions of the individual European countries from one another. Many reasons are offered to explain this distance, e.g. the fact that in the United States the mobilization of the subaltern classes was a prelude to industrialization rather than its result,[7] as opposed to what took place in most European countries. Since times and modalities of mobilization of the subaltern classes were universally essential in the formation of parties and party systems, the particular development of American parties can thus be explained.[8] In trying to understand the social environment in which party development came about, Barrington Moore's observations on the peculiarity of "the American Way" of political modernization are worth citing:

xvi   *Preface*

The United States did not face the problem of dismounting the complex and well-established agrarian society of either the feudal or the bureaucratic forms. From the very beginning commercial agriculture was important, as in the Virginian tobacco plantations, and rapidly became dominant as the country was settled. The political struggles between a pre-commercial, landed aristocracy and a monarch were not part of American history. Nor has American society ever had a massive class of peasants comparable to those in Europe and Asia.[9]

Since the factors that influenced the birth and organizational development of American parties differ significantly from the European factors, America has not been used as a case in evaluating the hypotheses developed in this book.

This book has been divided into four parts. In the first part (chapters 1, 2, and 3) I will elaborate those essential concepts which, in my opinion, are vital to the development of an organizational analysis of political parties. I will approach, by successive approximations, a conceptual framework – a network of concepts – that seem to me useful in developing realistic analyses of party functioning. My methodological choice has been to utilize the tools of analysis that the sociology of organizations has been elaborating in the study of the functioning of complex organizations, and to adapt them to the case of parties. More specifically, I've contrasted hypotheses, theories, and models of the sociology of organizations with the traditional political science literature on parties. My objective is essentially to demonstrate the superior explanatory capacity, with respect to the more traditional perspectives of an approach that treats political parties from the vantage point of the theory of complex organizations.

In general terms, this first part deals with *the conditions of the organizational order*: through what mechanisms and in what ways do party organizations deal with the innumerable pressures and challenges to which they are subject. An examination of the conditions of the organizational order requires, firstly, a definition of the order itself; and this, in turn, presupposes the recognition of the different factors determining it. This part will essentially be a study geared to the ordering of a series of concepts, with a view to laying out the tools for the successive historical-empirical analyses of particular political parties.

In the second part (chapters 4 to 9) the analytic picture brought into focus in the preceding chapters will be utilized to interpret the organizational evolution of a certain number of Western European parties. The fourth chapter, opening this second part, is still predominantly theoretical. Here I proceed to adapt the theory of institutionalization to the case of parties, and to elaborate a typology of relations between "genetic model" (the genetic characteristics of organizations) and level of institutionalization: a typology that will be put to an historical test in the following chapters. The theory of institutionalization is introduced at this point in order to permit a dynamic analysis of the organizational development of parties.

Chapters 5, 6, 7 and 8 contain an investigation, albeit synthetic, of the history of political parties selected as archetypical cases of the many forms that these organizations can assume, in as much as they are representatives of a very wide range (though not necessarily exhaustive) of possible *organizational orders*. None of the analyses of individual cases is in itself original nor do they offer new ideas with respect to the predominant historiographical theses. Furthermore, and for reasons already explained, related to the intrinsic difficulties of a comparative–historical analysis, the reconstruction necessarily follows only certain of the different possible interpretative perspectives that are currently being discussed in contemporary historiography. If there is originality in these chapters, it appears above all in the theoretical framework through which the different historical theses are filtered, and in the facility with which this framework allows one to pinpoint the similarities and differences between the different cases. In the ninth chapter I shall, in a certain sense, draw out the consequences: I will make use, at that point, of sufficient data to elaborate a typology, albeit provisional and surely partial, of party organizations.

In the third part (chapters 10, 11, 12) I will treat specific organizational problems which had only been considered in passing in the preceding chapters, but which are nonetheless important for the organizational theory of political parties: the role of the "size" of the organization, the problems connected to the division of labor and to organizational complexity, the role of environmental influences and pressure, the features of party bureaucracy and bureaucratization. As in the first part, the discussion will be predominantly theoretical, even if several empirical examples will be used to lend support to my argument.

In the fourth part (chapters 13 and 14) I will treat the problem of organizational change, of the processes of transformation that political parties sometimes undergo. I will deal with them in two different ways: (1) in chapter 13, proposing a model of organizational change and exploring the validity of such a model with respect to changes experienced by different parties in different periods. This model is simply an attempt to partially formalize (in non-mathematical terms) a perspective present throughout the book. (2) In chapter 14, on the other hand, I will examine certain changes taking place today in Western political parties and their repercussions and meaning for more general political processes.

I have deliberately *not* provided a concluding chapter. The analysis of parties as complex organizations is still in its infancy, and studies made in this area can but remain open to successive adaptations and revisions. On the one hand, only extensive and systematic empirical research can permit a more in-depth enquiry, through wider and more articulated use of organizational categories than is permitted in a largely theoretical endeavor. On the other hand, the absence of a conclusion also serves to underline this text's character as that of a work in progress, rather than as a finished product, as more an attempt to identify and pose the relevant questions than to find all of the answers.

Part I
Organizational order

1
Organizational dilemmas

Some years ago an American scholar, reviewing the literature on political parties, observed that: "Party organizational analysis is . . . one of the oldest in parties' research and one of the most frustrating."[1] And surely it is quite frustrating that seventy years after the publication of Robert Michels', *Zur Soziologie des Parteiwesens in der Modernen Demokratie*,[2] and thirty years after Maurice Duverger's *Les Partis politiques*,[3] the most intelligent and persuasive observations are still to be found in these old texts. Most contemporary analyses resist studying parties for what they obviously are: *organizations*. This resistance is partly due to the objective difficulties involved in an organizational analysis of parties. But it is also the result of widespread prejudices and attitudes in the literature on parties that create barriers between the observer and the object observed. Two prejudices are particularly common in this literature: I will define the first as the *sociological prejudice* and the second as the *teleological prejudice*. Both jeopardize serious organizational analyses of parties.

The *sociological prejudice* consists in the belief that the activities of parties are the product of the "demands" of social groups, and that, more generally, parties themselves are nothing other than manifestations of social divisions in the political arena. Expressions such as "workers' parties," "bourgeois parties," "peasant parties," etc. are not only utilized in this perspective for sociographical aims, in order to describe the prevalent social composition of the electorate and/or membership of different parties, but to explain the behavior of the parties as well. This orientation typically leads to reading internal party conflicts as though they were nothing but conflicts between representatives of different social interests.[4] It also tends to represent eventual divergences between the composition of a party's electoral following and that of its members, as well as between its members and its elected representatives, as being caused by "distortions" in the representation of social interests.[5] Another typical trait is the systematic underestimation of the ability of parties, in so far as they are organizations, to shape their own followings.

The sociological prejudice – through its highly imprecise and simplistic use of the term "representation" – prevents us from understanding the complex relationship that exists between parties and the "social inequality" system. In addition, it makes us forget that not only does the party not mechanically mirror, either in its organization[6] or in its politics, the system of social inequality, but that the party itself is a producer of inequalities within its own structure. I will define these inequalities as *organizational* in order to distinguish them from inequalities connected with the system of societal stratification. One of the theses of this book is that the principal cause of intra-party conflicts is to be found in the party's internal system of inequalities; this system is related to, but in no way the simple reflection of social inequalities.[7] *Qua* organization, the political party is a system which is at least partly autonomous *vis-à-vis* social inequalities, and the tensions that often persist within it are primarily the product of such a system. The sociological prejudice thus prevents us from correctly representing the complex relationships between the party and its electoral following, and from identifying the *specific* inequalities inherent in its organizational behavior.

The *teleological prejudice* is just as diffuse but perhaps more insidious than the sociological one. It consists in attributing *a priori* "goals" to parties which in the observer's mind represent the *raison d'être* of the party in question, of parties in general, or of some "ideological family" of parties. Having identified the goals of a party, one then either "deductively" determines its activities and its organizational characteristics, or measures possible discrepancies between these goals and the party's actual behavior. The idea behind this way of proceeding is that parties are organizations formed to achieve specific goals, that they are strictly committed to the realization of these goals, and that researchers can easily and definitively identify them. This approach to the problem leads to the elaboration of *definitions* of parties which – as is the case with the sociological definitions such as "bourgeois parties," "workers's parties," and so on – predetermine the direction and results of the analysis. Two versions of the teleological prejudice exist: the first privileges definitions related to the ideological aims of the party, while the second privileges so-called *minimal* definitions, i.e. based on those aims that all parties are supposed to share.

The first version of the teleological prejudice would include affirmations of the following types: (1) "The assumption which explains my focus of attention is that . . . it is a party's objectives, its *Weltan-*

schauung, which represent its most characteristic features and are most influential in molding its structure and mode of action,"[8] and (2) "A political party is an organized group, an association, oriented toward political goals, which attempts by its actions to maintain the status quo or to change the existing social, economic and political conditions by means of influencing achievement or conquest of political power."[9] The common sense distinctions between, for example, "revolutionary parties" (parties whose goal is that of revolution) and "democratic parties" (parties whose goal is that of defending democracy), fall into this category. Such definitions (and many others) are justified if we lend credence to two "self-evident" presuppositions: (1) parties are groups that pursue goals, and (2) a party's ideology is the best indicator of its goals.

The weak point in the first presupposition is that it takes for granted precisely what has to be demonstrated: that parties are goal-oriented groups. In other words, it takes as a simple matter of fact something which, as organizational sociologists well know and as we shall soon see, constitutes a *problem*.

The weak point in the second presupposition is more obvious. If we unquestioningly assume that parties are goal-oriented groups, and that the "declared goals" (ideological aims) are the "real goals," we simply and implicitly deny the relevance and utility of social analysis. If we consider it sufficient to rely upon the definitions that actors or institutions proffer of their own goals, we will never be able to go beyond simple descriptions of their ideological self-representations.[10]

The second version of the teleological prejudice is more insidious as it is more scientific in appearance. It entails postulating minimal definitions of the goals common to all parties. Scholars that adopt definitions of this type are generally wary of parties' declared ideological goals. They agree with Anthony Downs' assertion: "parties formulate policies in order to win elections, rather than win elections in order to formulate policies."[11]

According to this second version of the teleological prejudice, the minimal common goal of every party is accession to power through electoral victory. With respect to the first version of the teleological prejudice, the second reverses the relation between electoral and ideological aims. In the first, electoral victory is a means to the realization of ideological goals; in the second, the ideology is a means to electoral victory. In its various forms,[12] the minimal common definition of parties as organizations pursuing the aim of electoral victory, constitutes a simple clear definition in accordance with elementary common sense. But is it correct? It is not, because it cannot explain why – as Michels observed[13] – parties so frequently adopt courses of action predictably destined to penalize them electorally, or at least act in ways which will not procure them electoral gains. Such definitions cannot account for the numerous cases in which a party seems to deliberately avoid actions or choices that would lead it to electoral victory, or in which a party seems content – as has for a long time been true of certain Western European communist parties, e.g. the French Communist Party (PCF) – to be a permanent opposition without any chance of building a greater consensus, much less acceding to governmental control.[14]

In its different versions, the teleological prejudice always manifests the same logic: it attributes goals to parties, and explains party behavior on the basis of those goals. This is, as we shall soon see, a simplistic way of understanding the relation that exists, in any complex organization, between "goals" and organizational activities.

If party goals cannot, as I here maintain, be predetermined, how can we distinguish parties from other organizations? This is the very question that all the preceding definitions attempt (unsuccessfully) to answer.[15] The only possible response is that parties – like all other organizations – can be distinguished by referring to the specific *environment* in which they carry out a specific *activity*. Whatever other arenas they may share with other organizations, parties are the only organizations which operate in the electoral arena, which compete for votes. This allows us to distinguish them by an *activity* (tied to a specific environment) foreign to all other types of organizations, and allows us to leave open the question of their possible goals (given that the same activity can be motivated by different goals).[16]

Organizational dilemmas

Both the sociological and the teleological prejudice take as *givens* what in effect constitute *problems* which need to be investigated. The approach we use to examine these problems involves the identification of organizational *dilemmas*, contradictory needs with which every party, in as much as it is a complex organization, must in one way or another come to terms.[17] These dilemmas are derived from some theoretical models which define alternative ways of representing organizations.

The first dilemma: rational model versus natural systems model

This is the most classic of the existing alternatives in organizational theory. According to the *rational model*, organizations are primarily instruments for the realization of specific (and specifiable) goals. The organization's internal arrangement is comprehensible only in the light of its goals.[18] Each of the organization's members participates in the realization of the goals through his assigned role in the organization's internal division of labor, and only this aspect of his behavior is relevant for the functioning of the organization. If the organization is also a voluntary association, the identification of the participants with the organization's goals is explained on the basis of a common "cause." Organizational literature has been based for years upon this rational model, this "paradigm of ends,"[19] as one of its critics has defined it, of which the teleological prejudice is a direct expression. More recent literature has posed persuasive objections to the rational model.

First of all, the "real" aims of an organization are never determinable *a priori*. It has been widely demonstrated, for instance, that the aim of a firm is *never* the simple maximization of profits.[20] The activities of the firm are often subordinated to other goals, whose elucidation requires *ad hoc* investigations. These goals may vary from the maintenance of the stability of internal lines of authority, to a simple defense of the portion of the market already conquered by the firm.

Secondly, a plurality of aims are often pursued within an organization, sometimes as many as there are actors in the organization. The so-called organizational aims, therefore, either simply indicate the result, the complex effect which derives from the simultaneous pursuit of particular aims by the different actors (and in that case it would be equivocal to define such an effect as an "aim"), or else they are but abstractions lacking empirical reference.

Finally, as Michels has persuasively demonstrated, the true objective of an organization's leaders often is not that of pursuing the manifest aims for which the organization was established, but rather that of ensuring the organization's survival (and with it the survival of their own power positions).

An alternative to the rational model may be constructed on the basis of these objections: the model of the organization as a *natural system*. In the words of one of its proponents:

In contrast to the basic ideas of the rationalistic tradition, the systems perspective does not see the organization primarily as an instrument for the realization of the mandator's goals. Rather, the organization is perceived as a structure which responds to, and adjusts itself to, a multitude of demands from various stakeholders, and which tries to maintain balance by reconciling these demands.[21]

The role of the managers is also viewed differently than it was in the rational model. In the rational model, the managers are the ones who bear the greatest responsibility in guiding the organization towards the realization of its goals. In the natural systems model, on the other hand: "The organization's management acquires a kind of mediator role, i.e., a role of weighing the demands from different stakeholders against each other."[22]

The relation between organizational aims and the organization is inverted: whereas in the rational model the independent variable is the aims and the dependent the organization, in the natural systems model "goals are treated as a dependent variable, an effect of 'complex processes within the system,' and thereby, cannot be conceived as either the starting point for, or cause of, organizational action."[23]

The natural systems model implies, more specifically, three consequences concerning the problem of "organizational aims:" (1) The "official" aims are, in the majority of cases, but a facade behind which the real aims are concealed.[24] (2) The real aims can be conceived *only* as the result of each successive equilibrium reached within the organization between a plurality of demands and goals in a competitive context. (3) The only aim that the different participants have in common – and this isn't even always guaranteed – their lowest common denominator (which prevents an organizational "deflagration") is the survival of the organization. This is precisely the condition that allows the different actors to continue to follow their own particular objectives.[25]

The natural systems model and the rational model are usually presented as opposing models. The one would exclude the other: if the organization is a natural system, it cannot simultaneously be an instrument for the realization of specific goals, and vice-versa. Following Michels' example, researchers often present the two models in succession:[26] organizations are initially created to realize certain aims shared by their creators, and are thus structured on the basis of these aims (according to the rational model). With the passing of time, however, organizations develop both a growing tendency towards self-preservation and a growing diversification of aims on the part of the actors (according to the natural systems model). Michels' theory of the "substitution of ends" illustrates precisely this passage of the organization from being an instrument for the realization of certain aims (e.g. the original socialist goals of the party), to a natural system in which the survival imperative and the actors' particular objectives predominate. This hypothesis concerning organizational evolution (and the transformation over time of the organization-aims relationship), and the natural systems model in general, clearly offer a more realistic and persuasive account of organizations than does the rational model. In a well-established organization, the importance attached to the survival of the organization generally prevails over that attached to the pursuit of its original aims. It is also quite clear that the different organizational actors pursue a plurality of often contradictory aims. And, finally, there remains little doubt that organizational equilibrium depends on the way in which the leaders mediate the particular competing demands.

But does this mean that the rational model is unable to explain any dimension of organizational action? In other words, are the "official" organizational aims nothing but a facade? Or, at best, the contingent and precarious products of organizational equilibria? If we accept this conclusion, totally rejecting the rational model, we find ourselves faced with two difficulties: we cannot explain why many intra-organizational conflicts develop over contrasting evaluations of the organization's "efficiency," i.e. over its capacity to pursue the "official" goals; secondly, we cannot explain the persistence of organizational ideologies (which define official aims)[27] to which the leaders are often forced to appeal.

The "official" aims cannot be reduced to a mere facade nor to a contingent product of organizational equilibria.[28] The official aims continue to influence the organization, continue to play an essential role both in its internal processes and in the relationship between the organization and its environment even for a long time after the organization's foundation. This brings us to the second and third organizational dilemmas which can be conceived, in effect, as articulations of the rational/natural dilemma.[29]

The second dilemma: collective versus selective incentives

In the theory of voluntary associations – organizations whose survival depends neither upon paid nor coercively based participation[30] – participation is attributed to the "offering," be it manifest or hidden, of *incentives* (benefits or promises of future benefits) by the organization's leaders. There are two versions of the so-called incentive theory:[31] in the first, the incentives that the organization must distribute in order to assure necessary participation are above all *collective incentives*, that is, benefits or promises of benefits that the organization must distribute equally among the participants;[32] in the second, the organizational incentives are *selective incentives*, i.e. benefits that the organization distributes only to some of the participants and in varying amounts.[33] According to Olson's well-known theory, only this second kind of incentive can account for organizational participation.[34] The two versions correspond to the distinction between "public goods" and "private goods", and represent, according to Brian Barry's definition, the *sociological* approach (which interprets participation as the fruit of a community of values) and the economic or utilitarian approach (which interprets participation as the result of individual interests).[35]

The two versions classify organizational incentives in different ways. For example, the theory of collective incentives distinguishes between incentives of *identity* (one participates because one identifies with the organization), incentives of *solidarity* (one participates because one shares the political or social goals of the other participants), and *ideological* incentives (one participates because one identifies with the "cause" of the organization). The theory of selective incentives, on the other hand, focuses on power, status, and material incentives. Our position is based on the notion that parties are bureaucracies requiring organizational continuity and hierarchical stability,[36] and at the same time voluntary associations which rely on at least a minimum of non-obligatory participation: they must therefore distribute *both* collective and selective incentives (even if, as we shall see, their relative proportions can vary from party to party).

On the one hand, the theory of selective incentives aptly explains the behavior of party elites which compete for organizational control[37] and more generally for power, as well as of party *clients* who exchange votes for material benefits and of some party members who seek career benefits. On the other hand, such a "utilitarian" theory cannot explain the behavior of all of the organization's supporters. The participation of much of the rank and file can be more persuasively explained in terms of collective incentives, i.e. in terms of adherence to the party's official goals, in terms of organizational identification and solidarity. Analogously, the existence of the "electorate of belonging" (*elettorato di appartenenza*)[38] cannot be persuasively explained in terms of selective incentives. At best, selective incentives (collateral assistance services, leisure services, etc.) can only reinforce identifications produced by the distribution of collective incentives.[39] The fact that the party must necessarily distribute both types of incentives contemporaneously implies an organizational dilemma, for one type works against the other. If the organization distributes too many selective incentives, or does so in too open a manner, the organization's credibility as an instrument dedicated to the realization of its "cause" is threatened, and its capacity to distribute collective incentives is thereby diminished. If, instead, collective incentives are overly accentuated, organizational continuity (assured primarily by selective incentives) is compromised. The satisfaction of individual *interests* through selective incentives and the increase of organizational *loyalty* through collective incentives must therefore be carefully counterbalanced. Collective incentives are, however, always associated with activities aiming at the realization of official goals. Identity and solidarity diminish if confidence in the realization of these aims is shaken as, for example, when the organization's behavior clearly belies its official aims. While the interests – fed by the use of selective incentives – push the organization towards a "natural system" model (organizational maintenance activities, and the balancing and mediating of particular demands), the loyalties – fed by the collective incentives – pushes it instead towards the rational model. This double pressure helps us identify the different *internal* functions of an organization's ideology (the ideology which defines the organization's official aims and selects, as we shall see, its "hunting domain").

The first internal function of ideology is that of maintaining the identity of the organization in the eyes of its supporters. The organizational ideology is thus the primary source of collective incentives. The second internal function of ideology is that of concealing the distribution of selective incentives, not only from the eyes of those who do not benefit from them within the organization, but often even from the eyes of those who do.[40] This dissimulation is of the utmost importance, because excessively visible selective incentives would weaken the credibility of the party as an organization dedicated to a "cause," and therefore adversely affect its distribution of collective incentives.

So we can now understand why the "official goals," prescribed by the organizational ideology, are never purely and simply a facade, for the organization must always engage in at least some limited activities aimed at their realization; party activities which blatantly contradict the official goals often result in unacceptable organizational costs.

The third dilemma: adaptation versus domination of the environment

Every organization has a myriad of relationships with its external "environment," and organizational literature has often portrayed these relationships as being very heterogeneous. The two most common theories are (1) that the organization tends to "adapt" itself more or less passively to its environment,[41] and (2) that the organization tends to "dominate" its environment, to adapt and transform it in accordance with its own needs.[42] Two different sets of questions are involved in these theories, relating to how the environment influences the organization, in the first case, and how the organization modifies its environment in the second.

The various existing analyses in the literature on political parties usually boil down to one of these two theories. In Downs' theory, for instance, the party which always attempts to maximize its votes corresponds to the image of an organization that tries to dominate its (in this case electoral) environment. On the other hand, the party that limits itself to "staying on the market,"[43] i.e. to surviving in the space left unoccupied by larger and more powerful parties, corresponds to the image of an organization that tries to adapt to its environment. A party that limits itself to translating into political action the demands of the social groups that make up its electoral base, is another example of an organization that "adapts" to its environment, as it passively reflects the interests and demands of certain social sectors.[44] A "revolutionary" party, on the other hand, is (according to Leninist theory) an organization that attempts to dominate its own social base, to act upon and thus transform it.[45]

Once again, however, defining organizations on the basis of the strict alternative adaptation *or* domination misses the point. First of all, the fact that the organization tends to adapt to or dominate its environment depends obviously on the environmental features. Certain environments are rather easily dominated, while others force the organization to adopt a strategy of adaptation. Secondly, the so-called "environment" is, in reality, a metaphor used to indicate the numerous environments or arenas in which each organization operates; these arenas are generally interdependent and related to one another, but they are nonetheless distinct.[46] This means that an organization can easily develop strategies of domination in certain arenas, and of adaptation in others. The history of certain socialist parties, e.g. that of the German Social Democratic Party (SPD) at the turn of the century, illustrates rather clearly this possibility. As "social integration" parties,[47] these parties developed strong tendencies to dominate their own *classe gardée*; their relationships with their own followings cannot be qualified as adaptive; on the contrary, they reflected active relationships of formation, indoctrination, and mobilization. But at the same time, these parties tended to adapt themselves to the parliamentary arena, establishing a more or less precarious *modus vivendi* with the existing institutional system.[48]

The alternative, adaptation *or* domination, defines the third organizational dilemma with which every party must in some way come to terms. Every organization must, at least to some extent, develop a strategy of domination over its external environment. Such a strategy is generally manifested in a sort of "disguised" imperialism[49] whose function is to reduce environmental uncertainty, i.e. to safeguard the organization from surprises (e.g. the challenges made by other organizations) which may come from the environment. But a strategy of domination is at the same time likely to provoke violent reactions from the other organizations menaced by it. A strategy of domination adopted to *reduce* environmental uncertainty can thus turn out to be counterproductive: it can lead to an increase of environmental uncertainty. Every organization will thus be pushed by its relations with the external world in two different directions at the same time: it will be tempted both to colonize its environment through domination, and to "reach a pact" with it through adaptation. Whether one or the other of these strategies prevails and to what extent (and in what arena) – environmental conditions being put to the side for the moment – depends on how the organization has resolved or resolves in each case its other organizational dilemmas.

Being an organization set on assuring its own survival, balancing the demands of its numerous actors (according to the natural systems model) and thereby guaranteeing the *interests* of organizational continuity (produced and increased by selective incentives), the party must reach a "compromise" with its external environment, must "adapt" to it. The party leaders, from this perspective, have no interest in jeopardizing organizational stability with offensive strategies which might provoke equally offensive reactions from threatened organizations and groups.

But as it is also an instrument for the realization of its official aims – upon which the loyalties nourished by collective incentives depend (according to the rational model) – the party cannot passively adapt to its environment, but must inevitably develop domination activities. The party is, moreover, pushed in this direction by its organizational ideology, which defines its specific "hunting domain,"[50] i.e. the portion of the environment in which the organization stakes its claims, and with respect to which its organizational identity is defined both "internally" (in its members' eyes) and "externally" (in the eyes of its electorate). It is with respect to this same "domain" that the party's *conflictual* relationships (based on competition for the same resources) and *cooperative* relationships (based on exchange of different resources) with other organizations are established. Parties which define themselves as "workers' parties," "catholic parties," etc., for example, delimit *electoral territories* – workers, catholics – and accordingly establish conflictual and/or cooperative relations with all other organizations that "hunt" in the same territories. In delimiting the territory or domain, the ideology pushes the organization to control/ dominate this territory (over and against competing organizations). This is of the utmost importance, for success in the control over territory is intimately tied to the party's organizational identity.

Whereas *interests* of self-preservation fed by selective incentives push the organization to adapt to its environment, the *loyalties* tied to collective incentives and to organizational ideology push it to dominate it. Holding environmental conditions constant, the more the selective incentives prevail in the organization, the more the organization will tend to adapt. The more collective incentives prevail, the more the organization will develop strategies of domination.[51]

The fourth dilemma: freedom of action versus organizational constraints

In this case the division lies between the schools which emphasize the autonomous guiding role of the organization's leaders, and those schools which emphasize instead the limits imposed on the leaders' freedom of action by organizational imperatives. For the former, the leaders' freedom of action is quite extensive: they are in charge of all the key decisions, from the definition of organizational aims to the management of internal order of the party and of the relations with other organizations.[52] For the latter, the leaders' "freedom of action" is more apparent than real: the leaders move within rigidly defined limits, limits dictated by the needs of the organization; the leaders' possible courses of action are in reality pre-determined by the nature of the organization and by its environmental constraints.[53] Posed in this way, the alternative freedom of action or constriction, like our previous alternatives, misses the point. It reveals a serious misunderstanding of the organizational decision-making process. To maintain that decision-makers have "freedom of choice" means little or nothing when we consider that decision-makers are rarely single individuals. In the majority of cases we are dealing with *coalitions* of individuals and/or groups. Organizational decisions are therefore generally the result of internal negotiations in organizations, of reciprocal influences amongst many actors.[54] So-called freedom of choice or action is therefore restricted by the need to maintain equilibrium amongst divergent interests, by the negotiations within the "decisional coalition" itself. Every decision must be viewed as the outcome – implicitly or explicitly negotiated – of numerous forces within the coalition. Moreover, for every "majority" coalition, there is always (potentially) at least one alternative coalition ready to jump in and profit from every false step the majority coalition makes. This further limits, technical–organizational imperatives aside, every leader's "freedom of choice."

At the same time, organizations are arenas in which numerous "strategic games"[55] are played, for there are always many actors pursuing different goals. For this reason the leader's freedom of choice (as well as that of the other actors) is never totally non-existent. Within limits which must be determined for each particular case, leaders really do exercise a certain freedom of movement at the various organizational levels: the existence of many players and many games make possible, at least theoretically, numerous majority coalitions.

The problem of the *degree of the freedom of choice*, of which the majority coalition disposes, points to another crucial organizational dilemma. On the one hand, each such coalition has, besides its "internal" constraint (due to its being a coalition that must reconcile different interests), an "external" constraint as well: it must adopt strategies to realize organizational needs in its daily functioning and "anticipate" its opponents' reactions. These ever-present constraints limit its freedom of movement. On the other hand, however, the coalition (and every single leader in it) must continuously try to increase its own margin of maneuverability. In fact, a certain amount of freedom of movement (in "adjusting" organizational aims, in the management of its relations with other organizations, etc.), i.e. a certain amount of tactical and strategic flexibility is absolutely necessary to the survival of the organization (and thus to the maintenance of its internal power structure) in variable environmental conditions. If the margin of movement is restricted, the coalition's position on organizational problems becomes, by definition, rigid. Such rigidity makes adjustment to environmental changes more difficult, and winds up threatening the organization. And when the organization's survival is threatened in this way, the leadership is likely to be rejected or at least contested.

The fourth organizational dilemma is thus due to the powerful mechanism tending to limit the maneuverability of organizational leaders, and to the continual efforts made by these leaders to evade such limits and obtain as much freedom of movement as possible.[56]

This fourth organizational dilemma is very closely related to the others. For to deal with all the previously described contradictory pressures, the majority coalition must have sufficient "freedom of movement." If its maneuverability is too restricted, it will be unable to provide alternatives to dominative (or adaptive) strategies, rigidly and exclusively dictated by the internal organizational equilibria, *even when* a different strategy is called for by the environmental conditions. If, instead, its freedom of movement is quite extensive, it can more easily vary its strategy (adaptive or dominative) according to the environmental conditions and pressures, and thereby better defend its organizational stability.

The articulation of ends

The preceding discussion should allow us to develop a more realistic approach to the study of political organizations. It will above all enable us to deal flexibly with a series of problematic contexts – relating directly to the functioning of party organizations – in which *a priori* definitions that dogmatically resolve open questions are decidedly misleading.

We may now put into perspective Michels' thesis that in well-established organizations, a process of "substitution of ends" comes about (the official ends are abandoned and the organization's survival becomes the real end). The fundamental internal and external roles that the official aims continue to play – even in well-established organizations – allow us to redefine Michels' thesis in the following terms: whereas the official aims of the party may give way to other official aims (a process usually defined as "succession of ends")[57] as a result of consistent organizational transformations, no party can effect a genuine substitution of ends without such transformations. In well-established organizations a different process takes place, a process that Theodore Lowi calls *articulation of ends*. The organization's original official aims are never abandoned, nor do they ever become a mere "facade." They are adapted to organizational needs: "The rule seems to be that goals are somehow maintained but lose a little something in being translated into organizational requirements."[58] The organization continually engages in certain activities related to these aims, for it is precisely upon these activities that the party's *collective identity* and the leadership's legitimacy are based. The aims are always, however, pursued *sub condicione*, i.e. they are pursued only on the condition that their pursuit does not jeopardize the organization. In the course of their articulation, official aims become – with respect to the genetic phase of the party – vaguer. The organizational ideology, which was manifest (involving explicit and coherent objectives), often, if not always, becomes latent (involving implicit and contradictory objectives).[59] More importantly, a permanent gap opens between official aims and organizational behavior. The relation between aims and behavior never completely disappears; it attenuates. The correspondence of a party's behavior to its official aims is constantly reaffirmed by its leaders, but only these courses of action – amongst the many possible that the party may choose to achieve its official aims – which are compatible with the organization's stability will be selected. For instance, that recurrent pattern we find in the history of socialist and communist parties, i.e. the split between reformist praxis and revolutionary language, is better understood as the result of an articulation, rather than a substitution, of aims: on the one hand the original goal (the revolution/socialism) is constantly evoked as it is the basis of the movement's collective identity; but on the other hand, the chosen courses of action, pragmatic and reformist, guarantee organizational stability without taking credibility away from the notion that one is still "working" towards the official aims: daily reformist praxis is, in fact, always justified with the explanation that reforms do not deviate from, but are rather intermediate steps towards socialism.[60]

A model of organizational evolution

Up to this point I have emphasized a series of opposing needs that every party must counterbalance. The way these needs are in fact counter-balanced defines a central dimension of the party's organizational order. This order varies from party to party and depends on numerous factors, above all, as we shall see, the party's organizational history and the features of the "environments" in which it operates. In other words, there is no "iron law" of parties' organizational evolution (nor of any other organizations). A number of outcomes are possible and thus a number of organizational orders. However, it is possible to identify certain tendencies that appear to operate in many parties. Combining these tendencies, a model of organizational evolution can be constructed. In the course of this evolution, some organizational needs (which we have previously described) tend to grow in importance with respect to the others. The model I will now describe is virtually an ideal type of organizational evolution. Which is not to say, of course, that the organizational evolution described by the model corresponds to the actual evolution of parties. The advantage, however, of the Weberian methodology of the ideal type is that it allows us to establish a standard (an artificial/laboratory creation) with respect to which we can measure differences and deviations due to concrete historical developments. Having identified these differences, it is then easier, in any given historical case, to find the causes behind its real configuration.[61]

To illustrate this ideal type, I will draw upon two theories. Their combination gives rise to an hypothesis about organizational evolution, i.e. about the transformation over time of the way in which the aforementioned organizational dilemmas are resolved. The first theory I will use is Michels' theory of the oligarchical development of parties. According to Michels, every party is destined to pass from a genetic phase, in which the organization is entirely dedicated to the realization of its "cause," to a later phase in which (a) the growth of the party's size; (b) its bureaucratization; (c) the apathy of its supporters after their initial participatory enthusiasm; and (d) the leaders' interest in preserving their own power, transform the party into an organization in which the real end is organizational survival. We have already seen that the outcome described by Michels is too radical, but we can not deny that such a tendency really exists.

The second theory upon which I shall draw has been elaborated by Alessandro Pizzorno to describe the development of political participation.[62] It is based on the sociological distinction between "systems of solidarity" and "systems of interest." A system of solidarity is based on the concept of a "community" of equals in which the participants' ends coincide. A system of interest, on the other hand, is a "society" in which the participants' ends diverge. While the system of solidarity is "a system of action based on the solidarity between the actors," a system of interests is "a system of action based on the interests of the actor."[63] In the former, cooperation in the realization of a common end prevails. In the latter, *competition* between diverging interests prevails. When a political party is founded, it is an "association amongst equals" created to realize a common end, and can thus be considered as a system of solidarity. The birth of a party is therefore always associated with the formation of "areas of equality."[64] A typical aspect of party phenomena is that "one participates always amongst equals:" in this way the fact that the party is a system of solidarity explains the members' intense initial participation. In time, however, the party tends to evolve from a system of solidarity into a system of interests. Through its bureaucratization and progressive involvement in daily routine, the organization diversifies from within, and creates – on the "ashes" of the initial equality – new inequalities. Participation tends to decline, and we see here the passage from a *social movement* type of participation (corresponding to the party *qua* system of solidarity) to a *professional* type of participation (corresponding to the party *qua* system of interests).

What do these two parallel theories indicate? That parties, in the course of their organizational development tend to go from an initial period in which certain needs prevail to a subsequent period in which different needs prevail.

Let us assume that the transition from the first period to the second occurs because of the process of organizational *institutionalization*. It is not (for our immediate purpose) necessary to rigorously define this term:[65] we will simply say for now that it implies the consolidation of the organization, the passage from an initial, structurally fluid, phase when the new-born organization is still forming, to a phase in which the organization stabilizes, develops stable survival interests and just as stable organizational loyalties. Institutionalization is the process which marks this transition from one phase to the other, and which is described differently by the two theories. The organizational dilemmas described in the first part of this chapter can be easily related to this model. Institutionalization designates the party's passage from a system of solidarity oriented to the realization of its official aims (corresponding to the "rational model") to a system of interests oriented toward its own survival (corresponding to the "natural systems model"). The party goes from a phase in which collective incentives – related to the formation of organizational identity – prevail (involving participation of the social movement type), to a phase in which selective incentives – related to the development of a bureaucracy – prevail (involving participation of the professional type); from a phase in which organizational ideology is *manifest* (the objectives being explicit and coherent), to a phase in which organizational ideology is *latent* (the objectives being vague, implicit, and contradictory); from a phase in which the leaders' freedom of choice is broad (they are expected to define the ideological goals of the party, to select the social base of the party, and to mold the organization around these goals and social base)[66] to a phase in which the leaders' freedom of choice is drastically reduced (conditioned as it is by the organizational constraints in a well-established party); from a phase in which an aggressive strategy that tends to dominate/transform its environment prevails (characteristic of an organization in formation that must pave its own way amongst rival organizations and gain for itself a stable portion of the market), to a phase in which a strategy of adaptation prevails (characteristic of an organization already transformed into a system of interests, i.e. that has too much to lose by adopting an aggressive and adventurous policy).

We are therefore dealing with a three phase model: genesis, institutionalization, maturity. The characteristics of phase one (genesis) are symmetrically opposed to the characteristics of phase three (maturity). The model (Fig. 1), as we have said, does not pretend to describe the actual evolution of parties; the latter may radically diverge from this ideal type because of a variety of factors, the principle ones being that:

(1) Organizational features of the first phase generally continue to be present (though much less so), in the third phase, for the reasons we have indicated above. And it is precisely for this reason that the original official aims are "articulated" and not "substituted" in the course of the party's development.

(2) The modalities of institutionalization vary in accordance with the original organizational form. The particular combination of organizational factors present in the first phase influences both the degree of institutionalization that the party later attains (some parties become strong institutions, others hardly institutionalize at all) and the *forms* of this institutionalization. In other words, parties can present different combinations of organizational elements in the first phase, and these initial organizational differences contribute to the formation of organizational differences in the third phase. The organizational

Phase 1	Phase 2	Phase 3
System of solidarity 1 rational model: the goal is the realization of the common cause. Ideology is manifest		System of interests 1 natural systems model: the goal is survival and the counterbalancing of particular interests. Ideology is latent
	Institutionalization	
2 collective incentives prevail (participation of the "social movement" type)		2 Selective incentives prevail (professional participation)
3 broad freedom of movement for the leaders		3 restricted freedom of movement for the leaders
4 strategy: domination of the environment		4 strategy: adaptation to the environment

Fig. 1

variations can give rise, in their turn, to different modalities of composition of the various organizational dilemmas.

(3) Organizational development is strictly conditioned by the relations that the party establishes in the genetic phases and after by its interactions with other organizations and societal institutions. The organizational development of a party may, for example, significantly diverge from the model presented if it depends on other organizations, e.g. on a trade union, a church, the Comintern (i.e. if we are dealing with an externally-legitimated organization). Organizational development may also diverge from the model if the party comes into being as a governmental instead of as an opposition party; in this case it is likely to be constituted *ab initio* as a system of interests, to leave undefined (except in latent ideological terms) its organizational goals, not to undergo pressures to bureaucratize, and thus not to institutionalize considerably.

(4) Finally, and more generally, a party's organizational development is constantly affected by the incessant environmental changes, and these may alter the relation between the various organizational needs in ways which the model would not predict. A "natural history" does not exist which would be valid for every party. Surprisingly abrupt changes of direction can come about at any time. An ideal type of organizational evolution provides, nonetheless, a first approximation which can help us understand the organizational evolution of specific parties.

2
Power, incentives, participation

In order to examine a party's organizational order, we must first investigate its power structure: how power within the organization is distributed, how it is reproduced, how power relations get modified and with what organizational consequences. To do so we must have a sufficiently precise definition of organizational power: we must first of all know *what* organizational power *is*, what its properties are. Such a serious definition of organizational power is conspicuously lacking in the party literature. One example should suffice to illustrate this point.

Since the appearance of Michels' famous "iron law of oligarchy," many authors have taken positions either for or against his thesis.[1] The debate has not, however, been conclusive. Those who uphold the validity of the "iron law" cite as proof the fact that in many parties some leaders are able to hold the reins for a long time, to manipulate national congresses and other party gatherings through plebiscitary techniques, etc. On the other hand, those who deny the validity of the "iron law" use the argument that the leaders of a voluntary association must necessarily keep in mind the will of their followers, and that it is usually easy to find considerable agreement between leaders and followers on the political strategy to be pursued. The two theses are obviously presented as alternative choices: the validity of one precludes the validity of the other. There is here, however, no real alternative. The two positions, in fact, lead to different conclusions simply because they start from different premises. This is due to different conceptions of the properties of power within parties. While the defenders of the "iron law" see power as something very similar to a "property," to something that one possesses and exerts over others, its opponents see power, instead, as being a "relation of influence," with features (even if diluted and partial) of reciprocity. We can thus explain why both schools refer to dimensions of power which coexist in every party (and, in reality, in every organization) but accentuate only the dimensions singled out by the definition of power (implicitly) adopted. It is clear that leaders can extensively control and manipulate their party; and it is equally clear that leaders generally try to maintain the consensus of their following. What is thus in fact needed is an alternative definition of organizational power, one which can account for phenomena which are apparently contradictory.

A well known theory of organizational power captures the "sense" of intra-organizational power relations far better than the theories which can be found in party literature: the theory of power as an *exchange* relation.[2] In the words of two of its most representative supporters:

Power can once again be defined as a relation of exchange, and therefore reciprocal, but in the sense that the exchange is more favorable for one of the parts involved. It is a relation of force, in that one is advantaged over the other, but where the one can, however, never totally be defenseless with respect to the other.[3]

Power is therefore relational and asymmetrical, but also *reciprocal*. It manifests itself in an "unbalanced negotiation" in a relation of *unequal exchange* in which one actor receives more than the other. Power is, thus, never absolute: its limits are implicit in the very nature of the interaction. One can exercise power over others only by satisfying their needs and expectations; one thereby paradoxically submits oneself to their power. In other words, the power relation between a leader and his followers must be conceived as a relation of unequal exchange in which the leader gets more than the followers, but must nonetheless give something in return. The outcome of the negotiation depends on the degree of control that the different actors have over certain resources – those resources that Crosier and Freidberg define as the "trump cards" (*atouts*) of organizational power games. As we shall see in the next chapter, power resources are based on control over "zones of organizational uncertainty," that is, over factors which, if not controlled, menace or can menace the survival of the organization and/or its internal stability. The leaders are those who control the crucial zones of uncertainty for the organization, and can capitalize on these resources in internal negotiations (in power games), swinging them to their own advantage. In organizations, however (and especially in voluntary associations such as parties), every organizational actor controls at least a small "zone of uncertainty," i.e. possesses resources which can be capitalized on in power games. Even the lowliest party member possesses some resources: he can abandon the party and thus deprive it of his participation, he can give his support to an internal minority elite, and so on. Here we see the primary limit of the leader's power (a limit not taken into account by Michels' theory).

But this definition is not yet sufficient. A definition of power as an exchange relation does not allow us to isolate *what* is exchanged, the "objects" that are traded in the "unbalanced negotiations." We must identify the content of the exchange which constitutes organizational power. First of all, it is important to distinguish between negotiations among leaders (*horizontal* power games) and leader–follower negotiations (*vertical* power games): the content of the exchange is different in the two cases. In this chapter we will consider only the content of vertical power games, those that concern leader–follower relationships. The theory of incentives offers a correct, but only partial, account of their content: the leaders exchange incentives (collective and/or selective) for participation. One side offers benefits or promises of future benefits, and the other engages in activities necessary to the functioning of the organization. But this is not all. Incentive theory tends to neglect the fact that certain kinds of participation are of no interest to the leaders, e.g. participation in the form of protest or contestation of the leadership (which, despite appearances, is a form of participation). The leaders are interested in a type of participation which helps the organization function and which at the same time implies that the followers support the leaders. This kind of support amounts to a "carte blanche," i.e. freedom of action for the leaders. The unequal nature of the exchange consists in the fact that the followers obtain only organizational incentives whereas the leaders obtain both participation and freedom of action. The fact that the exchange results in a broadly defined mandate for the leaders corresponds, as we have already seen, to a vital need;[4] for the greater the leaders' freedom of movement, the greater are their *chances* of stabilizing the party's organizational order under changing environmental conditions. Consequently, the greater the freedom of movement won by the leaders in vertical power games (the more such freedom is configured as a "carte blanche") the stronger their trump cards wielded in horizontal power games *vis-à-vis* the internal opponents. In other words, the greater their freedom of action, the greater their invulnerability to attacks made by internal adversaries. This explains the circular and self-reinforcing character of power relations: some actors (the leaders) "enter" with resources, "leave" in an even stronger position, having finessed *both* the participation necessary for the running of the organization (and thus also for the maintenance of their leadership) *and* a wider consensus which, in allowing them to guide the party with a sufficiently free hand, protects them from their competing internal opponents. Vertical power games are thus the (logical) precondition for horizontal power games: and the outcome of the negotiations among leaders depends on the outcome of the negotiations between leaders and followers.

We have already mentioned that there are two types of organizational incentives: collective and selective. Contrary to common practice, it does not seem very useful to us to rigidly distinguish the different types of collective incentives; they are all, in fact, related to organizational ideology, to the party's official goals. If the official goals lose credibility, not only are the "ideological" incentives weakened, but so are the incentives of identity and solidarity as well: identity becomes confused and thus solidarity tends to crumble. I will therefore refer to all collective incentives related to organizational goals as *incentives of identity*. It is no easier, moreover, to isolate the different types of selective incentives: I will distinguish here only between *material* incentives (reward systems, welfare, and assistance services) and status incentives. My typology of organizational incentives will therefore include one type of collective incentive (identity) and two types of selective incentives (material and status).

Let us emphasize a few points here: (1) In order to assure participation every party must distribute all three of these types of incentives. (2) The incentive system, i.e. the particular combination of these three types of incentives, varies from party to party as well as, often, within the same party over time. (3) An organizational actor will tend to benefit from a combination of selective and collective incentives rather than from any one single type of incentive. Thus a distinction between, for example, party members whose participation depends upon collective incentives and party members whose participation depends instead upon selective incentives can only be theoretical. In reality, we will have to speak of organizational actors whose primary (but never sole) incentive is of the first or second type.

The party member who participates primarily because he identifies with the goals (collective incentive), generally tends to benefit from some kinds of selective incentives in the form of, for example, collateral assistance services or status. And those actors primarily attracted by selective incentives also benefit from certain collective incentives. We have said that one of the functions of ideology is to conceal selective incentives whose excessive visibility could compromise the image of the party as an organization dedicated to a "cause" (and could therefore weaken its capacity to distribute collective incentives of identity). But this dissimulation usually effects both groups: the party members primarily interested in collective incentives, but also those primarily interested in selective incentives. Ideology, in fact, takes on (among other functions) the important function of rationalizing and dignifying aspirations to individual success. One's increased status can be related to the "superior needs" of the cause and of the party. As Gaxie has observed: "the more the existence of a party depends on the gratifications offered to its members, the more the problem of their dissimulation becomes relevant, and the more the ideology that defines the party's 'cause' comes to play a determinant role in its functioning."[5] In other words, ideologies, as often happens, have the function of justifying underlying interests. The empirical distinction between actors primarily interested in collective incentives as opposed to those primarily interested in selective incentives does not at all imply a moral distinction between "idealists" and "opportunists." It is a theoretical and not a substantive distinction, and does not imply any type of moral judgement.

Believers and careerists

The image of concentric circles – electors, supporters, members – already employed by Duverger[6] is useful, as a first approximation, in the identification of the recipients of organizational incentives.

The outermost circle is composed of the electorate. In order to obtain a minimal form of participation (voting), party leaders must distribute incentives to the electorate as well, i.e. to the actors who are both formally and factually outside the organization. In terms of organizational consequences, the most interesting part of the electorate is represented by the part which "belongs to the party,"[7] the electorate that participates steadfastly in the party subculture, that is often involved in a network of associative ties revolving around the party and whose identification with the party is independent of its contingent political oscillations. This electorate primarily benefits from the collective incentives of identity. This identification constitutes the party's strongest "external" organizational loyalty reservoir. This electorate also benefits, at times, from selective incentives tied to assistance services, welfare services, etc.

Within this circle we see the party members, those who limit themselves to paying dues and participating now and then (usually silently) in party meetings. This kind of member – in the majority in every party – logically covers an intermediate area between the electorate which "belongs to the party" and the party's "nucleus." He often joins the party without having made a thought-out political choice. His membership is often due to friendly or familial ties, to conforming to the political views prevalent in his community.[8] Naturally, the more his entry is controlled by the party (i.e. the more his entry is subordinated to a presentation, to a meeting with the local party head, etc.) the more the member has an incentive to participate, to be an active member. In such a case, membership is seen as an honor, a status symbol to be flaunted on the job, with friends, etc. The selectiveness of the membership is therefore in and of itself an incentive to active participation. But the party member is usually not an active organizational actor. He is content to benefit from the organizational incentives; geared to getting him to at least renew his annual membership. As for the "electorate of belonging," the normal party member also primarily benefits from (collective) incentives of identity, but he benefits from selective incentives as well. The collateral assistance services and the organization of free time and recreation reinforce identification. Party members can more easily benefit from the "solidarity networks" which revolve around the party's organizations[9] than can the simple electorate, because they have closer contact with the party's active members.

We have assigned party members to that intermediate area between the "electorate of belonging" and the party activists. We can no more draw a clear-cut distinction between the simple members and the activists, than between the members and the electorate. In fact, much of the rank and file activity has a very discontinuous character: some members participate on particular occasions (e.g. during electoral campaigns), and the activists do not all participate with the same intensity. Some activists dedicate all their free time to voluntary political work for the party, others only a part of it, and still others alternate between periods of greater participation and periods in which they reduce their commitment without, however, withdrawing altogether.[10] The dividing line between simple members and activists is therefore rather unclear. We can speak of a *participation continuum*, but not of clearly distinct groups with completely different participatory characteristics. The activist "nucleus," the party's small minority which continually participates and whose activities enable the organization to function, is clearly the most important group. The leaders' exchanges with this group will have the most relevant organizational consequences. I will break this group down (but as I said before, only in an artificial way) into activists whose participation depends primarily on collective incentives of identity (and who I will term *believers*), and activists whose participation depends primarily on selective, material, and/or status-oriented incentives (and who I will term *careerists*).

It is the believers' presence that explains why the official organizational goals weigh heavily upon the organization, why the organizational goals are generally articulated but not replaced. The community of believers is by definition devoted to the official goals, and vehemently protests when the party betrays the official goals, jeopardizing the collective identity. The leaders must above all safeguard the believers' identity with constant and ritual references to the ideological goals, and with cautiousness in their choice of heterodox alliances (i.e. heterodox from the organizational ideology's viewpoint). The believers' presence keeps the party from acting exactly like those opportunistic animals described by Downs, ever ready to move from the political left to the right and from the right to the left for a handful of votes.

Careerists are active members primarily interested in selective incentives. Their presence has considerable organizational importance. The careerists constitute the main force behind the factionistic games, are often the human base for the schisms, and represent a potential source of turbulence and threat to the organizational order which the leaders must attempt to neutralize. The careerists constitute the pool from which future party leaders emerge. The selective incentives from which the careerist benefits are related to the system of internal inequality: the party hierarchy (its inherent system of unequal status) is one of the careerist's main sources of remuneration.

The internal hierarchy responds to two different needs: The first need is obviously of a technical–organizational character; it is imposed by the internal division of labor. The internal hierarchical system responds, at least in part,[11] to the organizational needs that were defined by Michels seventy years ago, and that have been confirmed by those schools of organizational sociology which are more attentive to the "technical" aspects of organizational functioning.

The second need which directly concerns us here is tied to a more purely "political" reason, one related to problems of the organizational control over internal differentiation processes.[12] The need for control brings about the formation of a *differentiated status system* that functions as an autonomous distributor of remunerations to the organization's activists, and, in particular, to those that I have termed careerists. The need for a hierarchical system that assures a symbolic and/or material distribution of incentives, is dependent (technical imperatives aside) upon the *voluntary* character of many of the party's activities. In the words of the scholar who has best identified this problem: "(D)efining a system of inequality from the symbolic point of view allows us to define a career, to attribute differentiated gratifications to a set of positions, and to increasingly remunerate the offices successively assumed by the most active supporters."[13]

There are three principal consequences of the differentiation of selective incentives tied to the party hierarchy, of the fact that remuneration increases as we ascend the hierarchy's ranks.

(1) A pressure exists (which is partially autonomous from the "technical" needs related to coordination or environmental constraints) to increase internal differentiation. In fact, the more differentiated and complicated the hierarchy, the more remunerations can be distributed.

(2) On the other hand, an increase in positions of responsibility unequally recompensed in a symbolic sense leads sooner or later to the "devaluation" of such remuneration: if there are too many positions of responsibility at various levels, they are not "scarce goods," and the marginal utility of each new position created is small.[14] The two opposing tendencies delineate the inherent tension in systems organized on a voluntary basis between (a) the tendency to multiply positions of responsibility in order to gratify as many active members as possible (i.e. the tendency towards hyper-bureaucratization in the attempt to increase participation) and (b) the consequent symbolic "inflation" that leads to the devaluation of roles of responsibility, and reduces the attractiveness of the positions (which is reflected in a decrease in participation).

(3) Finally, the differentiated distribution of selective incentives of status related to a hierarchical system implies that more important positions are symbolically remunerated better than less important ones. Dedication and activism thus tend to grow in intensity and constancy as one goes up the hierarchical ladder and to decrease as one descends.[15] A local party association leader will tend to be less dedicated than a regional party association leader, the rank and file activist less than a local leader, etc. This third consequence leads to an endemic scarcity of rank and file activism in many parties. On the one hand, hierarchical differentiation of status is necessary to make the organization work. This is why even party factions tend to organize themselves hierarchically. On the other hand, a devaluation of the lower levels is implicit in every hierarchical differentiation. The party's responses to these dilemmas consist, firstly, in a constant preoccupation with the collective identity (the distribution of collective incentives) and, secondly, in welfare activities and/or the development of a network of extra-political ties (assistance or recreational activities, etc.) that enable it to distribute *additional* selective incentives. In some cases the space reserved for these extra-political ties will be very great and we will thus have a *social integration* party; the vertical organizational links common to this type of party respond to the fundamental function of additive or compensatory remunerations for activists unable to accede to upper level party positions. It is with the aim of remunerating the activists that:

social activities tend to be carried out through the party which "furnishes the occasions for *loisir* and *detente*, favoring relations," contacts and exchanges and constitutes a sort of matrimonial micro-market for many of those who belong. Integration in a micro-society with all the psychological and social advantages associated with them appears to be the most general benefit obtainable from belonging to an organization and so it is logical to expect that party activities are greater the more the organization favors this integration.[16]

Whether the activism be primarily of a believer type or a careerist type, it is thus recompensated with a mixture of identity, material and status incentives. This is true not only on the rank and file level, but on all levels. For example, the intellectuals (part-time political professionals) are often recompensated with positions outside the party hierarchy (consultant positions or contracts in publishing, activities in party "cultural" organizations, etc.). In general, this is one way of escaping from one of the difficulties already mentioned. Given that it is not possible to differentiate the hierarchy beyond a certain point – what we might term the *line* hierarchical system – it is thus necessary to proceed in enlarging the pool of collateral roles (the *staff*) with the goal of distributing other symbolic and/or material incentives without depreciating the hierarchical system itself.[17]

The "mixed" character of the incentives on which each organizational actor's participation depends is further evidenced by the fact that, overcoming a certain threshold in the party hierarchy (at times even rather a low one, as in highly bureaucratized parties) activism ceases to be rewarded by status alone, and begins to be rewarded in material terms as well. Beyond a certain hierarchical threshold, activism becomes a full-time professional activity, directly rewarded (as in the case of party bureaucracy) or indirectly rewarded (stipends tied to elected public positions, the appointment to agencies or associations of various sorts controlled by the party). We should also point out that we speak of party hierarchy (in the singular) in an inappropriate way: various interwoven and complex systems act on one another within the party hierarchy, and function as sources of activist compensation. In addition to internal positions, we must take into account local public positions and positions in the party's collateral associations as forms of remuneration. Moreover, even factions, where they exist, are internally organized on a hierarchical basis. This results in a multi-hierarchical system.

In summary, activists of the believing and of the careerist types operate in every party, in varying combinations depending on the different types of incentives offered. From our analytical distinction, and from the observation that activists generally benefit from a combination of incentives,[18] it follows that the majority of activists conform to what we have referred to as the believer type and only a minority to the careerist type. This explains why, even in the parties divided into factions, one can find a great many sectors of activists who do not participate in factionistic games.[19] The believer, by definition, identifies with the party (and not with one sector of the party) – to which he is highly loyal – unless the leaders demonstrate that they don't take seriously the official organizational goals upon which his personal identity depends. The fact that in many cases most activists are of the believer rather than of the careerist type, explains why there is always a sort of natural majority supporting the leadership in power. The sentiment of deference analysed by Michels, the personality cult reserved for the party leaders, is explained by the fact that the leaders, as the legitimate holders of power within the party, represent the visible and tangible sign of organizational identity.

The careerist minority represents, instead, the potential risk-zone for the party leaders. It is within this group that the aspiration towards upward mobility is strongest; from this group the party's future ruling classes will come.[20] With respect to the careerists, the leaders have but two alternatives: to coopt them through the hierarchical ladder, or to encourage them in every possible way to "leave" the party. Otherwise activists from this group will emerge who will support the minority elites' challenges to the existing leadership. The fact that only some of the careerists can be coopted (due to the scarcity of distributable resources at any moment) explains in large part the practically endemic character of intra-party conflicts.[21]

Incentives and unequal exchange

An examination of the distributional processes of collective and selective incentives helps to explain how the organizational *loyalties* of the "electorate of belonging" to the party, simple members, and believer–activists, and the organizational *interests* of the careerist–activists form and grow. The existence of loyalties explains why an articulation rather than a true substitution of ends takes place in the parties. The existence of interests, on the other hand, explains why the party is a "natural" system which is dominated by organizational survival imperatives and continuously mediating a lot of heterogeneous demands. The combination of loyalty and of interests sustained by organizational incentives is the reason why the leaders are able to obtain, through exchanges and vertical power plays, the participation which is indispensible to the smooth functioning of the organization. But this is only one aspect of the problem. The leaders are not only interested in people's participation, but also want them to participate "in the right way." What the leaders try to obtain is a consensus granting them the widest possible freedom of movement.

What is it that makes the leader–follower exchange so unequal as to assure the leaders not only participation but also this widest possible freedom of movement? The explanation is a low *substitutability* of organizational incentives. The slighter the followers' chances of obtaining elsewhere benefits comparable to the remunerations distributed by the leaders, the more the vertical power games favor the leaders. The activists, having no alternative sources of remuneration, are heavily dependent upon the organization. And the more they depend upon the organization, the less they control certain zones of uncertainty, and thus the more the leaders can act independently. In fact, the exchanges are seriously unbalanced in favor of the leaders when the activists are heavily dependent upon the organization.[22]

Every party or movement that monopolizes a collective identity privileges its own leaders in this way. The more the party is a "community of fate," a community defined by a specific identity that has no equivalent in the external market, the stronger are the leaders' positions in the vertical power games. Even a formally voluntary organization can, in certain cases, be highly coercive. As has been observed: "In the case of social movement organizations and religious sects, one might speak of coercion when such organizations monopolize highly desired ends – when participation and conformity is perceived as the only way to achieve the transformation of the world or to attain grace."[23] The same mechanism functions in certain parties. As there is no "salvation" outside of the party in these cases – i.e. no substitute identity exists – the activist has no choice but to deferentially participate, to give the leadership a blank check (within the insurmountable limit, obviously, of safeguarding the party's identity). This explains why, despite the assertions made by some critics that power in a voluntary association can never be a relation of domination, Michels' thesis on the power relations within the SPD of his epoch is merely exaggerated, not mistaken. For a worker who was an SPD member or activist in that period, no alternative in fact existed outside of the party – neither in terms of identity and assistance services, nor of social mobility – and the leaders could therefore effectively exercise an "oligarchical" power, i.e. they could, in our terms, seriously unbalance in their own favor the exchanges with the rank and file. The same reasoning that holds true for collective incentives holds true for selective ones: the party bureaucrats, for example, who don't have alternatives to organizational incentives, are often extremely conformist, and compliant with the existing leadership.[24]

The opposite is obviously true as well. The more organizational incentives are substitutable (the more it is possible to find alternative remunerations on the external market), the greater is one's control over the zones of uncertainty, and the less unbalanced in favor of the leaders are the vertical power games, i.e. the more restricted is their freedom of movement. Activists can, in this case, look to other sources for an equivalent remuneration, and can therefore raise the exchange price and at least partly attenuate the imbalance which is *nonetheless* inherent in vertical power games.

It is therefore possible to imagine the unbalanced leader–follower negotiations within a party as being situated on a continuum where at one pole we have an exchange relationship strongly in favor of the leaders, thus resembling Michels' power–domination; and at the other pole a type of exchange which more closely resembles a relation of reciprocal influence. We never find pure cases of either of these: the vertical power games actually operating within parties tend to be located at a certain point along the continuum, a point determinable in relation to the degree of substitutability of the organizational incentives.

This reasoning allows us to understand why vertical power games tend, or at least tended in the past, to produce oligarchies more easily in those parties which organized the popular classes than in those parties which organized bourgeois classes. For the former the substitutability of the incentives was low and often nonexistent, whereas for the latter it was high. In the former, thus, the leaders' freedom of movement was extensive, in the latter it was more restricted. This also explains why the parties that organize bourgeois classes must often deal with many more problems due to scarcity of activism and discontinuity in participation levels than parties that organize popular classes. Individuals with a middle-class background often have alternative channels of mobility at their disposal. If they can't quickly climb the party rungs, they readily seek out other career advancement channels. Individuals of popular classes, on the other hand, don't have (or didn't have) analogous alternatives: party activism is their only possible path. They are thus more likely to remain within the party whatever their career advancement possibilities may be.

3
Dominant coalition and organizational stability

Having examined the content of the exchanges that constitute the power games, we must now isolate the resources of organizational power, i.e. the control of those factors that permits certain actors to swing these power games to their advantage. Such factors can be understood, according to the power theory to which I have referred, as *zones of uncertainty*, areas of organizational unpredictability.[1] The survival and functioning of an organization depend on a series of activities; the very possibility that a vital activity could be denied, that someone could walk out on the organization, that an interruption could take place in crucial activities, constitutes an uncertain situation for the organization. People who control the zones of uncertainty upon which the operation of the services depends, hold a trump card, a resource that is "spendable" in the internal power games. This way of defining zones of uncertainty is so vague, however, that any relation or organizational situation can be interpreted in these terms. Within a party, for instance, even the lowliest activist controls a small zone of organizational uncertainty. We can, nonetheless, group the principal zones of uncertainty on the basis of a rather limited number of organizational activities. There are essentially six factors which are central to the development of these vital activities: competency, environmental relations management, internal communication, formal rules, organizational financing, and recruitment.[2]

(a) Competency. It defines the "power of the expert," he who possesses a specialized knowledge as a result of the organizational division of labor, and thus controls a fundamental zone of uncertainty. Specialized knowledge is not, however, to be understood here as a set of skills obtained through educational training. The specialized knowledge which interests us here is that which derives from experience managing the party's internal and external political–organizational relations. It consists in the recognition by the other organizational actors that certain individuals possess the qualities corresponding to certain roles, i.e. that it is their competency that makes them indispensable to the organization in the roles they occupy. One of the most powerful mechanisms leading to the formation of oligarchy is, according to Michels, the activists' awareness that only certain men within the organization possess the expertise needed to guide the party, to carry out qualified political work in Parliament, etc. Competency is the first resource that any national leader in a party congress, or any functionary charged with presiding over a local assembly, displays to sway negotiations with the public to his advantage. Competency, understood both as an attribute of the actor and as the attribution of a quality to the actor by the others in the organization, is therefore a fundamental resource of organizational power. This represents a zone of uncertainty because of the widespread conviction that the loss of that specific competency could hurt the organization: leaders typically threaten to resign when they want to exploit their competency as a power resource.

(b) Environmental relations. The environment, from the organization's point of view, is the primary source of uncertainty. Whether we are dealing with a firm that must make predictions about future market trends, or with a party which must perfect its way of responding to changing electoral moods, organizations almost always face an external world over which they can exert but limited control and from which serious threats can arise. To control environmental relations is thus to control a decisive zone of organizational uncertainty. The stipulation, redefinition, or solidification of alliances with other organizations, and the choice of the issues to be disputed with still other organizations, are only some of the many tasks of environmental relations management that some of the organization's actors must necessarily undertake. Those who undertake such tasks find themselves in the position called *secante marginale*:[3] they participate in two action systems, one within the organization, and one at the juncture of the organization and the environment (or parts of the environment). The role undertaken in the second system of action provides a crucial resource that can be "spent," with reasonable expectations of profit, in the first.

(c) Communication. There is no need to refer to cybernetics to realize that organizations are communications systems. They function to the extent that there are channels through which information travels. The third crucial power resource is therefore the control of the communication network: he who can distribute, manipulate, delay or suppress information controls a fundamental zone of uncertainty, holds in his hands a decisive resource in power relations.

(d) Formal rules. The fourth is the control of organizational rules (their control and manipulation). To establish formal rules is to mold the "playing field," and to choose the terrain upon which confrontations, negotiations, and power games with other organizational actors will take place.

The rules constitute a zone of uncertainty. Few rules have a self-evident meaning; a rule almost always necessitates an interpretation. He who interprets the rule strengthens his position with respect to the other organizational actors. In addition, controlling the rules allows one to passively tolerate deviations from them. In every organization there are many rules which are not observed due to a tacit agreement that Downs has defined as the "institutionalization of deviation from the written norms."[4] There is, thus, plenty of room for maneuvering: deviations which are tolerated today might not be tolerated tomorrow. Certain rules which have officially been on the books for a long time but never enforced – with the tacit consent of those who institutionally should enforce them – can suddenly be revived in the course of particular conflicts. This allows for the possibility of implicit or explicit blackmailing. The establishing of rules, the manipulation of their interpretation, and their enforcement are thus zones of uncertainty, of organizational unpredictability whose control is another decisive resource in power relations. A party's statutes do not describe its organization any more than a political system's written constitution does. It is only a pallid trace, fleeting and imprecise, little more than a point of departure for the organizational analysis of a political party.[5]

(e) Financing. Money is indispensable to the life and functioning of every organization. He who controls the channels through which flow the money that finances the organization controls another crucial resource. But money can flow in many ways. There are two extreme cases; one in which there is a single external financier and the other in which there are many small contributors (memberships, self-financing campaigns, etc.). In the first case the external financier himself controls this zone of uncertainty and thereby exercises a certain amount of power over the organization. In the second case, none of the financiers is in this position, and control is thus in the hands of the internal actors who preside over fund-raising activities. Most parties occupy intermediary positions between the two extremes. Certain large external financiers (pressure groups, trade unions, the Comintern, etc.) usually have a certain degree of control over the organization, but so do those people within the party who raise the remaining funds. More generally, control over this zone of uncertainty often depends on privileged contacts that one organizational actor is able to establish with external financiers, i.e. control of this zone of uncertainty is subsumed under controls of organization–environment relations.

(f) Recruitment. The sixth resource stems from control over recruitment at the various organizational levels. The control over decisions as to who can and who cannot join the organization (e.g. acting on party admission criteria), and as to which of the many candidates can advance in internal "careers" and what the career advancement requisites are to be, are fundamental trump cards of organizational power; they are related to (as we shall see more clearly further on) the control of "organizational borders" and of the members' career "opportunity structure" respectively.

Power resources tend to accumulate: those who control a certain zone of uncertainty are likely to acquire control over others.[6] There is a tendency – characteristic of all parties – toward the concentration of power in small groups. But control over zones of uncertainty cannot be totally monopolized by any one group, for in that case there would be no exchanges, no negotiations, not even unbalanced ones. The powerless groups would not have the resources necessary to make an exchange possible, and the resulting power relations would be very similar (especially if incentive substitutability is minimal) to those of domination. This does not often come about, for "competencies" are usually diffused within parties. They go beyond the limits that divide the managerial group from the other organizational actors. They rest outside of the leaders' control. The communication system cannot be totally monopolized by an isolated elite; informal communication amongst the members of an organization, for example, goes on continually outside of official channels and can in no way be controlled.[7] Moreover, environmental relations are managed by numerous actors at different levels: financing may in certain cases take place through channels which are not controlled by the ruling elite.[8] Even recruitment is not entirely controlled, and the same goes for the formal rules, the official rules of the game. In the first place, the majority of internal formal relations are *givens*, i.e. they depend on the party's organizational tradition and history, and thus cannot be modified at the whim of the elite.[9] Secondly, various groups can propose other interpretations of the rules which may compete with or even contradict those supported by the elites: intra-party conflicts typically take the form of "procedural battles" (i.e. clashes between groups adhering to different interpretations of the same rule). And furthermore, while rules are instruments of control – resources in leaders' hands – they *also* represent a guarantee, for other organizational actors can appeal to the rule in order to defend themselves from the leaders' whims.

The dominant coalition

Keeping the preceding remarks in mind, we must nonetheless take account of the established fact (established by a lot of empirical research on parties) that the principal power resources tend to be concentrated in the hands of small groups. Michels' oligarchy, Duverger's "inner circle," Ostrogorski and Weber's "ceasaristic-plebiscitarian dictatorship," are just a few examples which bring this phenomenon to mind. Of the usual terms used to indicate a party's elite, I prefer the expression "dominant coalition"[10] for at least three reasons.

In the first place, even when a single leader seems to exercise an almost absolute power over an organization, observation often reveals a more complicated power structure: the leader, even if he leads because he controls crucial zones of uncertainty, must (more often than not) negotiate with other organizational actors: he is at the center of a coalition of internal party forces with which he must at least to a certain degree negotiate. Neither Adenaur's power in the CDU, nor that of Togliatti in the PCI nor of Thorez in the PCF was, for example, absolute: their power depended on their continually knowing how to control organizational zones of uncertainty, and on their flexibility in guaranteeing the other participants (those making up the dominant coalition) their requested compensations.

Secondly, organizational power within a party is not necessarily concentrated in the internal or parliamentary positions of that party itself, as the terms "oligarchy" and "inner circle" lead us to believe. The British Labour Party's real power structure must remain totally opaque to us if we don't take into consideration the role of the trade unions; the dominant coalition that has kept the party together for the better part of its history is composed of leaders of the most powerful unions (dominating the TUC) and of "centrist" sectors of the parliamentary group loyal to the party's leader.

Thirdly, in contrast to the expressions often utilized, the expression "dominant coalition" does not at all imply that only national party leaders take part in such a coalition: a dominant coalition includes the national leaders (or some of them) as well as a certain number of local or intermediate leaders. If we consider, for example, the power structure of the SFIO in the twenties and thirties, it is easy to pinpoint the dominant party coalition in the alliance that included a part of the parliamentary group (headed by Leon Blum), the national secretariat (controlled by Paul Faure), which dominated the central apparatus, and the leaders of the strongest federations (i.e. those with the most members) which dominated the national congress.[11] The concept of dominant coalition, broader than those often used, allows us a better description of the actual structure of party power, both when this implies the existence of a "transversal alliance" (between national and local leaders) and when it implies instead an alliance among national leaders and leaders of organizations which are formally external to and separate from the party. In light of the definition which we have given of organizational power, a party's dominant coalition is composed of those – whether inside or, strictly speaking, outside of the organization itself – organizational actors who control the most vital zones of uncertainty. The control over these resources, in its turn, makes the dominant coalition the principal distribution center of organizational incentives within the party.

Control over the distribution of incentives – incentives being the currency of exchange in vertical power games – constitutes another zone of uncertainty, another resource of organizational power within the horizontal power games, i.e. in the relations among the dominant coalition's leaders, and in the relations between the dominant coalition and the minority elites. The negotiations, in fact, do not only take place between the dominant coalition and its following, but also within the dominant coalition itself. Power equilibria within the coalition can be altered at any moment, because the control of some leaders over certain crucial zones of uncertainty grows, thus increasing their control over the distribution of incentives at the other leaders' expense. A dominant coalition is therefore always a potentially precarious construction. It disintegrates due to the pressure of external forces (minority elites) when it proves itself incapable of controlling organizational zones of uncertainty, or because of internal conflicts due to changes in its internal distribution of power.

The physiognomy of the dominant coalition is what distinguishes the "organizational order" of one party from that of another. The dominant coalition can be examined from three points of view: according to its *degree of internal cohesion*, its *degree of stability*, and the party's *organizational power map*.

A dominant coalition's degree of cohesion depends upon the fact that control over zones of uncertainty is either dispersed or concentrated. The principal distinction here lies between parties divided into *factions* (strongly organized groups) and parties divided into *tendencies* (loosely organized groups).[12] Factions – organized groups – may be of two types: groups which cut the party vertically, from the top to the rank and file (these being the true or "national" factions), and geographically concentrated groups, organized at the party's periphery (these latter I shall term *sub-coalitions*).[13] Tendencies can be characterized as aggregations at the top without organized rank and file (which does not necessarily mean without consensus).

In a party in which internal groups are factions (highly organized groups), control over zones of uncertainty is dispersed (subdivided among the factions) and the dominant coalition is not very cohesive (because it is the result of a compromise between certain factions, each of which maintains its own individuality *vis-à-vis* the others). In a party in which internal competition – manifested in horizontal power games – is based on tendencies (weakly organized), control over zones of uncertainty is more concentrated and the dominant coalition is more cohesive.

We must, however, observe that both cohesive and divided dominant coalitions are the result of alliances between groups; what varies are the degrees of organization in the groups (which, as we shall see, are inversely related to the parties' levels of institutionalization). Moreover, if we examine the groups (factions and/or tendencies), we discover that even these are usually the result of alliances between smaller groups. The difference is that if the group is a tendency, the ties between its sub-groups are weaker and more changeable than those between a faction's sub-groups. What is important is that the dominant coalition is always an *alliance of alliances*, an alliance between groups which are, in turn, coalitions of smaller groups.[14] Degree of cohesion is based upon the extent to which vertical exchanges (the elite–follower exchanges) are concentrated in the hands of a few, or are dispersed amongst numerous leaders. Degree of stability, on the other hand, is related to horizontal exchanges (elite–elite exchanges), and, in particular, to the character of compromises (whether stable or precarious) at the organization's upper echelons. A cohesive dominant coalition is generally also a stable one. The contrary, however, is not necessarily true: i.e. a divided coalition is not always unstable. We can site cases in which a dominant divided coalition is able to remain stable over time through mutually acceptable compromises between its factions. By "organizational power map" I intend both relations between the party's various organizational units (e.g. the predominance of the parliamentary group, the internal national leadership, or the peripheral leadership, etc.) and relations (of predominance, subordination, and/or cooperation) between the party and other organizations.[15]

Together the degree of cohesion, the degree of stability, and the organizational power map delineate a party's dominant coalition physiognomy, which I define here as its conformation. We must, however keep separate the coalition's conformation – which depends on the attributes indicated – from its *composition* (the people concretely involved in it). Changes in a dominant coalition's composition (due, for example, to cooptation, to physiological substitutions, etc.) do not necessarily produce alterations in its conformation.

Legitimacy

Following the tradition that has its origins in Weber and that, with Schumpeter, gave rise to the modern "economic" theory of democracy, it seems possible and useful to think of party leaders as "entrepreneurs" who either try to conquer political power or to maintain or expand already aquired positions.[16] The entrepreneur's primary objective is to keep control of his enterprise. Party leaders can pursue this objective only if they secure their control over the distribution of organizational incentives. Should they lose this power – for example, when other actors acquire control over certain crucial resources – they are unlikely to remain at the party's head. This line of reasoning can, within certain limits,[17] be reformulated in terms of *legitimacy*: the leadership's legitimacy is a function of its control over the distribution of "public goods" (collective incentives) and/or "private goods" (selective incentives).[18] When the flow of benefits is interrupted, the organization is in serious trouble: revolts break out, leaders are contested, and attempts are made to change the guard and thereby preserve the organization. The link between selective incentives and legitimacy is sufficiently clear. Let us take the case of a party with a strong clientelistic component, i.e. a party in which selective incentives linked to the distribution of material benefits (monetary remuneration, patronage-system, etc.) prevail. Its leaders sleep peacefully as long as they can assure continuity in the clientele's remuneration, for their power is recognized as "legitimate" by a satisfied majority. But if, for one reason or another – for example, an unfavorable economic situation which reduces the resources available for client-oriented ends – continuity in the flow of benefits is interrupted or becomes uncertain, an "authority crisis" is triggered off in the party. As another example, let's take the case of an opposition party with a strong bureaucracy. The bureaucrats that make up the party's backbone normally have a vital interest in its survival. As long as the leaders follow a political strategy that does not endanger the organization, the leaders exert a virtually undisputed authority over the party bureaucrats. But if – due, for example, to some consistent environmental change – the leaders have to pursue an adventurous policy that stirs up dangerous reactions (e.g. the threat of state repression), or if they simply continue to adhere to a policy that had in the past been successful but that now, due to environmental changes, no longer "pays" (thus weakening rather than reinforcing the organization), the bureaucrats' rewards will be compromised, and the leadership's "legitimacy" will disappear.

The relation between collective incentives and legitimacy is more complicated. Collective incentives depend, as we have said, on the official goals, on the organizational ideology. The official goals, however, in order to be credible, must be accompanied by an indication of the means to be used. One cannot identify with a "cause" if there are not at least credible proposals as to the paths to be taken for their realization.[19] The specification of the political and/or social alliances that are to be strengthened or consolidated, of the most opportune tactics, etc., i.e. of what might be called here a "political strategy"[20] – in other words, the indication of the means – is indispensable to the credibility of the "cause," and improves its ability to function as a symbolic center of identification. The official goals must therefore be translated into a political strategy.[21]

This implies a rather close relationship between political strategy and the leadership's legitimacy. Once a political strategy has been formulated and accepted by the party, the elite's ability to distribute identity incentives to its followers depends on its application: if the political strategy loses credibility, the party's identity suffers, at least until a new political strategy is adopted. This reasoning explains why party elites, both majority elites (the dominant coalition) and minority elites, are often prisoners of their respective political strategies, and are often obliged (by the same rules of the game) to pursue them consistently. It is this fact which leads many theorists to erroneously sustain that a utilitarian theory (one viewing the leader as entrepreneur, and the party office competition as playing a crucial role in intra-party conflicts) cannot explain the elite's behavior. The game works in such a way, in fact, that a minority elite very often remains faithful to a political strategy which allows it to challenge the dominant coalition *even when* the strategy turns out to be an impractical means of obtaining a central power position in the party. To abandon the strategy would entail losing credibility and would thus preclude the possibility of future victories. Even a minority's political strategy functions as a source of legitimation, for the minority elite distributes identity incentives to its own restricted following on the basis of its strategy. Abandoning a political strategy for an openly opportunistic strategy is to risk immediate loss of the support that the minority elite has been guaranteed within the party. Remaining faithful to a political strategy without apparent *chance* of victory is thus a way of continuing to profit from one's position (i.e. the leadership of the internal opposition). The maintenance of this position is the precondition for future victories.[22] But even the majority elite, i.e. the dominant coalition, is more often than not a prisoner to its "political strategy," on the basis of which it distributes identity incentives to its following. The majority elite has, in fact, tied its fate to a distribution of identity incentives based on this strategy and cannot drastically change its ways without disorienting its following (and thereby instilling in them an "identity crisis"). This introduces an element of rigidity into the party's internal conflicts and explains why, when faced with serious organizational crises demanding profound changes of political strategy and sometimes redefinitions of organizational ideology, dominant coalitions are often unable to reelaborate their political strategies and consequently fall prey to the minority elites.[23] This would always be the case if parties depended exclusively upon identity incentives. But certain elites are able to maintain their positions, surviving changes in political strategy, clinging to the reserve of legitimation assured them through the distribution of selective incentives.

We can thus also explain why "transformism" (frequent change from one political strategy to another for purely opportunistic reasons) can only be a profitable and practical strategy if the party's incentive system provides far more material incentives than collective incentives.[24] Since this is more probable as a rule in governmental parties that have greater possibilities for substituting material for symbolic resources and that in any case need less voluntary participation from the "believers," we should normally expect to find more transformism in governmental party elites than in those of the opposition: "political coherence" is a more profitable virtue when the available exchange currency is constituted by "symbols" rather than by "money."

Organizational stability

Our thesis that a primary objective of party leaders – as political entrepreneurs – is the safeguarding of their control over their enterprises, can be reformulated as follows: the party leadership's fundamental objective is to safeguard *organizational stability*. By organizational stability I mean the conservation of the party's internal authority channels, i.e. its configuration of legitimate power.[25] Such a configuration is continually threatened by environmental challenges which can, at any moment, endanger the organization and thus offer ammunition to the minority elites (who were waiting for just such an occasion to challenge the organization's power structure).

To sustain that the leaders' goal is to conserve organizational stability is to attribute to them a broader goal than that of simply ensuring the organization's survival. The latter is but a *precondition* for the defense of the party's stability, for the maintenance of its internal authority channels. The activities designed to realize organizational stability can be of different types, for to conserve the status quo can involve activities which are defensive and cautious in certain cases, and innovative and/or aggressive in others. Leaders try to ensure organizational stability in more than one way (and Michels was thus mistaken in thinking that it could only be done through growing political conservatism).[26] According to a well-known theory,[27] organization leaders, *qua* entrepreneurs, always attempt to increase their organization's power. According to this theory, the more the organization grows and bolsters itself *vis-à-vis* competing organizations, the more its leaders' prestige grows, and the more extensive its controllable resources become. From this point of view, an organization's imperative is to expand in such a way as to increase its control over the environment and thereby augment its leaders' power resources. What this theory's supporters forget, however, is that an organization's expansion can, in certain cases, destabilize it (in the sense discussed above): a rapid increase in a party's membership can, for example, undermine its internal cohesion[28] (because of socialization differences between the old members and the newcomers) and give rise to a crisis in the party's collective identity. This can also happen in an opposition party that achieves a strong electoral victory which suddenly gives it a good deal more parliamentary clout: the "messianic hopes" fed by collective incentives when the party was in the opposition, with no chance of becoming a governmental party, are quickly crushed by daily administrative needs. The political temperature in such a party rises and leads to conflict and confrontations concerning political strategies; in a word, the party's identity is undermined.[29] In these cases, the organization's stability is thrown into question, and with it the party leadership's preeminent position.

The strategy that will be chosen by the party's leaders to ensure organizational stability cannot, therefore, be predetermined; it depends on the characteristics of internal power equilibria (the dominant coalition's conformation) and on the organization's relations with its environment. In certain cases, the organization's growth strengthens its stability; it thus becomes a tool for the consolidation of the leading group, and the organization manifests tendencies towards expansion (as has, for a long time, been true of certain opposition parties, in particular socialist and communist parties). In other cases, expansion is a product of competition within a divided elite. In a party of factions, for example, the organization's expansion through the recruitment of new members – as was the case for the Italian Christian-Democratic party in certain phases of its history[30] – and the "colonization" of sectors of the environment (e.g. *state* institutions), can be due to the different factions' attempts to strengthen themselves *vis-à-vis* their adversary factions. In still other cases, however, organizations exhibit no growth tendencies. There are a lot of examples – from Mollet's SFIO (French Socialist Party) to the CDU (German Christian Democratic Party) – in which we can find no trace of activities geared towards expansion; growth is perceived by their leaders as a possible threat to organizational stability, and is therefore systematically discouraged. In the examples cited, it is the national and local leaders in the dominant coalition who slow down growth, discourage recruitment, and maintain the organization in a static condition.

Organizational stability can thus be defended by leaders through different strategies: in certain cases through expansion (and increasing environmental domination), and in other cases through the avoidance of expansion (and increasing environmental adaptation). How to ensure the party's organizational stability is often a subject of debate and/or conflict within a dominant coalition, for example, between leaders backing expansive approaches to assuring stability and those backing defensive ones. In such a case of conflict, we find vacillations and inconsistencies between the party and its external environment (at least until the conflict is resolved) which give rise to continuous changes in the dominant coalition favoring one of the contenders at any given moment.

Conclusion

The problem of *organizational order* can now be raised. Organizations often have very varied goals and interests. But whatever the goals pursued by the different organizational actors – I'm reformulating Michels' thesis here in other terms – the leaders' primary objective is to ensure organizational stability. Organizational order, as has been noted,[31] is always a *negotiated order*, an order depending on the equilibrium reached between varied pressures and demands. The leaders' goal of organizational stability – to which they must necessarily subordinate other possible goals – plays a decisive role in this negotiation. In fact, leaders are (by definition) those who, by controlling the most vital zones of uncertainty, can most forcefully impose their objectives. The internal compromises upon which the organizational order rests are thus always compromises between the different demands that arise within the organization on the one hand and the imperatives of stability on the other hand. These compromises lead to the articulation of ends, and render intelligible organizational activities and behavior. It is the "conformation" of the dominant coalition which gives the "tenor" to these compromises and defines their modalities. Different types of organizational orders are possible – as many as there are possible conformations of the party's dominant coalition. But the degree of performance of a certain organizational order always depends on the success (or lack thereof) of the compromise between the leaders' objective of stability and the other innumerable ends that might be pursued within the party.

Part II
Organizational development

4
Institutionalization

Our argument up until this point has been aimed at constructing a number of premises indispensable to an organizational analysis of parties. We have dealt, however, with a *static* analysis. We have, so to speak, imagined a party *x* grasped at a moment *t* of its history, and have tried to isolate the instruments most useful in examining its organizational physiognomy as well as the conflicting pressures with which it is confronted. But a party (like any organization) is a structure in motion which evolves over time, reacting to external changes and to the changing "environments" in which it functions. One might suggest that the most important factors explaining its physiognomy and functioning are its organizational history (its past) and its relations with changing external environments. But the thesis is obviously too general thus formulated. In order to specify its implications we must use analytical tools which can give us a sort of "motion picture" of parties' organizational evolution in changeable environmental contexts. Once we have isolated these tools, it will be possible to attempt an historical-comparative analysis of the organizational development of a certain number of parties (this analysis being, in its turn, indispensable to the elaboration of a typology of party organizations).

The concepts essential to our analysis are, *genetic model* (the factors that, when combined, give an organization its mark, define its genetic characteristics[1]) and *institutionalization* (the way the organization "solidifies"). We will now examine, separately and in order, the main factors which account for the diversity of genetic party models, and for the noticeable differences in institutionalization. Afterwards we will relate the two concepts, showing *which* type of genetic model is presumably associated with *which* type of institutionalization. At that point it will be possible to compare this typology with the historical development of a certain number of political parties.

The genetic model

A party's organizational characteristics depend more upon its history, i.e. on how the organization originated and how it consolidated, than upon any other factor. The characteristics of a party's origin are in fact capable of exerting a weight on its organizational structure even decades later. Every organization bears the mark of its formation, of the crucial political–administrative decisions made by its founders, the decisions which "molded" the organization. Although crucial, the problem of parties' formative paths receives little consideration in the current literature on parties. Party formation theory has been unable to go beyond Duverger's distinction between *internally created* parties (parliamentary) and *externally created* parties, between parties created by preexisting parliamentary elites and those created by "non-political" groups and associations.[2] As historical research on the origin of a large number of parties has already demonstrated, however, this old distinction is only partly adequate. It is above all unable to account for organizational differences between parties with the same type of origin (internal or external): a parliamentary origin permits many outcomes; analogously, party organization with extra-parliamentary origins (which for Duverger are primarily mass parties) vary very widely.[3]

We cannot, therefore, classify parties according to their origins using the internal/external distinction. A more complex model is required, one that can deal with the information that historians have gathered on the origins of many parties. A party's formation is always a complex process. It often consists in the amalgamation of many heterogeneous political groups. Though each party's genetic model is historically unique, it is nevertheless possible to identify certain similarities and differences between the different parties' genetic models. Three main factors help us define a party's genetic model. The first factor concerns the organization's construction and development. As two Scandinavian political scientists have observed,[4] a party's organizational development – the organization's construction, strictly speaking – is due to territorial *penetration*, to territorial *diffusion*, or to a combination of these two. Territorial penetration occurs when the "center" controls, stimulates, or directs the development of the "periphery," i.e. the constitution of local and intermediate party associations. Territorial diffusion occurs when development results from spontaneous germination: local elites construct party associations which are only later integrated into a national organization. This penetration/diffusion distinction does *not* correspond to Duverger's distinction between internally and externally created parties. Developments resulting from diffusion or penetration can characterize either of the latter two types of parties. As Eliassen and Svaasand note, both conservative and liberal European parties are for the most part internally created (parliamentarily), and yet almost all conservative parties develop primarily through territorial penetration, while many liberal parties develop through diffusion.[5]

At times "mixed" types of organizational development prevail: development initially takes place through diffusion: a number of local associations autonomously spring up in various parts of the country; later they unite to form a national organization. The national organization then goes on to develop local associations where these are still absent (penetration). Liberal parties have often had this mixed type of development.[6] It is generally possible, however, to identify a prevailing modality. For example, many communist and conservative parties developed primarily through penetration. Many socialist and confessional parties, on the other hand, developed primarily through diffusion. Sometimes a party is formed by the union of two or more preexisting national organizations (as was the case for the SPD and the SFIO): this is a type of diffusion.

To anticipate a point that relates the genetic model to institutionalization (and that I will take up further on) different organizational developments influence differently the dominant coalition's formation and degree of internal cohesion. Organizational development through territorial penetration implies, by definition, the existence of a sufficiently cohesive "center" right from the start. It is this center, composed of a restricted group of national leaders, which forms the first nucleus of its dominant coalition. A party which develops through diffusion is, on the other hand, a party whose leadership's formation process is normally much more turbulent and complex, because of the many local autonomous leaders who control their own associations and aspire to national leadership. Such a party's national organization is a *federation* of different local groups, and the party is quite likely (unlike parties which have developed through penetration) to give rise to decentralized and semi-autonomous structures, and consequently, to a dominant coalition divided by constant struggle for party control.

The second principle determining a party's genetic model is the presence or absence (at the party's origin) of an external "sponsor" institution,[7] for this affects the leadership's source of legitimation. If such an external "sponsor" institution exists, the party will be conceived as its "political arm." This leads to two consequences: (1) the party's organizational loyalties will be *indirect loyalties*, loyalties primarily to the external institution, and only secondarily to the party; (2) the external institution is, consequently, the leadership's source of legitimation, and this can tip the balance from one side to the other in the internal power struggle. We shall therefore distinguish between *externally legitimated* parties, and *internally legitimated* parties.

The third factor to take into consideration is the role of charisma in the party's formation, i.e. whether the party is or is not essentially created by, and a vehicle for, a charismatic leader. To be sure, there are *always* charismatic components in the leader–follower relation in a party's genetic phase: a party's formation always involves aspects of *statu nascenti*, of collective effervescence, in which charisma typically emerges.[8] Our concern here is with parties formed by one leader who imposes himself as the undisputed founder, conceiver, and interpreter of a set of political symbols (the party's original ideological goals) which become inseparable from his person. In this sense, the National Socialist Party, the Italian Fascist Party, and the Gaullist Party were, for all intents and purposes, charismatic parties, parties whose existence was inconceivable without reference to their leaders. This is not, however, true for the SPD or the Labour Party, regardless of the prestige of their leaders.

In some cases, however, we can speak of what Robert Tucker has called a "situational charisma" without resorting to Weberian characterizations. Determinant here are *not* the leader's messianic components (so important in the case of "pure" charisma) but rather a state of acute social *stress* that gets the people ready to perceive as extraordinarily qualified and to follow with enthusiastic loyalty a leadership offering salvation from distress. More specifically,

we might use the term 'situational charisma' to refer to instances where a leader-personality of non-messianic tendency evokes a charismatic response simply because he offers, in a time of acute distress, leadership that is perceived as a source and means of salvation from distress.[9]

According to Tucker, "situational charisma" was quite important in the cases of, for instance, Churchill and Roosevelt.

Situational charisma was certainly important in the case of Adenaur and the CDU, De Gasperi and the DC, Hardie and the Independent Labour Party, Jaurès and the SFIO, etc. Situational charisma, like "pure" charisma, makes the leader – in the eyes of the electorate and of a majority of the activists – the authorized interpreter of the party's policy, and ensures him great control over the forming organization. Situational charisma differs, however, from pure charisma in that the leader in question is less able to mold the organization as he likes. Hitler, Mussolini and De Gaulle were able to *impose* all key decisions upon their parties. Adenaur, De Gasperi and Jaurès had to *bargain* with many other organizational actors. A party based on pure charisma has no autonomous existence apart from its leader and is entirely at his mercy; a party based on situational charisma is not simply a leader's creation, but is the product of many different impulses and thrusts: other actors maintain a certain degree of control over the organization's zones of uncertainty.

Pure charismatic parties are rather rare, but not as rare as one might think. Often they are small parties which remain marginal with respect to large-scale political games; more often, they are parties which pass like a meteor over the political firmament, which spring up and die out without ever institutionalizing.[10] Institutionalization entails a "routinization of charisma," a transfer of authority from the leader to the party, and very few charismatic parties survive this transfer. The three factors creating conspicuous differences in parties' genetic models are thus (1) development through diffusion or penetration; (2) the presence or absence of an external "sponsor" institution; and (3) the presence or absence of an initially charismatic leadership.

Institutionalization

During the organization's formative phase, the leaders, whether charismatic or not, normally play a crucial role. They spell out the ideological aims of the future party, select the organization's social base, its "hunting ground," and shape the organization on the basis of these aims and this social base – taking into account, of course, available resources, different socio-economic and political conditions in different parts of the country, etc. During this phase, the problem of the leadership, of the political entrepreneurs, is that of "selecting the key values and of building an organization that is coherent with them."[11] This explains the crucial role that ideology normally plays in shaping the newly-formed organization, in determining its *collective identity*. To its supporters, the organization is still a *tool* to be used to realize certain ends:[12] their identity is defined exclusively with respect to the ideological aims selected by the leaders, not yet with respect to the organization itself. This is why an organization, during its formative phase, can be effectively analysed using the "rational model." As institutionalization begins, we can note a qualitative leap. Institutionalization is, in fact, the process by which an organization incorporates its founders' values and aims. In the words of Philip Selznick, this process implies the passage from a "consumable" organization (i.e. a pure means to certain ends) to an *institution*.[13] The organization slowly loses its character as a tool: it becomes valuable in and of itself, and its goals become inseparable and indistinguishable from it. In this way, its preservation and survival become a "goal" for a great number of its supporters.

The organizational goals (the ideological aims) of the party's founders shape the organization's physiognomy; with institutionalization these objectives are "articulated" (in the specific sense given above to this term) with respect to organizational needs. There are essentially two processes which develop simultaneously to bring about institutionalization: (1) the development of *interests* related to the organization's preservation (those of the leaders at the different levels of the organizational pyramid);[14] and (2) the development of diffuse *loyalties*.

Both processes are tied, as we have already seen, to the formation of an internal incentive system. In order to survive, an organization must, from the very start, distribute *selective incentives* to some of its members (prestigious positions, "internal" career possibilities) and this leads to the development of organizational interests. A procedure must be set up for selecting and recruiting leaders for the various organizational levels. Party founders can only partly and temporarily resolve the problem of finding the right people for the leading roles at the different organizational levels. Future elites must be "raised" (socialized to the role's tasks) and recruited as the organization develops.

The development of diffuse organizational loyalties depends on the distribution of *collective incentives* (of identity) to the organization's members (its activists) as well as to a part of its external supporters, i.e. the "electorate of belonging;" it is related to the formation of a "collective identity"[15] that is guided and shaped by the party's founders. The consolidation of an incentive system – comprising both selective and collective incentives – is thus very much tied to institutionalization: if such a system doesn't consolidate, institutionalization doesn't take place, and the organization cannot guarantee its own survival. The organizational loyalties which make the party a *community of fate* (for its activists and many of its supporters) and the organizational interests which help the organization become more autonomous *vis-à-vis* its external environment, these loyalties and interests provide the basis for permanent activity geared towards organizational self-preservation.[16]

Up until now we have discussed institutionalization as though it were a process or a collection of attributes that the organization may or may not develop in the period following its birth; thus we have distinguished parties which undergo institutionalization from those which do not (and which soon dissolve).

But the problem of institutionalization is more complex. For organizations don't all institutionalize in the same way or with the same intensity. Profound differences exist from one party to another. All parties must institutionalize to a certain extent in order to survive, but whereas in certain cases the institutionalization process gives rise to *strong* institutions, in other cases it gives rise to *weak* institutions. My hypothesis here is that parties can be distinguished primarily according to *the degree of institutionalization* they attain, this degree being in its turn dependent upon the way the party forms, on its type of genetic model (I leave aside here the type of environmental influences to which the organization is exposed). This implies that it is at least theoretically possible to "measure" the different parties' levels of institutionalization, and to place them at one point or another along an institutionalization *continuum*.

Institutionalization, as it has been used here, can be measured on two scales: (1) that of the organization's degree of autonomy *vis-à-vis* its environment, and (2) that of its degree of *systemness*, i.e. the degree of interdependence of its different internal sectors.[17] The autonomy/dependence dimension refers to the organization's relation with the external environment. An organization is necessarily involved in exchange relations with its environment: it must procure the resources (human and material) which are indispensable to its functioning; to obtain them it must exchange internally "produced" resources. A party must distribute incentives of different types not only to its own members, but also to external supporters (the electorate, its collateral organizations, etc.). A position of autonomy is reached when the organization can directly control exchange processes with its environment. An organization is, on the other hand, *dependent* when its indispensable resources are in part controlled by other organizations (e.g. the British Labour Party depends on the trade unions for the funding necessary to sustain it and conduct its electoral campaigns, and for the mobilization of worker support). Institutionalization always involves at least some "autonomization" *vis-à-vis* the environment. The difference between levels of autonomy in different parties is therefore one of degree. An organization which has little autonomy exerts little control over its environment, adapting to it rather than vice versa. A very autonomous organization, on the other hand, exerts a great deal of control over its environment and can transform it to meet its own needs. Only organizations that directly control their own vital exchange processes with the environment can develop that form of "latent imperialism"[18] which reduces the organization's areas of environmental uncertainty. The more control a party exercises over its environment, the more it can autonomously generate resources for its own functioning. The "ideal type" of the mass party described by Duverger has, considering its autonomy *vis-à-vis* the environment, institutionalized as much as possible. Such a party directly controls its financial resources (through membership), dominates its collateral associations – extending, through them, its hegemony over the *classe gardée* – possesses a developed central administrative apparatus (i.e. is strongly bureaucratized), and chooses its leaders from within (involving a minimum of external entries); its public assembly representatives are controlled by the party's leaders – the party's organization remains autonomous regardless of the degree of institutionalization of the parliamentary assemblies.[19]

At the other extreme we have the party with very little autonomy *vis-à-vis* its environment, depending on it (e.g. on interest groups) for its financing; it does not control its collateral associations, but is, rather, controlled by them or must bargain with them on an equal basis; its electoral lists include many candidates sponsored by interest groups who have never had previous careers within the party.

Both are ideal types: no party is ever totally dependent upon its environment, and no party can ever develop as much autonomy *vis-à-vis* its environment as Duverger's "mass party." We can, nevertheless, distinguish between those parties which conform more closely to the first model and those which conform more closely to the second. A characteristic easily associated with the level of autonomy *vis-à-vis* the environment is the level of indeterminacy of organizational boundaries: the more autonomous the organization, the more defined its boundaries. An autonomous organization allows us to establish fairly certainly where it starts and where it leaves off (i.e. who comprises it, what other organizations fall under its influences, etc.). A very dependent organization, on the other hand, is one whose boundaries are undefined: many groups and/or associations formally outside the organization are really part of it, have ties with its internal sub-groups, and "cross" its formal boundaries in a more or less concealed fashion. When boundaries are well defined the organization corresponds to the "closed" model, when undefined to the "open" model.

The second dimension of institutionalization, the degree of systemicity, refers to the internal structural coherence of the organization. When an organizational system leaves a good deal of autonomy to its internal sub-groups,[20] its degree of systemness is low. The sub-groups thus autonomously control (independently of the organization's center) the resources necessary to their functioning (i.e. their exchange processes with the environment). A high degree of systemness, on the other hand, implies a great deal of interdependency among the sub-groups assured by the centralized control of organizational resources and exchange processes with the environment. The higher the degree of systemness, the more concentrated the control over the party relations with the environment, but also (given the tendentially cumulative nature of power resources), over other vital zones of uncertainty. Reciprocally, the lower the degree of systemness, the more diffuse the control over the zones of uncertainty.

A low level of systemness generally leads to a very heterogeneous organization: the sub-groups differ from one another because they extract their resources from different environmental sectors. A high level of systemness, on the other hand, generally leads to more homogeneous sub-groups.

The two dimensions of institutionalization are related, for a low degree of systemness often implies little autonomy *vis-à-vis* the environment, and vice versa. In fact, the sub-groups' independence from the "center" is often tied to their dependence upon specific environmental sectors (as when a local association's independence from the party's national organization is assured by a strong controlling local interest group, an important local notable, etc.). This last example helps explain why undefined organizational boundaries typical of high environmental dependence *also* give rise to weak internal coherent structures and a low degree of systemness.

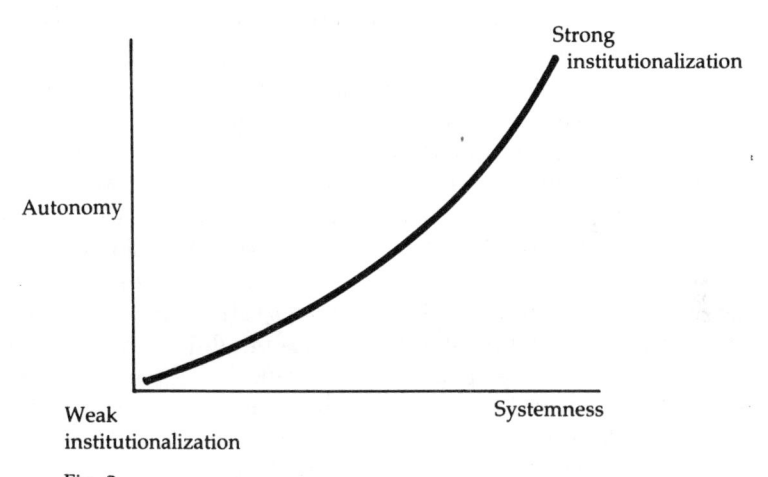

Fig. 2

A highly institutionalized organization normally possesses more defenses with respect to environmental challenges than a weakly institutionalized one, as its instruments of control over environmental uncertainty are concentrated in the hands of the "center" rather than dispersed among the sub-groups. All the same, a "strong" institution can be more fragile than a "weak" one. When an organization's systemness level is high, in fact, a crisis affecting one of its parts is destined to make itself quickly felt by all its other parts. When its level is low, the relative autonomy of the different parts allows for an easier isolation of the crisis effects.[21]

A highly institutionalized party drastically limits its internal actors' margins of maneuverability. The organization imposes itself upon the actors, it channels their strategies into specific and obligatory paths. A highly institutionalized party is one in which change takes place slowly and laboriously, one which is more likely to break up because of excessive rigidity (as was the case with the SPD in 1917) than to experience deep-rooted and unexpected changes. A weakly institutionalized party is one in which the actors have more autonomy in order to compete with each other; the competing organizational subgroups are assured autonomous control over the different environmental sectors and external resources. Such an organization can experience sudden transformations, as when, for example, a sudden regeneration of organizational and ideological leadership follows a long period of progressive sclerosis. Regenerations of this type are rarer in highly institutionalized parties.

We have at our disposal at least five indicators of the different degrees of institutionalization in parties.

Firstly, the degree of development of the central extra-parliamentary organization.[22] The rule is that a highly institutionalized party possesses a developed central bureaucracy, a strong national apparatus confronting the party's intermediate and peripheral associations. In a weakly institutionalized party, the central bureaucratic apparatus is weak and embryonic. It is hardly, if at all, developed, and the peripheral associations are rather independent from the center. This is the result of a different degree of concentration/dispersion of control over the organizational zones of uncertainty (*high* versus *low* level of systemness). For example, the British Conservative Party, more highly institutionalized than the Labour Party, also traditionally possesses a more powerful and developed central bureaucratic apparatus. A more highly institutionalized party is thus both more bureaucratized and centralized than a weakly institutionalized party. Centralization is a consequence of bureaucratization.

Secondly, the degree of homogeneity of organizational structures at the same hierarchical level: in highly institutionalized organizations, for example, the local associations tend to be organized in the same way throughout the national territory. In weakly institutionalized ones, the local associations are likely to be quite heterogeneous. This is obviously due to different degrees of systemness, of structural coherence.

Thirdly, how the organization is financed: the more highly institutionalized the organization, the more probable that it has at its disposal a revenue system based on a regular flow of contributions from a *plurality* of sources. The less institutionalized, the less continuous and regular its flow of funds, and the less diversified its financial sources. Regularity is indispensable to the maintenance of a bureaucratic structure that can preside over the party's structural coherence and keep its degree of systemness high. A plurality of financial sources safeguards the party from external control.

Fourth, relations with the external collateral organizations: We have said that different degrees of institutionalization lead to different levels of control over the environment. A highly institutionalized party dominates its external organizations, as has been the case (for the better part of their existence) for the PCI, PCF, SPD, and the SPÖ (the Austrian Socialist Party), in their relations with trade unions, or of the British Conservative Party in its relations with its collateral organizations: external organizations act as the party's "transmission belt." In weakly institutionalized parties, on the other hand, there are either no relations with external institutions (e.g. the SFIO in the first decades of this century, and the CGT), only precarious ones (e.g. the PSI and trade unions, 1906–22), or the collateral organizations are weak and not vital (CDU); or else, finally, the party is itself dependent on external organizations (the British Labour Party).

Fifthly, the degree of correspondence between a party's statutory norms and its "actual power structure." Such a correspondence tends to be greater in highly institutionalized parties. This does not mean, naturally, that strong institutions' statutes accurately describe their actual power distributions, but rather that actors in dominant party positions are there because their authority is formally recognized and not because they, for example, play important roles outside the organization. A highly institutionalized party's dominant coalition, like that of the British Conservative Party, revolves around a parliamentary leader whose preeminent role is formally recognized. The Labour Party's dominant coalition, on the other hand, *de facto* includes the trade union leaders whose roles are not formally recognized (i.e. the formal constitution attributes power to the trade unions, but not directly to the TUC, the unions' governing body). This phenomenon directly follows from the different degrees of indeterminacy of the boundaries associated with the level of institutionalization. If the institution is strong, the boundaries are clear and defined; people, groups, or associations formally outside the party cannot, by definition, play leading roles within the organization. If the institution is weak, the boundaries are undefined, autonomy *vis-à-vis* the environment is minimal, and actors who are formally outside can more easily "cross over" the boundaries.

Strong and weak institutions: two ideal types

A low degree of institutionalization generally gives rise to a dominant coalition which is not very cohesive (i.e. one which is subdivided into factions), whereas a high degree of institutionalization gives rise to a cohesive dominant coalition (i.e. one which is subdivided into tendencies). In other words, a high degree of institutionalization implies a concentration of control over the zones of uncertainty and thus over the distribution of organizational incentives. A low degree of institutionalization implies a dispersion of control over the zones of uncertainty, and thus the absence of a "center" that monopolizes incentive distribution.

The degree of institutionalization therefore shapes the party's dominant coalition, particularly influencing its degree of internal cohesion. With the exception (as we shall soon see) of charismatic parties – where the initial absence of institutionalization is accompanied by a cohesive dominant coalition – the two phenomena are generally closely linked: the less institutionalization, the more divided the dominant coalition, the more institutionalization, the more cohesive the dominant coalition. Thus an inverse relation exists between the party's degree of institutionalization and its sub-groups' degree of organization, for *the more institutionalized the party, the less organized are its internal groups*. Correlatively, *the less institutionalized the party, the more organized are its internal groups*. In the extreme case of maximal institutionalization, the groups are barely organized: they represent *tendencies* in a pure state. In the extreme case of minimal institutionalization, the groups are highly organized *factions*. As the difference in degree of institutionalization between parties (and within the same party at different times) is rather one of "more or less," so too the difference in degree of organization between their internal groups is one of greater or lesser organization (see Figure 3).

Given the degree of institutionalization, the "opportunity structure" varies within each party, or rather the modalities and channels through which internal political competition develops vary.[23] Consequently, the modalities of elite recruitment vary. In a highly institutionalized party, the recruitment of elites tends, in accordance with its dominant coalition's cohesive character, to have a *centripetal* movement: since there is a strong "center" in the party – a cohesive dominant coalition that monopolizes the zones of uncertainty and incentive distribution – there is thus only one way to make one's career in the party: *to allow oneself to be coopted by the center*. The opportunity structure is such that the "ambitious members" (careerists) must, in order to rise to the party's upper rungs, comply with central direc-

```
Strong institution              Weak institution
◄───────────────────────────────────────────►
    tendencies                      factions
```
Fig. 3

tives. The result is a sort of funnel-shaped structure, for personal mobility and success require a *vertical convergence at the center*; one must be supported by a restricted national elite and zealously conform to its will. In a weakly institutionalized party, on the other hand, the recruitment of elites has a *centrifugal* movement. Many groups at the top control important power resources and are thus able to distribute organizational incentives. Rather than speak of a group at the top, we should instead speak in terms of a plurality of groups which are either in alliance or at odds with each other. The climb has a centrifugal movement because, in order to succeed, one needs to politically define oneself as belonging to a group (a specific faction) which is "opposed" to all the other groups.

In regard to internal "opportunity structures," a strong institution tends to create an internal inequality system which is very autonomous and independent from the societal one (its inequalities being primarily dictated by the division of labor in its bureaucratic structure); a weak institution will have a less autonomous internal inequality system. Greater institutionalization means greater autonomy from the environment;[24] thus the criteria defining a highly institutionalized party's internal inequalities tend to be primarily *endogenous*, specific to a given organization. In the case of weak institutions, such criteria are at least in part *exogenous*, i.e. externally imposed. Concretely, this means that the more highly institutionalized a party, the more "professional" will be its internal participation (and thus the criteria regulating its inequality system will be those of a professional–bureaucratic structure). The less institutionalized a party, the more the internal participation tends to be of the "civil" type,[25] i.e. a transfer within the organization of external resources controlled by people well placed in the societal inequality system. In other words the weaker the institution, the more "important notables" and the fewer "political professionals" we find in its internal hierarchy, in the elected positions, etc.

We can reformulate this point in another way: in highly institutionalized parties, political activity tends to assume the form of a "true" career: one enters the party at the lower levels and one rises, after a long apprenticeship, step by step. In weakly institutionalized parties, on the other hand, few "careers" of this type exist; there is greater discontinuity at all levels;[26] and while there are few "conventional" careers,[27] in the strict sense, there are many rapid careers involving immediate entry to the middle–high ranks. More generally, we can say that a high degree of institutionalization corresponds primarily to "vertical integration" of elites:[28] people enter the organization at low levels and rise to the top, they are born and raised within the organization. In weakly institutionalized organizations, on the other hand, there is a "horizontal integration" of elites: people enter the party at high levels from the outside environments in which they already occupy elite positions, i.e. they convert other resources into political resources (as do local important notables, but also all those coopted within the party because of the power they wield over extra-party organizations).[29]

Being by definition less "permeable" to external relations, a highly institutionalized party usually has fewer clientelary relations with its followers than a weakly institutionalized one, as there are fewer important notables in it. (A weakly institutionalized organization is not, however, automatically clientelistic.)

On the other hand, the higher the degree of institutionalization, the stronger and more extensive is the party's subculture. Only a strong institution – one capable of dominating its social base – can develop the "social integration party's" characteristics. It is for this reason that the greater the institutionalization the more the party subculture resembles a "society within a society."[30] A weak institution, on the other hand, having to adapt to its social base, will not develop a strong party subculture. Religious parties, however, present an exception, for while they are normally weak institutions, they are often inserted into strong political subcultures. Such externally legitimated parties can take advantage of an associative subcultural network which actually depends (as does the party) on the sponsoring institution (the church).

We have spoken up until now about the differences between two ideal types of parties, those which are strongly and those which are weakly institutionalized. But these are *ideal* types: no party totally corresponds to the one or the other. The internal inequality system will therefore never be entirely independent from the societal inequality system,[31] nor totally dependent upon it. Recruitment will never be exclusively centrifugal nor centripetal, nor will the integration of elites be exclusively of the horizontal or vertical type. No party, furthermore, will be immune from clientelism nor totally clientelistic. Real parties can be located on an institutionalization continuum, but not at its extremes.[32]

In addition, the fact that a party is highly institutionalized is no guarantee that de-institutionalization, loss of autonomy *vis-à-vis* the environment, and decline in organizational "systemness" will not take place when its environment undergoes radical changes. Nor is a weakly institutionalized party necessarily condemned to always remain the same. The way that institutionalization, however, has taken place generally continues to weigh upon the party's internal life for decades, conditioning its internal competition system and political behavior.

Genetic model and institutionalization: a typology

Having defined institutionalization and the main elements of parties' genetic models, we shall now try to see how genetic model and institutionalization are related, i.e. how, a certain originary model influences the degree of institutionalization.

Organizational development through penetration and diffusion are related to institutionalization in an at least theoretically comprehensible way. Development through penetration tends to produce a strong institution. A cohesive elite, able to set in motion a strong developmental process in the nascent organization, is present by definition right from the start. Development through diffusion, on the other hand, tends to produce a weak institution because of the presence of many competing elites controlling conspicuous organizational resources; the organization is thus forced to develop through federation, compromise, and negotiation among a plurality of groups.

Analogously, we can easily determine the kind of relation that exists between the presence or absence of an external sponsoring organization and the degree of institutionalization that a party can attain. The presence of a sponsoring organization generally results in a weak institution. In fact, the external organization has no interest in strengthening the party (beyond certain limits) for this would inevitably reduce the party's dependence upon it. The very fact that the supporters' party loyalty is indirect (the party being externally legitimated), impedes strong institutionalization. Therefore, *ceteris paribus*, it is easier for an internally legitimated party (i.e. a party not sponsored by another organization) to become a strong institution. Communist parties, however, present an important exception, sponsored as they are by an external organization (the Comintern) and yet at the same time highly institutionalized. We can thus suppose that the sponsoring organization affects the party in formation in one way if the organization is part of the same national society in which the party operates, affecting the party differently if it is not. If the sponsoring organization is a trade union or a church, the formation of a highly institutionalized party will be impeded, implying as it would autonomization, i.e. "emancipation" of the party from the sponsoring organization. If, however, the sponsoring organization operates outside of the national society, a high degree of institutionalization guaranteeing the party's independence from the national environment is a probable outcome, but this independence is bought at the price of greater dependence on the sponsoring organization. The Bolshevization process of communist parties in the 1920s resulted in highly institutionalized organizations dominated by cohesive dominant coalitions, and yet their autonomy *vis-à-vis* the national environment was accompanied by subordination to an international institution which functioned as the source of their legitimation and the external support of their dominant coalitions.

When the sponsoring organization operates within the national society a "*double* organizational membership" phenomenon influences the party's institutionalization process, for party members are normally also trade union members or active in a religious community. The external organization's authority is directly exercised by its representatives (the trade union leaders, the ecclesiastical hierarchy). In the case of a sponsoring organization which operates outside of the national society, on the other hand, double membership cannot (by definition) play a role, and the organization's authority can only be exercised through the party. We can thus hypothesize different levels of institutionalization for the different types of legitimation (namely, internal, "national" external, "extra-national" external). If internal legitimation corresponds to strong institutions, and national external legitimation (e.g. labour parties) corresponds to weak institutions, extra-national external legitimation tends to be associated with institutions which are very strong (i.e. which are very independent from the national society, and show a high degree of internal structural coherence).

The discussion up to this point, of the relationship between the genetic model and level of institutionalization can be schematized as follows:

	penetration	diffusion
	Institutionalization	
	strong	weak
external legitimation	1	2
internal legitimation	3	4

Fig. 4

Case one is above all exemplified by communist parties. Their source of legitimation is external, and the dominant coalition asserting itself within the party against the adversaries of Bolshevism is politically cohesive. Their organizational development is predominantly characterized by territorial penetration (as well as by total reorganization of the local structures inherited when they split off from the socialist parties). The process results in a high degree of institutionalization.

Case two is represented by labour parties (the British Labour Party first and foremost) and by some religious parties (the Italian Popular Party, the Italian DC, the Belgian DC, etc.). Their organizational development is predominantly due to territorial diffusion and to the spontaneous germination of associations. An initial development through diffusion, along with the existence of a sponsoring organization, impedes the formation of strong organizational loyalties. The dominant coalition that forms is, moreover, divided and heterogeneous. The organization institutionalizes but only to a limited extent.

Case three is represented primarily but not exclusively by what Duverger terms "internally created" parties. The center which builds the organization through territorial penetration is cohesive, and is generally a parliamentary elite which rallies behind the banner of a very prestigious leader. The process results in a strong institution. Different conservative parties, with the British Conservative Party at the head of the list, have developed in this way (curiously, much more often than liberal parties).[33]

Case four primarily covers parties created by the federation of existing groups, parties such as the SFIO the PSI, the Japanese Socialist Party, the CDU, etc. The federation of two or more preexisting organizations, or an initial development through diffusion in a "pure" state (in the case of the CDU),[34] gives rise to a dominant coalition with weak cohesion, because different internal groups possess veto power with respect to the center's attempts to reinforce itself at the expense of the periphery. The organization institutionalizes in a weak manner.

Personal charisma: a deviant case

In the preceding discussion we only considered how two of the three aforementioned factors characterizing the different parties' genetic models (namely the type of organizational development and the presence or absence of an external organization) can be hypothetically linked to different degrees of institutionalization. We have not as yet spoken of charismatic leadership, for its role is more complex and must be treated separately. The presence of personal charisma gives birth, in fact, to partially deviant outcomes with respect to the analysis made up to this point. We may begin by saying that charisma can be associated with development through both penetration and diffusion (or federation). But the latter, considering the available historical cases, is the most likely association: a charismatic party is generally born through the federation of a plurality of spontaneously germinating local groups and/or preexisting organizations identifying with and submitting to the same leader. Charisma is, however, incompatible with the simultaneous presence of a sponsoring organization. The latter only tolerates what I have defined, following Tucker, as "situational charisma," which is, in effect, but a diluted form of personal charisma. Pure charisma and sponsoring organizations are mutually incompatible: either one or the other exists (though often, naturally, neither the one nor the other is present). The party cannot simultaneously be a leader's tool, shaped entirely by him, *and* the political arm of an external organization. But the singularity of pure charisma consists in the fact that it contextually produces a cohesive dominant coalition despite the absence of a process of organizational institutionalization. Charisma therefore presents an exception to our hypothesis that the stronger the institutionalization, the more cohesive the dominant coalition (and vice versa): the dominant coalition is cohesive from the very start, though composed of various tendencies (which are often secretly but virulently fighting among themselves). The leader represents the cement, and the struggle between the different groups aims at greater protection by and more benefits from the leader. Cohesion is assured by the fact that only those who benefit from the leader's support and faith have authorized access to the party's "inner circle." In such a party, as in strong institutions with powerful bureaucracies (but for different reasons), the recruitment of elites thus has a centripetal movement, and the organization is highly centralized – at any rate, this is the case *before* the eventual routinization of charisma, i.e. prior to institutionalization. In a charismatic party (before the routinization of charisma), the absence of institutionalization and the presence of a very strong centralization of authority (which, in non-charismatic parties can only be found under conditions of strong bureaucratization) are associated.

The centralization of authority – or rather the concentration of control over the zones of organizational uncertainty in the leader's hands – appears outside a context of bureaucratic development because, in general terms (following Weber here), charisma and bureaucratization are antithetical organizational phenomena.

Personal charisma is, besides, generally associated with strong resistance to institutionalization. The leader, in fact, has no interest in organizational reinforcement which would inevitably set the stage for the party's "emancipation" from his control. In a certain sense, the charismatic leader and the external sponsoring organization occupy analogous positions *vis-à-vis* the party, for they tend to discourage institutionalization.[35]

This reasoning helps explain why institutionalization is very rare in charismatic parties – why, in other words, charismatic parties generally cannot survive their founder, cannot go through the process of routinization (or objectivization) of charisma. In the few cases in which this has happened, the original stamp remains: a charismatic party which has institutionalized will probably maintain its highly centralized internal authority pattern – which is, in turn, the prerequisite for a relatively high degree of institutionalization.

	Genetic Model	Institutionalization
1	territorial diffusion	weak
	territorial penetration	strong
2	internal legitimation	strong
	external national legitimation	weak
	external extra-national legitimation	strong
3	charisma	absent/strong

Fig. 5

Conclusion

The preceding discussion has allowed us to develop a typology of party formation. We must now "empirically" test this typology, which in this domain means developing an historical-comparative analysis using the available information on the birth and formation processes of a number of concrete parties.

We must, however, qualify what we have said. The above typology excludes the role of environmental factors by introducing the clause "under equal conditions." It limits itself to identifying certain hypothetical relations between genetic models (the independent variable) and degrees of institutionalization (the dependent variable). The typology was obtained by selecting certain plausible factors and trying to discover what effects they have upon other factors selected in the same way. When such a typology is tested (empirically checked), the clause "under equal conditions" no longer applies. We then find ourselves faced with a great variety of environmental conditions which operate as intervening (and troubling) variables between parties' genetic models and their degrees of institutionalization, variables which can favor very different outcomes from those hypothesized. These factors – which we excluded while constructing our typology – must be taken into account when we undertake an historical-comparative control of the hypothesis.[36]

5
Oppositional parties (1)

It is a common belief that the organizational characteristics of parties which are in opposition for a good part of their existence are different from those of parties which stay in power for a long time. The former have a greater need for strong and solid organization than the latter. They cannot rely on the state bureaucracy for support, cannot utilize *pro domo sua* the state and its agencies, and they do not have at their disposal the abundant financial support that interest groups reserve for parties in government. They can, for the most part, only count on themselves. Strengthening their organization, making it able to mobilize the party's supporters efficiently and continuously, is usually the only practicable way to overcome their disadvantage in the competition with governmental parties. The opposite is true for governmental parties. These parties have at their disposal a multiplicity of public resources in political competition, and these resources are often an efficient substitute for supporter mobilization. Pursuing this line of reasoning we should expect parties that form and develop in opposition to be more prone to becoming strong institutions, and parties that gain national power immediately after their formation – thus undergoing organizational consolidation while in power – to become weak institutions. This is often the case. In effect, the control of state resources (or lack thereof) in the crucial consolidation phase often weighs heavily upon the modality of institutionalization. This is not, however, always true. Different degrees of institutionalization can occur among "opposition parties" (i.e. parties that consolidate while in opposition), just as they can occur among "government parties." No *rigid* relation exists between the level of institutionalization and the party's initial place with respect to national government.

The initial position can, however, be important, and so I shall use it as a sort of litmus paper test: I will examine separately the initial organizational developments of some "oppositional parties" and some "governmental parties" so as to allow for a comparison among the different cases. In this way, it will also be possible to test the hypothesis about the relationship between genetic models and levels of institutionalization, which we have already laid out.

The first series of comparisons (in chapters 5 and 6) involve parties that have two common characteristics: (1) they are all parties that institutionalized during a long period of opposition; (2) they are parties (namely socialist and communist) situated on the same side of industrial society's fundamental "cleavage," the class cleavage. Despite these similarities, they are parties which have developed with marked differences as far as their organizational profile is concerned.

In this chapter I will examine the development of three parties (SPD, PCF, PCI) which have become "strong institutions." In the following chapter we will examine three cases of "weak institutions."[1]

The German Social Democratic Party

The SPD, the first mass party in Europe, had a singular fate: it became a symbol of both the virtues and defects of organizational power. The SPD, the political organization which Friedrich Engels viewed favorably,[2] was also a model inspiring most European socialists:[3] its political programs (from Gotha to Erfurt) were copied exactly by many other socialist parties; its charter became the model of many others; and its organizational and electoral success were seen for decades as the proof of the imminent advent of a socialist society. Beginning with Michels' analysis, the SPD became the symbol of the bureaucratic and oligarchical degeneration of big organizations as well.

Not all of the organizational power developed by the SPD during the imperial epoch (and which gave rise to many contrasting opinions) has gone today. After the vicissitudes of Weimar, the clandestinity of the Nazi period, Bad Godesberg, and even after a long period in power (1966–82), the SPD maintains, albeit in an inevitably diluted form, many features of its antique splendor. One must refer to its distant past in order to understand the origin of certain characteristics differentiating the SPD from many other political parties of analogous inspiration.[4]

When the ADAV (General German Workers' Association), founded in 1863 by Ferdinand Lassalle, and the SDAP (the Social Democratic Workers' Party), founded in 1869 in Eisenach by Wilhelm Liebknecht and August Bebel, merged in Gotha in 1875, they were – despite their youthfulness – two rather highly organized political sects.[5] The ADAV was organized in an especially highly centralized form, and was guided with a heavy authoritarian hand by its charismatic founder and leader, Lassalle (and, after his death, by Johan Babist von Schweitzer). The two organizations united in Gotha, the result, as the historians tell us, of a series of circumstances:[6] the death of Lassalle, who would never have agreed to a fusion in which his domination would not be accepted, in 1864; the discontent with and resistance to his successor's just as authoritarian direction (but lacking in charisma); the Franco-Prussian War and the Paris Commune which radicalized the German workers; and, above all, the growing state repression: Liebknecht and Bebel were arrested in 1871 for high treason and sent for a certain time into forced exile; in 1874 (a year before Gotha) the Lassalle organization was outlawed (on the basis of an 1861 anti-subversive law) and its leaders and supporters were persecuted.

The success of the Gotha unification can be explained by a mounting collective tension initiated and fed by the war, the events immediately following the war, and an ever-growing external threat (namely, state repression). The new-born party's platform (which Marx and Engels sharply criticized) was an ingenious mixture of Marxist ideological elements (imposed by the "Eisenachians") and Lassallian visions of socialism. Eisenachians and Lassallians were, moreover, equally represented in the party's leadership groups.[7] But the success of its Gotha unification was above all demonstrated by the events which followed. Even though Bebel remained the central figure of the new party's dominant coalition, the internal conflicts (with the isolated exception of Bebel's opposition by an unrepentant Lassallian, Wilhelm Hasselman) did not coalesce around the Eisenachian/Lassallian cleavage; the two original groups amalgamated perfectly under the pressure of an external challenge.

The party platform approved at Gotha by the delegates was, from the point of view of its organizational ideology and political leadership, one that combined elements of the two original groups' physiognomy: strong centralization and a disciplined organization based on the ADAV model but tied to a central collegial leadership based on the SDAP model.[8] Such elements constituted the basis for the organizational development experimented with by the SPD after the abrogation of the anti-socialist laws in 1890. Before 1890, however, the party leaders had to let drop many of their organizational plans, pursued as they were by Bismarck's repression. The approval of the anti-socialist laws in 1878 forced the Social Democrats to adopt emergency measures. The basis for a high degree of institutionalization had been established all the same. After Gotha, sustained organizational and electoral growth occurred: at Gotha, there were 24,4433 members; at the congress a year later, the 98 delegates already represented 38,254 members and 291 local associations;[9] at the elections for the *Reichstag* in

1877 the SPD obtained 49,344 votes (about 10 per cent of the total) and won 12 seats.

Its financial situation was also relatively stable:

> From June 1875 to August 1876 the Treasury took in 58,763 Marks, from August 1876 to April 1877, 54,763 Marks, and from February to October 1878, 64,218. With these funds, the party was able to pay its leaders (i.e. the members of the Central Electoral Committee), sustain professional political agitators, and provide funds for the publication of daily papers and periodicals.[10]

A large number of daily and weekly publications revolved around the party. In 1878 the SPD had at its disposal forty-seven newspapers – national and local dailies, weeklies, and monthlies – and thus possessed a very powerful communication network.

The enforcement of the anti-socialist laws blocked the party's organizational development, or better, channeled it in ways different from those established at Gotha. The parliamentary group (*Fraktion*) was then the party's only legally existing political center. The local associations had to organize autonomously (and clandestinely) – and were encouraged to do so by the national leaders – on the basis of local conditions without central coordination.[11] Moreover, they functioned under the guise of electoral associations (tolerated by the law). The independence of the "periphery" from the party's "center" was, however, more apparent than real: the relation between *Fraktion* and the local clandestine associations was, in fact, ensured by the *Vertrauensmänner* (the "faithful men") who – for the entire twelve years that the anti-socialist laws remained in force – illegally and despite difficulties and risks maintained communication between the party's periphery and center, guaranteeing the (informal) control of the latter over the former. The official political communication network, i.e. the party press, was destroyed. But the clandestine publication of the *Sozialdemokrat* printed in Switzerland under Bebel's political control, and distributed throughout Germany by the "faithful men," contributed to the maintenance of the party's ideological cohesion.

The plans of the party's founders drawn up at Gotha established the *Fraktion*'s subordination to the internal party organs. Because of the anti-socialist laws, however, *Fraktion* became the party's ruling center.

But only up to a certain point. Bebel, while not in parliament between 1881 and 1883, always participated in an important position in *Fraktion*'s meetings. As did Liebknecht, absent from the Reichstag from 1887 to 1889.[12] No one dared question the right of these two popular and prestigious leaders to participate in party decision making. In other words, even though the party's legal structure at that time suggests an at least potential development in the direction of a parliamentary party (i.e. domination of the parliamentary group over the party) and a high degree of independence of the local associations from the "center" (an evolution which is, as we shall see, typical of weakly institutionalized parties), such a possible development was impeded by the solid intermediate, though informal, structure of the "faithful men," and by the presence of leaders (Liebknecht and Bebel) whose power and organizational control depended on their popularity among party supporters and *not* on their official organizational roles.

The "faithful men" were volunteers, i.e. they were not paid. They were the predecessors of the bureaucrats (in the period following the party's return to legality) whose conformist and conservative attributes Michels interprets as the fruit of the inevitable *embourgeoisement* of militants from worker origins, and as a primary cause of the oligarchy's formation. The "faithful men" were made of different stuff. The difficult conditions of their political work strongly radicalized their feelings. Throughout the period of clandestinity, they continually criticized *Fraktion*'s "soft" behavior, its "ambiguous parliamentarianism"[13] composed of practical reformism (parliamentary activity aiming at concrete measures favoring the workers) and "revolutionary language." The "faithful men," in other words, put up resistance to *Fraktion*'s separation of ideological statements and actual behavior foreshadowing an essential aspect of the following period's "negative integration." Throughout this period, the party remained a "system of solidarity," i.e. an organization which can be examined in the light of the "rational model" described in chapter 1: collective identity incentives were still the only true organizational glue. After 1890, with the Reichstag's refusal to prolong the anti-socialist laws, the party's organizational situation changed drastically. The dominant coalition, which will subsequently be defined as the "Marxist center" (or the "swamp," using Luxemburg's pejorative definition), had already consolidated.

In the course of the 1880s, Bebel "liquidates" the leftist challenge posed by a heterogeneous coalition of anarchists and the Lassallian, Hasselman. Then, at the St Gall Congress (1887), he won a decisive showdown against the "moderates" (the parliamentarian reformists) after a hard struggle which anticipated the conflicts and polemics against revisionism of the subsequent decade.

In 1883 Karl Kautsky founded the *Neue Zeit*, the party's ideological magazine, to which the best German socialist intellectuals contributed. The journal, thanks to Lautsky's prestige as a Marxist theoretician, became the principal focus for the ideological "rationalization"[14] of Bebel's "ambiguous parliamentarianism" – that political strategy of petty reformism hidden behind "anti-parliamentary" and "anti-system" rhetoric. The "Marxist center," of which Bebel was the political and Kautsky the ideological focal point, came to represent the majority view within the party. From 1887 on, Bebel and his men controlled *all* key positions in the party, challenged only by a marginal right-wing parliamentary group from the southern regions, and by a handful of organizationally powerless left wing intellectuals.[15] At Erfut in 1891, the "Marxist" Bebel, by then safely at the head of the party, revised the party's platform, eliminating all the "impurities" (from the standpoint of Marxist ideology) which had been imposed by the political–organizational compromises with the Lassallians at Gotha.

The Erfurt "Marxist" platform – sanctioning the Messianic wait for the "inevitable" revolution which would assuredly come about, but *only when* the contradictions of capitalism had exploded (so that in the meantime one could simply organize and wait), furnished the ideological cover for the successive organizational development and for that kind of "negative integration" within the political system, aptly described by Gunther Roth.[16] With some prudence, and without forcing the issue, we can maintain that the organization's institutionalization process unfolded during the fifteen year period between the return to legality (1890) and the Jena Congress in 1905 (when the party's bureaucratic development accelerated). The organization progressively developed *interests* at all levels, interests fed by a selective incentives system related to the consolidation of internal hierarchies and to the growth of vertical ties with the *classe gardée*. At the same time, *loyalties* fed by the hope of revolution and reinforced by the "assistance services" and by the other collateral activities, took root, encrusting themselves upon the organization.

In the 1890s the party's dominant coalition had to confront challenges to its organizational stability mounted by leftist "radicals" and rightist "revisionists." The Marxist center fended off the radicals using their own revolutionary language, and fended off the revisionists (represented by Bernstein and Vollmar) through appeals to parliamentary reformism.[17] In other words, the party's organizational stability was assured by the policy of "parliamentary ambiguity." Thanks to this policy, the dominant coalition was able to ensure its survival and the development of the organization, setting up a *modus vivendi* with a hostile state; and to simultaneously defend internal authority from periodic "stage-coach holdups" by the right and left.

Many historians mistake the SPD's internal struggles – endemic, as in all parties – for *factional* struggles, but they were far more akin to struggles between *tendencies*.

The groups that opposed the Marxist center were unorganized. A faction is a highly cohesive group that cuts the party vertically. Neither the radicals nor the revisionists were organized in this way. They were, rather, opposition leaders known within the party (but with only weak and irregular connections with local supporter groups), who periodically – in particular in the national congresses, but occasionally even within the two primary leadership party organisms, the *executive* and the *commission of control* – challenged the dominant coalition and grouped people around their own positions on those occasions.

The intra-party conflicts were, therefore, conflicts between weakly cohesive and fluid *tendencies*, the fruit of episodic and discontinuous aggregations of groups rallying behind the banner of one or another of the adversaries. The fact that the opposition leaders were always the same should not mislead us: it is not the leadership's continuity that makes a group a faction, but rather its duration and its organizational solidity. For a long time neither one nor the other were attributes of the groups opposing the Marxist center. The Marxist center (i.e. the party's dominant coalition) in that period was very securely in power. The fact that the radical leadership was only able to establish more permanent ties with its own followers in various local seats (thereby organizing a true faction) in 1912, when internal political polarization was already very advanced, is symptomatic. In that year (1912) for the first time: "we find the radical organizations of Bremen and Stuttgart submitting similarly worded motions to the party congress."[18] In other words, the radical groups' "factionist" coordination only began in 1912. And only in 1913 had the faction established its own independent channel of communication when "Luxemburg, Mehring and Karski set up an organ for their wing, the 'Sozialdemokratische Korrespondenz'."[19] But at that epoch the organization was already on the verge of breaking up: the party was just waiting to split in two after the famous vote on war credits.

The "tendency" character of intra-party conflicts in the SPD was the result of its dominant coalition's high degree of cohesion. And this, in its turn, was the precondition for a development which, at the turn of the century, made the SPD that strong institution so admired for its power by all European socialists of the time.

Organizational consolidation and bureaucratization proceeded throughout the nineties. It took a long time for the rips in the organizational fabric, resulting from the years of clandestinity, to be patched. A new statute was adopted at the Jena Congress in 1905 in which the executive was reinforced and the groundwork was laid for a further organizational "qualitative leap".[20] The party's bureaucratic development (which had been set in motion many years before by Bebel) was completed just a few years later by Ebert who entered the secretariat at that same Congress (1905). The organization underwent centralization, the intermediate regional structure was completed and reinforced, and organizational homogeneity was imposed on the local associations. In the meantime, a parallel growth of the organizational *size* proceeded (measured in numbers of members, collateral assistance activities, etc.).

By 1909 the process was complete: the SPD was a powerful bureaucracy, self-financed, centralized, with a bureaucratic structure extending from the center to the periphery and ensuring the dominant coalition's tight control over the party (according to those modalities well described by Michels and by many others after him).

Nevertheless, no organization can institutionalize beyond a certain point; no institution can become completely independent from its environment. In fact, the SPD's organizational reinforcement at the turn of the century was balanced by a significant shift in power relations between the party and the trade union.

The German trade union played no part in the party's foundation. Throughout the eighties the union associations were weak and not coordinated nationally. Only in the nineties did nationally scaled centralization, expansion, and organizational reinforcement begin. In 1893, with 223,530 members, the union was still very weak. Under such conditions it was logical for the party to totally dominate the union. The party itself encouraged the reinforcement of the union structure. In the nineties the unions were rather undistinguished among the many collateral organizations depending on the party.

But starting in 1896 the unions began to develop organizationally. By 1900 there were already 600,000 members in the trade unions, and the balance of power between party and union rapidly shifted. In 1906, while the SPD could count 384,327 members, the union boasted 1,689,709 members. In 1912, as compared to the 4,250,000 Social Democratic votes, there were 2,530,000 union members.[21] This process altered the power relations between the two organizations' elites, producing two effects: First, the union elite, already heading a powerful organization, could liberate itself from the party's protection and establish with it a relation between equals. Second, in growing in size and enlarging its recruitment horizons, the union became a politically heterogeneous organization. While at the beginning of its organizational history its members were exclusively Social Democrats, the union's activity and concrete *worker* assistance began to attract many non-socialist-oriented workers, and these latter put up stronger resistance to the party's political use of the union.

The union's organization thus grew both more powerful and more heterogeneous. Its leadership had to balance and mediate between conflicting internal demands: e.g. socialist union sectors versus non-socialist ones. Socialist sectors wanted the party's supremacy maintained, while non-socialists wanted the union to be independent from the party. This resulted in a search for compromise and finally in a joint union–party relation designed to "contain" the conflicting demands and ensure the union organization's stability.

By the beginning of 1900, the union had institutionalized, and, as always happens, institutionalization implied an at least partial "emancipation" from the mother organization, i.e. from the sponsoring organization (in this case the party), in the form of a redefinition and re-equilibration of relations between the two organizations.

This produced a significant change in the SPD's dominant coalition, a change manifested in the debate concerning the "general strike" at the 1905 Jena Congress. While the radicals proposed the general strike as a "revolutionary tool" and the union opposed this political tactic, it was, as usual, the Marxist center's compromise position which prevailed: Bebel had the Congress approve a resolution in which the general strike was accepted, but only as an extreme "defensive weapon."[22] At the Mannheim Congress a year later, the power shift solidified: the move from the party's domination of the union to a joint relation between the two organizations was made official. Despite Kautsky's dissent[23] (he was still defending the praxis of the nineties, i.e. union subordination to the party), Bebel succeeded in getting a motion passed requiring consultation with the union before resorting to a general strike. The organizations' "equal dignity" was at that point already accepted, and the dominant coalition, as became clear in the years which followed, had changed. In the nineties the dominant coalition was entirely *in* the party, i.e. its actors' organizational power depended on their roles *in* the party. After Mannheim, the "new" Marxist center included leaders from both the SPD and the union. Even the party's tendency struggles were reshaped by the new equilibrium. Union anarcho-syndicalist sectors began to back the "radicals" struggles with the dominant coalition, while the union right wing established close ties with the parliamentary "revisionists." The dominant coalition's change, i.e. the shift from the old to the new Marxist center, was also a move to the right. This became clear at the Second International Congress in Stoccard in 1907, in Bebel's and Jaurès' dispute over worker internationalism and anti-militarism.[24]

The new Marxist center (the alliance between the SPD and reformist union leaders) makes of the SPD a bastion of the conservative front within the International, preparing the party for its 1914 nationalist choice.[25] Even if, contrary to what some affirm, the unions *never* truly controlled the party (because even the party was a very powerful organization) the party's political choices were undoubtedly the by-products of a system of mediation and inter-organizational exchanges between the elites of the two organizations.

On the whole, the case of the SPD confirms the relation between the genetic model and the degree of institutionalization already indicated. The fact of being an internally legitimated party from its birth, i.e. neither sponsored nor forged by a charismatic leader, favored a high degree of institutionalization. The unfavorable factor – its being the result of a fusion of two pre-existing organizations – was, for all effects and purposes, annulled by a concomitant and very grave external challenge (i.e. state repression). Its role as permanent opposition party (after the return to legality) reinforced a type of organizational development to which the party was already predisposed by its genetic model's characteristics.

The French Communist Party

As we have seen, the SPD was an internally legitimated party, its birth was not sponsored by a preexisting association, nor did it, in the entire course of its history, fall under another organization's control. The Second International was no more than an international frame of reference which the different parties had to take into account, i.e. it was a system of loose interdependent relations among "worker parties," *not* an organization capable of imposing its will on single participants. If anything, the contrary was true: the leaders of the SPD – the most powerful socialist party of the time (with its organizational and electoral victories and its great international prestige) – played a somewhat hegemonic role in the International.[26] The relation between communist parties and the Third International was completely different. The Third International was an organization which – by virtue of the total control exercised by Soviet communists – was able to impose itelf upon the different parties, able to dominate them and to direct their organizational development[27] (even if the Comintern, as we shall see in examining the Italian Communist Party, had to take account of the different national settings in which each communist party developed). Bolshevization is a term habitually used to indicate the process by which parties born through schisms with preexisting socialist parties (as a result of the latter's refusal to accept Lenin's twenty-one conditions) model themselves on the Russian Bolshevik party and internalize its political control. In our perspective, Bolshevization is this but is *also* a particular manifestation of the institutionalization process. Rupture and/or interruption of this process (due to diversity in national settings) can explain the *contemporary* differences among the various European communist parties (or at least among those that did not remain small, uninfluential sects).[28]

As the comparative history of the different parties demonstrates, Bolshevization was neither a painless nor instantaneous process. It was the fruit of an international charismatic leader, Lenin (and later Stalin who continued his work), and of the enormous burst of collective enthusiasm produced in all socialist European movements by the October Revolution. The leading Russian group capitalized on its prestige so as to ensure Bolshevization and to be able to completely control the leaders of the different communist parties (to such an extent that any dissent expressed by a leader with respect to the Comintern's position would automatically lead to his political liquidation). And yet, as we have said, the process was long and complicated. The PCF's history shows this in an exemplary way.[29]

While the party was born out of the schism at Tours in 1920, the Bolshevization process only began in 1924, and was completed by the early thirties with the dominant coalition's consolidation (with Maurice Thorez at its head). It thus took over ten years for it to consolidate around the Comintern's directives, and for it to actually become a docile organizational instrument at the Comintern's service.

This process coincides with the party's institutionalization. It should be noted that the PCF's birth involved a highly ambiguous element: the majority of the SFIO's delegates at Tours *didn't* vote for Lenin's twenty-one conditions. They voted instead (3208 to 1022) for Cachin-Frossard's motion to join the Third International. The battle between "Bolsheviks" and "leftist socialists" began then. These two groups together brought the majority of the SFIO's leaders and members to the Third International, and initially guided the new-born party. Under pressure from the Comintern the alliance broke up and an open battle ensued between the centrist group (guided by Frossard, the party's first secretary), and the 'Bolsheviks' (led by Boris, Souvarine, Fernand Loriot and others). Frossard was forced to resign and abandoned the organization along with other centrists who had tried to bring the party back to a pre-Tours situation (i.e. to a new unification with what remained of the SFIO). The centrist group then split: the right wing headed by Frossard left the party, and the left wing joined up with the Bolsheviks. After the succeeding expulsion of other sectarian groups (e.g. the extreme left) the party was ready to initiate the Bolshevization process. The formation of the dominant coalition therefore involves a complex process of convergence and fusion of the more centrist sectors of the two original groups, and of expulsion of the two extreme wings.

From 1924–6 the reorganization process began. It was a reorganization because the PCF had inherited a large part of the old local and intermediate SFIO structures and had to redefine its physiognomy. Concretely, it moved from an organizational model based on territorial section to a model based on the cell. Furthermore, the reorganization affected the relations at the top, the intermediate levels, and local associations, involving the adoption of "democratic centrism."

The party was thus constructed in watertight compartments. Rigid discipline at all levels (unknown in the SFIO) and centralized control were assured by a special kind of bureaucratic apparatus (whose members were *trained* as "professional revolutionaries"). The process was finally completed through "territorial penetration," i.e. through the creation of new and intermediate associations where the party had not yet taken root.

It is interesting to note that while Bolshevization was taking place, the PCF was reduced to a small sect. In 1920, as we have seen, the SFIO majority chose to join the Third International. The SFIO was therefore reduced to a small organization by the communist schism. Most of the old party's local leaders and structures were appropriated by the new organization. But in the course of time, while the SFIO (under the leadership of Léon Blum and Paul Faure) constantly recovered terrain until it once again became (in 1924) stronger than the PCF, the latter lost a good deal of organizational force during the Bolshevization process. This can be demonstrated by comparing the two parties' membership figures in the years immediately following the schism:[30]

Table 1

	PCF	SFIO
1921	110,000	50,000
1922	79,000	49,000
1923	55,000	50,000
1924	60,000	73,000

The change in power relations between the two organizations continued: in 1932 the SFIO counted 138,000 members, the PCF barely 30,000. The PCF had to wait until the Popular Front epoch (1934–6) and the consequent difficulties of the SFIO as a government party to make that qualitative jump to a mass party boasting 300,000 members.

Bolshevization, however, was not only reorganization by cells according to the Leninist model; it also involved the internalization of control of the Soviet leadership. This latter process was completed when Maurice Thorez assumed the leadership of the organization in the early thirties. Only at that time did the party become almost completely institutionalized. Thorez' career advanced extremely rapidly (as successful careers always do in young organizations),[31] by constantly using the "Soviet card" against internal rivals. As opposed to Gramsci and Togliatti in Italy, Thorez was not one of the party's founders; he did not play an important national role at Tours, and thus at that time had little personal prestige. He only entered the Central Committee in 1924 while the aforementioned expulsions were taking place and the Bolsheviks had just about finished politically eliminating the Comintern's internal rivals. In 1925 he was given the office of organizational head, a key role in a phase of organizational restructuring. In the same year, he entered the party's Political Bureau. By 1929 he was in the party's secretariat – due to secretary general Senard's arrest. He was, in his turn, arrested, and upon release in 1930, he attacked the new party leadership (Henri Barbé and Pierre Célor) for their opportunism; which in the communist lingo of the time meant sluggishness in fulfilling the Comintern's directives. With the Comintern's support he became, in the early thirties, secretary general. In 1934, Stalin's choice of Thorez became definitive, and Jacques Doriot, Thorez's main rival, was censured by the Comintern and then excluded from the party's Central Committee. From then on the party became controlled by a ruling group which was completely dependent on the externally sponsoring organization, and whose legitimacy within the party relied upon its fidelity to Stalin.

In the course of the twenties and first half of the thirties, the PCF was but a small sect with a decreasing number of members. Both the Stalinist class-against-class tactic and the polemics against social fascism after 1928[32] had their share in the continued loss of party members (even if the shrinking membership also largely corresponded to a deliberate choice made by the party's dominant coalition).[33] In 1933 the PCF could count only 28,000 members, and the CGTU, the communist trade union, had also shrunk so much as to be unable to compete with the CGT (which had made great progress between 1922 and 1930).

With the coming of Popular Front the situation changed. The PCF was the principal beneficiary of the enthusiasm which came from the leftist victories; its growth was very rapid, but its centralized structure was able to control and channel the growth (from 28,000 members in 1933 to 280,000 in 1936). In March 1936, the CGTU and the CGT amalgamated, and in a very few years the PCF acquired control over the entire trade union.[34]

The PCF was henceforth a strong institution with a powerful bureaucracy, able to organize its own *classe gardée* into a true "counter-society:" "it underwent a profound transformation. From a small, well structured sect of professional devotees to the cause (on the Bolshevik model), the party arrived at forming an entire community with its own force."[35] With an apparatus of around 100,000 members, with an overwhelming number of full time bureaucrats;[36] a financial system combining members' dues, conspicuous contributions by the International (before the war), and development of import–export commercial activities (after the war);[37] and a network of tightly controlled collateral associations; the PCF is perhaps the European party which comes closest to the "strong institution" ideal type in which maximum independence from the national environment is combined with a very high level of "systemness," of organizational coherence. The original Leninist model – deeply engrained in the organization's Bolshevization process – underwent changes due to growth and to transformations in the external situation,[38] but continued to characterize the party with a strength unknown to those communist parties which couldn't institutionalize in the same historical period.

The Italian Communist Party

Even in the PCI Bolshevization was a tortuous and complicated process. However, it was interrupted by the rise of the fascist regime (this did not happen in the PCF).

This was why the organization's reconstruction, already during the partisan war and immediately thereafter (i.e. in a changed historical period), followed at least a somewhat different path. The PCI's genetic model was the same as the PCF's: external legitimation, formation as a result of a reorganization of local and intermediate structures inherited from the PSI at the schism of Livorno (in 1921), and territorial penetration interrupted by the fascist victory. The process of Bolshevization was led by the Gramsci–Togliatti group under the Comintern's directives (as in the case of the PCF).[39] As in the PCF, the Bolshevization of the PCI involved serious internal conflicts, especially between the Gramsci–Togliatti group and Bordiga.[40] At this point the development of the two parties diverges. In fact, the PCI's institutionalization process (in the communist variant of Bolshevization) was abruptly interrupted by its passage to illegality. After Matteotti's assassination and Mussolini's speech to the House on 3 January 1925, the fascist offensive against all opposition rapidly destroyed what remained of the PCI's organization.

After the fall of the fascist regime, the PCI's genetic model had a strong influence on the organization's rebirth (1944–8). But Togliatti – a very prestigious leader in the International, one of the founders of the PCI, and its secretary in the period of illegality (thus possessing a partial autonomous control of the organization's zones of uncertainty) – was able to lay the foundations (with the organizational formula of

"Partito Nuovo" – the new party) of a development that significantly deviated from the Leninist model. In turn, the modality of organizational consolidation in 1944–8 explains the PCI's successive "deviations" from its original root matrix; this was the structural precondition for the PCI's response (different from the PCF's) to the crisis of 1956 at the Eighth Congress.[41]

The PCI's difference from other communist parties should naturally not be exaggerated, as, for example, Italian communist historiography tends to do.[42] And it is not to be exaggerated because, despite the historical breakdown produced by fascism, the continuity of the ruling class was substantially maintained,[43] and many elements of the party's genetic model were incorporated by the organization during the postfascist reconstruction. As a result of this continuity of leadership, Stalin's control over the PCI was just as strong as in the twenties and thirties. In the meantime, the myth of Stalin grew among party followers. He was no longer simply Lenin's successor, but also the victor in the struggle against Nazi fascists.

From 1944 to 1948, the PCI was in fact a Bolshevik party undergoing reconstruction. But a Bolshevik party with a difference. This difference, symbolized by Togliatti's formula of the "new party," accounts for the ever widening gap between the PCI and the PCF, as well as the PCI's slow movement towards a mode of functioning more typical of socialist parties (e.g. the SPD and the Austrian Socialist Party (SPÖ), both strong institutions but weaker than classical communist parties).

The party's structure was similar to that of the PCF, but there were two very important differences. In the first place, the factory cells, although defined in the statutes (until 1956) as the most important base unit, were actually supported by a number of local cells of the territorial and functional type (i.e. composed of young people, women, etc.).[44] These cells were numerically significantly superior to those of the PCF, and resulted from the party's decision to branch out into wider social sectors (sectors beyond the traditional *classe gardée*, the factory worker). In the second place, the criteria for recruiting members were much less rigid than in the PCF, which explains the PCI's enormous organizational growth in the reconstruction years. In 1946, in a moment of intense political mobilization both in France and Italy, the membership of the PCF reached a high of 800,000 members while the PCI already had 1,800,000 members and continued to grow to over 2 million.

The difference was essentially one of level of institutionalization. The "Bolshevik party" of which the PCF was for years one of the most faithful incarnations,[45] was a very strong institution in which a formidable internal structural coherence was accompanied by a great deal of autonomy *vis-à-vis* the national society. These features were ensured by the predominance of the cell system over every other base unit, by a system of democratic centralism faithfully reproducing Leninist catechism, and by an impotent bureaucratic apparatus whose cohesion was entrusted to a combination of centrally distributed selective and identity incentives. Socialist parties (which are internally legitimated parties), on the other hand, sometimes become strong institutions, but they *never* become this strong: they are less independent from their national society and less internally cohesive. Togliattian organizational choices resulted in a party more rooted in Italian society than the Bolshevik model would have permitted. The party's mass character – i.e. the inevitable internal social and political heterogeneity of a mass party established in a society with very strong socio-economic and political territorial differences[46] – impeded both an autonomization from the national society as strong as the PCF's, and the attainment of a high degree of structural coherence.

In the period immediately following organizational reconstruction, the PCI suffered from many problems related to its "hybred" character, i.e. being both a revolutionary sect and a mass party.[47] It was eventually driven toward the *second* solution, that of a mass socialist party.[48] The "new party" thus positioned itself, in terms of level of institutionalization, between the PCF and the SPD (in the imperial post-1905 period), and tended toward the SPD's position more than towards that of the PCF.

Its slow emancipation from its sponsoring organization (the PCUS) accelerated in the mid-seventies with the passage from external legitimation to internal legitimation, and with the transferral of authority from the PCUS to the organization's internal organs. This brought about a still lower level of institutionalization: a reduction in its autonomy and a diminuation of its internal structural coherence. The parabolic movement ends in recent times with significant progressive weakening of the dominant coalition's degree of cohesion and an incipient transformation of the traditional tendencies into factions (albeit still weakly organized, but ever more coordinated nationally and vertically).[49]

In summary, in the first phase (1921–5), the evolution of the PCI was very similar to that of the PCF, except for the obvious difference in national political situation and the increasing fascist aggression against the new-born organization. As in the PCF, the Bolshevik dominant coalition slowly emerged through progressive expulsion of the left (Bordiga) and of the right (Angelo Tasca). The fascist regime's consolidation, however, led to an interruption of the organization's continuity. This differentiates the PCI not only from the PCF which enjoyed organizational continuity in the consolidation phase, but also from the SPD whose development under the anti-socialist laws (1878–90) involved some deviation from its originally established course. With Togliatti's return to Italy in 1944, the organization was, in a certain sense, reborn. This explains the leadership's, at least partial, freedom of action in (re)modeling the organization. If the organizational consolidation had not been interrupted twenty years earlier, the organization experiencing only a brief period of clandestinity during the war period (as happened to the PCF), this freedom of action would not have existed. The organization would have been rebuilt around the pre-war base of *interests* and *loyalties*. The Togliattian leadership was able to forge the organization (by introducing the "difference" mentioned earlier) on the wave of a collective tension connected to the partisan struggle, and to an at least partial redefinition (related to its participation in the "national solidarity" government) of its ideological goals. This partial redefinition of goals – combining both a Soviet linkage and an attempt to adapt to Italian societal conditions – posed the premises for what was termed the "Italian road to socialism" (after 1956). Once loyalties and organizational interests had been consolidated, this difference became an integral and constitutive part of the new PCI. Its effects became more and more palpable in the course of time.[50]

Conclusions

We have thus far compared the typology developed in Part I of this book with the historical genesis and consolidation of three parties with a common characteristic: they were created and institutionalized (with the partial exception of the PCI during the postwar "national solidarity" government period) as opposition parties. All three organizations became strong institutions, though not all to the same degree: while the SPD's dominant coalition eventually included trade union leaders, nothing of the kind happened during the institutionalization of the PCI or PCF. The CGIL and the CGT remained for a long time nothing but the two parties' "union arms." As was true for all other collateral organizations as well, the loyalties of the union members and activists were not to the union but to the party, and this undercut the unions' (and other collateral associations') possible vitality and autonomy.[51] The degrees of institutionalization of both the PCI and the PCF were, however, quite different, as the evolution of party–union relations indicates.

The Italian communist trade union, during its organizational reinforcement in the late sixties and early seventies, partially emancipated itself from the party, following the SPD trade union model. (During the decline of the unions in the late seventies, it reverted to a situation of dependence upon the party.)[52] Nothing similar happened between the CGT and the PCF.

The three parties' different degrees of institutionalization (highest in the PCF, and lowest in the SPD) can be explained by the different genetic models: the SPD was not sponsored by an external organization; the PCI and PCF were.

The outcome which our model would normally predict is modified in the case of the PCI, because of an organizational breakdown and the fact that institutionalization recommenced under historically changed conditions. The party was temporarily in government, and its leaders, in rebuilding the organization, had to mediate between this specific "environmental position" pushing it towards "renewal" and those factors (e.g. its genetic model's characteristics and Stalinist power) pushing it towards "continuity."

Aside from the differences discussed, the three parties present many similarities. This legitimates our grouping them under the heading of "strong institutions." They are all powerful bureaucratic organizations with highly cohesive dominant coalitions, and their systems of collective and selective incentives are all in the hands of restricted elites. Their internal struggles are *tendency struggles*, i.e. conflicts between barely organized groups. When tendencies begin to organize – as happened in the SPD after 1912, or in the conflicts preceding the revision of Bad Godesberg[53] – we can be sure that a de-institutionalization process is taking place (i.e. the level of institutionalization is decreasing) due to environmental pressure which even strong organizations can control only up to a certain point. An absence of organized factions, in the PCI for example, does not simply correspond to a formal statutory prohibition. For example, we find such prohibitions in the statutes of the British Labour Party and the Italian Christian Democrats. But the Labour Party is a factional party, and the Christian Democrat's factionalism (along with that of the Japanese Liberal Democratic Party) is cited as exemplary by all the international literature on parties. The PCI, PCF and SPD (but many other parties as well, e.g. the Austrian Social Democratic Party, SPÖ)[54] are parties in which internal struggles are tendency rather than factional struggles. This is because strong institutionalization implies that to make a career, it is necessary to conform to the central directives (elite recruitment being of the centripetal type), in order to deal with a cohesive center which monopolizes incentive distribution. They are tendency-type parties because they are developed bureaucratic organizations in which conventional bureaucratic careers predominate.[55] The incentives enjoyed by bureaucrats are not substitutable: the bureaucrats usually cannot recycle the skills they learn working for the party in other parties or in extra-political jobs. The conformity upon which the dominant coalition can count at all levels of the organizational pyramid is reinforced by a centralized distribution of collective identity incentives, incentives which are unavailable elsewhere. Under such conditions (using Hirschman's well-known categories)[56] to "exit" at the various hierarchical levels involves heavy costs; loyalty is high and the mechanism keeps peoples' "voice" under control, i.e. the dissenters are never allowed to come together and organize.[57]

This is not, however, true for all parties that form and consolidate in opposition. In certain cases, even "opposition parties" weakly institutionalize. This will be the thesis of the following chapter.

6
Oppositional parties (2)

The three cases examined in the preceding chapter involve parties "born and raised" in opposition, parties which were created and matured in opposition, parties which have developed into powerful organizations capable of mobilizing thousands of supporters, with imposing bureaucratic apparatuses, and with strong vertical organizational ties to their respective *classes gardées*. These parties have been able to exploit the only resource at their disposal: the organization.

This is not, however, always the case. Certain parties may weakly institutionalize even if they were initially and even for a long time in opposition, even if their genetic models' characteristics are such as to inhibit strong organizational development. We shall now examine the history of three such parties: the Labour Party, the SFIO, and the PSI.

The British Labour Party

Like the SPD, the British Labour Party is an emblematic case of a workers' party. It presents, however, an organizational model whose characteristics are diametrically opposed to those of the SPD. The Labour Party was created at the beginning of the century through the encounter between the unions and a small, well organized sect, the Independent Labour Party (ILP), guided by one of English socialism's prestigious leaders, James Keir Hardie.[1] This happened when, in the late 1890s, the unions decided to break off their already tenuous alliance with the Liberal Party and to independently organize.[2]

They decided to do so, however, at the cost of serious internal conflicts which shaped the Labour Party's organizational future. Along with George Marnes, secretary of the TUC (Trade Union Congress, the union's central government), the railway workers were the main driving force behind the experiment. The defenders of the Lib–Lab alliance were, on the other hand, guided by the powerful cotton picker and miner unions' leaders. A motion favoring the formation of an autonomous party was presented to the TUC's general assembly in 1899. The motion passed with a margin of only 112,000 votes (546,000 to 434,000),[3] an unequivocal sign of the favor still enjoyed by the Lib–Lab alliance. The party's founding conference was set for February 1900.

The preparatory commission was composed of delegates from the Unions, the Fabian Society, the ILP and the SDF (the Social Democratic Federation, a small sect of Marxist orientation). During the preparatory work, one could already glimpse the first traces of the future stable alliance between Hardie – the leader of the strongest and most prestigious socialist organization – and the unions. Hardie dominated the preparatory work, and assured his organization an important position with respect to the other socialist associations. At the Labour Representation Committee's founding conference Hardie obtained five of the executive committee's twelve seats, and was able to hand the job of secretary to Ramsay MacDonald.

The organizational force mustered up by the unions at the party's origin explains why the Labour Party was created and why it was destined to remain the unions' political arm, externally sponsored and weakly institutionalized. The ILP's role should not be underestimated. It was the grafting of this small but organized political association onto the union body which was to provide most of the new party's parliamentary personnel and which eventually facilitated the organization's institutionalization.

The new organization's beginnings were rough. Financial resources were lacking, there was no central office, and the secretary was not paid. Furthermore, the new-born party had to pass the electoral test in the same year as its foundation (1900).

Electoral results raised serious difficulties for Labour during its formative stage. The small group of Labour members was in fact forced by the general political situation to align with the Liberals in opposing the South African war and on a number of other political questions. This caused an immediate problem of identity. In a country in which the working class had for a long time been loyal to the Lib–Lab alliance, and in which most of the unions, and first and foremost the mineworkers' unions, were still against the new party, Labour risked being swallowed up by the liberal left. The political alignment with the Liberals involved the risk of dissolution due to the party's inability to develop a distinct political identity to which electoral loyalties could adhere.

The initial difficulties were therefore very great. MacDonald was, however, a very capable organizer, and from the outset obtained the support of Arthur Henderson, a man who dedicated all his energy to the party's organizational development. The main problem was the excessive time it took many unions to abandon the Lib–Lab alliance and request party affiliation. Until the completion of this process, the party's survival could not be guaranteed, and at least ten years passed before all the most important unions came over to Labour.

Aside from financing, the immediate problem for MacDonald and Henderson was the constitution of local associations. It is symptomatic of the party's dependent and externally legitimated character that such action was manifested by encouraging local initiative, and only in small part by direct intervention from the center. In 1901 a special commission on organizational problems, directed by Henderson, opposed "any uniform system of organization for the whole country," on the ground that "some of our affiliated societies are already organized in certain constituencies. We think that these attempts should be encouraged by us, and be made the basis for a complete organization later on."[4]

The local associations thus developed in a rather haphazard way throughout the country. The Labour Party was a party under construction in which (1) development took place almost exclusively through territorial diffusion, i.e. through spontaneous local initiative. (2) The center limited itself to encouraging and stimulating the process, neither guiding it nor centrally controlling it. (3) The party's construction really began with the work of its local unions. For many years and in many areas, the party associations were simply local union councils.

Diffusional development, indeterminate organizational boundaries, externally legitimated character and dependence of the party's "periphery" on the trade unions, are all natural consequences of the modalities through which the party was founded. But this is only a partial picture which must be completed by consideration of the old ILP's local associations (the ILP having affiliated with the party), and above all by the decision of MacDonald and Henderson – cautiously manifested so as not to provoke the unions' veto – to guide the party's formation at least in the case where local unions' autonomous initiatives were lacking. At the annual conference in 1905, they succeeded in getting a resolution passed allowing local associations created by the "center" to affiliate with the national party "and by 1906 the number of such bodies has been variously estimated at between 70 and 100. Thus by the time of the general election, MacDonald, Henderson and their colleagues had succeeded in creating at least the skeleton of a national political machine."[5]

Labour obtained a great electoral success in 1906, seating twenty-nine deputies in parliament. Hardie was elected chairman of the parliamentary group. In spite of his great prestige, the election was tough: Hardie beat David Shackleton, his rival, by only one vote. We can thus immediately detect the weak cohesion and intense factionalism which were ever present in English labor history. It was the logical effect of a genetic model which combined a diffusional development with dependence on an external institution, such that every parliamentary representative was tied more to his electoral ward's unions (to which he owed his victory) than to the party leaders. The problem that thus arose, a typical and constant subject of internal political conflict in the years which followed, was whether the parliamentary group should be guided by a leader from its own ranks, or whether it should depend on congress, i.e. on the annual party conference, and thus on the unions controlling the congress. Hardie's adversaries (guided by deputy Ben Tillet) supported the latter thesis. Hardie, however, was able to defend the autonomous role of the parliamentary group. He had the union leaders on his side because they were afraid that the conference's control of the parliamentary group might displace them, putting the party in the hands of the rank and file union delegates.[6] The typical Labour dominant coalition, which controlled the party for almost the whole of its existence, had already formed. The coalition was based on a delicate mechanism of cross-cutting alliances and reciprocal guarantees: the leader's job was to control the parliamentary group in exchange for a certain amount of independence from the annual conference, and the union leaders had the more or less informal job of guaranteeing such independence, i.e. keeping the party's union delegates under tabs (preventing them from interfering too much in parliamentary activities), in exchange for a share in the management of the party. The left/right divisions in the parliamentary group soon began to appear. But as the party was in its formative phase, i.e. in a state of structural "fluidity," these divisions still took on the character of "tendencies." This did not, however, last for long: the external sponsoring organizations (the local and national unions) provided the tendencies with organizational reference points which eventually facilitated their transformation into factions. The "left wing," guided by the deputy Victor Grayson, repeatedly attacked the parliamentary leadership, and with particular force from 1907 onwards. The parliamentary "right wing" was just as combative, beginning at the 1905 conference when it tried to obtain the expulsion of the socialist associations of Marxist orientation. MacDonald's role as mediator was crucial at that point. His election to chairman of the parliamentary group in 1911 ended the era of two-year rotations to the chair (occupied by Hardie from 1906 to 1908, Henderson from 1908 to 1910, and Barnes from 1910 to 1911), and institutionalized the leader's role. The Labour Party found its first true leader in MacDonald, who was accepted by both the left and the union leaders.[7] But the organization was still very fragile and constantly on the verge of splitting up because of internal conflict. It was only after the organizational reform of 1918, and after having overcome a crisis which could have destroyed the party, that institutionalization was completed. The crisis arose at the beginning of World War I. Labour, like most other European socialist parties, was violently shaken by conflict between nationalists and pacifists. It was through the mediation of MacDonald, Henderson and the union leaders most dedicated to the party's construction that this crisis was slowly resolved. In 1917 the party was still a weak machine, weakly based in London, and organizationally heterogeneous from region to region: there were at least seven different types of local organizations in the country.[8]

As party affiliation still had an entirely collective form, Labour suffered from a chronic lack of funds. In 1918 Henderson designed and had passed – with the support of trade union leaders – a decisive organizational reform. This reform was the signal that party institutionalization was under way. Labour soon consolidated, assuming a physiognomy which remained substantially unaltered (aside from periodic ajustments) forever after. Direct individual membership was added in 1918 to collective membership (i.e. membership based on one's union affiliation).[9] From that time on, the party could count on a certain amount of direct rank and file activism other than that accorded by the unions. This did not, however, commit the party to complete emancipation from the unions; but it did furnish an essential element in the organization's institutionalization: a reserve of direct loyalty, loyalty which was not mediated by an external organization. The 1918 reform also consecrated the asymmetrical relation – as opposed to that found in the SPD, and especially in the PCI and the PCF – between the parliamentary group and the extra-parliamentary party already established by Hardie. In the SPD, PCI and PCF, the "internal leadership" dominated, and the parliamentary group was in a subordinate position. In the Labour Party, on the contrary, the parliamentary group dominated. This was simultaneously the cause and the effect of a decisively weak bureaucratic development (as we shall see further on), symbolized by the exclusion of party bureaucrats from public activity, their "ghettization" in purely administrative tasks.

The 1918 reform brought about a formalization of the relation between the unions and the other associations affiliated with Labour (e.g. the cooperative movement, the Fabian Society, etc.), a formalization assuring the union a majority in the national conferences and in the party's national executive organ, the National Economic Council

(NEC),[10] in addition to the representation of the different affiliated associations, and of the individual members.

The 1918 reform led to the formalization of Labour's composite and federal character as well as of union control over the party. There are three paradigmatic aspects of the Labour Party's weakly institutionalized character. The first relates to financing. The 1918 reform ended the era of uncertainty and financial instability, but self-financing was *not* yet possible: the party's percentage of direct membership financing remained marginal. The party's dependence on the unions was, instead, reinforced and formalized. From then on, the unions contributed three-quarters of the party's necessary funds.[11]

The financial dimension of individual and collective membership and the Labour Party's complex financial situation in general were summarized in the seventies as follows:

> Financially it is true that the individual member pays £1.20 per year, against 10p. for the affiliated member, from 1 January 1972. But only a small proportion of the individual members' subscriptions comes to the central organization of the party, which is financed at present by 88 per cent from trade union affiliation fees and the remaining 12 per cent from the individual members and other organizations. Trade unions, in addition to their annual affiliation fees, also contribute to local parties and are almost wholly responsible for financing the general election campaigns.[12]

The second factor to be considered is the weakness of the central, intermediary and peripheral bureaucratic structures, especially when compared with the Conservative Party which has, as we shall see, a more developed and professional bureaucratic apparatus. It is not simply a question of the size of the apparatus. It is also a question of internal relations: the fact that the regional agents (those in charge of the intermediate organizations) have much more autonomy with respect to the NEC (on which they officially depend) than their Conservative counterparts (who were tightly controlled by the Central Office), is a revealing sign of Labour's low internal structural coherence.[13] Its organizational weakness is also revealed by the small number of Labour associations which have a permanent bureaucrat (i.e. an electoral agent).[14]

The third aspect of Labour's weak institutional character relates to its method of parliamentary candidate selection. The selection comes about on the basis of two lists of possible candidates prescribed by the NEC (in which, as we have seen, the unions are in the majority). The first list includes the candidates the unions are willing to directly sponsor (financing their campaign) and who, if actually chosen and elected, become the unions' "official" representatives in parliament.[15] The second list is composed of candidates among whom the local associations choose their own representatives. In each association, the organ proposing the selection (which was then ratified by the local assembly), the General Management Committee, is composed of delegates from all the locally affiliated associations. The unions are quite influential there as well, whereas individual members cannot feasibly control the selection process.[16] The result is decisive: leaving aside those deputies directly put into parliament by the unions, it is quite rare for a candidate to be chosen if he has not been assured trade union support. Moreover, the NEC always has veto power over unwanted candidates (traditionally utilized, when the dominant coalition's equilibrium favors the right, at the expense of the leftist factions).

In conclusion, the Labour Party is a weakly institutionalized organization and its genetic model's characteristics explain why. It is subdivided into *factions*, i.e. into a number of power centers which control crucial zones of organizational uncertainty, and distribute selective and/or collective incentives to its own supporters. Their organizational possibilities depend on their stable ties to a union, an affiliated association, or occasionally (as is traditionally true of the party's left wing) even to individual members. The availability of relatively dispersed organizational resources explains the longevity of various groups in the party. It naturally also explains the relatively divided nature of the dominant coalition. I say "relatively" divided, because what generally prevents Labour factions from organizing in as solid a way as, for example, the factions in the Italian DC, is the external control exercised by the unions. As long as the trade union leaders keep the respective organizations under control, the party's organizational stability is generally assured. The dominant coalition remains composed of trade union leaders and the parliamentary leader, and this system of *crossed oligarchies* allows for a controlled management of internal conflicts. When, however, the union leaders sense that they risk being (or are in fact) supplanted by their own rank and file, the dominant coalition's pact of internal cooperation falls apart and the factionistic games regain strength and vitality. This is the effect of the party's dependence upon the trade union. The party's organizational stability is a function of the union's organizational stability.[17] This explains why the Labour Party's dominant coalition manifested greater stability when it was in opposition than when it was in government. Up until recently, Labour's typical dominant coalition when the party was in opposition, included leaders of the most powerful unions (i.e. those controlling the TUC) and a parliamentary leader selected from the center–right factions. The cooperation pact was reciprocally satisfactory: the dominant coalition was able to put up a common front against both the Conservative government's and the left Labour factions, thereby guaranteeing the party's organizational stability.[18] When the Labour Party governed, however, it was never – with the one exception of the Attlee government (1945–51) – able to defend its own stability.[19] The dominant coalition generally did not hold up under the strain of the inevitable difficulties of governing; the rank and file unionists fled to the "left," pursuing the discontented worker fringes, thereby swelling the left factions' ranks while the unions lost cohesion and stability. In the end, the cooperation pact between the union leaders and the parliamentary leader dissolved. The party's resulting destabilization ended in an organizational crisis typified in the confrontations between the "party" (namely, unions plus leftist factions) and the parliamentary leader.[20]

The French section of the Workers' International

The SFIO's birth, like that of many other socialist parties, was the product of a long gestation process during which several small organizations were founded and broke up into splinter groups which fought among themselves.[21] When the SFIO was created at the Paris Congress in 1905, the conditions for its future weak institutionalization were already present. The SFIO was in fact founded through the federation of five main currents of French socialism – each more or less organized into an autonomous political association – along with a few minor groups. The five organized tendencies were: the Guesdistes, the former French Workers' Party (POF), followers of Jules Guesde, of Marxist orientation; Paul Brousse's *Possibilistes*; Jean Allemande's Allemandistes; the Blanquists, headed by Edouard Vaillant; Jean Jaurès and Alexander Millerand's Socialistes Indépendants. Among these small sects, the most organized was, without a doubt, the POF, founded by Jules Guesde and Paul Lafargue in the early nineties.[22] The Guesdistes' organizational superiority secured them a leading role in the first phase: when, at the 1906 Congress, the SFIO was given a charter (which lasted for its whole lifetime), it adopted lock, stock and barrel the Guesdistes' by-laws from the nineties (which were modeled on the German Social Democrat charter).

The POF, in spite of Guesde and Lafargue's efforts to build a powerful and centralized organization, was a small sect which for the whole of its brief existence bore the traces of French socialism's early difficulties. It came about through territorial diffusion, organizationally heterogeneous from region to region, and its intermediate structures – the Federations – were very much independent from the party's center.[23] It was certainly a powerful and well-organized sect in comparison to other French socialist groups, but insignificant indeed when compared, for example, to one of the SPD's predecessors, the Lasalle organization. The POF's organizational character reappeared as one of the SFIO's organizational constants because of Guesde's important role at its creation. The crucial traits of the SFIO original models were (1) its birth from the federation of many groups, necessitating a political compromise among heterogeneous tendencies, and (2) an organizational model inheriting decentralized traditions and weak structural cohesion from the POF.

Though the Guesdistes had the lion's share in the new party's organization, they were unable to reap the fruits of this triumphant beginning. They were severely penalized by the electoral geography, i.e. by the type of electoral loyalties formed around the new organization. The POF, which had a certain following among industrial workers in Paris and elsewhere, could not – despite its leaders' intensive efforts – build a trade union dependent upon the party (like the SPD in the nineties).[24] The CGT, the workers' trade union, born in 1895, but dominated right from the start by an anarcho-syndicalist tendency, was very hostile to political parties.[25] The SFIO inherited from the POF weak and sometimes negligible relations with workers' unions. This meant that, with the exception of the working-class milieu in Paris and a few other cities, the most important area of the party's electoral (and even organizational) expansion was rural France. The SFIO was thus a more serious competitor for the radical socialist party (whose *classe gardée* was in the countryside) than for workers' syndicalism. The effect on the party's internal power structure was the rapid rise to power, at Guesde's expense, of the other prestigious leader involved in the 1905 unification, Jean Jaurès. His humanitarian socialism, mixed with republican ideology – at the crucial moment of the selection of the party's social base, i.e. of its "hunting ground" – provided the organization with a political identity better adapted to its social area of electoral expansion than was Guesde's workers' sectarianism. Within ten years: "the SFIO had obtained its most substantial gains in the rural zones. Jaurès' rural sort of socialism – reflecting a still peasant-based France – replaced the old POF's socialism which founded its hopes on the factories and cities."[26]

These figures "show a rhythm of vigorous growth, but also show its limits and lead us to examine the SFIO's nature. A voter party more than an activist party, the SFIO could not count on workers' votes. It thrived mostly in regions of rural radicalism."[27] Whether this was due to Jaurès' type of leadership – i.e. his particular set of identificatory symbols – or rather to the CGT's monopoly on workers, is, to a certain

Table 2. *SFIO: member's, voter's and parliamentary seats in the pre-war period*

	Members	Voters	Seats
Period preceding unification	34,688		
1906	51,736	877,999	51
1910	56,164	1,106,047	74
1914	76,667	1,398,000	103

Source: M. Perrot, A. Kriegel, *Le Socialisme français et le pouvoir*, p. 85

extent, a moot point. The two factors no doubt reinforced each other. But this development – the selection of a *classe gardée* with strong rural characteristics – does help explain the outcome of the party's internal power struggle, i.e. the fact that, although the "workerist" Guesde was initially stronger, he couldn't stop Jaurès from gaining control over the party.

The workerists thus, after a brilliant start, became a minority faction (strong only in the northern federations) while Jaurès' leadership "spread." The organizational structure – modeled, as we have already seen on the POF – crystallized in this period and survived intact all the subsequent vicissitudes of French socialism and transformations in the dominant coalition's composition: from the era of Jaurès and that of Blum and Faure between the two wars, right up to Mollet's post-war era. Many traces of these organizational characteristics can be found in the new PSF, born from the 1969–71 reorganization.[28] We have once again therefore, a classic and paradigmatic case of the persistence of the genetic model's characteristics. The SFIO's organizational structure, which emerged in the early years, was, as we shall see further on, quite similar to that of the PSI. Like the Italian socialists, the French socialists unsuccessfully tried to imitate the envied and admired SPD.

The new organization's essential traits were: heterogeneity and variability of organizational forms from region to region; a very weak central apparatus (or rather, until Paul Faure became secretary in the twenties, no central apparatus at all); highly independent intermediate structures, viz. the federations, immediately organized into autonomous fiefdoms strong enough to stave off the center's attempts to interfere. At the same time, and in contrast to these characteristics, the internal leaders' formal control over the parliamentary group (a tradition inherited from the POF, which had borrowed it from the SPD) was never completely realized. In fact, the internal leaders' supremacy over the parliamentary group can only be actualized if the former are national leaders running a vast bureaucracy. In the case of the SFIO, the internal leaders were, instead, the federation's peripheral leaders. The SFIO thus formed and consolidated with characteristics of a hybrid organization, half-way (to use Duverger's terminology) between the parliamentary party composed of notables, and the mass "socialist" party. The central apparatus' inability to control the intermediate structures and local associations (e.g. in the crucial moment of candidate selection), and Jaurès' "situational charisma" – Jaurès became, for thousands of voters and most activists, a symbol of French socialism – tended to favor the supremacy of the elected officials, i.e. of parliamentarians. This tendency was balanced by the relatively strong concentration of organizational power resources in the federations which dominated the national congresses (in proportion to the number of their members) and controlled the weak executive organ.[29] The power equilibrium continually oscillated between the parliamentarians and the internal leaders (in this case, the federation bosses) because of the incessant struggle between the former – who tried to secure their own political independence and autonomous electoral power bases – and the latter, who attempted to control the former.

The foundations for weak institutionalization were thus laid: the combination of a weak central apparatus of semi-autonomous and in certain cases independent deputies (as well as those elected to local public offices) and the federations' independence from the party's center rendered the organization incapable of achieving much autonomy *vis-à-vis* its environment, incapable, for example, of controlling its own *classe gardée* through a tight network of vertical ties typical of "social integration parties." Throughout its existence, the SFIO remained an opinion party with weak and intermittent electoral loyalty, and strongly dependent upon the whims of a poorly organized electorate.[30]

The party was predisposed to such a development by its birth through the federation of groups with autonomous organizational power resources (which thus impeded the growth of a central bureaucratic apparatus), but *also* by the workers' unions' political independence. This independence prevented the SFIO from controlling a resource which was, in other parties (e.g. the SPD and the Austrian PS) essential to the construction of a solid party sub-culture.

The party was so dependent on the environment (due to its weak institutionalization) that the slightest environmental change – in its relations with the electorate or in its position within the political system – had a direct and dramatic impact on its internal affairs. Being hardly autonomous *vis-à-vis* its external environment, the SFIO was thus also – because of its weak central apparatus, and of the federations' autonomy – lacking in structural coherence among the different parts of the organization. Its organizational forms differed widely from region to region, and the party's financing was primarily controlled by the periphery, i.e. by the federation leaders, but also, in certain cases, by the mayors and local notables.

The logical corollary to this development was the dominant coalition's low degree of cohesion and rather intense factionalism. The internal groups, except during the brief phases of reconstruction following the 1920 communist schism and at the height of Mollet's influence in the fifties, immediately gave themselves a sub-coalition structure through a "partition of influence" over the different federations.

The uncohesive nature of the SFIO's dominant coalition for the whole of its existence was demonstrated by the fact that no leader could emerge within the party without the consensus of the most powerful federation leaders, and without getting involved in a system of exchanges and reciprocal compensations with the peripheral and national leaders. I will more systematically discuss later (e.g. in examining the somewhat analogous case of the CDU in the Adenauer era) the fact that this development never allowed for much membership expansion, a typical aspect of feudally organized structures. The leaders of the various federations, whether absolute monarchs or, less often, sub-leaders of a national faction, had little interest in expanding the organization beyond a certain minimal point by proselytizing. For excessive expansion of the membership could have compromised the organization's stability: the entrance of an excessive number of new (and especially young) members, could have produced even conspicuous and unexpected alterations in the intra-federation power relations; and the difference between the political socialization of the old activists and that of the newcomers could have led to acute conflicts within the federations. And, worst of all, membership expansion could have brought about the formation of extensive groups of activists open to political mobilization by adversary factions. The party's organizational stability depended for a long time (except during the post-twenties' reconstruction period) upon the absence of proselytizing, i.e. upon an organizational stasis (which reached its peak around Guy Mollet's time) which is perfectly explainable in terms of power equilibria.

A partial reconstruction of the organization's internal relations took place after the 1920 communist schism; it was necessitated by the serious challenge which the schism posed to the survival of the party.[31] The SFIO was reduced to a small party. Most of its local and intermediate structures were taken over (and later reorganized according to the Leninist model) by the PCF; which gave rise to a series of meetings and struggles between the two parties for the systemization of the organizational and financial problems opened up by the schism.[32] The SFIO held on to the oldest federations (primarily in the rural regions), as well as most of the local public office holders and almost all of the parliamentarians, i.e. just enough resources to keep the party afloat. The "rebirth" that soon led the SFIO to surpass the PCF (preoccupied as it was with domestic struggles) in organizational force, was primarily due to Paul Faure's organizational abilities.

In the period immediately following the schism the party was very weak. In addition, Jaurès, the father of French socialism, was assassinated in 1914, and it took some time for Léon Blum to emerge as the new prestigious leader. Paul Faure's election to the secretariat (an office not provided for by the charter which, as we have seen, penalized the central apparatus) was, under such conditions, a decisive factor in understanding the SFIO's speedy comeback. Paul Faure was able, as the party's "organization man" in the twenties and thirties, to create for the first time an extra-parliamentary center of power and prestige. His administration created a central apparatus which controlled the party's printed matter as well as its finances.[33] It was nothing compared to the SPD's bureaucratic development, but it represented the beginnings of a central organization.

Faure had moved away from the "left:" at Tours he had sided with the "leftist socialists" favoring the Third International though still opposing the twenty-one conditions.

Only a break at the last minute with the Bolsheviks stopped him from moving, along with Frossard, to the other side. This act increased his acceptance by the internal left wing, and more generally by the party membership – less "moderate" on the average than the electorate. Faure, controlling an at least partially revitalized central organization and being politically well accepted by the party members, became the true fulcrum of the dominant coalition which stabilized the party for the fifteen years which followed. The second key figure in the dominant coalition was Léon Blum. Blum, of moderate persuasion, but attached to no particular faction, was soon reputed to be the incarnation of French socialism's humanitarian tradition. His prestige accounted for the power he wielded over the parliamentary group.

The alliance between Blum and Faure, initially tacit and later more manifest, was irresistible: Faure was able to overcome the federation leaders' resistance (because the communist competition had made them more dependent on the center) and to establish a durable internal compromise involving reciprocal compensations among the federations, parliamentary leaders, and the national secretariat. The new party's dominant coalition which permitted the SFIO to overcome the problems of the twenties was now composed of an extra-parliamentary center (namely, Faure), the leaders of the strongest federations allied with Faure, and the majority of the parliamentary leaders controlled by Blum. The Blum–Faure alliance was the fulcrum of this coalition and, as long as the two men remained united, they were unbeatable. The factionistic games did not disappear altogether (in fact, in 1933 the right-wing parliamentary leaders split off), but they were kept under control.

The SFIO, however, remained a weak organism; its low degree of institutionalization rendered it highly susceptible to environmental changes.

Along with the birth of the Popular Front, and with the PCF's greater competitive capacity (it went on to obtain a spectacular electoral victory in 1936), the party's dominant coalition began to show its first signs of breakdown and factionistic games resumed their normal intensity.[34] The leftist government, along with the PCF which was in a phase of strong political upswing, caused a serious identity crisis in a weak institution like the SFIO. Factionalism regained strength, being fed by both the parliamentary right (tied to an anti-communist electoral clientele) and the "revolutionary" left (the groups of Pivet and Zyromski) which was especially strong in those peripheral sectors of the party which, having a worker base, were more exposed to the communist challenge. Faure and the leaders of his larger allied federations stepped up their anti-communist polemic, increasing their opposition to the leftist factions in order to defend the party's organizational identity. Blum, on the other hand, being at the head of a government kept in power by the PCF's support, had to tone down the polemic and manifest a conciliatory attitude towards the communists.

Thus began the divergence between Blum's and Faure's political positions (due primarily to the diversity of their organizational roles). A few years later the dominant coalition totally fell apart giving rise to ever more intense internal factionalism. Faure, the party's center of gravity in the twenties and thirties, ended his career as the organization's most right-wing leader.[35]

Guy Mollet emerged as a star in the postwar reconstruction period, but he did not modify the party's essential structure. Nor did his changeable political tactics. He won the 1946 Congress on a left Marxist platform (namely neo-Guesdism) and then led the SFIO to break with the PCF and steered the party into government: a change in political strategy that Mollet effected successfully only because he was able to use the governmental apparatus to substitute the symbolic resources which helped him gain control of the party (e.g. collective identity incentives) for material resources (e.g. material selective incentives).[36]

The process succeeded so quickly because it was carried out in a weakly institutionalized organization, highly permeable and sensitive to changes in the environment. In a "strong" institution endowed with a powerful bureaucracy, incentive conversion cannot be effected so rapidly, and any dominant coalition which tries to do so (as Mollet did in 1946–7) soon runs into serious problems.

The organizational sclerosis of the Mollet era (e.g. decline of membership, aging of the cadre, etc.)[37] "falsifies" the theory that organizations always tend to expand according to an "entrepreneurial" logic. Neither the secretariat nor the "despots" of the most important federations were interested in risking organizational stability by adopting an aggressive political strategy. The internal power structure remained substantially stable for the whole of the Fourth Republic.

The Italian Socialist Party

The PSI, like the SFIO, took the SPD as a model in its formative years.[38] And like the SFIO, the PSI was never anything but a bad copy of the German socialist organization. The party's genetic model was in this case too a faithful indicator of the later weak level of institutionalization. At the 1892 Genoa Congress, the Milan Workers Party (a small party similar to the Lassalian and Guesdiste organizations), which had by then abandoned its original workerist sectarianism, joined with at least 200 socialist cooperatives and socialist local mutual aid associations throughout the country.[39] After that Congress, many other local associations sprung up autonomously. The party's birth thus involved the fusion of a multitude of preexisting local organizations and subsequent territorial diffusion.

Since it was not individual activists but rather *associations* which converged in Genoa, the party began with a collective base (i.e. involving group, not individual, affiliation). It was only in 1895 that, thanks to the efforts of Turati and other Milanese socialists who directed the organization's construction, the party organized on an individual basis. But the original character of this weak central organization (which had to lean on other groups and associations) weighed heavily upon the party for decades. Though its model was that of the SPD: "the party's function was conceived in a more toned-down and general manner: the party was more the coordinator than the guide of the various organisms into which the workers' movement was subdivided, and had to move in step with them and give expression to their different maturation levels."[40] This is the political consequence of the specific mode of formation and type of relationship which the PSI (as opposed to the SPD) was forced to establish with other organizations of the socialist movement.

In 1896, after a financial effort which was impressive for a party as weak as the PSI, the newspaper *Avanti!* was born. It was the only nationally distributed party publication, and the only center of organizational power which represented an at least partial alternative to the parliamentary group.

The organization's characteristics which consolidated at the end of the century and remained for a long time unchanged, can be summarized as follows:

(a) A voter-member ratio which, at its best, was twenty to one (as compared to the SPD's four or five to one ratio).[41] Up until the organizational expansion which followed the 1912 "maximalist" faction's victory, and especially after World War I, the PSI, like the SFIO, was more a voters' than an activist's party. Like the SFIO, it immediately had a social base in which the rural component was very strong. The *classe gardée* of the PSI always included a significant number of agricultural day laborers (even when, after the World War I, the party's ability to increase its support in the worker sectors increased). After the introduction of universal suffrage in 1913, while the national average of socialist votes was 17.7 per cent, it was 38.3 per cent for the Emilian agricultural day laborers.[42]

The socialist party was thus forced, because of the conditions in the countryside, to choose a social base which was more "popular" (like the SFIO) than "workerist" (like the SPD).

Very strong regional differences divided the party, and political differentiation of the geographical base always intersected but never completely coincided with national political divisions of left and right.

(b) The national extra-parliamentary organization was very weak. The Direzione Nazionale, the party's central national organ from one congress to another, never had sufficient means to hire a bureaucratic staff. It just barely managed to pay the salary of the political secretariat and only for very limited administrative services.[43]

(c) A very strong organizational differentiation from region to region – the effect of its emergence through a territorial diffusion which was not balanced by a "central power" – existed side by side with undefined organizational boundaries (both of these factors being symptoms of weak internal structural coherence). For example, it was the party's common practice to select candidates for public office through the local sections, union headquarters, cooperatives and other socialist organizations all together.[44] This led to the party's strong dependence on local external organizations.

(d) Given that there was no central bureaucratic apparatus (and none existed up until Rodolfo Morandi's reorganization after World War II), the selective incentive system upon which the party's support was based primarily utilized two channels: the municipalities with socialist majorities ("municipal socialism"),[45] and single deputies who won state concessions favoring their own constituencies.[46]

(e) The relationship established between the trade union, the Confederazione Generale del Lavoro (founded in 1906), and the party was a complicated,[47] torturous and ambiguous one. Rather than an absence of relations (as in the case of the SFIO) or an initial subordination of the trade union followed by slow emancipation (as in the case of the SPD), or even a dependence of the party on the trade unions (as in the case of the Labour Party), a relationship of formal mutual independence and informal collaboration developed on an egalitarian basis between the Turatian parliamentary group and the CGL's reformist leaders. This alliance, however, was always on the verge of breaking down due to maximalist pressure in the party and the CGL's revolutionary syndicalism (which was quite strong in the Camere del Lavoro, the local Union Headquarters).

Alongside the weak extra-parliamentary organization was a dominant parliamentary group. Dominant, in the first place, for a contingent reason: Turati, one of the party's founders, was also one of the most prestigious figures in Italian socialism; this prestige placed him at the parliamentary group's "center" and thus placed the parliamentary group at the party's "center" (exactly as Jean Jaurès had done in the SFIO). But the parliamentary group dominated for more structural reasons as well, e.g. because of the weakness of the central organization, the fact that selective incentives were distributed to party followers by the parliamentarians through the state bureaucracy (according to the typical model of Italian parliamentarianism), and the existence of "municipal socialism" (i.e. the flow of benefits which passed under the guise of a political relationship between Turati and Giolitti).[48] Moreover, the parliamentarians were almost all notables (especially lawyers and other professionals) able to personally and directly control their constituencies, and able to transform them into veritable personal fiefdoms (as was demonstrated by the constant reelection of the same candidates in many electoral colleges).[49] The notable (rather than bureaucratic–professional) character of socialist parliamentarianism was also due to the fact that until 1912, the deputies enjoyed no parliamentary indemnity.[50] The parliamentarians' control of the local sections could not be infringed upon, as in the SPD, by a central bureaucracy, nor, as in the SFIO, by a strong intermediary structure.

(f) The predominance of the parliamentary group and the weakness of the central organization, characteristics shared by the PSI and SFIO, were complemented (unlike the SFIO) by the weakness of the intermediate structure. The territorial section (not the federation) was the true seat of organizational power at the peripheral level, albeit with exceptions, as it was totally independent from the central party.[51] This characteristic explains two closely related phenomena: first of all, the ability of many parliamentarians to construct their own local fiefdoms; secondly, and consequently, a fragmentation of the party's national elite group which is even more pronounced than in the SFIO. In fact, if organizational power is concentrated at the federation level, there are few peripheral leaders with whom the national leaders can negotiate (as Paul Faure and then Mollet did in the SFIO). But if the intermediate structure is weak, as in the PSI, and organizational power is based on territorial sections, there are many local leaders, and no solid internal alliance can form.

This explains why the PSI's factions were more fluid than the SFIO's. Each of the former's factions had its own solid power base: the maximalists had theirs primarily in the party sections (opposition) and in the union headquarters; the reformists had theirs in the alliance (during the Giolittian decade) between the parliamentary group and the CGL's reformist leaders, in the peripheral and collateral associations (e.g. cooperatives, etc.) where the party dominated the local governments (as in Emilia), and also in those party sections which the parliamentarians/local notables had been able to make into personal fiefdoms.

It was just this highly fragmented and localized character of the party – not held together by a solid intermediate structure – which explained the factions' fluidity; people often moved from one faction to another at the top as well as at the base, and the boundaries between factions were poorly defined.[52] The SFIO's factions were more clearly defined, because they consolidated through the control of different federations. This also explained the flagrant lack of discipline in the PSI's parliamentary group.

As opposed to what happened in the Labour Party, it was only a convergence of interests which allowed the overwhelming majority of the parliamentarians to remain aligned with Turati's positions. In the Labour Party, the parliamentary leader and the unions decided together which of the deputies could run for office. In the PSI, on the other hand, each deputy decided for himself, relying on his personal prestige and his ability to procure material favors for his constituency. As the parliamentarians owed their reelection to the distribution of selective incentives to the voters, they "naturally" favored Turati's reformist policy: they could only distribute favors by accepting reformism.

The extremely weak condition of both the central and intermediate organizations explains why the maximalist victory at the 1904 Bologna Congress did not change the power structure nor stop the reformist parliamentarians from remaining the party's true motor force.[53] The maximalists' inability to fortify their own positions by acquiring control of the parliamentary group accounts for their rapid decline and the reformists' triumphant return to the party's head in the space of two short years. But if the 1904 maximalist victory was ephemeral, it was also an eloquent testimony to the weak cohesion of the PSI's dominant coalition. The reformists were far from unified, staying together as they did more because it was convenient (as we have already mentioned) for individual parliamentarians than because of a centrally controlled organizational mechanism. With changing political conditions – the decline of Giolittism, on which the credibility of Turati's political strategy hung – the reformist coalition was plagued by internal centrifugal forces (e.g. the Salveminian left, the Bissolatian–Bonomian right, and the Turatian center), until the dissolution and the final maximalist victory of 1912, influenced by the Libyan war.[54]

Throughout the reformist era the party avoided proselytism and remained a weak organization with but 20,000 to 30,000 active members. Its electoral strength was due more to the external support of other organizations of the Italian socialist movement, than to the party's autonomous organizational power. The absence of proselytism was partly due to the lack of a strong extra-parliamentary center able to promote and sustain with continuity an organizational expansion effort. But it was also, and perhaps especially, the result of the reformists' deliberate preservation of the internal power balance, i.e. their defense of organizational *stasis* (as was the case in the SFIO). In the SPD, on the other hand, numeric expansion was controlled by a strong central bureaucratic apparatus which could, for example, "pilot" the party congresses:

In Italy, the sovereignty of the national congresses doesn't run into serious obstacles or forms of mediation. The main if not only guarantee of the political platform's stability resides in the relatively small number of members and in their extremely slow turnover; those, therefore, most sensitive to tradition and to the most prestigious and authoritative leaders always prevail in the end.[55]

This situation changed somewhat at the 1912 Reggio Emilia Congress and with the maximalists' rise to power. The dominant coalition's new leader, Benito Mussolini, launched a serious campaign to increase party membership. Two years later – by the 1914 Ancona Congress – "the number of members had almost doubled. The old guard was submerged, dissolved in the vast new organism which now could only be controlled by the same force which had created it."[56]

The reason was clear: the new dominant coalition, having its pivot point in the (weak) Direzione Nazionale (from which the reformists were expelled) and in *Avanti!* had – in order to liquidate the parliamentary group's power – to reinforce the extra-parliamentary organization, i.e. balance and annul Turati's prestige using other organizational power resources, as quickly as possible. This scheme was ambitious, but the genetic model's strength could not simply be completely dismissed even by a leader as aggressive as Mussolini. And in fact, the reformists (a minority faction at that time) still autonomously kept the party's parliamentary political strategy going, ridiculing the maximalists' constant interference and energetic attempts to subordinate the parliamentary group to majority political choices. Having lost their predominance over the party, the reformists could still count on the support of the trade unions and other socialist organizations. And despite Mussolini's organizational efforts, the party remained weak compared to other "autonomous centers"[57] of the socialist movement. In 1913 the PSI, for example, still had only 45,000 members while the CGL had over 300,000.[58] Only after the postwar mobilization did the PSI become a mass party, totalling just over 200,000 members in 1920.[59] By that time, the maximalists (by then deprived of Mussolini's leadership) had succeeded in advantageously rebalancing their relations with the parliamentary group, and the political decline of the reformists had already run its course. Up until then

the PSI was the organizational incarnation of the reformist ideal of decentralization, its fulcrum being at the municipal level. The party was composed of a varying number of local independent sections, and the vertical ties with the party leadership were only weakly developed . . . Until the end of the First World War, when the party became a mass party, the reformist group, composed of politically eminent personalities, occupied a very influential party position.[60]

But the maximalists' definitive victory and the reformists' decline coincided with the more general decline of the party as a whole. As in the SFIO, the new situation was brought about by the Russian Revolution, and the party's affiliation with the Third International led to its breakdown (into three parties).

With its rebirth after World War II (the party was officially reconstituted in 1943 in Rome), the socialist organization only partly succeeded in emancipating itself from its past history. Along with the genetic model's characteristics – which played an important role in the party's reconstruction (a fusion of old and new groups[61] which only partly amalgamated) – the highly competitive PCI helped to stop the PSI from becoming a strong institution. Caught between parties having their own international positions in the polarized postwar conflict, it was virtually impossible for the reborn party to develop an autonomous identity.

The PSI, a frontier organization perched on the crest of the Cold War, oscillated continually from right to left, tore itself apart through constant internal struggle and paid for its untenable situation with repeated schisms. Nevertheless, the organizational break provoked by fascism led the PSI (like the PCI but for different reasons) to partially restructure. The PSI's 700,000 members in 1946 were the result of the political mobilization which took place during the partisan war. It was on this base that Morandi* attempted, after 1949, to build up the organization. Under Morandi the PSI made its most consistent effort (as did the DC under Fanfani – on this point see the next chapter) to become a strong institution. The attempt (as in the DC) was only partially successful, both because no party can entirely escape its organizational inheritance, and because the characteristics of the environment in which the organization was operating (i.e. its position with respect to national and international divisions) did not allow for the development of a solid identity (nor did it allow for the choice of and stable control over an autonomous electoral hunting ground).

After the ephemeral victory of the autonomist faction, "Riscossa Socialista" (whose leaders were Lombardi and Jacometti) as a result of the 1948 electoral defeat, the dominant coalition which affirmed itself at the 28th Congress (1949) through a political strategy of renewed cooperation with the PCI, was based on Rodolfo Morandi's organizational abilities and Pietro Nenni's great prestige. This coalition kept the party going until Morandi's death (1955), and in fact, until the 1957 Venice Congress. This was the period of greatest instability for the party's inner circle. Examination of the Direzione Nationale's composition between 1945 and 1966 demonstrates that "minor turnover between 1949 and 1957 corresponded to the period in which the socialist party most consistently followed a political platform (acceptable or not) without undergoing the crises endemic in its previous and subsequent history."[62]

Morandi's energetic attempts to transform the PSI into a strong institution, into a mass party modeled on the PCI, took form in this phase.[63] The Direzione became the party's central organ, and a (previously nonexistent) central bureaucratic apparatus developed at the expense of the territorial sections' traditional independence. The party also attempted to gain control over the collateral associations.

But the Morandian attempt was only partially successful. The

* Rodolfo Morandi, along with Pietro Nenni, was the most influential leader of the Socialist Party in the 1940s and 1950s.

bureaucratic apparatus never equalled that of the PCI in unity or size. As the political scientist Zarinski observed in 1962, commenting on the reasons for Nenni's change after 1957, an attentive investigation of the PSI's bureaucracy reveals: "a bare skeleton composed of 500 salaried officials. Many of its alleged functions – i.e., legislative reference, research – were apparently being performed in a remarkably sporadic and haphazard fashion, or in some instances were not being performed at all."[64]

The organization was never able to entirely replace its pre-fascist network of notables with a bureaucratic structure. Consequently, even though the federations grew much stronger than in the pre-war period, they were never strong enough to subdue the local notables. The new preeminence of the Direzione Nazionale over the parliamentary group was in itself ambiguous. Along with the strengthening of the Direzione, a rapid parliamentarization of the national leadership followed.[65]

The party's control over the collateral associations was never really assured. The socialist component of the trade union organizations, for example, lacking a powerful party to guide it, was influenced by the majoritarian communist component (which was the "syndicalist right hand" of a strong institution).

Consequently, even in the dominant coalition's period of maximum cohesion (1949–57), the party's factionistic life continued. The ruling group constantly had to confront a minority but combative right-wing faction with an autonomous base within the organization and among the local notables.

In 1957 the dominant coalition began to dissolve, giving rise to a stand-off between the Nennian right (a weak pro "center–left" majority group) and a strong leftist minority. We could term this a bi-factionalist epoch: the two factions were similarly constituted amalgamations of groups and matched up all across the board, as two-party systems often do.[66]

The center–left governments of the sixties and the new availability of public resources – which access to the government guaranteed and which could be capitalized upon in internal competition – quickly led the weak PSI to internal fragmentation. Its evolution paralleled that of its governmental partner (the DC) during the center–left governments: the PSI came up in the sixties against more pronounced factionalization than it had ever before experienced. In this phase the factions attained a maximum of institutionalization.

The PSI had to wait for the end of the center–left governments and the emergence of a threat to its own political survival (which came from the communists' electoral advancement in 1975–6) in order to engage in, with Midas'* generational turnover (1976), a new phase of recomposition under the direction of a more cohesive dominant coalition.[67] Even though some organizational transformations took place in the "catch-all" party's direction, and a more professional and aggressive stance was adopted in the field of mass communication, the party's weakness was not overcome. Its weakness was the result of factors going back a long way in time.

Conclusion

The three parties here presented are all cases of weak institutionalization. They are all highly dependent upon their environments: the Labour Party (and even to a certain extent the PSI) upon external organizations, the SFIO upon an electoral environment over which it exercises no direct control (control guaranteed the SPD, PCI and PCF by their strong organizations). They have to "adapt" to what happens "outside." They were unable to develop "imperialistic" strategies of environmental domination (like those developed by the strong institutions). Moreover, they all have little internal structural coherence, i.e. a low degree of systemness: they are, in other words, organizations which over time take on a wide variety of forms in different regions, demonstrating the significant indeterminancy of their organizational boundaries (especially in the cases of Labour and of the PSI). It is often difficult to figure out where the organization ends and where external organizations begin.

They differ from the SPD, PCF and PCI in that they could never develop strong central bureaucracies. Their bureaucratic organizations were more or less negligible in the SFIO and the PSI (up until the postwar period), and only embryonic in the Labour Party.

Their weak institutionalization entails a number of consequences. All three are factional parties, made up of organized groups contending for party control. Their opportunity structures are thus centrifugal. With the partial exception of the Labour Party (whose internal inequalities are a function of its sponsoring organizations' physiognomy) there is a direct correlation between internal and societal inequality systems. In the SFIO, and even more so in the PSI, the logic of the division of labor within a bureaucratic structure does not determine the distribution of trump cards and power resources. It is rather the societal inequality system which does so. The notables play a role here unknown in the SPD, for instance. The scarcity of "professional" participation is offset by massive doses of "civil" participa-

* Midas was originally the name of the hotel where the party's national gathering took place in 1976. A new generation of socialist leaders came to power as a result.

tion by these notables, as typically happens in cases of weak institutionalization. The structure of their participation involves predominantly clientelary selective incentives as opposed to the material rewards distributed by the bureaucracies.

Though all three parties weakly institutionalized, they are not identical on all points. The Labour Party's genetic model was that of an externally legitimated party, a party which for the whole of its existence remained the "political right hand" of a sponsoring organization. The SFIO, on the other hand, was an internally legitimated party. The PSI stands mid-way between the two: neither the political right hand of an external organization, nor totally independent from other socialist associations. This was foreshadowed by its initial formation involving indirect and collective types of affiliation, as well as by its ambiguous party–trade union relations.

Another difference lies in the degrees of cohesion of the dominant coalitions, and consequently the degree of organization of the internal factions. In the PSI, the factions, at least throughout the Turatian era, possessed a consistency inferior to that of the SFIO: they were less organized, had more fluid boundaries (though not to the point of being classified as tendencies). This was probably due to the diversity of the two parties' organizational structures. While in the SFIO the federations constituted the party's backbone (with the factions having a solid base around which to organize), in the PSI the territorial sections fulfill this function (and this makes the factionalistic struggles more diffuse and less easily coordinated).

The PSI was, in this respect, more like the Labour Party (in which, as we have seen, factionalism did not acquire – except during acute organizational crises – the rigidity and degree of organization seen elsewhere). This may be partly due to the fact that in both parties (though quite strictly and formally in Labour's case, and only informally and sporadically in the PSI) there was a functioning alliance between the parliamentary group and the union leaders (as well as between the party's left wing and the union's left wing). These intersecting inter-organizational alliances (lacking in the SFIO) can at least partly explain the rather unsolidified character of the internal factions of both parties. In fact, relations of force among the internal groups are subject, in organizations which are largely externally dependant, to changes in political orientation which take place outside (strictly speaking) of the party organization, i.e. which take place in other organizations (on the national as well as the local level).

The analogy between the Labour Party and the PSI should not, however, be taken too far: their difference is based on the fact that the unions had power to intervene in Labour's internal affairs which was greater than that of Italian union organizations over the PSI (even during the Turatian period).

I want, in conclusion, to underline one last point. An obvious difference between the three strongly institutionalized parties (the SPD, PCI and PCF) and the three weakly institutionalized parties (the Labour Party, SFIO, and PSI) examined thus far, is that only in the latter does the parliamentary group play a leading role, i.e. it wields much more organizational power than any other party level (even in the SFIO where it was balanced by the federations' power). We should not, however, jump to the conclusion that strong institutionalization is synonymous with the predominance of internal leaders, and weak institutionalization with the predominance of parliamentarians. Cases exist (and we shall discuss them further on) of parties which are, due to certain of their genetic model characteristics, relatively strongly institutionalized and also have a predominant parliamentary group.

7
Governmental parties

Further evidence supporting the analytic schema I have developed can be found in the history of three parties that institutionalized from a central rather than peripheral position, parties which acceded to national government just after their formation (and before organizational consolidation) and which remained in power for a long time. As I have already maintained, governmental control during the phase of organizational consolidation should, under normal conditions, favor low degrees of institutionalization. The public resources which state control places at the disposal of governing parties often seriously inhibit strong organizational development. Nevertheless, just as being in opposition does not guarantee a high degree of institutionalization, control of the government during consolidation does not *inevitably* condemn a party to a low degree – it makes it probable but not absolutely necessary. Certain genetic model traits (e.g. development through territorial penetration and, as we shall see in the following chapter, charismatic origin) may predispose even governmental parties to a high degree of institutionalization. Aside from the characteristics of the party's genetic model other factors play an important role, for example the nature of the state bureaucracy and the degree of competitiveness in the political system.

In the first place, the quantity of public resources available for "private" ends (in party competition) is important: the more public resources available, the less the leaders' need to highly institutionalize the organization. Where, due to the characteristics of the bureaucracy, distributable public resources (in the form of incentives) are widely available, we find weakly institutionalized governmental parties. Easy availability of public resources discourages strong organizational development, leaders are not interested in creating a party bureaucracy, and selective incentives pass through other channels (e.g. governmental ones). Where, on the other hand, the bureaucracy has the opposite characteristics, it is not easily colonized (e.g. in the case of a powerful public administration elite, independent of the parties, with a strong *esprit de corps* on the Prussian model), public resources are scarce, and we must therefore expect more sustained organizational development in governmental parties: the leaders, having no alternative resources, must strengthen their party's organization. Governmental parties can be situated along a *continuum* from a maximum to a minimum of private disposal of public resources. The Italian DC is, among the parties here considered, the governmental party disposing of the most public funds. The English Conservatives, governing almost uninterruptedly for twenty years (1886–1905) – with a brief Liberal intermission (1892–4) – in the phase of organizational consolidation, can be situated at the opposite pole of the *continuum*, with quite limited access to public resources. The different levels of institutionalization are influenced by the differences in bureaucratic systems, party government–bureaucracy relations, and state intervention in the respective national economies.

The second important factor is the political system's degree of competitiveness. The German Christian Democrats (up until the SPD's ideological revision at Bad Godesberg) and the Italian Christian Democrats are organizations which have gone unchallenged for a long time by oppositional parties, and were not seriously threatened in their roles as governmental parties during their organizational consolidation. The British Conservatives, on the other hand, were constantly threatened by a credible competitor: the Liberals.

In this chapter we will examine the formation of three governmental parties. Two of these (the CDU and the DC) became weak institutions, only one (the British Conservative Party) became a strong one. This comparison raises even more delicate substantive and methodological problems than those raised in the preceding chapters.

Two of the parties to be examined, the CDU and the DC, were born after World War II, and their genetic models reflect this fact. But as is true of many organizations which "start from scratch" in environmental contexts which have undergone institutional breakdowns – in this case, changes in the political regime – there is a problematic relation between the new organizations and their predecessors. Both the CDU and the DC had predecessors (the Catholic *Zentrum* and the *Partito Popolare* respectively) which operated in the pre-authoritarian regimes. Though posing more problems for the DC than for the CDU, some elements of their genetic models must, no doubt, be pre-dated, i.e. sought in the past and in the subterranean continuity (of ruling classes in particular) from the old organization to the postwar one. This is a problem which we will not be able to adequately treat here, but which certainly presents itself when one tries to define the origins of these organizations.

A second problem concerns the Conservative Party, and is related to the definition of its genetic model. We have decided to begin with the moment of the Conservatives transformation from a parliamentary elite to a modern political party. We have done so because only modern political parties which dispose of a national extra-parliamentary organization (be it solid or fragile), are the focus of our analysis here. The Conservative Party's origin, however, as a parliamentary group, dates back to a much earlier period and at least certain aspects of its genetic model must be sought much further back in the past (space does not, however, permit us to do so here).

Another problem is related to the significance of historical lag in the three cases examined. The most important point is that while the CDU and the DC consolidated as governmental parties in an era of expanding state intervention in the national economies of their respective countries – and thus had access to (state) resources which discouraged institutionalization – the Conservative Party consolidated in a phase of competitive capitalism (the late 1800s), i.e. in environmental conditions very different from those in Europe just after World War II. We must keep this fact, as well as the traditionally competitive character of English democracy (which never allows the ruling party to let down its guard) in mind in explaining the different organizational outcomes.

The Christian–Democratic union

The constitutive factors of the CDU's genetic model can be summarized as follows.

Firstly, legitimation which is, unlike most other denominational parties, only minimally "external." The CDU is a new party, not the inheritor of the old Catholic *Zentrum*.[1] At the end of the war, the *Zentrum* was widely discredited (as were most of the Weimar era parties) and conservative politicians sought to create a new political organization. As a result, though *Zentrum* tried to rebuild and compete with the CDU, it had little success.[2] The CDU's novelty consisted in its being a multi-denominational party including both Catholics and Protestants. The need to maintain a balance between the two faiths explains why the religious organizations' influence on the new party was great but not overwhelming.[3] Its leaders constantly had to hold off a schism along the Catholic/Protestant split which would have inevitably occurred if one of the churches were to hegemonize the party's political choices. The CDU thus differed not only from the old *Zentrum* but from all other christian-democratic parties as well. While the religious organizations had a certain influence over the party, it was no greater than that exerted by many other interest groups. In this sense, the CDU can be considered to be an internally legitimated party. This would have predisposed the organization to highly institutionalize had other factors not intervened.

Secondly, a birth through *territorial diffusion*, in its purest form. The party's local and regional associations formed and consolidated autonomously without any central coordination and with almost no horizontal contact between zones. Between 1945 and 1950 (the year in which the Federal Party was formed), the local, intermediary, regional and zonal associations developed and consolidated as autonomous power centers. This development explains the federal character of the future organization.[4]

Thirdly, an organizational development which accompanied Konrad Adenauer's growing prestige in the party and the country as a whole. His situational charisma and the development through territorial diffusion led together, as we shall see, to a low degree of institutionalization.

Fourthly the formation of a parliamentary party group and of a CDU dominated government *before* the unification of the various associations into a federal party.

An examination of its first phase of development is, as in many other cases, crucial if we wish to understand its organizational logic during the long period in which the CDU controlled the national government (1949–69).

The embryo of what later became the CDU was formed – right at the end of the occupation – by the autonomous initiative of a number of political groups scattered throughout the country.[5] The first group which was able to successfully organize locally (with the support of the Christian trade union) was the Berlin Group. Its leaders (Andreas Hermes initially, and Jacob Kaiser afterwards) tried unsuccessfully to exploit their initial organizational advantage to take control of the entire party. Hermes organized the first party conference in order to bring together all the local and regional groups which had sprung up by the autumn of 1945 at Bad Godesberg. Hermes, however, having fallen out with the Soviet command in Berlin, did not obtain the necessary authorization to go to Bad Godesberg himself, and thus could not dominate the meeting. The only important decisions made there concerned the adoption of a name for the new party (the Christian–Democratic Union) and the creation of a new liaison office whose task it was to coordinate the various associations. No "center" able to monopolize control of the party's organizational development could come forward in this phase because of the communication problems among the zones under occupation and of the local leaders' unwillingness to accept centralized direction. The CDU's fate was sealed right from the start. Most important developments took place on a zonal and not on a national level, especially in the English zone where Adenauer soon emerged as the undisputed leader; this was largely due to the energy he put into the CDU organization in his zone as the primary and most promising political interlocutor with the allies (like De Gasperi in Italy). His organization became the most important nucleus of the future federal party. Because of Adenauer's "private" use of the party in this phase, his zone's secretariat (controlled by Adenauer's right-hand men) informally functioned as the party's national secretariat from 1948–50. Adenauer also rapidly rose to power in the English zone by exploiting his image as the "new" man: he had held no national political position during Weimar and was not thus discredited as were the old guard. In a few short months he became the undisputed leader of the Rheineland organization. He was able to attract different interest groups ranging from Catholic syndicalists to conservative Protestants. In allying with the Wesphalian CDU leader, Holzapgel, he was able to get the whole organization to rally behind him. The Adenauer–Holzapgel accord allowed the Rheineland and Westphalian parties to build, and later hegemonize, their zones' organizations. A Zone Council, i.e. a deliberative and executive party organ for the entire English zone, was created under Adenauer's control. The Council's secretariat was entrusted to one of his men, Joseph Löns, who made every possible effort to homogenize and centrally coordinate all the local and regional associations in the zone; and by 1947, their organization was the best organized in the entire country.

Throughout 1946 the party's development on a local and federal level proceeded without any central control or coordination. Adenauer and the other zonal leaders were far more concerned with strengthening their respective organizations (and their personal control over them) than with creating an efficient national organism. The first step towards real national coordination was motivated by an external event: the SPD's rapid reorganization under Schumacher's guidance in the years 1945–6.[6] The reconstruction of social democracy with the same centralized features of the pre-Nazi era was very rapid. By the end of 1946, the SPD had become a very dangerous competitor for the CDU. This challenge forced the CDU's most prestigious notables to make a first attempt at unification. In Frankfurt in November 1946, the different leaders held a preparatory meeting with the aim of coordinating their efforts in order to deal with their common enemy. The conflict between the prestigious leaders of the two best organized groups,

Adenauer and Kaiser (the Berlin Organization) immediately erupted at the Frankfurt meeting. At stake was the party's national leadership; the crucial issue was the nationalization of the heavy industry in the Ruhr. Kaiser and the left, supported by the trade unions, were in favor of it. Adenauer, who on this issue rallied the whole of the CDU's center–right as well as the industrial community behind him, was against it. In Konigstein in February 1947, a national conference was finally held. A central party organ was formed (the *Arbeitsgemeinschaft*) whose first secretary was Bruno Dorpinghans from Frankfurt. But despite the platform put forward by the Berlin group, no real national organization was formed. Adenauer himself went to Konigstein with the intention of blocking any solution which would divest the zonal organizations of their authority. And other regional leaders went with similar intentions. The CDU's birth through "pure" territorial diffusion explains the failure at Konigstein, i.e. the fact that the leaders of the separately formed and consolidated local, regional, and zonal organizations were unwilling to cede their organizational power to a superior agency. The *Arbeitsgemeinschaft* thus could not become the center of the national organization. It remained a weak organism throughout its brief existence (1947–50), totally lacking in authority and depending even for its financing on the regional leaders' good will.

The organizational features developed by the CDU in this phase remained practically unchanged up until its internal reform in the seventies. The party's financing, membership, and bureaucratic staff had as their seat not the national center but rather the CDU organizations in the *Länder*: the organization was thus but a collection of autonomous and independent potentates, each developing separately.

Paradoxically, "national" loyalties eventually coalesced around the division between Kaiser's left and Adenauer's right. This occurred, in part, because external groups, from trade unions to religious associations, and entrepreneurial and financial associations, gathered around one leader or the other. In 1947 an Anglo-American initiative led to the constitution of the Frankfurt Economic Council. The SPD and the CDU were jointly represented there, having forty seats each. The CDU's parliamentary group was thus formed *before* the national organization. It is interesting to note that the CDU's organizational development was the opposite of the SPD's. The latter was rapidly rebuilt and was already a strong organization by 1946. Its power allowed it to firmly establish itself in the local representative councils in most of the *Länder*. The CDU, on the other hand, was too weak to compete with the SPD on the local level. It could only hope to win control over the central government.[7] The party's unification was thus delayed, both because of the local notables' resistance and because the problem of national leadership had not been resolved. It was only in 1948 that Adenauer won out over his rival Kaiser in the struggle for party control. The blockade of Berlin and the autonomous administrative unification of the zones under Western control made it clear that the unification of Germany (supported by Kaiser) was impossible. Adenauer's political platform (representing that of the commercial and industrial sectors) of a political unification which would at least temporarily not include the Soviet zone, became the only realistic position. Kaiser lost more ground later on account of the Catholic Church's sharp opposition to his very advanced socio-economic reform proposals. Adenauer became the only significant party leader of national renown, partly because he was able to ally with the right interest groups, and partly because of circumstances. He was the man upon whom the Western allies banked.

Meeting no appreciable resistance, Adenauer nominated himself president, in June 1948, of a new *ad hoc* national party organism: the Council of the *Länder*'s presidents. Thus was constituted the party's typical dominant coalition throughout the fifties consisting in an alliance between the future Chancellor (and the party president), and the leaders of the federal organizations. At the 1949 elections, the party boasted an efficient coordination system composed of regional leaders and a single national center: Adenauer. In September 1949 Adenauer became national Chancellor. In this way: "In late 1949 the CDU found itself in the curious position of having achieved office without even having formally unified itself into a party."[8] But Adenauer in 1949 rejected propositions from several sides to set up a real federal party. He was still afraid that various internal oppositional leaders (Werner Hilpert from Hessen, Gunther Gerke from Lower Saxony, Kaiser from Berlin, etc.) would thereby be able to unify and get the upper hand. By 1950, however, his control over the central government had consolidated enough that he could allow the party to form without putting at risk his privileged position. At the time "The immense patronage now at his disposal in the Federal Government put him in an extremely strong position."[9]

The national party's constitutional congress was finally convoked in October 1950 at Goslar. It was there that the party adopted its first statutes and organized on a national scale.

Although there were a few minor revisions afterwards, the party's physiognomy determined at Goslar (actually the fruit of a simple ratification of already existing internal organizational power relations) lasted practically up until the reorganization which followed its shift into opposition (starting in 1969). In certain respects, the CDU resembled the SFIO.

In the first place, the party had a "federal" structure which reflected its birth through territorial diffusion and its adaptation to the federal order of the German state. Federal structure signifies highly autonomous intermediate organizations, and a lack of central control over the organization. For the whole of its twenty years in government, (thanks to its close relations with the federal bureaucracy and many interest groups – especially the industrial associations – which placed at the disposition of the party leaders a constant quantity of usable resources for campaigns), the CDU was never seriously forced to develop a strong organization. It maintained, instead, the character of an electoral association composed of many poorly amalgamated groups, held together by their common government benefits and by Adenauer's image – the focus of all moderate German public opinion.

Secondly, *Fraktion*, the parliamentary group in the *Bundestag*, was – as is always the case when there is no extra-parliamentary bureaucracy – the central national organ. Its organizational power was, however, limited by the ministerial elite's predominance (consisting at that time of Adenauer's right-hand men), and dominated by the Chancellor (who got himself elected party president at Goslar). Like the SFIO, it was also limited by the power of the intermediary leaders heading semi-autonomous regional organizations.

Thirdly, the extra-parliamentary organization was very weak. Its headquarters (the *Bundesgeschäftsstelle*) began to function in 1952. It had, however, only administrative tasks, and only operated within a very limited ambit; it had no financial means of its own, and depended for support upon the regional leaders. The organization had no central membership system, and its finances were entirely controlled at the regional and local levels. And it had no central bureaucratic structure (not even an embryonic one), as neither the Chancellor nor the regional leaders wanted to strengthen the party organization, fearing a challenge to their power positions.

Fourthly, the result of its weak extra-parliamentary central organization (as in the case of the SFIO) was a strong intermediary structure. The *Landesverbände*, i.e. the regional organizations, were veritable autonomous fiefdoms, able to successfully ward off "central" party interference. They had their own bureaucracies and financial resources.[10] The local associations depended on these intermediary organizations, and the center had no direct contact with the "periphery." For years the regional leaders succeeded in aborting all of the extra-parliamentary center's attempts to build itself up. They even went so far as to prevent, for a very long time, the creation of a central card-index of party members, refusing to give the list of regional organizations' members to the headquarters.

The party president and the regional leaders together controlled (according to the statutes) the two main national organs, the federal committee (*Bundesausschuss*) and the federal executive (*Bundesvorstand*).

The CDU could never highly institutionalize. It was heavily dependent upon its external environment, a dependence demonstrated by the *direct* involvement of interest groups at all crucial moments in the organization's life. For example, the industrialists', merchants', and farmers' collateral associations directly participated in the *Länder* level in selection of parliamentary candidates.[11] The result was that a fairly high number of the deputies came from outside groups and/or organizations. What's more, the organization's financing depended on the interest groups. There was neither centralized enrollment nor a regional enrollment important enough to influence the party's budget. In 1961, for example, only 50 per cent of the members paid dues (compared with 94 per cent of the SPD's members).[12] Being an electoral organization deprived of a central bureaucratic structure, the party was financed at the national level by interest groups (above all by industrial associations), and especially during electoral campaigns. The CDU was characterized by not having either regular financing or a diversity of financial sources (two indicators of strong institutionalization).[13]

Its dependence on the external environment is demonstrated by the importance of the local and regional notables within the leadership. The integration of the CDU's elites was of a "horizontal" type. It was not possible to rise up in the party by making a career within it. One generally entered the organization through local, state, or federal elected office in virtue of a previous prestigious position, or a privileged external position (e.g. being a leading local notable or an interest group representative on the regional or national level).[14] This heavy dependence on the environment led to a very low degree of internal structural coherence. Lacking a central bureaucracy – i.e. a unified center able to control the development of the various parts of the organization – the party developed in very different ways as a result of local conditions and of regional and local leaders' choices. The crucial difference here hinged on the fact that the party was either in government or in opposition in the different *Länder*: when the party was in government, the dominant "regional" coalition was generally guided by public representatives; when the party was in opposition, it was guided by the *Landesverbande*'s presidents.

As in all weakly institutionalized parties, control over zones of uncertainty and distribution of organizational incentives was quite scattered within the party. The party's dominant coalition was thus anything but cohesive. This was reflected first of all in the relative lack of discipline in *Fraktion* (which, though docilely accepting Adenauer's foreign policy choices, was much less united on domestic politics).[15] The parliamentarians, in fact, were either representatives of many different interest groups (supporting conflicting positions), or ex-high-ranking state bureaucrats. They had personal connections in the state apparati or were elected not because of the Chancellor's decisions, but because of their ties with regional organizational leaders. Adenauer's prestige and the regional leaders' enjoyment of government benefits were the only factors keeping the organization together in the fifties. As the SFIO's dominant coalition was composed (after 1905) of a parliamentary leader, Jaurès, and the leaders of the strongest federations, the CDU's dominant coalition was composed of Adenauer – in his double role as Chancellor and party president – and the leaders of the most powerful *Landerverbande*. Adenauer both symbolized the party's organization and controlled the distribution of material goods at the federal level. The regional leaders, despite Adenauer's national political role, were still the true party bosses. The dominant coalition, due to the extreme dispersion of control over its power resources, was held together by a delicate equilibrium. In spite of his great prestige, Adenauer was never able to outweigh the regional leaders' will.[16] When, for example, in 1956 he attempted to prevent the election of his main adversary (Karl Arnold) to the vice-presidency, he was decisively overruled by a majority led by the principal regional leaders. Every decision had to be negotiated within the organization. Even when Adenauer's prestige was at its height, powerful internal groups still existed which could adopt opposing positions and take advantage of the existence of many autonomous centers of organizational power. A minimal *modus vivendi* among the various organizational components was, however, maintained until Adenauer could assure the party's electoral victory.

In the fifties and sixties, the internal power structure owed its stability – as was true of the SFIO and the PSI – to the absence of proselytism, to the decision not to increase the organization's size. There were 215,00 members in 1954, and still only 280,000 in 1968, one year before the CDU's exclusion from government. The CDU had to move into opposition to become a mass party of almost 700,000 members. Throughout the Adenauer era, and even in the years thereafter, both the Chancellor and the regional leaders preferred organizational stasis to prevent a broadening of internal participation which might have endangered the party's power structure. Organizational stasis allowed both the Chancellor and the regional leaders to exercise uninterrupted control over the organization. With Adenauer's political decline (he withdrew from national politics in 1963) and the increase in political danger posed by the SPD – which after Bad Godesberg had become a potentially governmental party – the CDU's organizational equilibrium began to break down. Pressures to "reform" the party – to more highly institutionalize – began to make themselves felt, pressures exerted by a new generation of emerging leaders who saw in "organizational reform" a way to liquidate the old guard. These maneuvers could not, however, be successful as long as the CDU continued to control substantial public resources through the federal government. It was only when it was forced into opposition that the CDU could more highly organize. This transformation, as is always true of organizational transformation, was associated with a transformation of the party power structure.[17]

The Italian Christian Democrats

The CDU was only partly the secular wing of a religious institution. As opposed to the Catholic *Zentrum*, it was a multi-denominational party, and its need to maintain a balance among the different churches made it dependent on the religious institutions (Catholic and Protestant), but no more dependent than it was on industrial, commercial, agrarian and other interest groups. The Italian DC was, on the other hand, a uni-denominational party: it was created by a single religious institution. The DC was an externally sponsored and legitimated party – like the Labour Party and communist parties, but more so than the CDU. If the CDU's weak institutionalization resulted from birth through territorial diffusion in the "pure" form (facilitated by the country's division among the different occupying powers), the DC's was primarily due to its external legitimation. It resulted from the Church's "maximum pledge" and "maximum participation"[18] in the transitional phase following the decline of fascism. The Church hoped to create a solution to the Italian political upheaval in harmony with its own institutional interests.

The Church not only legitimated the new-born party but also furnished some of its fundamental organizational resources: (1) The network of Catholic associations (and its base structure – the parishes) served as the DC's external support; and the parishes and civic committees often reinforced its grass-roots electoral organizations, substituting for them where they didn't yet exist. (2) It also furnished the political personnel from which the Christian Democratic ruling class emerged: the laicized youth (politically raised in *Azione Cattolica*)[19] and the old ex-*populari* politicians, both groups with very close ties to the ecclesiastical hierarchy.

But the legitimation and the commitment of an external institution are not, alone, enough to give life to a party. Partially autonomous political entrepreneurs with the know-how and authority necessary to undertake mediatory roles between the external institution and other groups and organizations are also needed. While the Labour Party's formation was sponsored by the unions, Hardie, MacDonald, and the personnel of the ILP also played a decisive role; analogously, an important role was played in the DC's formation by Alcide De Gasperi, the most prestigious political exponent of liberal Catholicism.[20] De Gasperi was the political entrepreneur who, in aligning himself with the external institution, gave a strong push to the organization's construction, the definition of its ideological goals, and the selection of its social base.

The external institution, however (as in the case of the socialist and communist parties), controlled the party. The DC's predecessor, the *Partito Popolare* (1919–26), was born through the efforts and will of Luigi Sturzo, more because of the Church's "authorization" than because of his own considerable commitment. But the *Partito Popolare* was so dependent on the Church that it immediately folded when the Church decided to set up a direct dialogue with fascism.[21] The DC's heavy dependence can thus be explained by the Church's direct massive intervention. The party's peripheral development through territorial diffusion also contributed to the party's low level of institutionalization. Under the Church's orchestration and supervision, the first initiatives came from the center: the party resulted from the encounter between De Gasperi and the group of the so-called neo-Guelfs (a Catholic group of intellectuals) in mid-1942.[22] The first central organ constituted was a Provisional Commission, replaced in 1943 by a Central Directive Commission, and finally in 1944 (in accordance with De Gasperi's proposal) by an Executive Committee.

The rapid and premature formation of the national organs was *not* followed by subsequent development of the periphery through territorial penetration. From 1944 to 1945, the initiatives to implant the party in the various zones proceeded without central coordination. Its rapid diffusion corresponded to the progressive liberation of Italian regions from German occupation. The formation of the local Christian Democratic associations was often due *not* to the activists' independent action, but rather to the initiative of the local clergy following central orders.

We can therefore speak of two simultaneous but largely independent processes: the formation by De Gasperi and other ex-*populari* of a center, and the autonomous formation of the periphery:

> At the peripheral level, the initiative began in the Catholic movement and the clergy often played a key role. The initiative was frequently so uncoordinated that the central directory commission of the DC decided to initiate a kind of census and asked the section and provincial committee organizers to establish contact with the center. Already in 1945 there were more than 500,000 members; but there was no way to bring all of the peripheral organizations under national party control.[23]

In Naples in July of 1944, the inter-regional Congress was held with the participation of delegates from all of the already liberated zones.[24] The First National Council and the Directorate were constituted there. The office of secretary general was inaugurated, and De Gasperi was unanimously elected secretary. The fact that the party charter was not approved is indicative of the dispersed and federal nature of the organization at that time, as well as the premature setting up of local centers of autonomous power. Heated debates over the DC's organizational form delayed the approval of the charter for several years. As in many other parties, the approval of the DC's charter represented the *ex post facto* ratification of the power relations between the organization's different components which informally began to take root in the party's very first years of life.[25] At the first national congress held in Rome in April 1946, the Republican proposal was adopted.* Although this was the party's most important political decision, relevant organizational events were not lacking. The distinctly fragmentary nature of the new-born organization and the existence of numerous internal power centers – effects of its genetic model's characteristics – had political consequences: for the election of the National Council, eight different lists, comprising 200 candidates, were presented for 60 councilor positions. Only De Gasperi's authority allowed for a partial political unification: his proposal to fuse the different party lists just barely passed. Though De Gasperi was the center of the party's dominant coalition, the type of organization formed prevented him from controlling it entirely. The postponement of the charter's approval due to serious conflicts[26] is a good indicator of his only partial control.

The Italian DC, whose main features remained unchanged despite the subsequent reorganization engendered by Fanfani, was thus another example of a weak institution resulting from external legitimation and development through territorial diffusion. The party was

---

* This is in reference to the so-called "institutional debate," i.e. the problem of the choice between monarchy and Republic which was a central national issue at this time.

structured primarily as an electoral organization with fragile and uncertain boundaries, totally lacking a solid central apparatus. If the extra-parliamentary organization seems a bit stronger than the CDU's (and the SFIO's and the Turatian PSI's), it is probably because the national center's constitution accompanied rather than followed the peripheral development (and a special type of bureaucrat, paid on a regular basis by the Catholic associations, worked in the national headquarters). Its local and intermediary structures were very weak and dominated by external organizations (the Catholic associations and the clergy), especially in the traditional strongholds of the Catholic mass movement.[27]

Where Catholic associationalism was traditionally weak (for example, in Southern Italy), the development through diffusion facilitated the party's rapid colonization by notables. The DC thus consolidated as an organizational hybrid, controlled in certain zones by the Catholic associations, and shaped in other zones by the traditional network of notables. The party thus always depended on either religious organizations or individuals and local groups in socially privileged positions. Weak organizational articulation[28] and the absence of a strong central bureaucracy were the other characteristics accounting for the low level of internal structural cohesion during the De Gasperian period. Throughout that period, Luigi Gedda's Civic Committees'* and the local clergy's direct participation in the political and administrative electoral campaigns, the active role of the notables (especially in the rural areas of the south) and the massive pro-Christian Democratic ideological intervention of the ecclesiastical hierarchy explain why the party's national leaders, disposing of external organizational resources, had no interest in strengthening the organization.

The DC's political activism (at the grass-roots level and at the top) was provided by external Catholic organizations, and its financing came from external interest groups (as in the CDU).[29] The *Confindustria* – an association of private entrepreneurs – was the DC's most important financier during the De Gasperi era. These conditions predisposed the party to a heavy dependence on external organizations.

Being an externally legitimated party born through territorial diffusion, its weak institutionalization was reinforced by its early dominant position in the national government. Interest groups consequently coalesced at the top, and notables at the base. A low degree of institutionalization brought about the domination of the parliamentary

---

* The *comitati civici* were local electoral organizations directed and coordinated by Gedda, a right-wing Catholic politician with strong ties to the clergy, completely independent from the party and with a strong influence on the electorate.

group over the rest of the party and, as the DC was a governmental party, of the prime minister and the other ministers over the parliamentary group.

The low degree of institutionalization favored deep divisions within the leading group. At the Second Congress (Naples, 1947), the problem of already formed internal factions (called "currents") was debated. In this phase the main division between left and right amounted to a generational conflict: De Gasperi and the other ex-*populari* who controlled the party's center–right (i.e. the majority) were counter-balanced by the youth coming from *Azione Cattolica*'s ranks. The two leftist factions, having their own publications and embryonic organizations, were led by ex-syndicalist Giovanni Gronchi (from the *Politica Sociale* faction) and Giuseppe Dossetti (from the *Cronache Sociali* faction). The Dossettian group developed the more aggressive and coherent political stance opposing De Gasperi, proposing the transformation of the DC into a real mass party (a proposal which was later taken up, in a different context and with different alliances, by the ex-Dossettian, Amintore Fanfani). Dossetti fought for the subordination of the publicly elected assembly officials to party control. The majority leader, De Gasperi (whose behavior was quite similar to that of his German counterpart, Adenauer), successfully defeated this proposal. Prevailing organizational policy in every way discouraged the strengthening of party structures. Dossetti's offensive failed immediately after a temporary partial modification of the party's dominant coalition so as to include individuals from minority factions in the directive organs (e.g. of Dossetti in the vice-secretariat). This failure led Dossetti to quit in 1951, and to withdraw from political life.

One of the most important reasons for Dossetti's withdrawal was the hostility he and his political strategy provoked in the ecclesiastical hierarchy. In an externally legitimated party, the internal power struggles are decided by the external institution. De Gasperi's famous letter to Pius XII calling for the Pope's intervention against Dossetti, was a clear indicator of the DC's externally-dependant character.[30]

The most serious attempt to reinforce the organization was made while Fanfani was secretary (1954–9). While little data is available on the extent of the strengthening of the central bureaucratic apparatus (a crucial indicator of degree of institutionalization), it is generally thought that it became stronger at all levels. The Fanfanian center tried to increase the structural coherence of the intermediary and peripheral organizations, to reduce the party's dependence on external organizations, to unhinge the network of notables, and to professionalize the ruling class at the central and peripheral levels. Fanfani's action led the DC to institutionalize and develop an at least partially autonomous party loyalty (i.e. not solely or primarily to other organizations). The process was accompanied by increasing independence from the Church (which was beginning to take new political positions),[31] and partial disengagement from the *Confindustria*'s and other interest groups' financial protection; self-financing began through the control of public firms (e.g. semi-autonomous state firms).[32]

The Fanfanian attempt to make of the DC a mass party was only partly successful. By the end of the Fanfanian experiment, the organization was much stronger than during the De Gasperian period, but still largely corresponded to the ideal type of a weak institution. Fanfani's defeat in 1959 – due to the break-up of *Iniziativa Democratica*'s majority faction and to the birth of a new anti-Fanfani faction (the "Doroteans")[33] – can also be seen as due to organizations' inability to escape their organizational heritages (the weight of their genetic models) to any great extent.

The acceleration of state colonization (*occupazione dello Stato*)* undertaken by Fanfani, contained the seed of the DC's future development: the strengthening of the internal factions more than of the party as a whole. The factions, expanding in reciprocal competition within the public and semi-public state apparatuses, developed complex systems of autonomous connections with many external power centers.[34] This led to the dominant coalition's fragmentation and the institutionalization of its factionalism. The factions' greatest institutionalization occurred just before and during the ten years of center–left governments:** the adoption of an internal electoral proportional system in 1964 was not the main *cause* of the strong Christian Democratic factionalism, but was, on the contrary (as usually happens with organizational game rules), the *ex post* ratification of the dominant coalition's conformation. This conformation had been favored by the party's weak institutionalization and by the "colonization" – on the part of many internal party groups – of state apparatuses.[35]

So despite Fanfani's efforts, the DC remained a weak institution dependent on private groups and the Church (though less so than in the De Gasperian period), on the new managers of public industry,

---

* Translator's note: *Occupazione dello Stato* is translated as "state colonization." In Italian political jargon this expression refers to the transformation of the state apparatus into a clientelary reservoir of governmental parties by means of the recruitment and promotion of state functionaries loyal to these parties and through the use of the state bureaucracy and public firms to advance party ends.

**Translator's note: The "center–left" was the political formula for the governments of the sixties and early seventies which were characterized by the participation of the Socialist Party together with the DC and its older governmental partners. The birth of the center–left governments was preceded by a long and complex process during which the breakdown of the alliance between two opposition parties (the PCI and the PSI) and the slow thawing between the PSI and the DC took place.

and on powerful pressure groups such as *Coldiretti* (the Catholic farmers association).[36]

The recruitment of elites was still of a "horizontal" type: the leaders continued to come from external organizations or from the ranks of the traditional notables (though due to the state's *occupazione* and the simultaneous expansion of the public economy, they had to cede their positions in many areas to a *sui generis* network of notables tied to state bank credit, to the Cassa del Mezzogiorno, etc.).[37] The DC's partial emancipation from the Church's support was thus counter-balanced by a rather tight link with public structures. Indeterminate boundaries, external dependence, and low internal structural coherence continue to characterize the organization.

It is indicative of its still primarily notable rather than professional character that, in the early sixties, only 25.3 per cent of its national leaders (as opposed to 65.5 per cent of the communists' leaders) were willing to define themselves as "political professionals."[38] And the party's institutional weakness is indicated by the fact that, in the same period, the overwhelming majority of DC activists declared themselves more "loyal" to the Catholic associations than to the DC, i.e. they identified more with the external sponsoring institution than with the party.[39] In time, the state's "colonization" had new effects on the organization. In particular, a new type of political professional emerged: bureaucrats from public and semi-public institutions who were in fact full-time party activists. The public bureaucrats operating in the DC were usually (as in many other Italian parties as well) "hidden" political professionals placed by the DC in public roles in the bureaucracy.[40]

The DC's physiognomy did not undergo significant subsequent changes (though some changes were made with the "refoundation" attempts in the seventies).[41] The DC can not undergo reform as long as its symbiotic tie with the state remains intact: substantial transformation can only take place if the party finds itself in opposition for a relatively long period of time.

A significant characteristic of the DC's organizational dynamic is that it has often – as opposed to the CDU among governing parties, and to the SFIO and Turati's PSI among opposition parties – been highly expansionist and "imperialistic" *vis-à-vis* its environment. We have spoken of the state's process of "colonization." But the same is true of the DC's member recruitment policy.

The DC – unlike the CDU and SFIO – was not a party whose dominant coalition chose organizational stasis in order to preserve its internal power balance. Though weakly institutionalized, it pursued a policy of expansion. The major expansive phases (followed by lapses) coincided with either external electoral deadlines or moments of renewal of internal offices (at sectional, provincial, and national congresses, etc.). The DC pursued an expansionist policy – involving proselytism and party colonization of the state apparatus as well – because of the competition among its different factions, i.e. their incessant efforts to grow stronger, their competition for public resources and supporters.[42] We have already seen cases of: (1) highly institutionalized parties with cohesive dominant coalitions (e.g. the SPD and PCI) – their expansionist strategies result from restricted elites' deliberate choices – and (2) cases of environmental adaptation strategies producing organizational stasis (e.g. absence of proselytism, aging of the cadre, etc.) typical of weakly institutionalized parties guided by divided dominant coalitions in equilibrium (CDU, SFIO, PSI). The DC suggests a third possibility, the expansion and colonization of the environment, not on the basis of deliberate strategies developed by the party's center, but as secondary effects of internal competition (of ruling groups which are so divided as to only rarely reach even the shakiest of compromises).

The British Conservative Party

The Conservative Party, like other European conservative parties,[43] was able to become a strong institution despite being in power for almost twenty years (1886–92 and 1894–1905) during its crucial institutionalization phase.

According to Robert McKenzie, both the Labour Party and the Conservative Party were dominated by their parliamentary leadership.[44] Labour's case was, however, more complex: its dominant coalition revolved around an alliance between parliamentary leaders and the most powerful trade union leaders, and its cohesion depended on the ability of the latter to keep their respective organizations under control, to prevent the rank and file union activists from taking on too autonomous a role within the party. McKenzie is, however, largely right concerning the Conservative Party. Its parliamentary leader was, until quite recently,[45] a sort of autocrat, governing alongside a small group of important national notables, and who did not have to compete for control with extra-parliamentary organizations. He was the central point of a dominant coalition which was concentrated in a parliamentary group, and had vast powers: the party was a machine under his direct control, and he personally selected the people who were to occupy the most important positions.[46]

The Conservative Party was therefore dominated by a parliamentary group which was, in its turn, subordinate to the leader and to his small *entourage*. Unlike other parties dominated by parliamentary elites (e.g. the SFIO, Labour, DC, and PSI), it was and continues to be a strong institution. To understand how and why this is the case, we must once again return to its transition from a parliamentary faction to a modern political party, i.e. to the 1867 Reform Act passed under Disraeli's leadership.[47] In the last thirty years of the eighteenth century, the Conservative Party became a relatively powerful organization with a central, intermediate, and peripheral bureaucracy which constantly grew in strength; with well organized local organizations throughout the country; and with many supporting organizations which operated like transmission belts or efficient channels for the electorate's political socialization. This came about for three major reasons.

Firstly because the Conservative Party was internally legitimated, a genetic model characteristic which, as we have seen, tends to produce (if not counter-balanced by other factors) a high degree of institutionalization.

Secondly because the party was organized by a pre-existing parliamentary elite centered on a prestigious leader. The party's drive came from its center (not from the periphery as in the PSI and CDU). Though the local associations developed their own traditions (but not entirely independently of the center, as we shall see), the central elites' efforts were so important that the Conservative Party's development can be defined as one of territorial penetration.[48]

Thirdly, because of the British state bureaucratic system. Unlike the French and German bureaucracies, the British bureaucracy does not have a tradition of autonomy – it is subordinate to political power (first to the crown, then to the government) – nor do its high-level bureaucrats enjoy particular prestige in British society.[49] When the Conservative Party was in government, there was a "normal" quotient of clientalistic activity common to all governmental parties, but the leaders established a relationship with the state administration which was characterized by neither colonization nor dependency. Naturally, it was not only the particular character of the British bureaucracy which contributed to this outcome – the increase of state intervention in the economy (which characterized a later phase in the development of industrialized countries) had not yet begun. But in any case, the Conservative Party could not control a very large pool of public resources. Its dominant coalition could not thus splinter into many different power centers, each having its own ties to different state bureaucracy sectors and incentive distribution possibilities. The party leaders, in this situation, had no alternative to vigorous organizational development.

The Conservative Party shows us (1) how prolonged control of national government does not necessarily lead to a low level of institutionalization; (2) how a party's development is only partly conditioned by the party's kind of ideological goals and/or by the sociological nature of its social base. Contrary to the common sense thesis that strong organizational development only occurs in "leftist" (revolutionary) parties which aim at mobilizing the subaltern classes against the existing political order, the Conservative Party shows how even a party with a social base mainly composed of privileged classes, can be highly organized. This strikingly demonstrates the inadequacy of the approaches based on what we have termed "sociological prejudice" and "teleological prejudice" in accounting for parties' organizational developments.

The birth of the Conservative Party – i.e. its transition from a loosely-knit parliamentary group with local electoral machines in the hands of single parliamentarians, to a modern political organization – began immediately after its 1868 electoral defeat. In that year, J. E. Gorst was selected as party agent (replacing Markham Spofforth). Gorst was a young ex-MP highly respected by Disraeli, and a staunch defender of the Conservative Party's need to "open itself up" to the working masses (and thus compete with the Liberal Party). A reorganization of the party was, however, needed to do so, and Gorst, with Disraeli's approval, dedicated himself to this task. He formed the Conservative Central Office (the CO), the organization's headquarters; and when the National Union was founded in 1867 – unifying and coordinating the local conservative associations – Gorst managed to get himself designated as its honorary secretary. In this way, both the Central Office and the National Union were unified under the control of one man (who enjoyed the full support of the party's leader). With such a propitious start, Gorst's efforts to develop the organization led to rapid and conspicuous results. Here is how a historian describes the achievements of the Central Office in 1869–74 under Gorst's direction:

The ordinary routine of Gorst's office consisted in collecting information, stimulating activity in sluggish constituencies, seeking out the local leaders, finding candidates, issuing literature over the name of the National Union . . . Links with the press were formed, and Gorst himself acted as political representative for *The Standard*, the London conservative daily. A list of Conservative agents and associations in England and Wales, published by the Central Office in 1874, reveals an impressive organizational set-up throughout the country, in the creation of which the Central Office had no doubt played a notable part. . . . Party Organization is never in itself enough to ensure victory at a general election, but Gorst's new headquarters, with the stimulus to local effort it provided, was in advance of anything the Liberals had.[50]

In 1874, this impressive effort was finally rewarded: the Conservatives won by a landslide and took up their former governmental role.

The party's development then stopped momentarily. Gorst found himself in conflict with the party leaders – due to personal rivalry and to the old parliamentarian's resistance to organizational transformation – and lost his position. After the 1880 defeat, he was called upon to help revive the party. He held his office for but a short while, for his political ambitions were too strong for him to indefinitely submit to the parties' leaders. In 1885, after an uneventful interlude in which Gorst's position had been filled by G. C. T. Bartley, R. W. E. Middleton (a conservative electoral agent in West Kent) was chosen to take the office:

In Captain Middleton the right man for the job was at last found. By experience it had been learnt exactly how much political weight the man who filled the post of party agent should carry. Middleton managed to establish . . . harmonious and fruitful relations both with the constituencies and with the party leaders, and he continued in office until 1903.[51]

Though the conservatives ruled almost uninterruptedly from 1886 to 1905 (which led to little interest in the party's organizational problems), the work started by Gorst was continued by Middleton. In 1886 he decided to establish an intermediary structure (regional organizations) to ensure stable relations between the Central Office and the local associations.[52] Ten provincial divisions were constituted (eight in England and two in Wales). The control over the intermediary structure was centralized. In order to facilitate central control, the Central Office's main agent and one Conservative parliamentarian (the vice-whip) were *ex officio* members of the deliberative and executive organs of each provincial division. After the 1906 defeat, the party underwent an organizational restructuring. As is usually the case, the reorganization was the effect of a drastic modification in the party's internal power relations due to an external challenge (namely, the electoral defeat). The defeat led the party leader, Balfour, to lose ground and prestige to his rival Joseph Chamberlain. The dominant coalition lost its former cohesion and the party factionalized. The 1906 reform involved a certain amount of de-institutionalization. Along with this reform, the Central Office's power was drastically reduced and the National Union's sphere of influence was accordingly increased. The Central Office's main agent was no longer honorary secretary of the National Union: the two organizations were thus formally separated. The provincial divisions were then abolished, and the local associations began to autonomously elect their own secretary rather than rely on the Central Office's agents. The National Union assumed a series of tasks (concerning, for example, documentation, propaganda, the coordination of the local associations, and so on) which until 1906 had been performed by Central Office, and a committee headed by the

National Union assumed the control and supervision of the local agents.[53]

The regional agents (responsible for the intermediary organizations) became bureaucrats paid by the local associations. The Central Office was eventually made to pay £8,500 to the National Union for its yearly activities, in addition to its electoral expenses.[54]

The 1906 reform marked, in Conservative Party history, the only real setback in the organization's bureaucratic development. It was due, as we have said, to a power struggle which led to the development of factions in the party's dominant coalition. In fact:

> Central Office was the major centre of organizational resistance to Chamberlain and the Tariff Reform, and, with the Balfourites remaining firmly in control at Central Office, Chamberlain and his followers were obliged to turn elsewhere in their attempts to topple the old guard, so they attempted to undercut the powers of Central Office by widening the authority of the National Union.[55]

But the 1906 reorganization was a provisional one, the result of a political stalemate between groups contending for organizational control. As these power relations changed, a new reorganization had to result. The 1910 electoral defeat was the external challenge which led to a reshuffling of the cards. At the organizational level this implied the annulment of all decisions made in 1906, the restitution to the Central Office of all powers temporarily ceded to the NU, and the beginning of a new phase of powerful organizational development. Balfour's definitive political decline and Chamberlain's withdrawal from politics after the 1910 defeat mark the end of the dominant coalition's period of greatest division. Demand grew for a reorganization which would make the party efficient, and for a change in the national leadership. A commission concerning itself with organizational problems was thus established (namely, the Union Organizational Committee) which laid out essential aspects of the reform. But more important than the work of this commission were the political changes effected. The combination of a prestigious leader (Disraeli) and a capable organizer (Gorst) had, earlier on, rapidly transformed the party into a modern political organization and laid the foundations for subsequent institutionalization. The combination of a new authoritative leader (Bonar Law) and a new bureaucratic chief (Steel-Maitland) led to the completion of the organization's consolidation.

When Steel-Maitland was taken on, he was young and virtually unknown. Balfour picked him to head the Central Office rather than a more prestigious man in a last-ditch attempt to maintain control over the party. He wanted to prevent important political personalities from occupying this position which was the old leaders' last stronghold. At Steel-Maitland's nomination, no one foresaw that the young organizer would, in a few short years, profoundly influence the Conservative Party. The real reorganization began in 1911 when Balfour was replaced as party head by Bonar Law; the latter adopted an aggressive stance towards the Liberals. Other main party offices changed hands at this time as well: Lord Balcarres became chief-whip, and Lord Farquhar became party secretary. Balcarres, Farquhar and Steel-Maitland enjoyed Law's full confidence and plotted the party's new course. The headquarters hired three new specialists: John Boraston, a professional organizer who was designated head agent, William Jenkins, put in charge of the organization and of agent recruitment, and Malcolm Fraser, editor of the conservative daily (*The Standard*) who became honorary public relations counselor and then head of the party press office.

Steel-Maitland, Boraston, Jenkins and Fraser made up a team of experts, all of sufficient status to deal with politicians who might call into the office; the work of the office was departmentalized for the first time and the heads of department brought together into a supervising board.[56]

A new propaganda system was adopted which applied to all local associations.[57] The reorganization involved even the financial system:

Expenditures on Central Office, district offices and the London office doubled from £32,466 in 1909–10 to £68,957 in 1913–14; the total expenditures of the party organization from central funds also doubled from £73,000 to over £150,000. To pay for this outpouring, a great drive was mounted for additional income by Farquhar and Steel-Maitland. In 1912 ordinary subscriptions still brought in only £12,000 a year and it proved difficult to raise them to anything like what was needed. The method adopted was to canvass for capital donations that could then be invested to bring in a regular income. . . . Systematic collections were made from peers and from the City; by the outbreak of the war the invested funds amounted to £671,000 – twice the sum in 1911 and worth four years' expenditure – and there was a special cash deposit of £120,000 for the coming election.[58]

There were still further accomplishments. The communication system was rationalized by an increase in the influence of the Central Office over the conservative press and in financial support. The Central Office secured its influence and control over the majority of organizations coming into the Conservative orbit (the "Primrose" League, the League for Tax Reform, the anti-socialist union, etc.).[59]

The local associations had a tradition of independence from the center. Their reform thus had to be discreetly effected through the intermediary and peripheral financial system (involving regional and local agents) which directly depended on Central Office. Steel-Maitland was able to bring about a considerable organizational uniformity in the periphery. Through services and political assistance provided by the Central Office to the local associations, the periphery's financial dependence grew: "By 1913–14, over £25,000 was being given away in this manner and in return the Central Office agents were able to ensure the appointment of suitable constituency agents and the choice of good candidates."[60] Though the local associations' autonomy was not attacked, they lost power to the center. This did not stop certain local associations from being the personal fiefdoms of important notables (Derby in Lancaster, Neville Chamberlain in Birmingham, etc.). But it was very different from the situation of the CDU, SFIO and PSI. The Conservative Party's national center was authoritative enough to be able to exercise control, albeit indirect and limited. Bonar Law and Steel-Maitland made the Conservative Party into a strong institution; it definitively consolidated between 1923 and 1930 with the new direction, associated with Baldwin's rise to power in 1923, known as the "New Conservatism."

The reformist activity of Law and Steel-Maitland's was interrupted in 1914 by the outbreak of the war: the government coalition with the Liberals (1915–21) led to a phase of serious internal party conflict. The dominant coalition's dissolution led (as happened before, 1906–10), to a political stalemate between the different groups, to a phase of retreat and organizational stasis. Baldwin's election, the 1924 defeat, and the birth of the new Labor government all contributed to the re-invigoration of the previously stagnant situation.

The period of neo-conservatism during Baldwin's leadership led to an expansion in the staff of Central Office and further rationalization of its financing. Herbert Blain (the new head agent), Davidson (the party chairman), and Younger (the treasurer) designed the changes.

The later expansion also led to all those problems typical of excessive bureaucratization. In the late twenties, the Central Office:

> had become more effective but was now suffering from all the strains that are inherent in a large organization. The staff, which had been so tiny in 1910, had grown to over two hundred, and with another fifty or so scattered about the country in eleven district offices. It would be surprising if Central Office agents did not sometimes resist a plan of which they disapproved by pleading entrenched local opposition, or if departments in Central Office did not use their specialized knowledge for the same purpose. . . . It was becoming difficult to exert the authority of Central Office as a united force in the party because it had become too large to have a united view. By 1930 Central Office had become an entrenched bureaucratic force in the party, set against the social and political forces represented by the National Union and by the parliamentary party.[61]

Table 3. *Number of bureaucrats employed by Central Office*

	1926	1927	1928	1929
Organization and administration	60	75	123	127
Propaganda departments	43	65	54	50
Woman's department	16	15	29	22
Others	25	30	22	19
Total	144	185	228	218

Source: J. Ramsden, *The Age of Balfour and Baldwin, 1902–1940*, Longman, 1978, p. 229.

Table 4. *Central Office expenditures, 1926–9*

	1926	1927	1928	1929
Department L.	4,140	1,729	1,049	851
Organization	9,150	7,467	7,234	7,350
Speakers	7,618	8,696	5,936	5,141
Propaganda	22,269	29,586	49,599	49,786
National Union: finances and secretariat	6,088	5,494	2,611	3,837
Woman's department	7,547	8,664	11,853	11,161
Miscellaneous expenses	9,422	11,090	12,568	15,219
General administration	22,887	25,874	24,759	21,740
Total	89,127	98,600	115,609	115,085

Source: As for Table 3.

At the same time, the Central Office emphasized its regional and local agents' professionalization:

Under the aegis of Central Office, and especially of Herbert Blain, the professional party agents took a long step forward in the 1920s towards the achievement of a full professional status. Improvement had gone on ever since the change from lawyer–agents in the early years of the century, but it was the reshuffle of agents in 1924 and decisions taken in Blain's time that made the real difference. By the 1930s Conservative agents had professional standing in their own eyes, in the official eyes of the party and in the eyes of outsiders. This advance can be traced through several features common to professions: a professional journal, pensions, a qualification and examination system, equality within the profession, and financial status.[62]

The 1929 electoral defeat gave the party the form which it maintained (with periodic adjustments and revisions) right up until the seventies. After 1930 the most important developments took place at the intermediate and peripheral levels:

A uniform pattern of administrative units was adopted throughout England and Wales and, with the exception of a major reorganization in London, this pattern has remained largely unaltered. . . . The standardization of Central Office influence at the provincial level was an important feature of the 1930s, affecting every organizational unit.[63]

One of the consequences of this standardization was the definitive insertion of the Conservative Workers Organization, understood as an important instrument in the competition with the Labour Party,[64] and under the direct control of the Conservative Party bureaucracy.

Taking shape in successive stages (starting from initial territorial penetration based on a pre-existing cohesive parliamentary elite) the Conservative Party thus became a highly institutionalized party with a strong extra-parliamentary organization, solid central, intermediate and local bureaucracies, a solid financial system, and a parliamentary leader controlling the entire organization. Candidates' funds for electoral campaigns were limited in 1949 so as to definitively block the notables' personal control over the local associations.[65] The Conservative Party developed features of a strong institution despite the fact that it was frequently in government. But the features of the British state bureaucracy inhibited the leaders from converting public resources into party incentives; a strong party organization was thus necessary.

As opposed to other parties which, like the Conservative Party, depended for financial support on industrial and financial circles, the Conservative Party was able to create a solid financial system based on regular contributions. This led to the precocious construction of a solid central, intermediate and peripheral bureaucracy.[66]

A comparison of the Conservative Party's and the CDU's financial systems at the end of the sixties[67] clarifies the difference between a strong institution whose autonomy is guaranteed by a solid financial system, and a weakly institutionalized party, dependent on and colonized by external interest groups. While the Conservative Party had a regular revenue system and continuous political activity, the CDU alternated, as do all "pure" electoral parties, from great activity during electoral campaigns (thanks to the considerable financial contributions given at these moments by industrial, financial and commercial circles), to phases of almost total inertia and inactivity (due largely to the drying up of party funds) between electoral campaigns. The difference boils down to the Conservative Party's superior capacity for autonomous activity, and the CDU's decisive subordination to the interest groups which financed its campaigns. Also important is the difference between the two parties in terms of self-financing through the membership. From 1959 to 1969, over 50 per cent of the CDU's expenses were covered by public funds and the remainder came from interest groups; the members played no important financial role whatsoever. In the Conservative Party – a mass organization boasting almost 3 million members in 1948 – members were expelled if they hadn't paid at least 26 per cent of their annual dues.[68]

Such an organization gives rise to a cohesive dominant coalition (in this case, one dominated by a parliamentary leadership) which monopolizes the internal incentive system, and whose internal divisions do not lead to the formation of sub-groups with autonomous power resources. This is why Richard Rose asserts that the Conservative Party's internal divisions have the features of tendencies, not factions.[69] Though this assertion must be qualified as there are occasionally pressures towards factionalization,[70] it is nonetheless valid in principle. Aside from certain critical moments (which led to the replacement of declining leaders), the Conservative Party is generally united behind the banner of the current leader. Its centripetal opportunity structure, typical of strong institutions, explains the standard selection of bureaucratic and parliamentary personnel loyal to the leadership, as well as the traditional solid party discipline. It moreover explains the adoption of an aggressive strategy *vis-à-vis* the party's environment, at least as far as the expansion of its membership is concerned. The Conservative Party, with an oscillating membership after World War II (with almost 3 million in 1948, and around $1\frac{1}{2}$ million in the seventies), is one of the biggest conservative organizations in the Western world.

Its high level of internal structural coherence (ensured by a solid bureaucracy) corresponds to considerable independence from the environment (ensured by the financial system discussed above), a sure sign of which is the lack of institutionalization in the interest groups at the crucial moment of candidate selection (which was not true for the CDU). Two aspects of the organization seem to contradict the image of a strong institution: (1) the fact that the party leaders and parliamentarians are *not* of bureaucratic origin (as they are in the PCI, PCF and SPD), i.e. have not made their careers within the organization (the organization thus lacks the requisite "vertical integration of elites"); and (2) the local associations' traditional political independence. The non-bureaucratic character of its political careers (party bureaucrats are excluded from participation in public political activity) actually makes the Conservative Party a weaker institution than the parties cited above. It is a very strong institution except in this one respect. But we must also observe that both parliamentary candidates and future political leaders are mostly chosen for their renown in the business and professional world, and that selection mechanisms block or at least limit the formation of advantageous notable positions.[71] The local associations' candidate choices tend to fall on well-known people able to attract electoral consensus – i.e. on notables – but the latter are, generally, nevertheless unable to make political careers through direct control over the association (in accordance with typical modalities of notable–political party relationship). This explains why associations tend to select socially representative and relatively young men with aggressive and dynamic images. Many comparative studies on the composition of European parliamentarians show that conservative parliamentarians are, on the average, younger than those belonging to parties traditionally composed of notables.[72]

The political independence of local associations is more apparent than real. The Conservative Party shows us how centralization can be easily "concealed" behind apparent decentralization. Central control can be maintained in various ways: firstly, through the recruiting of local agents – this is the prerogative of Central Office and its regional agents.[73] In the voluntary associations where participation is weak and sporadic, controlling the bureaucrats often means controlling the entire association. Control is strong and efficient in these cases because career advancement can only take place through the center's choices. Candidate selection depends on a sort of discrete centralized control: it takes place at a local level on the basis of a list of potential candidates established by a special commission of the National Union (the Standing Advisory Committee on Candidates). Each association then apparently freely chooses its own candidate, and the Central Office (through its regional agent) restricts itself to a simple formal control (i.e. it checks whether selection happened in accordance with the official procedures). In reality, however, it happens rather differently. When candidates selected were opposed by the party leadership (which only happened twice between 1949 and 1969), the center was able to block their candidature and refuse to support them.[74] In other words, the Conservative Party is so unified and cohesive that its local associations tend "naturally" to select candidates who have the leaders' confidence without explicit intervention from above.[75] In the rare cases in which this did not happen, the leader's latent centralized control through Central Office became manifest, and the center – despite traditional and ritual assertions of the political independence of the associations – prevailed.

The organization is unified enough to do without an explicit procedural system: strong cohesion is maintained by a combination of solid and professional (but not overbearing) central, intermediate, and local bureaucracies, and harmonious political relations between activists and elites (a harmony which is not accidental, but is rather the result, in the Conservative Party as in the PCI, SPD, and PCF – of strong organizational institutionalization). This allows for a maximum reduction in procedure formalization. In the Labour Party, on the other hand, an explicit system of norms responds to its continuous need to appease, discipline and smooth over internal conflict in a highly factionalized national and local leadership group. The Conservative Party's dominant coalition's cohesion makes a formalization of procedures superfluous. The clearest sign of the dominant coalition's unity (which is due to strong institutionalization) is the highly "apolitical" character of the criteria habitually used by local activists in choosing parliamentary candidates: what tips the balance in favor of one candidate or another are not political criteria – i.e. the candidate's personal political positions – as is the case in the Labour Party, but rather the candidate's social status. The distinction between left and right which plays such an important role in the selection of elites in factionalized and divided organizations, does not play an important role in this unified party: "It is doubtful, therefore, that any applicant for a candidacy is selected or rejected because he is regarded in a general sense as left wing or right wing. Particular issues may, however, have some bearing but these are usually non-political or quasi-political matters . . .".[76]

Only in moments of crisis, i.e. when the party's dominant coalition vacillates or there are problems clearly dividing the national leadership, does candidate selection become politicized. This happened, for example, during the Suez crisis.[77]

Conclusion

The three cases examined in this chapter are all cases of "governmental parties." All three underwent organizational consolidation when they held government power. But whereas the Conservative Party became a strong institution, the other two became weak ones. The genetic models' characteristics are largely responsible for this, but the different historical conditions, political regimes and state institutions under which they consolidated also played an important role. The two weak institutions were not however identical: the CDU was internally legitimated, the DC externally; the party and state bureaucracies were more autonomous in the former (though there was still some patronage and party control over public resources), and more symbiotic – due to "colonization" by a weak and inefficient state bureaucracy – in the latter.

A partially different relation to the state apparatus is probably the main cause of another fundamental difference: the DC's coalition was far more fragmented than the CDU's. In the literature on factionalism, the DC is compared to another governing party, the Japanese Liberal Democratic Party (LDP). As was true for the LDP (created, like the DC, in the aftermath of World War II, 1955) the DC's internal factions became highly institutionalized (especially in the sixties); and both have been characterized as "clientelistic mass parties."[78] Whatever the value of this comparison may be, we should not forget what differentiates the DC from both the CDU and from more or less pure clientelistic parties (like the LDP). In time the DC comes closer to being a "clientelist" party than a "conservative" party like the CDU. The DC, however, started out very differently from both types, forming and consolidating as a "solidarity system" of the Catholic world, as the Church's secular arm. Traits of a mass clientelist party were eventually superimposed onto its original characteristics, but without making them completely disappear.[79] As was true for the Labour Party and so many other externally legitimated parties, the DC could never completely give up control over its original hunting ground (namely Catholics) because that would have involved giving up an important aspect of its organizational identity. The conjunction of more than one identity – hardly amalgamated and yet constrained to work together – along with the state's "colonization" and the necessity to share government control with other parties[80] is what explains the permanent conflict in the DC leading group (i.e. the impossibility of stabilizing the dominant coalition) as well as the many difficulties involved in examining its organizational system.

8
Charismatic parties

The two cases to be examined in this chapter can be clearly differentiated from the parties heretofore discussed on the basis of one of their genetic model characteristics. They are exemplary cases of organizations founded by single leaders who used them for their own purposes. A lot has been written on the theme of charisma since Weber formulated his theory of charismatic power. This concept is all too often employed as a passe-partout, used to describe any form of personal power.[1]

What is usually termed "charisma" is, in the majority of cases, one of the most common occurrences in politics: a successful leader's considerable influence over his followers. Charisma is, in this case, used as a synonym for prestige or authority. What is lacking here is the *technical* and *delimited* meaning of the Weberian concept which is no mere synonym for prestige and/or authority (though it is often the source of these qualities); charisma, in fact, involves:[2]

(1) A principle of organizational legitimation of a "revolutionary" and "extra-economic" nature. Charisma is the opposite of "ordinary" administration founded on the observance of rules or respect for tradition. It is the antithesis of both rational–legal (i.e. bureaucratic) and traditional power, and is always subversive–revolutionary in relation to the socially dominant relations. As such, a charismatic organization "lives in this world but is not of this world."

(2) An organization founded on exclusively *personal* ties, on the direct loyalty of the "disciples" to the leader – as in the case of traditional (e.g. patriarchal) power relations. Unlike *traditional* personal ties, however, loyalties here are based on a "state of grace," on a "mission" to which the leader is called and which instils a spirit of missionary zeal in his disciples as well. It is this revolutionary nature of charisma which distinguishes charismatic from traditional personal ties: the relations of deference and power in the latter are the fruit of a

pre-existing system of inequalities sanctioned by tradition; the relations of deference and power in the former *oppose* tradition. According to Weber, charisma represents the main source of social and political innovation, the only "authentically" revolutionary force in history.[3]

(3) As opposed to other forms of power, charismatic power gives rise to an organization of social relations characterized by an absence of "rules," internal "career patterns," and a clear division of labor. The direct loyalties and the personal and arbitrary delegation of authority by the organization's leader are the only criteria for the organization's functioning. The charismatic organization therefore substitutes total uncertainty and instability for the stability of the expectations that guide bureaucratic and traditional organizations. The choice of a leader and his continual demonstration of faith to his subordinates are the only criteria upon which the organization's "opportunity structure" depends, and are the only criteria molding the internal (informal) hierarchy. Though Weber doesn't explicitly say so, the primary effect of this organizational modality is a continuous competition among the subordinates to win favor in the leader's eyes in order to rise up (at the others' expense) in the power hierarchy.

(4) Being an extra-economic force, a charismatic organization shuns normal forms of financing, at least at the beginning. According to Weber, the charismatic organization is usually financed through "patronage" and/or the spoils of conquest. (This helps delay the organization's bureaucratization.)

(5) Charisma is intrinsically unstable, and is sooner or later eliminated by routine administrative needs. After the situation of *statu nascendi*[4] (which produced the charisma) has passed, the followers develop interests in stable remunerations: routine sets in and its accompanying expectations replace the initial missionary spirit. At that point the organization has but two options: the dissolution or "routinization" (i.e. objectivization) of charisma. When charisma disappears, success no longer shines on the movement, and faith in the leader's "state of grace" ceases. When this occurs in an organization in which the leader was successful in preventing the routinization of charisma (in order not to lose his total control), the movement ends and the organization dissolves. Or, alternatively, charisma is objectified and the organization overcomes the crisis through the transformation of personal charisma into official charisma.[5] In this latter case, the organization institutionalizes. The routinization of charisma can also take two paths (or even a third which is a combination of the two): "rules" replace personal charisma in regulating internal relations (i.e. legalization) and the organization becomes a bureaucracy; or the

original charismatic relation "traditionalizes." In this latter case, influential notables replace the charismatic force, their legitimacy stemming from the "continuity of their ideals" with those of the organization's founder.

Adapted to political parties, Weberian theory implies that the leader founds the party, proposes its ideological goals, and selects its social base *by himself*. He becomes – in the activists' and external supporters' eyes – the only interpreter and living symbol of the "doctrine," as well as the only possible means to its future realization. *A total overlap of the leader's image and party identity is the sine qua non of charismatic power*. The founding leader thus monopolizes control over the zones of organizational uncertainty and the distribution of incentives. Whenever a party's genetic model is based on personal charisma, the organization forms with certain fixed characteristics:

(1) A cohesive dominant coalition held together by loyalty to the leader. As long as the followers only recognize the leader's authority, the leading group cannot divide into factions which cut the organization vertically: neither rank and file activists nor external supporters are open to recruitment by factions; and therefore they will not identify with any particular internal group. The dominant coalition is thus cohesive, and internal competition assumes the form of competition among tendencies. Divisions affect only the sub-leaders; they do not reach the party's periphery. Its opportunity structure is therefore characterized (as is true of strong institutions) by centripetal competition and elite recruitment: one must conform to the leader's whims to make a career in the organization. In such an organization, no one can openly oppose the leader and hope to win. Competition among the different tendencies may get very intense, but it takes place at a level *below* the leader's: it doesn't directly involve him. The sub-leaders and tendencies struggle among themselves to get closer to the leader. Their objective is to occupy the second, third, or fourth place in the internal power hierarchy. This is the main indicator of the existence of charismatic power. In every party there are very prestigious leaders capable of controlling important zones of uncertainty through a direct relation with the organization's following. But when there is no charismatic relation, conflict with and open opposition to the leader can occur without necessarily leading to the end of the adversaries' political careers. Dossetti and Gronchi openly opposed as authoritative a leader as De Gasperi; the maximalists opposed Turati; Jaurès suffered minority faction opposition in the SFIO; and Hardie and McDonald were seriously challenged in the Labour party. Such things never happen in charismatic parties: open opposition to the leader automati-

cally leads to the end of the adversaries' political careers (e.g. their "excommunication") or at least to their political isolation (their marginalization as "heretics").

The charismatic leader has the same relation to the organization as an external sponsoring institution would have: he has the final say, and can determine the outcome of the tendency struggles going on around him. He has, in other words, the same control that Pious XII exercised over the top positions in the DC, and that Stalin exercised over the communist parties and their internal power structures; Activists' and voters' allegiances are to the external sponsoring institution, when there is one, and only secondarily to the party: this explains the strict dependence of the latter upon the former. In charismatic parties, analogously, the followers' loyalties are to the leader, not to the party.

(2) The charismatic party does not present bureaucratic characteristics. There may be a group of bureaucrats (in the special form of professional agitators) and even an "official" division of labor between different organizational offices – this was true in the Nazi party during Weimar and in the Russian Bolshevik party before Lenin's death. But reality is always more complex: bureaucracy presupposes the existence of paid bureaucrats, stable hierarchies, formalized procedures, stable career expectations, and career advancement based on fairly well defined criteria. In charismatic parties, on the other hand, the division of labor is constantly redefined at the leader's discretion, career uncertainties are considerable, no accepted procedures exist, and improvisation is the only real organizational "rule." Charismatic parties also generally have no stable income: their irregular revenues depend on the leader's ability to ally with external financers and/or on his personal control over public funds.

(3) A charismatic party is, moreover, a very highly centralized organization. A charismatic leader has the same effect as a powerful extensive bureaucracy: all key decisions are made at the top of the organization – i.e. by the charismatic leader. Financial centralization almost always gives rise to a pervasive control over the money delegated to the various organizational levels.

(4) The charismatic party is often, if not always, the focus of groups and organizations with undefined and uncertain boundaries which cluster around it. The tendency conflicts are often inter-organizational conflicts between leaders of various formally autonomous associations which comprise the "charismatic movement."

(5) Whatever the charismatic party's ideological orientation may be (conservative or progressive, reactionary or revolutionary, liberal or socialist, etc.) the "revolutionary" nature of charisma, which always subverts the political and/or social status quo, explains the organiza-

tion's *anti-party* character. The charismatic party always presents itself (within the constitutional rules or outside of them depending on the leader's "chosen" ideological goals) as an alternative to the existing parties, offering a Bonapartist political solution.

(6) While in externally sponsored parties institutionalization involves at least partial emancipation from the sponsoring organization, in charismatic parties it involves an objectification or routinization of charisma, a transfer of loyalties from the leader to the organization, and a growing divergence between the party's organizational identity and the leader's personal political fortune. It also implies a movement from a solidarity system towards a system of interests, and the adaptation of the original goals to the daily organizational needs. Institutionalization is not, however, very likely in a charismatic party: the leader often deliberately tries to block the process; charisma cannot be objectified, and the organization is forced to fold at its leader's political eclipse.

The aforementioned characteristics apply to all charismatic parties, i.e. to all those parties in which there is a total symbiosis between the leader and the organizational identity.

Charismatic parties can, however, differ in certain ways. In this chapter I shall schematically examine two charismatic parties, the Gaullist party of the Fifth Republic and the National Socialist party of the Weimar period. They differ for many reasons: one was a governmental party, the other an anti-regime party; one a democratic–conservative electoral organization, the other a paramilitary one; one playing the leading role in the transition from one democratic regime to another, the other giving birth to a totalitarian dictatorship. These differences explain their conspicuous organizational divergence. Those who prefer the Weberian to the "journalistic" use of the term "charisma" will, however, easily find many similarities as well.

The Union for the New Republic

The UNR came into existence in 1958, shortly before the September referendum which ratified the Constitution of the Fifth Republic. Different offshoots of the *Rassemblement du Peuple Français* (RPF) – a mass organization which had been the first important incarnation of political Gaullism (1947–53) – contributed to its formation.[6] The Gaullist party was one of the rare charismatic parties in which charisma was successfully objectified. So successfully, in fact, that after the loss of its leader, it institutionalized to a relatively high degree. Michel Crozier, in a recent examination of French parties, ranked the Gaullist party (immediately after the PCF and before the socialist party) among the best structured and established organizations on the French political scene.⁷ This is, no doubt, largely justified. The Gaullist party, born in the movement of transition from the Fourth to the Fifth Republic (and since then called by different names, the first being *Union Pour la Nouvelle République*, the most recent being the *Rassemblement Pour la République*),⁸ evolved into an institution which was perhaps weaker than the British Conservative Party, but much stronger than the DC or the CDU in their governmental phases. And yet most of its genetic model characteristics and the government control (that it was forced to assume in the consolidating phase) were unfavorable to an outcome of this sort.

In the first place, the Gaullist party was born as a charismatic party whose only *raison d'être* was to serve De Gaulle and the ideas identified with the General from the days of the resistance (e.g. that "certain idea of France").⁹ It was forged as an anti-party movement, opposing the "party-dominated regime" of the Fourth Republic.

Secondly, it was born through the fusion of many groups and movements headed by important figures, each with his own way of interpreting Gaullism. It was, in other words, an oligarchy splintered into a number of political tendencies which were, nonetheless, groups under the same Gaullist umbrella.

Thirdly, the party was formed while De Gaulle was in power. This means that the party was a governmental party right from the start and for a long time afterwards.

The presence of a charismatic leader, the fusion of a number of heterogeneous political tendencies (on the sole basis of their personal allegiance to him and to a vague "national doctrine" which, ideologically speaking, constituted Gaullism), and governmental party status, are all factors which in theory produce very weak institutionalization (assuming that institutionalization is even possible under such conditions). But the UNR's history shows quite a different development. The evolution of a party can be considered as the product of the interaction of its genetic model's characteristics, its place in the political system (i.e. in the government or opposition) during the phase of organizational consolidation, and, finally, the configuration of its "environments." These factors reinforce and/or annul each other in different ways: certain of the genetic model's characteristics can be counter-balanced by other factors. For example, we have seen that "internal" legitimation, taken alone, favors strong institutionalization. When combined, however, with development through territorial diffusion (as in the SFIO and PSI), or with diffusion *and* governmental party status (as in the CDU), it cannot bring about the formation of a strong institution. Analogously, internal legitimation combined with development through territorial penetration may very well produce a strong institution *even if* the party institutionalizes while in control of the national government (as was true of the British Conservatives). The various factors either reinforce, counter-balance or annul one another, defining each party's organizational trajectory; they can only be evaluated through an historical examination of each case.

In the UNR, the aforementioned factors – which all theoretically could have contributed to the party's very weak institutionalization – were counter-balanced by the institutional order, i.e. by the type of political regime and by the character of the state bureaucracy. The result was an organization which should be located mid-way on the weak/strong institution continuum.

In order to better understand this development, we shall recapitulate the facts. The UNR was officially born in 1958 through the fusion of many Gaullist movements: the *Centre National des Républicains Sociaux* (led by Jacques Chaban-Delmas and Roger Frey); the *Convention Républicaine* (led by Marie-Madelaine Fourcade and Léon Delbecque); the *Union Pour le Renouveau Français* (led by Jacques Soustelle); the *Comités Ouvrières* (led by Jacques Veyssières and Albert Marceuet), and other groups led by other prestigious Gaullists.[10]

The party's first directory committee was composed of thirteen "historical Gaullists" (*compagnons de toujours*) – men who had been faithful to De Gaulle since World War II. The most organized and powerful of these groups was led by Soustelle (De Gaulle's Minister of Information).

In exploiting the superior organization of the *Union Pour le Renouveau Français*, Soustelle played a leading role in the organization's early phases. He managed to "place" many of his most trusted collaborators in important positions. The Soustelle–De Gaulle rivalry exploded later over the Algerian problem, resulting in Soustelle's "expulsion" from the party. Up until that time, competition existed among the various leading figures (and the tendencies they represented) for De Gaulle's favors alone. Soustelle, encouraged by his "central" position, wanted to accede to the office of party president, but De Gaulle blocked the way by keeping the office vacant.

The selection of candidates for the legislative elections (1958) proved that the UNR was entirely under General De Gaulle's control, and that in the Central Committee, Jacques Soustelle and even Leon Delbecque were but equals among equals – rather than being the heads of parallel movements.[11]

Soustelle was dangerous to De Gaulle because he was heading a tendency with a clear and definite position about the crucial problem of the time, Algeria. Soustelle's strength in the organization's genetic

Organizational development

phase could have made the UNR something other than what De Gaulle wanted, i.e. a docile instrument, a politically maneuverable mass.[12]

After the election to parliament of De Gaulle's followers,[13] the preparatory work for the following year's national Congress began. In the meantime, the party's leadership began to take shape. The central committee (which met in September 1959 to prepare the Congress) was made up of the thirteen founders, representatives of the federations, and a large number of *de jure* members (ministers, presidents of parliamentary groups, etc.) – over sixty people in all. Control resided in the hands of the ministers and parliamentarians. The UNR was, thus, a parliamentary party – as are most parties which consolidate while in government, regardless of their degrees of institutionalization (e.g. the Conservative Party, CDU, DC, etc.). Its parliamentary character never disappeared despite successive transformations. The Soustelle conflict exploded at the first National Congress (in Bordeaux, 1959): Soustelle's opposition to De Gaulle's decisions concerning Algeria came out. Competition was no longer restricted to the various Gaullist notables, but directly involved the party's leader. Soustelle lost the battle and was expelled from the government and eventually (in 1960) from the party as well (only thirty deputies followed him). His experience was typical for opposition leaders in this type of party: those who openly oppose the charismatic leader's decisions are thrown out.

Both the new regime of the Fifth Republic and the party consolidated from 1958 to 1962. These were years of incessantly high levels of conflict:

From 1958 to 1962 a power struggle took place at the head of the movement recalling the instability of the Fourth Republic: five secretary generals and five presidents in four years, as well as changes in the ministry and leading agencies. More than half of the UNR's General Assembly changed over every year; it was easier to hold on to one's position in the central committee, but even there the conflicts were numerous. By November 1962, however, a ruling group had formed which was able to keep the movement under control.[14]

After the elections in 1962, the organization stabilized, but its stabilization also transformed the party. The Gaullist success brought a growing number of new politicians into the party who played at Gaullism so as to better defend their own traditional positions of power.

The consolidated parliamentary party was controlled by De Gaulle's ministers (the party's real "inner circle"). It was hardly a "mass" party; Charlot provides the following estimates:[15]

1959   7,000 members
1960   35,000 members

1961   50,000 members
1963   86,000 members

The organization was dominated by governmental and parliamentary personnel with a very high member–voter ratio. It was, however, highly centralized, compact and disciplined organization.

The oversized central committee delegated almost all of its power to the political commission and secretary general. The close connection between the parliamentary group's directive organs and government personnel established a sort of "inner circle," putting the party in the "historical" Gaullists' hands. This group instilled cohesion through the control it exercised both over the parliamentarians (subjected to rigid discipline) and the "internal" extra-parliamentary organs. Even the secretary general was but an administrator carrying out the group's directives.[16]

The peripheral departmental federations – whose electoral power was incommensurate with its number of members – were reorganized after 1963. The UNR's federations (unlike the SFIO's) had no political-organizational independence from the party's center. This is demonstrated by the fact that the departmental secretary was chosen by the secretary general rather than being elected locally. The fact that the secretary general sent a subsidy to each federation and required precise financial statements every five months further evidences the center's rigid financial control.[17]

The federations were controlled by the center through two channels: through the local constituency deputy (in turn subordinated to the parliamentary group), or more often through the *chargés de mission*, real *missi dominici* that took the directives from the center to the periphery. The *chargés de mission* were similar to the "right-hand men" who were the true cohesive force behind the German Social Democratic organization at the time of the anti-socialist laws: "The *chargés de mission* had to have authority over the local cadres and maintain a certain independence of judgement with respect to the departmental parliamentarians. They were, thus, mostly experienced men who had worked with the *Rassemblement du Peuple Français*."[18]

Financial resources and political activism were channeled through a network of ties to various commercial, industrial, and agricultural interest groups, which were integrated into the party by the collateral Gaullist associations.[19]

This centralized and compact organization – the Gaullist party from 1962 to 1967 (i.e. until the Lille Congress which was a turning point, leading to a changing of the guard) – was rather similar to the British Conservative Party: the parliamentary group dominated the organization, and the party was cohesive and disciplined at all levels. The

Gaullist party had, however, no strong central apparatus (though data on the apparatus' consistency is lacking), and was more organizationally consistent at its top than at its base.[20]

In this respect, the Gaullist organization could not be a mass party like the British Conservative Party. It had few party members and was unable (unlike the DC and CDU) to rely on a pre-existing network of notables. Tarrow has shown that the French center–right mayors clearly tended towards "non-partisan politics."[21] The mayors who were sympathetic to Gaullism were not party members. The Gaullist party – a dominant political movement on a national level – could not supplant the French right's traditional network of notables. They remained more or less extraneous to the movement; this explains the Gaullist's defeats in local elections and their inability to gain control of more than a very few municipalities.[22] This was partly due to the Gaullist tendency to "nationalize" the municipal electoral campaigns and to utilize national issues (e.g. the image and accomplishments of the General) in areas where this type of propaganda was rather inappropriate.[23] There is, however, a deeper explanation: the permanent incompatibility between traditional power (that of the notables) and De Gaulle's charismatic power, which in itself explains the French notables' distrust of Gaullism, and the contempt in which the Gaullists held the notables. Traditional power depends upon and is fed by the maintenance of the existing system of social relations; charismatic power depends, instead, on its ability to modify and upset this system.

The party's weakness at the local level was also due to an explicit choice not to expand the party's membership beyond a certain limit. This prevented the formation of a mass organization (like that of the old RPF) which might have restricted the General's autonomy, increased internal political heterogeneity, and thus destabilized the organization.[24]

Cohesive and efficiently centrally organized in the federations, the UNR remained very weak at the local level, especially in rural areas (which were important electoral reservoirs for the party at national elections). From the departmental level on up, however, the Gaullist party was surely the first powerful organization the French right had ever had. Its dominant coalition had a pyramidal structure: De Gaulle (who never accepted a party office) was at the top, in a formally detached position; below him were the "historical Gaullists" who wielded the organizational power – they constituted an inner circle access to which was possible neither through cooptation nor political merit. Entry into the dominant coalition was rigidly determined by an "ascriptive" criterion: only De Gaulle's old comrades in arms could take part in it. Immediately under them in the power hierarchy were the parliamentarians who were too young to have participated in the resistance, and who subscribed to Gaullism during the Fourth Republic. At the bottom were the "new" Gaullists in the federations and the local elected offices.

The party's organizational evolution can be explained by the relations among the historical Gaullists. They were divided by ambitions, personal rivalries, and differentiated political positions; loyalty to the General was their only common denominator. The competition among them (and the different Gaullist tendencies they represented) was incessant, though below the surface. The dominant coalition's cohesion was, therefore, imposed from above, i.e. by De Gaulle himself. He prevented the group from organizing openly into factions and struggling for power within the party. He forced them to cohabit and cooperate: open rebellion meant (as for Soustelle) political demise. This explains the party's strong centralization.

The Gaullist party was, thus, a charismatic party, an organization with no identity or life of its own. A poll taken immediately after the 1958 elections showed that 93 per cent of the UNR's electorate had voted for the party just "to support De Gaulle's actions."[25] The UNR remained a charismatic party (at least in its internal relations), not only in the beginning of the Fifth Republic (1958–62, in the period of plebiscitary Gaullism – while De Gaulle was the president of "all the French"), but in the phase immediately thereafter as well (while De Gaulle, then leader of a French "faction," had to rely all the more openly on the party).

All of the aforementioned characteristics of a charismatic organization were present: opposition between the notables and Gaullism; various tendencies revolving around the party which had loyalty to the General as their only common denominator;[26] a centralized organization that guaranteed De Gaulle's faithfuls iron-clad control; and an intense polemic against traditional organizational forms of party politics.[27]

The objectivization of Gaullist charisma took place in a number of stages: from 1958 to 1962, the UNR was a sort of "clandestine" party, prohibited by De Gaulle from using his name in electoral campaigns; in the succeeding stage it was openly recognized as the Gaullist party and could thus consolidate. When, in the presidential elections of 1965, De Gaulle had to suffer the "humiliating" test of an appeal (not having won the first time around), the party's role *vis-à-vis* the President was reinforced. Generational changes within the organization, the main institutional features of the Fifth Republic, and the UNR's growing importance as focus of electoral concensus, forced De Gaulle to allow the party to institutionalize. Institutionalizing and becoming a relatively strong institution (as the UNR did) are not identical. While De Gaulle was alive and running things, organizational centralization was perhaps due simply to his personal control, and the subsequent objectification of his charisma should have produced a more splintered, weak, and "federal" organization than in fact resulted. The actual result can probably be explained by the Fifth Republic's institutional order and the French bureaucracy's characteristics. These two factors forced the Gaullists to construct an organization which was more solid than the party's genetic model would have indicated. The following factors contributed to relatively strong organizational development.

First, a very important role was granted to the Head of State[28] by the Constitution, strengthening De Gaulle's already strong position (having successfully survived the founding phase of the new order, and resolved the Algerian crisis), and encouraging him not to obstruct an at least partial objectivization of his charisma. Since institutionalization took place before his succession, the organization incorporated the strong centralization generated by the General's leadership. This kind of organizational consolidation explains the subsequent party cohesion.

This was also made possible by the existing institutional system. Though neither the DC nor the CDU were charismatic parties (and thus the comparison is not ideal), we can nonetheless note that whereas their organizational development would surely have limited De Gasperi's and Adenauer's maneuverability (and they both impeded such development),[29] in the case of the UDR the strong constitutional position of the French Head of State made the party's organizational development infinitely less dangerous for De Gaulle.

The second condition was the parliament's weakness *vis-à-vis* the government and the Head of State. This weakness, implying the parliamentarians' subordination to the government, gave the deputies fewer occasions (in comparison with the number they had during the Fourth Republic) to appropriate resources for their own constituencies. This made the Gaullist parliamentarians very dependent on the party for re-election, and resulted in a group discipline previously unknown in the French right-wing parliamentary groups.[30] This also prevented the party elite from breaking up into a number of autonomous power centers.

The third environmental factor which influenced the party's development was the force and the prestige of the French state bureaucracy. It was much less susceptible to colonization and blackmail than other bureaucracies. Top bureaucrats established close ties[31] with the Gaullist party, and many of them served (as in Germany) in the parliament and government. The bureaucratic structure did not, however, possess "Italian" characteristics: it was not so weak as to be easily controlled by party factions. By the time of the Congress in Lille in 1967, the Gaullist party had already institutionalized. Its institutionalization was accompanied by a change of the guard. At that Congress (which decided upon a new name for the party: *Union des Démocrates pour la République*) the historical Gaullists had to cede some of their power to the upcoming generation. Power relations within the inner circle gradually changed in the course of the sixties. Initially the historical Gaullists had been over-represented in the high party offices; forty old-time Gaullists had controlled the organization in the form of a "closed group," i.e. into which one could not enter on the basis of cooptation and political merit. In the course of time, however, and especially at the parliamentary level, the number of new Gaullists grew.[32]

These developments could but result in a generational turnover. The occasion arose due to an external challenge: the noticeable loss in the Gaullist impetus in the 1965 presidential elections (the two electoral rounds between De Gaulle and Mitterrand) and then in the party's 1967 electoral defeat and loss of many seats. The changing of the guard at Lille led to an important party reorganization.[33]

The central apparatus was strengthened, and greater power was given to the secretary general, providing him with the force to recruit, and leading to a doubling of the membership with respect to that in 1963.[34]

The organization had thus consolidated and could suffer the eclipse of historical Gaullism without vanishing. It survived its founder, and then, in the Giscard era, the loss of control of the presidency and government.[35] An objectivization of charisma, not hampered by De Gaulle and favored by the environmental conditions, explains this development.

The German National Socialist Party

The NSDAP, the Nazi party, was – during and after the fall of Weimar – a case of a "pure" charismatic party in which the organizational dynamics already seen in the UNR were clearly manifested.[36] The NSDAP and the UNR had a number of common traits:

(1) A centralized organization in which the principle of "loyalty to the leader" prevailed and in which the organizational identity and the leader–founder were completely co-extensive.

(2) A lack of bureaucratic organizational ties accompanied by irregular financing by external patrons (who became less important

after the failed 1923 *putsch*, only to expand again after 1929), and capillary financial control.

(3) The existence of numerous political–ideological organizations with uncertain and poorly defined boundaries (the SA, Hitler Youth, etc.) revolving around the party and its leader.

(4) The existence of different and competing ideological tendencies representing different ways of interpreting the National Socialist doctrine. Under National Socialism's unifying banner – whose creator, uncontested interpreter, and living symbol was Hitler – many groups and tendencies gathered: the racist tendency represented by Rosenberg, Röhm's para-military movement (the SA), the "socialist" tendency of the Strasser brothers (the equivalent of Italian "leftist fascism"), the nationalistic groups and the conservative groups linked to industrial circles, etc.[37] National Socialism was (as was Gaullism, but in a democratic context) sufficiently vague to allow for many conflicting interpretations. Hitler personally encouraged this ideological pluralism both because it allowed the party to appeal to all sectors of the society, and because division of the leading groups into tendencies competing with each other secured his own power and prevented the formation of adversary coalitions. In this way, the NSDAP was a docile instrument at Hitler's beck and call.

The differences between the NSDAP and the UNR were, however, significant and were related to their diverse natures (totalitarian and democratic respectively):

(1) While the UNR was an electoral party, the NSDAP was structured like a para-military organization, like the "militia party" described by Duverger.[38]

(2) The NSDAP was organized as a "state within a state," similar in many ways to extreme-left organizations (e.g. the German communist party).[39] After 1925/6, the NSDAP internally reproduced existing state divisions of offices and functions (though, as we shall see, its formal charter never corresponded to the organization's actual functioning).

(3) Finally, while the NSDAP strongly tended to expand, quickly becoming a mass party, De Gaulle's choice was to keep the organization as small as possible. This difference was obviously at least partly due to the fact that Hitler was trying to take power, whereas De Gaulle already controlled the government when his party was consolidating.

The history of the Nazi party before its conquest of power can be divided into two phases: the phase preceding and the one following the failed 1923 *putsch*. The first phase was dominated by the struggle of Hitlerian groups in gain control of the DAP (the German Workers Party founded by Anton Drexler in 1919) and to ensure their hegemony over all the extreme right movements that sprang up in the early twenties.

Hitler (rapidly emerging as DAP's best orator) together with Röhm (whose following included many ex-military officers) won control over the party in 1921. The party was renamed, and reorganized on authoritarian bases through the adoption of the *fuhrer-prinzip*, the unconditional submission of all the movement's followers to Hitler's will. It is interesting to note that: "The NSDAP, though wanting to differentiate itself from the *volkisch* sects, never wanted to be simply one party among many, but rather a *sui generis* "movement" above the other purely "party-political" organizations."[40] The failure of the attempted 1923 *putsch* led to Hitler's imprisonment and the dispersal of the political movement. Until 1923 Hitler hadn't given much attention to building a mass movement, hoping instead for an immediate seizure of power. In 1924, once released, Hitler changed his strategy, deciding to build a real national party. In a few short years the Nazi organization, which had formerly been relatively strong only in Bavaria, had taken root throughout the country. Local organizations cropped up and consolidated in the north of the country where the movement had been completely absent.

The organization spread like wild-fire, through territorial diffusion involving the efforts of both local activists and various groups that made up the variegated Nazi movement. The organization's general headquarters was established in Munich (under the direction of Philip Bouhler) and it exercised a centralized control over the periphery. Both dues and the financing of local associations (which, in their turn, were organized into districts) were centrally controlled:

The exclusive right of the central office to issue membership cards enabled it to keep accurate accounts of party membership in each district. Since the number of members determined the financial obligations of the local organizations to Munich, this knowledge enables Bouhler to exercise strict control over local party finances. Local party organizations were required to collect one reichsmark for each new member and fifty pfennings each month thereafter. The initiation fees and half of the monthly membership dues were to be forwarded by the local organizations to the district offices if these existed, otherwise directly to Munich. The district party leaders were also required to forward to Munich the initiation fees and ten pfennings of each member's monthly dues. In addition, all extra contributions that local and district party leaders may have received from private citizens or groups were to be sent intact to Munich.[41]

But membership fees always represented a very modest part of the organization's financing; the latter depended far more on the contributions Hitler was able to get from industrial circles. In 1924 the NSDAP still had only 50,000 supporters.[42] The publication of *Mein Kampf* and the fame Hitler acquired during his trial for the failed *putsch* (a trial

158 Organizational development

transformed by Hitler's oratory abilities and the court's benevolence into a sounding board for his ideas), led to the party's irresistible popularity among extreme right movements.

By 1928 there were 100,000 supporters and membership snowballed the following year. The organization was transformed from a subversive sect attracting outcasts of any sort, into a mass party of the middle classes – without losing any of its original characteristics. By the end of 1929 there were 170,000 members; by Spring 1930, 210,000.[43]

The NSDAP won only 2.6 per cent of the vote in the 1928 elections, but a full 18.3 per cent in 1930, putting it one short step away from taking power.

The organizational restructuring from 1924 to 1926 was thoroughgoing. The SA was taken out of Röhm's hands (because of his autonomous political ambitions – he withdrew from the movement for a few years), and totally subordinated to the party. The SS and the Hitler Youth[44] were created. Furthermore:

> In 1926: . . . A Reich direction was created (with Hess as its secretary, F. K. Schwarz as its treasurer and P. Bouhler as its head administrator) on which a series of commissions depended. The Reich's direction had, in the beginning, more than twenty-five employees and three automobiles at its disposal. A vast organization rapidly formed that misled (the Germans) as to the true nature of the party. Offices for foreign policy, the press, business, agriculture, economics, internal affairs, legal questions and the technology and politics of work reproduced the state apparatus on a small scale. Purely national socialistic institutions sprang up – e.g. those for "race and culture" and for propaganda – and their activities quickly took on a primary role. Beginning in 1926, the foundation was laid for other auxiliary party organizations: the *Hitlerjugend* (HJ); the *NS-Deutsches Studentenbund* (National Socialist League of German Students (NSDSB) under Baldur von Schrach (who in 1931 also became head of the HJ and the Reich Youth); the *NS-Schulerbund* (League of National Socialist Scholars) which had the task of increasing the party's attractiveness to youth, and later to professional associations (of teachers, lawyers, and doctors); and the *NS-Frauenschaft* (National Socialist Women's League).[45]

This description might lead one to believe that a bureaucratic organization existed, but in fact, the charismatic organizational principle obstructed it. Hitler maintained total control over the party by prohibiting the formulation of "rules":

> Hitler's aversion to rules and his insistence on the unconditional authority of his will precluded the organization of the party on bureaucratic principles. . . . He correctly recognized that any bureaucratic order, no matter how authoritarian it may be, limits arbitrary power and gives some protection to the subject and the underlying administrations.[46]

Continuous overlapping of spheres of competency, exclusively personally based relations, and the absence of clear and defined hierarchies characterized the organization before and after it took power.

In place of the formal procedures for making decisions, Hitler introduced the principle of "absolute authority and freedom towards below and duty and complete obediency towards above" . . . which meant, above all, that the leader had "unrestricted authority" over the whole movement. He was not subject to any controls in the form of requirements for a majority, procedural rules, or lines of authority. He could exercise his authority in any manner he chose, or he could delegate any portion of it to whomever he chose. His authority was arbitrary, derived not from any institution but from his person, in accordance with the indivisible nature of charismatic authority: both in theory and in practice only one authority was decisive in the movement, and that was the will of the leader.[47]

Power was delegated directly by Hitler, without any codified procedure, on the basis of personal loyalty. This led to constant insecurity at all organizational levels: everyone's fortune and career possibilities depended on Hitler's benevolence. The competition between individuals and groups was completely bent on winning Hitler's support and discrediting one's adversaries. This happened at both the national and local leadership levels, and local leaders often proclaimed themselves to be Hitler's direct representatives. This was usually true: the local leaders were in power because Hitler supported them. The delegation of authority on the intermediate and local levels took place through personal contact. The district leaders:

developed networks of followers and protegés, whom they constantly attempted to get into positions of power. This increased the intrigue and competition, since, in the absence of any strictly defined competences, their power was limited only by Hitler's trust in them. . . . The cleverness of the subleader and his ability to secure Hitler's confidence was the only determinant of his power.[48]

Delegation of power on a personal basis favored competition and division; and the deeper the divisions, the more they emphasized Hitler's role as the only guarantor of the organization's unity:

The intriguing aspect of Hitler's organizational principle was that, although the sub-leaders had absolute authority within their delegated spheres they did not necessarily have exclusive jurisdiction in their areas of operation. Hitler assigned overlapping jurisdictions without any institutional coordination and in the meantime emphasized absolute autonomy: the result was confusion and duplicated efforts.[49]

The Hitlerian organization was therefore the antithesis of a bureaucratic organization. But, as in bureaucratic organizations, its internal dynamic favored centripetal elite recruitment, i.e. cooptation on the basis of a personal tie with Hitler, playing the same role as career advancement in bureaucracies. This led to highly conformist and deferential attitudes.

As in the UNR, the various groups' tendencies fought among themselves to gain Hitler's support for their "political strategies" (i.e. their particular interpretations of National Socialism). In certain cases leaders of one or another tendency had (as did Soustelle in the UNR) to directly oppose Hitler. When this happened (Röhm in 1924 and 1934, Strasser in 1926, 1930 and 1932) the leader either capitulated – Goebbels, for example, who was originally part of Strasser's group, allowed himself to be coopted by Hitler into a leadership position after a personal meeting with him in Munich in 1926 – or he was politically liquidated (and, given the nature of this movement, often physically liquidated). Political divisions divided the leading group but did not cut across the entire organization: the mass of members and external supporters identified only with Hitler and were only willing to follow leaders who clearly enjoyed Hitler's confidence. A dominant coalition rendered cohesive by its founding leader, centralized control over the party's periphery, and an absence of institutionalization through objectivization of charisma (i.e. through a shift of loyalty from the party's supreme leader to the organization – Hitler explicitly opposed and resisted it) made the NSDAP an exemplary case of a charismatic party. Its subversive right-wing nature did not rule out its being an organizational system whose features can be found in every party whose genetic model is characterized by a charismatic origin.

Conclusion

The two cases examined differ due to deep-rooted differences in their original ideological goals and environments. What distinguishes them is what makes every party (charismatic or not) historically unique – its being the product of particular and unrepeatable conditions. What unites them and legitimately allows for their treatment as sub-types of a more general category, is their unequivocably charismatic origin. The organizational logic of such parties remains completely incomprehensible if we ignore this. It is no accident, for example, that the foremost scholar of Gaullism, Jean Charlot, utilizing the traditional Duvergerian categories, is unable to place the UNR either among the "cadre parties" or among the mass parties and is forced to return to the not very original category of "electoral party;"[50] which is completely incongruent with the Duvergerian typology which (like mine) is organizational (that is, a typology which distinguishes parties as they are internally organized). Duvergerian categories in fact are not very useful in examining charismatic organizations.

Charismatic parties differ a great deal from one another. They can be "militia parties," like the para-military organizations described by Duverger (but not all militia parties are charismatic parties) or they can be "electoral" organizations: they can adopt an aggressive strategy of organizational expansion (like the Nazis) or choose to keep the organization's size to a minimum (like the Gaullists). Whether we are dealing with Nazis, Gaullists, Bolsheviks,[51] Italian fascists (in the phase that Renzo De Felice has defined as "movement-fascism"),[52] Poujadists,[53] or any other such group (whatever its political–ideological thrust and social base), they all present certain common traits. These common traits are, in an organizational perspective, at least as important as their differences.[54]

A comparative study examining a number of historical cases of charismatic political parties, could, in the light of Weberian theory, furnish responses to questions which are currently unanswerable. The main problem is certainly to isolate the conditions which allow charismatic parties to institutionalize and charisma to be objectified. Under what conditions does the leader accept that partial *diminutio capitis*, that reduction in his personal power which is indispensable to organizational institutionalization?

The second problem of particular interest deals with the forms assumed by charismatic parties when they institutionalize. Do they become strong or weak institutions, bureaucratic–professional or traditional organizations? Do they become parties with dominant coalitions divided into factions which fight over the founders' "spiritual inheritance," or parties with cohesive dominant coalitions, united under the banners of new leaders? The answer is not self-evident. The case of the UNR (not alone sufficient) makes us think that traditionalization and legalization are likely to occur, i.e. the dominion of national notables deriving their influence from a spiritual inheritance tied to strong bureaucratic–professional traits. Jacques Chirac's *Rassemblement Pour la République*[55] seems today to be an organization of this type, and seems to indicate that if institutionalization takes place, the centralization of power – originally brought about by the charismatic leader – facilitates the formation of a relatively strong institution (even though charismatic parties more often form through diffusion and federation than through territorial penetration). His initial centralizing thrust seems to be so strong that it overcomes every factor working against it. Whether the charismatic leader is replaced by another individual or by a collegial direction, the resulting organization remains very strong and highly centralized – and this should facilitate the party's bureaucratization. If a charismatic party institutionalizes (and few do so), its level of institutionalization should

Organizational development

be higher than the level that would be indicated by other characteristics of its genetic model and environmental factors.

In charismatic parties, dissolution for lack of institutionalization is the most likely result, formation of a relatively strong institution is the next most likely, and the formation of a weak institution the least likely.

The latter should not, however, be completely neglected. Objectivization of charisma occurring, for example, when ample public resources are available, may offset the high degree of centralization (initially established by the charismatic leader), and even completely annul its effects – facilitating the disintegration of the leadership group and the formation of factions involving all levels of the party.

9
Organizational order: a typology

The time has come to draw conclusions, to weigh the results obtained. It should be observed, firstly, that the two models of strong and weak institutions we have used to re-read the organizational history of a certain number of political parties, trying to make their similarities and differences intelligible, is the result of an attempt to systematize ideas which are still only partially sketched out in party literature. The use of a binary classification to describe similarities and differences between parties is certainly not new. For example, the organizational differences between the DC and the PCI in the sixties justified, according to a certain study,[1] their placement under completely separate "headings" (despite their both being, in Duverger's terms, mass parties, externally created, and based on a "direct structure"). The widespread tendency in party literature to counterpose the model of "stratarchy" (elaborated by Samuel Eldersveld)[2] to Michels' model of "oligarchy" belongs to the same tradition. Oligarchy and stratarchy correspond, if only to a limited extent, to the institutional categories "strong" and "weak" (for oligarchies and stratarchies can be classified as institutionally strong and weak along the centralization/decentralization axis).[3]

Our analysis has been based on two hypotheses: Firstly, that an organization's birth and consolidation strongly influence its subsequent organizational "state." Party analysis (and probably organizational analysis in general) must go back to the party's formative phase and introduce the historical dimension as central.

Secondly, that the interaction between a party's genetic model, its position during its institutionalization phase, and the environmental characteristics, provides better explanations than those presented in the traditional literature. Such analysis goes beyond, for example, Duverger's traditional classifications (externally and internally created parties, direct and indirect parties, etc.), which are too broad, grouping very different parties together. It also helps to dispel many common misconceptions, most notably, the sociological prejudice (i.e. the notion that parties are organized according to the composition and interests of their social base) and the teleological prejudice (i.e. the notion that parties are organized as they are because of their *Weltanschauung*, their political objectives, etc.). It explains why all charismatic parties have certain common characteristics regardless of their "ideological goals" and social base (declassed petit bourgeoisie, marginalized group, or multi-class movement, etc.). The fact is that parties with similar ideological goals and social bases (socialist parties, for example) can seriously differ from one another, just as parties with different ideological goals and social bases can present similar traits. This doesn't eliminate the importance of either the ideological goals or the social base of a party, but rather circumscribes their role.

The organizational evolution of political parties

Our examination of a number of representative cases of a wide gamit of organizational situations has obviously not been exhaustive. Each case would require a deeper study than we have space for here. And cases were selected for "reasons of convenience" (e.g. relative availability of data, good historic monographs on the different cases, etc.). Whether they are, in fact, representative thus remains an open question. Other cases may involve organizational evolution which contradict our thesis.[4] The generalizations made here apply thus only to the cases here considered; and, by extension, to parties with very similar political contexts and genetic characteristics. We have, nonetheless, a considerable set of cases, and we can now more closely compare them with the ideal type of organizational evolution described in chapter one. The variability and complexity of parties' organizational forms will thereby become more evident. A comparison with the ideal type allows for a more precise notion of the different ways in which each case deviates from and falls short of it.

Let us summarise the salient features of the ideal type. In the passage of institutionalization from the genetic phase to organizational maturity, we see the following transitions: (a) From a solidarity system to a system of interests, i.e. from an organization forged to realize its participants' goals (according to the rational model) to an organization bent on guaranteeing its own survival and mediating heterogeneous objectives and demands (according to the natural model). (b) From a phase of manifest ideology to one in which organizational ideology becomes latent. A parallel modification in the incentive system accompanies this transformation: from primary collective identity to material-selective incentives in the form of regular remunerations to a bureaucratic body. This leads to a transition from a "social movement" type of participation to professional participation. (c) From an expansive strategy of environmental domination to a cautious and circumspect strategy of environmental adaptation. (d) From a phase in which the leaders have maximal freedom of movement (in defining objectives, selecting a social base, and, more generally, in the organization's formation) to a phase of maximal restriction of their freedom of choice and maneuverability.

At least one case among those examined here fits this ideal type almost perfectly: the SPD. This is not coincidental, for we have utilized Michels' theory in defining this ideal type, which analyzes in detail the organizational evolution of the German Social Democrats. Another case which comes close to this ideal type is the British Conservative Party. It, however, already diverges slightly from the model in that the Conservative Party did not simply shift from social-movement participation to bureaucratic–professional participation. Alongside this process and right from the start there was a great deal of notable "civil-participation" (not foreseen by the model) which was due to the party's genetic character. The organization bureaucratized all the same, and professional participation became a central, though not dominant element, with the expansion of the power of the Central Office. While bureaucratization in time led to a decline of the notables' importance (e.g. the local associations were no longer their personal fiefdoms), the parliamentary elites continued to be recruited from the prestigious men in the "civil" professions, not from the party's political professionals.

The PCI and the PCF are close in many ways to the ideal type, but they deviate because of their particular genetic models involving an external sponsoring organization. Being external to the nation *as well*, the Russian CP pushed these parties to highly institutionalize. Party loyalties remained indirect, being first and foremost to the PCUS, Lenin, and Stalin. Consequently, the communist parties formed as, and remain externally legitimated parties. Their strong institutionalization (and consequent independence from the national political system) are explained by the fact that the relation between the rank and file and the external institution was mediated by the party (and its leadership). The "normal" transition from manifest to latent ideology did not take place in the PCI and PCF, and they retained many attributes of the solidarity system (though they also bureaucratized and developed many characteristics of the interests system). Ideology remained manifest because it was the ideological manipulation and continual emphasis on the goals of the international communist movement which ensured the external institution's control of the party. The maintenance of a relatively high level of participation (like that found in the social movements) even after institutionalization, and the fact that the party bureaucrats received, up until recently, identity incentives (the mystique of professional revolutionaries) as well as selective-material and status incentives indicate that much of the initial solidarity system is still intact. A considerable transfer of authority – as in the PCI currently – from the external institution to the party (although not owing completely to the presence of a strong pool of pro-Soviet activists)[5] gives rise to a phenomenon not accounted for by the ideal type: the party at least partially de-institutionalized with the incipient factionalization of its leadership and the decline of participation level. The repercussions on the organization – foreseen by the model – are that organizational ideology becomes more latent (reducing the role of collective identity incentives), and that incentives of patronage become more important. The organization's parliamentarians and elected representatives at all levels (mayors of the big cities, etc.) then have more room in which to maneuver. Other deviations from the ideal type can be found in the somewhat similar cases of the SFIO and PSI, where the presence of a solid political notabilary structure and the absence of bureaucratization give rise to a situation where clientelary incentives and, in general, patronage, acquire an important role right from the outset. These are, moreover, organizations that do not demonstrate expansive tendencies even in their genetic phase (as opposed to the cases mentioned up to this point).

Organizational stasis and strategies of environmental adaptation precede institutionalization (rather than following it, as the ideal type postulates). In dealing with weak institutions, founding leaders (e.g. Mussolini and the Maximalists after 1912, Morandi in the PSI after 1949, and Paul Faure in the SFIO after 1920) always have incomparably more freedom of maneuverability than their successors. This occurs, of course, because weak institutions are less "cumbersome" than strong institutions, and organizational game rules can thus be more easily modified.

The PSI also diverges from the ideal type due to a similarity with externally legitimated parties like the Labour Party and the DC which have indeterminate boundaries and are permeated by and highly dependent upon external organizations. In the case of externally legitimated parties – the Labour Party and the DC – institutionalization implies a transition from a solidarity system to an interests system as well as an "emancipation" from the external institution (as in the case of the communist parties). Such emancipation can happen in more than one way, and may even stop before being completed. The Labour Party emancipated itself only partially. The reform of 1918 (potentially the moment of emancipation) set unsurpassable limits: the introduction of membership and direct affiliation procured the organization only a marginal share of "direct" loyalty. The organization remains inexorably dependent on the unions, never having acquired true autonomy. In a certain way, the Labour Party resembles charismatic parties in which the objectivization of charisma has been interrupted, leaving the organization in a kind of limbo. The loss of direct members and de-bureaucratization (i.e. reduction in the number of bureaucrats) that the Labour Party suffered in the course of the sixties[6] and its resulting organizational stasis are signs of the party's inability to develop autonomous instruments of organizational self-maintenance.

The DC, on the other hand, was able to emancipate itself more thoroughly from its external institution (the Church) through institutionalization undergone during the Fanfani period, and especially through "state occupation." The DC was a hybrid organization right from the start: an externally directed organization – colonized by traditional notables – which combined solidarity system traits dependent upon the external institution's trust as well as interest system traits.

Moreover, with institutionalization, the DC increased its deviation from the ideal type. The social movement type of participation by Catholic personnel weakened as professional participation (which here has the characteristic of hidden political professionalism)[7] and civil participation by notables increased. The DC pursued an expansive strategy of environmental colonization even after institutionalization (and in part because of institutionalization) due to internal competition between its divided ruling elites.

The CDU also diverged from the model: it was born with strong interest system tendencies, postponed institutionalization for a long time, and practiced a strategy of organizational stasis (like the PSI and SFIO) and thus environmental adaptation before institutionalization. The organizational strengthening that followed its shift into opposition after 1969 coincided with the acquisition of solidarity system traits (a result not foreseen by the model). These were accompanied by increased social movement participation and reduced civil participation, but *also* by a contemporaneous bureaucratization.

The case of the UNR is very particular: (1) because Gaullism (like all charismatic doctrines) was too vague to be termed manifest (ideology had less importance as De Gaulle himself was the symbolic identification center); (2) because along with institutionalization, the party bureaucratized (as the model predicts) but also "traditionalized," i.e. formed a network of notables whose authority depended on the maintenance of tradition (the founder's doctrine); (3) because the UNR tended to expand only after institutionalization was complete (i.e. after the Lille Congress of 1967), when it had already become an interests system.

It was clear that we would find a wide variety of divergences from the ideal type of organizational evolution: this ideal type could not in fact take account of the different genetic models and environments influencing party development. Analyzing these factors has allowed us to obtain a more complete picture of the various possible party developments, and the ideal type has enabled us to highlight these possibilities.[8]

Dominant coalition conformation: cohesion and stability

Institutionalization, as we already know, affects the dominant coalition's degree of cohesion. A strong institution has a cohesive dominant coalition (with weakly organized groups/tendencies) whereas a weak institution has a divided dominant coalition (highly organized groups, national factions, or sub-coalitions). The degree of cohesion, however, is only one of the factors defining the conformation of a party's dominant coalition. The other factors are the *degree of stability* and its *map of organizational power*, which we shall now discuss.

The degree of cohesion/division refers to the concentration/dispersion of control over the zones of uncertainty, and thus over incentive distribution; it also refers, therefore, to the vertical power games (elite–follower exchanges). Stability/instability refers, on the other hand, to the way in which the *horizontal* power games are played (among the elites). It refers, more specifically, to their ability to make long-lasting compromises concerning spheres of influence within the party. There is naturally a relation between a dominant coalition's degree of cohesion and its degree of stability, for the cohesive dominant coalition of a strongly institutionalized party is also stable. Such a strong "center" ensures its stability by coopting its inner ranks when necessary, and marginalizing (to its left or right) the opposition's tendencies.

In the case of weakly institutionalized parties, on the contrary, the dominant coalition's modalities of organization can vary, and may be associated with differing degrees of stability/instability. Two examples are (1) a dominant coalition that revolves around a strong center despite institutional weakness, or even a lack of institutionalization, and (2) a dominant coalition without a strong center.

The first applies best to charismatic parties. Their dominant coalitions' stability is ensured by strong centers (the charismatic leaders) which unify the different sub-groups and oblige them to compromise. Externally legitimated parties such as Labour, the DC under De Gasperi, and even to a certain extent the PSI under Turati also fit into this category, but for different reasons: their centers were strong not because they monopolized control over zones of uncertainty, but because of the support of external institutions which monopolized them. Thus even here, weak institutionalization can be associated with (relative) stability.

If a strong center which monopolizes the zones of uncertainty or has the support of external monopolizing organizations is absent, the divided dominant coalition will probably be unstable. The absence of a strong center in a dominant coalition, however, can be partly compensated for by other factors which may attenuate the potential instability. In particular:

(1) The presence of a strong intermediary structure associated with a very prestigious national leader (e.g. Jaurès and Blum in the SFIO), and external constitutional order that favors the stability and the preeminence of a national leader, or a combination of the two (e.g. the CDU under Adenauer).[9] In these cases, the dominant coalition is rendered stable through an agreement and a division of spheres of influence between the national leader and the intermediary leaders. The factions are primarily sub-coalitions (groups with strong organizations, but on regional and not national bases), and compromise between the national leader and regional leaders is (relatively) easily reached.

(2) An institutional order that favors party stability and leader preeminence in the case of governmental parties. A strong executive tends to make the governmental party's dominant coalition relatively stable whatever be its internal groups' degree of organization. The factions that have allied against other factions in creating the dominant coalition at the moment of the choice of the premier, cooperate until the next crisis of succession.[10]

We can schematically distinguish three cases as indicated in Fig. 6.

		Cohesion	
		high	low
Stability	high	+	+
	low	−	+

Fig. 6

We thus have three distinct possibilities:

(1) Cohesive–stable dominant coalitions
(2) Divided–stable dominant coalitions
(3) Divided–unstable dominant coalitions.

We are obviously dealing with three purely hypothetical configurations. A dominant coalition is never simply cohesive or divided, nor stable or unstable, but more or less cohesive or divided, and more or less stable or unstable. Empirical analysis must take account of the fact that different degrees of cohesion can be associated with different degrees of stability, and that a great (but not infinite) number of real possibilities exist. Parties' different ways of functioning correspond to these three possibilities.

Different types of dominant coalitions are, moreover, associated with significant differences in organization–environment relations and in the members' level of participation/mobilization. The first type (cohesive–stable coalition) generally tends to be associated with an aggressive organizational strategy toward the environment and a strong and continuous mobilization of the membership. The second type (divided–stable coalition) is invariably associated with an adaptive/defensive environmental strategy aimed at discouraging or altogether stopping expansion alongside of low levels of internal participation. The third type (divided–unstable coalition) refers to an organization in which the drive towards expansion and organizational reinforcement is due less to a deliberate central strategy than the strategies of competing internal groups. This type is characterized by periodic participation alternating from mobilization to immobility in accordance with the political movement.

In the first case the cohesion and stability of the dominant coalition ensure the cohesion and stability of the entire organization. The dominant coalition can therefore pursue a deliberate expansive policy, enlarging, for example, its membership base without sacrificing the new arrivals' socialization. The centripetal character of recruitment allows for the minimization of *voice* risks, i.e. of organized protest, since the hypothetical dissidents do not have fixed reference points within the national elites' divisions. Internal cohesion can thus be maintained despite expansion or consistent and deliberate attempts to expand (at least within certain limits).[11] The level of participation tends to be rather high. A strong and continuous mobilization of the activists does not endanger the organization's stability, as there are no factions that can exploit it to destabilize internal power relations.

The cohesion and stability of the dominant coalition allow for organizational expansion and strong mobilization without boomerang-effects hampering the party's stability. On the contrary, a policy of expansion which encourages internal participation is, in fact, good for stability: the leaders can point to expansion as "proof" of the validity of their political strategy.[12]

In the second case, the combination of stability and division within

Type of dominant coalition

Strategy	Cohesive–stable	Divided–stable	Divided–unstable
	expansion/domination	stasis/adaptation	expansion/domination
Participation	high	low	variable

Fig. 7

the dominant coalition reinforces organizational stasis and blocks expansion. The dominant coalition's divisions make compromise fragile: even slight perturbations can alter power relations and give outsiders access to power. Stability is thus based on the dominant coalition's tacit choice to halt party expansion. The coalition's different components respect the compromise, avoiding imperialistic strategies of environmental colonization and closing the organization in on itself. While the cohesive–stable dominant coalition expands to ensure its stability, the divided–stable one ensures its stability by adapting to the environment and accepting organizational stasis (manifest in its disinclination to enlarge its membership base, in the aging of its activists, etc.). The SFIO, the PSI under Turati, the "center–left" period PSI, and the CDU under Adenauer fit the latter description. A low level of participation due to the leaders' choice not to mobilize the members so as not to risk losing party control is related to organizational stasis.

The third case illustrates a condition of "every faction for itself," where the compromises between factions are extremely precarious: since long-term agreements cannot be reached, each individual faction tries to augment its power by expanding. The result is an expansionistic organizational strategy which is not the fruit of stability and cohesion, but rather of extreme instability and division (e.g. the DC in certain phases). Internal participation tends to grow when there is a show-down between different factions (at congresses and general elections, for example): it is only at such moments that a faction mobilizes its whole following. Participation tends to decrease subsequently, and is at its lowest between one test and another.

In overly simplified terms,[13] the three types of dominant coalition can be described with traditional power theory concepts as oligarchy, monocracy and polyarchy. *Oligarchy*, according to a recent author's definition: "is a form of domination where a small coalition tends to exercise a disproportionate influence over a group's collective decisions. The leaders' powers are not necessarily identical, but profound differences cannot, by definition, divide the oligarchs."[14]

Monocracy, on the other hand, is a form of domination characterized by a predominant influence of one person over the group's decisions. The entire organization tends to identify itself with him. He, of course, needs the support of other important leaders, but their dependence on him is clearly greater than his on them.[15]

Finally, *polyarchy* is characterized by the existence of two or more organized groups, none of which can alone hegemonically control the organization.[16]

Relating these concepts to our typology, we find that a cohesive–stable coalition is always either an oligarchy or a monocracy. A divided–stable or divided–unstable coalition is always a polyarchy. Introducing the criterion of institutionalization, we derive the following conclusions: (1) an oligarchy is always associated with strong institutionalization – as in the PCI, PCF and SPD; (2) a monocracy can lead to either strong institutionalization – as in the Conservative Party, the PSF under Mitterrand, and the RPR under Jacques Chirac, etc. – or an absence of institutionalization, as in charismatic parties; (3) a polyarchy is always associated with weak institutionalization. Fig. 8 allows us to schematize these correlations:

	Dominant coalition	Institutionalization
Oligarchy	cohesive–stable	strong
Monocracy	cohesive–stable	strong/absent
Polyarchy	divided–stable/divided–unstable	weak

Fig. 8

The most complex case is that of polyarchy. It is a type of organization that requires decomposition into sub-types. It seems to us necessary to distinguish between a polyarchy composed of sub-coalitions and one composed of national factions. In the first case the polyarchy may even, at first sight, seem to be a monocracy: the dominant coalition is in fact usually formed by a very prestigious central leader who is thus quite visible, and by peripheral leaders of sub-coalitions (e.g. the CDU under Adenauer, the SFIO under Jaurès, the SFIO under Mollet). In the second case, the dominant coalition is an alliance of many factions, with the leaders (the factional heads) in the foreground. Polyarchies can be further classified on the basis of number of factions, their relative power, etc. This method does not, however, tell us much about the dominant coalition's stable or unstable character. The dominant coalition's stability depends too much on environmental factors (e.g. the institutional order of the political regime, the type and intensity of environmental challenges, etc.) to not consider them when examining the causes of stability or instability.

The dominant coalition's conformation: the map of organizational power (1)

The third and last factor to consider in sketching conformation of a party's dominant coalition (and thus classifying the different types of parties), is what I call the map of organizational power, i.e. the configuration of relations among the party organs. The organization's actual (not formal) organogram must be understood: on the control of which offices does the dominant coalition's power over the organization depend? Two factors contribute to the map of organizational power:

(1)   The relations (control/subordination) among the organization's different offices;
(2)   The relations between the organization and other organizational and/ or institutional centers.

Let us consider the first point. Duverger's prediction that a shift of the power center from the parliamentary group to the internal leaders' offices would take place in most parties proved itself true of only a few. The cases I have examined point to a wider range of possibilities. As Duverger himself observed,[17] there are three theoretical possibilities: domination by the internal leaders, domination by the parliamentarians, or an unstable balance of the two. In highly institutionalized parties, the first two are both possible: the predominance of internal leaders (as in the SPD, PCF, and PCI) or of parliamentarians (as in conservative parties). The dominant coalition will thus be cohesive–stable when either the internal leaders or the parliamentarians are predominant.

Weak institutionalization is always associated either with parliamentary preeminence (e.g. the Labour Party and the PSI under Turati) or with an unstable combination of internal leaders and parliamentarian preeminence (e.g. the SFIO). The parliamentary groups' power depends on the fact that a strong central bureaucracy is lacking; it thus disposes of autonomous resources with which it dominates the party. In certain cases, in the SFIO and the CDU for example, this tendency was tempered by a strong intermediary structure (party federations). In other cases – as in the post-Fanfanian DC – a stalemate prevails between internal leaders (national ones in this case) and parliamentarians.

These facts demonstrate that the relation between internal (national) leaders and the parliamentary group is only one of the important factors. A second is the configuration of the local and intermediary levels. The problem is whether the intermediary structure is weak or strong. If it is strong, as in the SFIO and the CDU, the intermediary leaders can counter-balance the parliamentary group's power. If it is weak, the parliamentary group (e.g. in the PSI 1895–1912) dominates for lack of institutional counterweights.

Why should the relations between organizational offices be treated as a component of the dominant coalition's conformation? Why do different control/subordination relations between the different offices, and between the diverse organizational sub-units, bring about differences of modality in the vertical and horizontal power exchanges? It isn't enough to know if a dominant coalition is cohesive and/or stable or rather divided and/or unstable, to differentiate between the party's organizational orders; one must also know through which intra-organizational relations the dominant coalition's power is exercised.

The map of organizational power can conform to various physiognomies; the five organograms represented in Fig. 9 are the most common.

Organograms 1 and 2 correspond to the maps of organizational power of highly institutionalized parties. Organogram 1 refers to the SPD (of the imperial period), the PCI (up until a few years ago) and the PCF. Organogram 2 refers to the Conservative Party, and in part to the UNR. Both involve high centralization of power (cohesive–stable coalitions), but internal leaders dominate in the first, while the parliamentarians dominate in the second; vertical integration of elites is thus ensured in the first case, but not in the second. If power resides in the hands of the internal leader, we find careers of the conventional type (i.e. entrance at the lower levels and slow promotion). If power resides in the parliamentary group, this possibility is excluded (one enters directly at high levels). Although both types involve strong institutions, institutionalization is greater in the first organogram.

Organograms 3, 4, and 5 are maps of organizational power for weakly institutionalized parties. Organogram 3 corresponds to a party whose parliamentary group and intermediary leaders share power fairly equally and whose local associations are controlled by the latter (e.g. the CDU and the SFIO). In 4, organizational separations between parliamentarians and base (local) structures are weak or nonexistent. The parliamentarians directly control the base associations, and

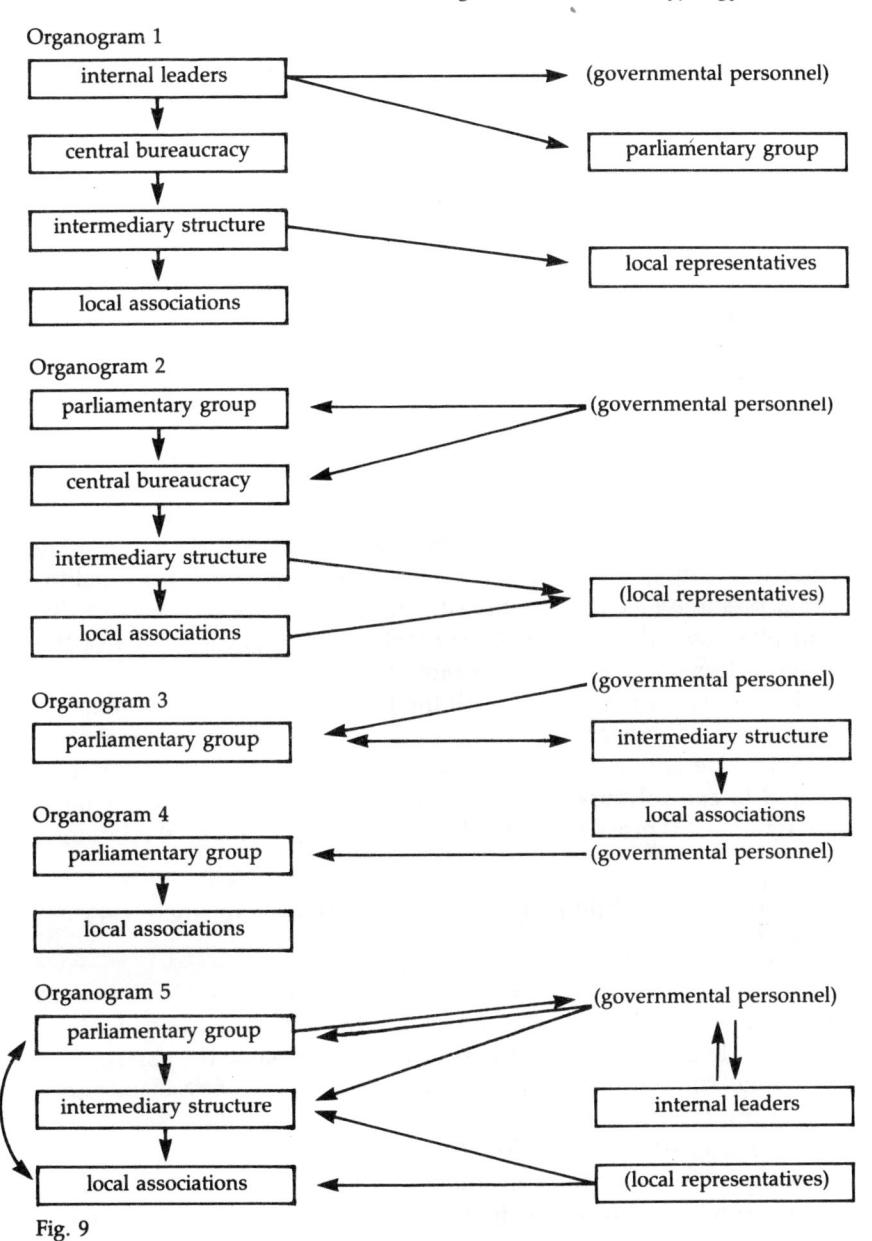

Organizational order: a typology 175

Organogram 1

internal leaders → (governmental personnel)
↓ ↘
central bureaucracy → parliamentary group
↓
intermediary structure → local representatives
↓
local associations

Organogram 2

parliamentary group ← (governmental personnel)
↓ ↙
central bureaucracy
↓
intermediary structure
↓ ↘
local associations → (local representatives)

Organogram 3

(governmental personnel)
↙ ↘
parliamentary group ↔ intermediary structure
↓
local associations

Organogram 4

parliamentary group ← (governmental personnel)
↓
local associations

Organogram 5

parliamentary group ← (governmental personnel)
↓ ↕
intermediary structure ← internal leaders
↓
local associations ← (local representatives)

Fig. 9

Note: The arrows indicate the direction of the relationship of control/subordination among the different organizational levels. In the attempt to make the chart easier to follow, indications of the retroactive process from the subordinate to the control level have not been provided. Such a process is always present in reality and depends on the nature of unequal exchange, not domination, of organisational power.

organize them as personal fiefdoms (e.g. the PSI during the Turatian era).

Organogram 5 refers to a party with a highly fragmented internal power structure. It closely corresponds to Eldersveld's model of "stratarchy;" various "strata" at different organizational levels control important resources and there is competition among groups at the same level as well as at differing levels[18] (e.g. the DC in many phases of its history).

Different maps of organizational power are associated with different dominant coalition conformations. Organograms 1 and 2 imply cohesive–stable coalitions (oligarchies and monocracies). Organogram 5 is always related to divided–unstable coalitions because of the stalemate between the different organizational levels and their internal divisions. Organograms 3 and 4 correspond to dominant coalitions which, though divided, exhibit different degrees of stability according to the institutional context in which the parties operate. The PSI under Turati has a relatively stable coalition due to the support of the trade unions (organogram 4). In the CDU, stability depended on institutional preeminence and on the consequent stability of the executive controlled by Adenauer in the context of the political regime of the Federal German Republic (organogram 3).

These observations, along with the fact that none of these maps of organizational power can adequately describe the Labour Party's structure, demonstrate that a party's organizational map must not be limited to control–subordination relations among different organizational offices. It must also consider the inter-organizational relations.

The dominant coalition's conformation: the map of organizational power (2)

The factors we have hereto examined do not always suffice in tracing the dominant coalition's conformation. There are situations in which groups or leaders of organizations formally external to the party play a directional role within it which cannot be accounted for by an examination of the relations between the different organizational sub-unities alone. We must therefore isolate the existing connections and the nature of such connections – if and when they exist – between the party and external organizations. It is necessary, in this light, to make a special comment.

A cooperative relationship between two organizations (like power relations between people) *always* implies an exchange of material and/or symbolic resources between them.[19] The collaboration between an organization X and an organization Y is based on the need each has for the other's resources and its inability to autonomously procure such resources on its own (without resorting to inter-organizational exchange). A union and a party collaborate by exchanging resources: the party, for example, gives political legitimacy to the union in exchange for mobilization of union resources in support of party activities. An interest group and a party collaborate if the party needs financial resources from the interest group and if the latter needs the party's support to obtain favorable legislative measures. Each party is, to varying degrees, connected to many groups, associations and organizations. These connections can take on three forms:

(A) The party controls the organization. In this case, a relation of unequal exchange exists between the party and the organization. There is an exchange of resources, but it is a rather lopsided one. The party gains more than the external organization and, as in a classical imperialistic relationship, unequal exchange reinforces the organization's dependence on the party. An extreme case of this is the "hierarchical association":[20] the external organization is so weak that it has no resources to exchange with the party: material and/or human resources flow to it from the party to keep it alive. The party can do without the external organization, but the organization cannot do without the party. A hierarchical association is akin to the case of a great power economically maintaining a poor and small but strategically important country through the flow of free aid. The difference between unequal exchange and hierarchical association is that whereas the latter does not imply tension and conflict between the two organizations, the former does, and thus represents a potentially unstable relation.

A relation of unequal exchange which is added to and is the result of an initial situation favoring the party, tends to perpetuate the organization's dependence on the party. The organizational leaders depend on the resources obtained in the exchange with the party in order to maintain organizational stability, but the party is not as dependent on the resources it receives from the external organization. In such a case, the organization's leaders should *not* be considered part of the party's dominant coalition.

(B) The second possibility is that of "equal exchange": the party leaders reap benefits of equal importance to those reaped by the external organization's leaders. There is a relation here of "equal dignity" between the party and the external organization. When equal inter-organizational exchange is more institutionalized than sporadic, each set of leaders needs the other set's resources in order to defend its own organization's stability. In such a case, the organization's leaders, formally external to the party, should be considered a component of the party's dominant coalition; and the party leaders naturally take part in the external organization's dominant coalition (e.g. the union–party relation in the SPD after 1905, and to a lesser extent in the PSI in the Turatian era).

The relationships between certain parties and interest groups are often, if institutionalized, quite similar.

(C) The third possibility is unequal exchange (or even hierarchical association) this time favoring the organization and not the party. This applies to all externally legitimated parties. The sponsoring organization's leaders are an integral part of the party's dominant coalition (e.g. the role of the ecclesiastical hierarchy in the selection of parliamentary candidates in religious parties), but are not, as opposed to case (B) merely one component among others; they are, instead, the focal point.

Relations between parties and external organizations can, of course, evolve and change. The SPD–union relations, for example, shifted from hierarchical association in the early nineties (i.e. the unions were very weak and dependent) to unequal exchange (as the union's position strengthened), and finally to equal exchange (after 1905). An identical parabola (even if the exchange never became completely equal) characterized the CGIL–PCI relationship from the early fifties to the mid-seventies (later unequal exchange re-emerged as the CGIL began to weaken).

On the basis of this analysis, we can formulate three general propositions.

Highly institutionalized parties can have relations with external organizations of both the A and B types; type C is, by definition, excluded in that it implies a degree of environmental dependence (more specifically, on another organization) which is incompatible with strong institutionalization. The standard exception here is the communist parties–PCUS relationship.

Weakly institutionalized parties tend to have relations of the B and/or C type. A is excluded in that the party must control its own environment (specifically, another organization); this is by definition incompatible with weak institutionalization.

Regardless of their levels of institutionalization, governmental parties are most likely to develop inter-organizational relations of the B type (i.e. involving equal exchange). If they are weakly institutionalized, relations of the C type are most likely (i.e. unequal exchange favoring the external organization). This is because interest groups tend to collect around governmental parties and to tighten ties with party internal sub-groups; and different components of the dominant coalition can easily develop stable organizational ties with various sectors of the state apparatus. This depends on the fact that in governmental parties "boundary personnel" proliferate: i.e. politicians who play mediatory roles between the party and external organizations. This explains why opposition parties which have developed into strong institutions invariably, at least to some extent, de-institutionalize when they move from the opposition to the government.

Conclusion

The dominant coalition's degree of cohesion and stability and the map of organizational power, give rise to a taxonomy of parties' dominant coalitions and thus to a taxonomy of the parties themselves. Not every type of organogram (1, 2, 3, 4, 5) can co-exist with every type of party – external organization relation (A, B, C). Nor can it coexist with every degree of cohesion/division or stability/instability of the dominant coalition. The possible relations between the different factors are schematized in Fig. 10. The possibilities are varied, and the taxonomy created could be the beginning of a more complex typology covering all possible combinations.

The different factors usually tend to reinforce each other. For example, a cohesive–stable dominant coalition and inter-organizational relations of the A and/or B type correspond to organograms 1 and 2. The dominant coalition's cohesion/stability safeguards the existing map of power: the organogram remains unchanged and inter-organizational relations of the C type are excluded. Organogram 5, for

Institutionalization	Map of organizational power	Dominant coalition
strong	Organogram 1 Interorganizational relations A/B[a]	cohesive–stable (oligarchy)
strong	Organogram 2	cohesive–stable (monocracy)
	Organogram 3 Interorganizational relations B/C	divided–stable (polyarchy)
weak	Organogram 4	divided–unstable (polyarchy)
weak	Organogram 5 Interorganizational relations B/C	divided–unstable (polyarchy)

Fig. 10
[a] The relationship between the communist parties in the pre-Stalinist and Stalinist eras and the Comintern (type C) is an exception.

Organizational development

example, is always associated with divided–unstable dominant coalitions (because of the fragmentation of power that this map entails). A party with a divided–unstable dominant coalition may change – e.g. the coalition, although remaining divided, may become more stable, thereby modifying its map of power (moving from organogram 5 to 3 or 4). This introduces the questions of factors affecting organizational change which I shall explore in the following chapters. Modifications in degree of cohesion and stability are always possible, but always imply modification in the map of organizational power (whether in terms of the organogram or of the inter-organizational relations). Dominant coalitions change and thus transform parties. These changes are absolutely inseparable from changes in the more general organizational order.

Part III

Structural contingencies

10
Size and organizational complexity

The analytical framework established in the course of this study and the "test" attempted in examining the historical vicissitudes of several political parties, is part of a perspective in which the role of power, conflict, and alliances within organizations is more important in explaining organizational dynamics than are the so-called technical factors – e.g. division of labor, number of hierarchical levels, organizational size, internal specialization in relation to different sectors of the environment – which are traditionally treated by organizational sociology. These and other technical factors, however, cannot be omitted from an analysis which privileges the dimension of organizational power over all others. In part three we will examine the role (or possible role) of some of these factors in the structuring of party organizations.

Organizational size, environment, and technology are the most important factors influencing organizational dynamics, according to a scientific orientation first developed in industrial sociology, which then found application in other organizational contexts: so-called *contingency theory*. According to this theory, organizational functioning is essentially a product of one or more of the three variables just mentioned; variations in organizational physiognomy thus depend on contingent variations arising in relations with the environment, in the state of technology, or in the size of the organization. Some authors have especially emphasized the role of technology,[1] some that of size, and others that of the environment. Still others have hypothesized the existence of a combined action of the three variables upon organizational physiognomy.[2] For all of these authors, the three factors influence the organizational physiognomy: level of bureaucratization, extent of the division of labor, hierarchical levels, etc.

In its various versions and ramifications, contingency theory has been submitted to serious criticism. Two objections are, for us, especially relevant. First of all, the critique of determinism (technological, environmental, etc.), i.e. of the fact that the theory hypothesizes the existence of a rigid causal link between the dependent variable (organizational physiognomy) and the independent variable (size, technology, environment) without leaving any room for the leaders' "freedom of choice"[3] and/or for the mediation – between structural contingencies and organizational physiognomy – of "power games" in the organization.[4]

The second objection overturns the definition of the organization as a sort of "passive object" at the mercy of contingent variations of size, technology and environment; it views the organization, in certain cases, as an "active subject" able to manipulate these same variables (by which, according to contingency theory, it is manipulated). The organization can, for example, in certain cases influence its own environment, adapt the environment to itself, increase or decrease in size, and choose among the available technological alternatives the one which best fits its own physiognomy. If these objections are justified, contingency theory only deals with one side of the problem: it helps us isolate the types of pressure technological, environmental, and dimensional changes can exert on the organization, but it does not help us determine the organization's *reactions*, i.e. it does not tell us which changes are actually produced.

The attempt we have made here integrates a series of technical imperatives into a framework which emphasizes the problem of organizational power; we will now consider the interaction (and its consequences) between technical imperatives and intra-organizational power games in political parties.

Why bring up these themes? Because in spite of many studies of parties which seem to ignore the very existence of the contingency theory approach to the study of organizations and its application, there are nonetheless many hypotheses (generally in the form of vague opinions) and a considerable number of observations concerning, for example, the organizational and behavioral differences between big and small parties (emphasizing thus the importance of size), and the influence of the party system, electoral behavior and changes in class structure on party organizations (emphasizing thus the role of environment and environmental changes).

In this chapter we will take up the problem of the possible influence of organizational size on party functioning. In chapter 11 we will examine some aspects of party–environment relations. And in chapter 12 we will analytically discuss the phenomenon of party bureaucracy and bureaucratization, attempting to situate this crucial theme within the more general question of political professionalism.

Party size

According to Michels, the party's magnitude is the primary independent variable explaining the formation of an oligarchy. In his perspective, organizational size both directly and indirectly affects power relations within the party. *Directly* because the organization's growth influences its leaders' degree of maneuverability:

> In theory, the leader is merely an employee bound by the instruction he receives. He has to carry out the orders of the man, of which he is no more than the executive organ. But in actual fact, as the organization increases in size, this control becomes purely fictitious. The members have to give up the idea of themselves conducting or even supervising the whole administration, and are compelled to hand these tasks over to trustworthy persons specially nominated for the purpose, to salaried officials.[5]

Above a certain numerical threshold,[6] any assembly inevitably succumbs to control by the few. According to Michels, this is partly due to mass psychology (the "manipulatability" of the crowd) but also partly to purely technical–organizational factors: "The regular holding of deliberative assemblies of a thousand members encounters the gravest difficulties in respect of room and distance; while from the topographical point of view such an assembly would become altogether impossible if the members numbered ten thousand."[7] This explains the necessity of the delegate system and, in time, the end of democracy. But organizational growth also has an *indirect* effect on the distribution of power within the party, bringing about an increase in its complexity: growth in size is correlated with growth in internal division of labor (i.e. functional specialization), multiplication of hierarchical levels, and bureaucratic development. An increase in organizational complexity also leads to centralization of the decision-making process.[8] Michels certainly asserts[9] that an oligarchy's formation is based on three interrelated causes which fall under mass psychology (i.e. mass apathy and deference towards the leaders), leader psychology (i.e. the desire to conserve one's own power), and strictly technical–organizational factors. But organizational size clearly stands out here as the primary causal factor from which the other psychological and technical–organizational effects derive.[10] As Michels tells us, big parties – those which organize and control large numbers of people – manage to combine internal complexity and oligarchical power. Michels' theory is, in effect, mono-causal: growth in size (not the environment or certain genetic model characteristics) is considered to be the cause of every change a party undergoes. Max Weber's critique of Michels stems primarily from a disagreement over this point.[11] An important contemporary school of organizational theory derives, however, from

Michels ground-breaking work on organizational size. A great deal of empirical research has since paved the way for an organizational theory which takes size as the main independent variable of an organization's internal order.[12]

Size is generally measured in terms of number of members. But in the case of parties, this criterion is not easy to apply. It is common to say "many" and "few" when referring to number of votes (i.e. the electoral force) and/or number of members. These are, however, two very different things. There are examples of parties with many votes and few members. In the fifties, the CDU was smaller than the SPD in terms of membership but much bigger in terms of votes. We must thus establish which of the two ways of measuring party size is more relevant to organizational functioning. As Duverger demonstrated, no univocal relationship exists between the two factors.[13] *Both* factors can affect the organization; but we are dealing here with different kinds of effects. The number of votes has an *indirect* effect on the organization, influencing its relations with the environment[14] (e.g. determining its governmental options, its attractiveness to interest groups, etc.). If, however, we are concerned with the *direct* effects of size on party organizations, we must use membership as a size indicator, although this can often be a rather approximate and even inaccurate criterion. Recruitment criteria for members can, for example, vary greatly from party to party; the number of members has, thus, a completely different meaning in a party which carefully scrutinizes its members than in a party which artificially inflates its membership to meet internal electoral deadlines. Despite its approximate value for empirical research,[15] this criterion (the number of party members) is indispensible for measuring organizational size.

Size as an independent variable

Although almost no empirical research has been done on the influence of size on parties (with an exception to be considered later), party literature is full of observations about it. Many authors seem to feel that size is an important factor in relation to:

(1) internal cohesion
(2) participation/mobilization of members
(3) bureaucratization

Internal Cohesion. It is commonly held that size differences are directly responsible for behavioral differences. The classic sect–church distinction is utilized to show the fundamental difference between a small and a large political organization in terms of their different levels of internal cohesion. According to this view, shared political values and tight organizational ranks are easier to attain in small organizations.

Studies on political sects offer numerous examples of small, highly centralized groups made politically cohesive by rigid entrance conditions (i.e. careful selection of new members).[16]

A similar line of reasoning takes size *variation* as effecting cohesion.[17] Kirchheimer, for instance, holds that one of leaders' main concerns is to prevent excessive party expansion in order to minimize internal conflicts.[18]

These authors equate small size with internal political homogeneity (and thus with cohesion of the ruling group), and vice-versa. But not all small organizations are sects (if we accept Von Doorn's definition of sect). The little that is known about small parties suggests great variation in level of internal cohesion.[19]

Large organizations, on the other hand, are not all lacking in internal cohesion: the PCI and the British Conservative Party are both quite cohesive. Small size does not guarantee internal cohesion (i.e. is not a sufficient condition), nor is it a necessary condition for it. Secondly, without isolating size thresholds (namely, small, medium and large) there is no way of knowing how much importance to attach to it. All that we can say is that a relationship between size and political homogeneity probably exists, affecting the level of internal cohesion; big organizations are, for example, more generationally stratified (i.e. in terms of members' age, periods of recruitment, types of political socialization, etc.)[20] than small ones.

More important, however, than the real size/cohesion link, is the fact that the leaders themselves believe in it, and act accordingly. Certain dominant coalitions' decisions to halt or impede membership expansion stem from the fear of possible de-stabilizing effects resulting from increased political heterogeneity.

Participation. Since Michels, organizational growth has been widely thought to have a depressive effect on internal participation/mobilization, i.e. political apathy on the part of the members is characteristic of big organizations. Growth is thought to correspond to increase in the division of labor, and the bureaucratization and centralization of authority. And these transformations are thought to lead to the decline in participation.[21]

Relating size and participation in this way leads to two claims: (1) small organizations are more "participatory" than big organizations, and (2) changes in size lead to inverse changes in level of participation. There is almost no data to substantiate the first claim. One could just as well maintain that the participant/total member ratio tends to remain constant in organizations of different size (and that if it varies, it is because of *other* intervening factors). And there are studies which contradict the second claim. For example, the PCI's membership dropped in the fifties, but so did participation.[22]

it is significant that, along with a decline in the absolute number of members enrolled in the party, there has been a concomitant, and often greater, decline in members' activism as well. Sources both inside and outside the PCI indicate that the average attendance at section meetings was running, at the end of the 1960's, to perhaps ten percent of the total membership, with 25 per cent considered truly exceptional.[23]

Participation levels seem inexplicable in reference to party size alone. Olson's theory,[24] which suggests high participation in small groups, *also* maintains that if big groups distribute enough selective incentives, their participation levels can be just as high. Small size is not, therefore, a necessary condition for high participation. As we have seen, a party in its formative phase tends to mobilize its members, but not because it is a small organization. It does so because it is a "solidarity system" geared to attaining its manifest goals. As the party institutionalizes (independently of its size), it becomes a system of interests; and its internal voluntary mobilization declines as bureaucratic–professional participation (i.e. that of professional politicians) grows. This explains why, in the case of the PCI, there was a correlation between decreasing size and decreasing participation.

Bureaucratization. Since Michels' time, size, complexity and bureaucratization have been taken as directly proportional co-variant factors. Peter Blau is the first scholar to have problematized this notion. In one of his early writings he observes that, contrary to popular opinion, large organizations do not necessarily suffer from bureaucratic hypertrophy.[25] While growth tends to increase complexity, and thus division of labor – both *horizontal* differentiation (i.e. the number of offices at the same hierarchical level) and *vertical* differentiation (i.e. the number of hierarchical levels) – it is negatively correlated with the administrative (bureaucratic) component. In a later study,[26] Blau points to the existence of contradictory affects of size on bureaucratization. Size affects bureaucratization in two opposing ways. On the one hand, growth augments internal vertical and horizontal differentiation. This necessitates increased coordination, resulting in administrative expansion. On the other hand, once having passed a certain threshold, growth permits an economy of scale and a consequent decrease in administrative personnel. The result of these two forces is an increase in the administrative–bureaucratic component with decreasing rates.[27]

Too little data prevents us from checking this theory. Comparative empirical research on division of labor (using real and not just official figures) and the consistency of party bureaucracies is lacking. The little data available seems to confirm Blau's theory. A significant and constant increase in membership seems to require greater division of labor (i.e. the creation of new offices, the splitting of pre-existing offices, more hierarchical levels, etc.) *and* more bureaucracy. This is, however, only true up to a certain point, beyond which growth does not necessarily influence either complexity or bureaucratization.

It is easy to show how growth during a party's formative phase is positively correlated to increasing complexity. The PCI, for example, during its very rapid expansion between 1944 and 1950, worked to channel and control the expansion, thus accelerating an increase in complexity (as shown by the large number of coordinating organs created – factory, local, zonal and regional committees) through organizational decisions. It ratified a series of related proposals at the Sixth Congress (January 1948):

> A more complicated and well-articulated structure began to arise than in the preceding one, above all in terms of the subdivision of members in specialized groups by sex and age (girls, women and youth groups) and the creation within the cells of subdivisions (10-member groups) and of supervisory roles even at this level.[28]

Significant horizontal differentiation accompanied the growth in complexity: the local base unit, the cells, grew in number from 30,000 in 1945, to 50,000 in 1947.[29] The Argentinian socialist party, to cite another example, underwent a similar development as its membership expanded.[30]

Size initially parallels complexity. One should not, however, confuse finding a correlation with discovering a causal relation. One could argue that increased complexity in the formative phase is only minimally due to growth; it is rather the effect of the need to channel and control the intense participation generated by the "solidarity system" accompanying an organization's début. There is certainly a connection between participation and membership, at least in the initial stage. But, according to this hypothesis, the real cause of structural complexity lies elsewhere.

Even if growth were the main cause of internal complexity, we still could not substantiate the close connection between them asserted by Michels and Blau. We would still have to demonstrate that (1) when size decreases, complexity and/or the level of bureaucratization diminish at the same time; (2) that a big organization is always more complex than a small one. To respond to the first point we can note that the PCI underwent a significant drop in membership between 1954 and 1966 (from over 2,000,000 to about 1,500,000) and yet its internal structure didn't become proportionally simpler.[31] When a party loses many members, there is a series of cuts – closing or regrouping sections or cells – which brings about a partial horizontal reconvergence (de-differentiation); the reconvergence is not necessarily great enough, however, for us to postulate a clear causal connection between size and complexity.

As for the second point, even if only the level of bureaucratization (i.e. the number of full-time bureaucrats) is considered, variations from party to party are clearly almost totally independent of size: for example, the British Conservative Party in the fifties (with around 2,500,000 members) had a bureaucracy much smaller than that of the PCF (with around 300,000 members).

There are also cases of very small organizations which are considerably more bureaucratized than middle-sized and large organizations. The small West German Communist Party (KPD), for example, with 70,000 members in 1956 had, in the same period, one full time bureaucrat for every 40–50 members, as opposed to the SPD's (about 600,000 members) one to every 1,500.[32]

The available data thus seems to indicate that the theories using size as an independent variable in explaining party physiognomy largely miss the mark. Size in and of itself does not seem responsible for significant variations in political style, participation, complexity or bureaucratization (though it does seem to influence internal cohesion). More important factors must be involved. We shall therefore look elsewhere.

Size as a dependent variable

The train of thought leading from Michels to modern contingency theory, assumes size as a *given* and attempts to examine its autonomous effects on organizational functioning. What is left aside is that size, in parties and other organizations, is often manipulated by the leaders. To reverse the reasoning we have hitherto followed, we can ask why leaders try to expand the party at certain moments and to halt its growth or even reduce its size at others. The question then becomes what effect the power structure has on organizational size.

According to Howard Haldrich,[33] what distinguishes leaders is their control over organizational boundaries, i.e. their ability to change size by tampering with membership recruitment (be it open or selective). The leaders decide who enters, who does not, and who is to be ousted. By controlling the organization's boundaries, the leaders can make it grow or shrink. During conflicts with other organizations, leaders (according to Haldrich) use two tactics to ensure the members' support and consensus. A first strategy:

> may take the form of constricting boundaries by strengthening the requirements of participation, with more asked of each member by way of conformity to organizational rules and ideology. . . . Tightening and strengthening an organization's boundaries means either raising performance standards or appealing to members' loyalty to the organization. Increased centralization gives authorities more direct control over members' energy and time, allowing them to reallocate resources rapidly.[34]

The second strategy consists in expanding the organization's boundaries, that is: "to take persons from the challenging groups and organizations inside organizational boundaries. They may be absorbed, co-opted, or amalgamated into the local organization."[35] The first strategy has the advantage of increasing cohesion, but the disadvantage of isolating the organization from its environment. The second strategy has the advantage of increasing the organization's ties with its environment, but the disadvantage of generating internal conflict through admission of new, insufficiently socialized members.

Using this theory one could maintain that the French and Italian Communist Parties have often used these two strategies alternately. By observing the fluctuations in the PCF's membership and keeping in mind that it is a strongly selective and controlled organization (on the Leninist model), we can note that the important reductions in membership occur when the party is pushed by the USSR towards highly sectarian political stances (from the "class-against-class" strategy of the twenties and thirties to the sectarianism of the Cold War). We can thus hypothesize that drops in membership are due to deliberate choices – to a strategy of contraction of boundaries. Being forced into a sectarian political position, the party must shrink (thereby increasing its internal political cohesion) in order to defend its organizational stability. Using Hirschman's categories, the PCF had, during those periods, to favor *exit* (through the contraction of boundaries) in order to shelter itself from *voice* (as possible internal reactions to sectarianism), expelling untrustworthy members and relying only on supporters of proven faith and loyalty.

In the seventies, the PCI, with the increase in membership accompanying the strategy of "historical compromise" (an increase of 300,000 members from 1969 to 1976,[36] deliberately expanded to guarantee the organization's penetration into many social environments, and to involve formerly peripheral groups in support of the strategy.[37] The internal conflicts aggravated by heterogeneity[38] (the massive entrance of new members with different political experience) were costs the leadership was willing to pay, because a failure of the consociative strategy would have more seriously disturbed its internal stability. Analogously, the PCF's deliberate boundary expansion after the 1976 Eurocommunist Congress (at which it abandoned its dogma of the dictatorship of the proletariat, and distanced itself from the USSR), contributed to the fact that: "in 1977 the PCF had practically doubled its supporters with respect to the sixties, passing from around 300,000 to 543,000 at the end of 1977. The objective it set after 1976 was the one million mark of members which could accelerate the party transformation from that of an essentially cadre party to a mass party in the light of the PCI which the PCF had always tried to follow without always succeeding in terms of its strategy of innovation on several fronts at once."[39] Not all the effects of boundary changes can be attributed to deliberate decisions (namely, to variations in recruitment criteria): the adoption of a sectarian stance leads many members to leave of their own accord, regardless of leader pressure. A more accommodating political stance can, on the other hand, attract people simply because they agree with that policy.[40] Size can sometimes vary independently of the elites' decisions to change it, but their deliberate choices still play a greater role on most occasions.

Our thesis is that party size mainly depends on each party's internal power structure, i.e. on the conformation of its dominant coalition. Thus a cohesive–stable, dominant coalition is more likely to increase party size (the deviant case, that of the PCF, depended on externally imposed political choices, i.e. of the sponsoring organization) in order to safeguard its organizational stability. A divided–stable coalition, on the other hand, is more likely to maintain party size stationary. A divided–unstable coalition, finally, tends to increase party size as a result of the competition between its different factions.

The decisive variable here is the party's power structure, i.e. the conformation of the party's dominant coalition. This allows us to understand why it is useless to search for a one-to-one correspondence between organizational size and internal complexity. It is true that growth requires some increased complexity, but complexity is mainly related to the problem of distributing selective incentives to careerists. As we saw in chapter 2, the main reason for increased internal differentiation is the pressure to augment the activist's remunerations in the hope of safeguarding organizational stability. The variation in levels of organizational complexity is consequently due more to the different dominant coalition conformations (which, in turn, are linked to different strategies for safeguarding the organization's stability), than to variations in size.

Organizational thresholds

While the role of size alone is not to be overestimated as it often depends on leaders' choices, there are, however, certain special and rare conditions under which it becomes crucial. This problem can be formulated in terms of "critical thresholds." Elites certainly actively control size to ensure organizational stability. But the environment doesn't always allow them to vary the organizational boundaries as they might like. The leaders of a small, newly constituted organization, for example, are often interested in increasing its size, but the environment may be too hostile to let them do so. And the opposite might occur in a very large organization, where smaller size would be seen as reinforcing internal cohesion and thus elite control, and yet its structure could be so complex or so rigid that it impairs their ability to do so. In other words, while size depends upon the leaders' choice, it depends on other factors as well which may sometimes annul their efforts. Thresholds can thus be hypothesized, above and below which size plays an autonomous and preponderant role.

A *survival threshold* would represent the point below which, lacking resources necessary to institutionalize, a party is forced to fight for its survival. When a party is born, its leaders normally have to adopt an aggressive stance toward the environment because it is only through its growth that the party obtains enough resources to survive. But the environment can be so *hostile* (or, as we shall see in the following chapter, so complex and unstable) that it frustrates these efforts, and even threatens the organization's survival. This happens where, for example, the human, symbolic and material resources which the party needs have already been swallowed up by pre-existing parties, as when a small extreme left party forms where a large and solid communist party already exists. In such a case the survival threshold might not be crossed. The party cannot expand enough to guarantee its control over the resources required for its survival. Not crossing this critical threshold leads to:

(1) A lack of necessary resources for institutionalization. The party wavers between rapid dissolution and the perspective of a long-term frenetic struggle for survival.

(2) As institutionalization is out of the question, the leaders try to maintain some of the organization's "solidarity system" traits. Under these conditions, the alternative, the formation of an interests system, is by definition precluded. A consequence is that the organizational ends, i.e. the manifest ideological goals, are not "articulated" or adapted to daily organizational needs. The leaders' only choice is to

use every available occasion to realize the original goals. This leads to high internal cohesion (characteristic of the solidarity system) and highly ideological external behavior. Since the organization continually attempts to expand by realizing its original goals, environmental hostility continues to grow: the new-born organization would like to annex part of the pre-existing party's "hunting ground" (its *domain*), but the latter reacts aggressively, further isolating the organization. The combination of a hostile environment and failure to cross the survival threshold creates a vicious circle of sectarianism:[41] the more the organization is isolated and thus struggles to ensure its precarious daily survival, the more it must attack its adversaries head-on. This escalation of aggressiveness isolates it even more and further reduces its chances of crossing the survival threshold. The organization is thereby destined to dissolve sooner or later. The sects described by the various authors we have cited in this chapter refer to organizations of this type, i.e. organizations whose inability to cross the survival threshold forced them into a position of "total opposition" *vis-à-vis* their environments.

Naturally, there is no once-and-for-all determinable survival threshold for every party. It varies from case to case in accordance with many environmental factors[42] and the genetic model. This explains why not all small organizations are sects. A small organization may also cross its own *specific* survival threshold, i.e. it may control the specific resources which allow it to institutionalize. To ascertain a party's survival threshold requires *ad hoc* evaluations.

It is also possible to hypothesize the existence of a maximal threshold, which, if crossed results in a return to the autonomous effects of size, involving a growing rigidity due to the leaders' inability to control the organization's complexity. Growth creates pressures which, in turn, increase the complexity (even if the leaders' response is not automatic). If, in the presence of a pressure caused by increase in size, the dominant coalition considers increased complexity to be consistent with the goal of organizational stability, then complexity increases. Beyond a certain threshold, negative effects due to extreme fragmentation, heterogeneity and bureaucratization begin to appear. We shall define this critical threshold as the *threshold of rigidity*. This is what Downs termed the "syndrome of ossification." It manifests itself clearly at the end of a cycle of progressive increase in rigidity:

when an operating bureau (or set of bureaus) greatly expands. The larger it gets and the faster it grows, the more likely it is that the entire cycle will occur, though total size is a more powerful cause than speed of growth. As the bureau grows, its top officials suffer from an increasing leakage of authority. Their efforts to counterset such leakage constitute the second phase of the cycle. This in turn leads to the third phase: a growing rigidity of behavior and structure within the bureau.[43]

In the cases of parties examined in this study, however, we have rarely seen this type of syndrome. It is therefore possible to assume that these phenomena can appear only under exceptional conditions, i.e. when a party reaches a (non-determinable) point of no return in terms of size and complexity. Parties rarely reach that level of complexity. But when they do (following an enormous membership expansion, for example), ossification may actually take place in accordance with Downs' description. We can thus explain why parties, which in the course of their histories have practised "imperialist" organizational expansion, often stop growing once they have reached a certain size. The traditional explanation for this is that the party has encountered a "natural barrier," i.e. its supply domain for members has been exhausted. Our alternative explanation (which of course does not entirely deny the validity of the other) is that once having reached a certain size, the leaders opt to halt further growth to preclude ossification.

In conclusion, size exerts an autonomous role on the organization only *below* the survival threshold and *above* the threshold of rigidification.

Let us assume, for the purpose of explanation, that party size can vary from 1 to 100 and then we place all possible sizes on a *continuum* as in Fig. 11.

Survival threshold			Threshold of rigidification	
1	10		90	100

Fig. 11

Arbitrarily placing the survival threshold at 10 and the threshold of rigidity at 90, our hypothesis states that in the intervals between 1 and 10 and between 90 and 100, size plays a decisive role in influencing intra-organizational dynamics and the relation between the organization and the environment. Between 10 and 90, however, it ceases to be decisive, and different party sizes are compatible with different organizational orders (as the cases examined in part 2 unequivocally demonstrate). Between these two thresholds, elites manipulate size to defend organizational stability under variable environmental conditions. The conformation of the dominant coalition (and thus the distribution of power) is more important than size here in explaining organizational dynamics.

The size of sub-units

Even if, in the majority of cases, party size does not significantly determine organizational dynamics, we can nonetheless assert that the size of the party's internal organs – its sub-units – may influence party functioning. This hypothesis is partially confirmed. Internal power relations, however, come into play here. Sub-unit size (understood as a "technical" factor) interacts with power relations in influencing organizational dynamics. Three problems merit consideration in this regard:

(1) Influence exerted on the organizational power map, i.e. on the organization's organogram, by the size of its sub-units.
(2) The mechanisms favoring the expansion of sub-units of the organization.
(3) The relation between sub-unit size and level of internal participation.

Empirical evidence on the first point shows that small units prevail over big ones, independently of the existing formal hierarchical relations. At all levels (whether we are dealing with the relations between national, intermediary or peripheral organs) the rule is that the formally executive organs (small) prevail over the formally deliberative organs (big).[44] This is really due to sub-unit size. Only small groups can function according to the committee method.[45] Since their members interact frequently or regularly, these organs can operate by bargaining through "deferred reciprocal compensations,"[46] and unanimous decisions. The executive organ's cohesion and, even more so, the secrecy of its activities, i.e. the lack of publicity[47] (publicity characterizing decisional processes would permit outsiders to follow and comprehend them), leave the deliberative organ no choice but to ratify the decisions adopted. In addition, it must be understood that the majority of the executive organ's decisions (made with time constraints) are not even subject to ratification by the deliberative organ (that, due to its considerable size, generally meets at long intervals).

The relation between the executive and deliberative organs is one of control/dependency *only if* there are no serious divisions within the executive organ. In order to function as described, a committee must base itself on unanimity. If it is divided into a majority and a minority, it risks paralysis; and if the division systematically penalizes the minority, it will inevitably make known its dissension outside of the executive organ: the publicizing of dissension and the circulation of information destroys the executives' trump card (secrecy). The deliberative organ comes to be invested with real decisional power. For instance, the selection of parliamentary candidates in Labour and Conservative local associations, normally takes place in small, *ad hoc* commissions, and the candidates are then ratified by a general assembly.[48] Unanimous decisions are rarely rejected by such an assembly. When the commission does not reach an agreement, however, or there are serious conflicts, the assembly must deal with the problem thereby acquiring real decision-making power.[49] The hypothesis can thus be restated: small organs prevail over the big ones when the dominant coalitions controlling them are cohesive, and the internal minorities are not represented in them. Otherwise, there is a constant oscillation based on the issues at hand and the cleavages which result from them.

As concerns the second point, there are two types of mechanisms governing the growth of certain organizational units: *cooptation* and individual or group pressure for career advancement. The tendency for ruling party organs to expand is well known. The CDU's executive organ (the Federal Committee), for example, grew from 17 members in 1950 to over 50 members in 1955.[50] In examining the national organs of Italian parties in the period from 1946 to 1966, Giacomo Sani detects: "the existence of a general tendency of a party's ruling organ to grow, interrupted, however, by moments of stability and even contrary tendencies."[51] Similar tendencies have been noted in ruling organs of certain French parties.[52]

The ruling organ's tendency to expand can be hypothesized as due to the competition among its internal components. Expansion here is a by-product of attempts by different groups (i.e. factions or tendencies) to modify power relations in their favor by coopting the most loyal members within the ruling organ. Moreover, the tendency to expand should be stronger the less cohesive and stable the dominant coalition. In principle, we could say that we find growth when the dominant coalition is divided and unstable, stability in phases of equilibrium (among the dominant coalition's different components), and contraction when a divided coalition becomes more cohesive. Increased cohesion pushes leaders to reduce the ruling organ's size in order to restrict the minority's margins of maneuverability. Other factors are, however, also at work, in particular, an autonomous external pressure exerted by those attempting to enter the ruling organ. The periodic expansion of certain ruling organs depends, therefore, on their internal dynamic. But it *also* depends on the dominant coalition's imperative to periodically enlarge its pool of resources to distribute to the careerists. If too many careerists "crowd around" and push on the ruling organ's doors, the refusal to enlarge its size could destabilize the party (e.g. push the frustrated careerists into the minority camp). This coincides with Sani's opinion that:

> the tendency to grow is perhaps due to the combined pressure of leaders to hold on to their positions, and of the new generation to enter the upper ranks. Growth would thus result as a mechanism allowing for a "renewal of continuity."[53]

If these are the causes of expansion in certain ruling organs (in particular of the collegial type), we may find other causes in other organizational units. Leaders of certain sub-units often deliberately try to increase the size of their sub-unit in the hope of securing more power than other leaders on the same hierarchical level. This usually happens when their mobility through other channels is temporarily blocked. One makes one's career in two ways: by passing directly to the next hierarchical level, or by increasing the importance of the office already held.[54] Competition between leaders at different levels largely explains the growth tendency of certain offices. Every ambitious leader tries to reinforce his prestige by enlarging his sphere of activity (often requiring an increase in personnel), at the expense of other offices, so as to control enough resources for further career advancement. The competition among section, federation, and other party offices to send their own delegates to congress explains a lot of the energy put into new membership recruitment campaigns. Increased unit size leads, in these cases, to a considerable increase in party size. In other cases, sub-unit growth takes place at the expense of other sub-units (for example, when some of the functions and the personnel of an office for organizational affairs are replaced by the office of "propaganda and communications"), and thus doesn't affect the party's size.

A leader, however, works to expand his role and the importance of his office only if there are no other immediate and less costly career advancement possibilities. We can therefore reformulate our hypothesis: sub-unit size tends to vary inversely with the availability of its leaders' career advancement possibilities.

These hypotheses can be made intelligible in the light of a theory of intra-organizational exchange. Increasing the importance and size of his office, the leader restructures his internal exchange bases and increases his control over zones of uncertainty; in doing so he modifies power relations with other actors to his advantage. And when expansion of the sub-unit is directly guided and planned by its leader, he can often neutralize the effects of an increase in political heterogeneity by coopting faithful supporters. Disproving the hypothesis that larger organizations are always more heterogeneous, the PSF's large federations are more cohesive (dominated by individual prestigious leaders) than its smaller, more factionalized federations.[55]

As for the third point, size influences internal participation. According to Olson's well-known thesis, only small groups are capable of sustaining participation, while big groups must resort to selective incentives to obtain the same results.[56] Selective incentives, however, don't vary in proportion to size: a thousand member section, for example, generally doesn't have many more positions to distribute than a fifty member section. Given equal selective incentives, Olson's theory predicts higher participation in small sub-units.[57] Parties in which participation is higher are therefore organized into a high number of small base associations rather than a small number of large associations.[58] Manipulating base unit size means increasing or decreasing members' participation levels. Manipulation naturally occurs in one or the other direction according to the type of dominant coalition and to the different strategies that each type of coalition develops to safeguard the party's organizational stability.

Complexity and electoral control

We have repeatedly referred in the course of this chapter to the problem of "complexity" without, however, defining it. It has become clear that the problem is in part different for political parties than it is in firms or public administration. An organization's complexity is often measured by the following parameters:[59]

(1)   level of *specialization*, the division of labor measured by the number of offices at the same level (horizontal differentiation)
(2)   degree of *standardization* of procedures
(3)   degree of *formalization* (development of written communication systems)
(4)   number of *hierarchical levels* (vertical differentiation)
(5)   level of *bureaucratization*, i.e. the ratio of administrators to total number of organization members

An apparently anomalous fact should be observed. There is a well supported theory which states that while these dimensions of complexity are all positively correlated (i.e. the more an organization specializes, the greater its level of bureaucratization, etc.), complexity is inversely correlated to degree of decision centralization.[60] The more complex an organization, the less centralized is its internal decision process. This would seem to contradict my thesis that strong bureaucratization is accompanied by equally strong centralization of authority. But the contradiction is only apparent: the more bureaucratic an organization is, the more hierarchical levels it has. This brings about a decentralization in the decision-making process. Many micro-decisions are made by bureaucrats at the various hierarchical levels without consulting the leaders. But these are administrative and routine decisions which are made automatically, based on directives from above. The political or strategic decisions (decisions regarding the governing of the organization) are always centralized in bureaucratic organizations (though not necessarily *only* in bureaucratic organizations, as charismatic parties demonstrate).[61] The high number of hierarchical levels determines the elevated volume of daily decisions.[62] If we don't distinguish between administrative and political decisions, we are bound to have the impression that a very complex (and therefore very bureaucratic) organization has a decentralized decision-making structure. This is in part correct, but the decentralization only refers to administrative decisions. Highly bureaucratized parties are certainly decentralized: the bureaucrats of the SPD, PCI, PCF and British Conservative Party really do make autonomous decisions about a variety of daily problems, but they do so in conformity with directives from above (in accordance with an "opportunities structure" which rewards centripetal more than centrifugal forms of competition).

The different dimensions of "complexity" listed above can not all be easily adapted to the case of parties. For example, according to the available data, level of formalization (production of written norms and rules) seems higher in *less* bureaucratized parties. The rules for parliamentary candidate selection are more formalized in the Labour Party than in the Conservative Party, even though the level of bureaucratization in the former is lower. In the LDP, the Japanese Liberal Democratic Party, which has very few bureaucrats, the procedure for the distribution of funds among its different factions is highly formalized.[63] Many other examples could be cited. Everything leads us to believe that formalization can, in certain cases, be an alternative to bureaucratization, rather than a component of bureaucratization itself.

A second factor shedding doubt on the usefulness of certain indicators in measuring party complexity is the ambiguity of the concept "administrative component" in a political party context. Two types of bureaucracy can exist in parties – *executive* and *representative* (as we shall see in chapter 12). British parties, for instance, are typically characterized by an executive bureaucracy, i.e. a paid administrative corps not allowed to hold political office, bureaucrats who are *appointed* from above to carry out exclusively administrative activities. The representative type of bureaucracy is common to mass communist and socialist parties. Here paid bureaucrats *also* hold political positions (many of which are elective). While the executive bureaucracy corresponds in part to those bureaucracies found in firms and public administration, the representative bureaucracy of certain parties (but also of many trade unions) is rather a *sui generis* phenomenon. Parties, like trade unions, are "mixed" organizations that combine principles regarding the functioning of both non-voluntary and voluntary associations. Their structure is "characterized by penetration and coexistence of bureaucratic and electoral elements, which are at times contradictory and at times harmonious."[64] The many elective positions at the different rungs of the hierarchy explain why "complexity" is a different phenomenon in parties than in other bureaucracies. Michels asserts that the electoral principle is annuled by a combination of member apathy and party bureaucratization. But Michels understood organizational power as a dominator–dominated relationship. Conceiving of power as an (unequal) exchange relationship, one's evaluation of inner-party elections changes. The latter are certainly manipulated by the leaders. Regular electoral deadlines, however, help prevent a complete monopoly of power by small groups. Though the leaders and "representative bureaucrats" can manipulate elections – primarily through "indirect suffrage," as Duverger notes[65] – they are forced to take internal elections seriously, and to dedicate time and energy to create rank and file consensus. Electoral control mechanisms affect the organizational level of complexity. In a recent study on a group of English trade unions it was found that: ". . . the associations in which elections play an important role [have] administrative systems which are less specialized and less standardized and formalized, with less hierarchical subordination and [are] in general less bureaucratized than those where the election of functionaries plays a less important role."[66] Authority is highly centralized in these associations.

The conclusions of this study on trade unions correspond to the findings on many parties' internal orders. Party complexity levels seem lower than those of non-representative organizations. Even very differentiated parties (horizontally and vertically) like the PCI or the PCF seem less complex than firms of a similar size. We already know that excessive party complexity is discouraged because it tends to diminish the symbolic value and status of every new position created, reducing the party's ability to distribute selective incentives. We can now add that systems of electoral control also discourage complexity. In analyzing the dominant coalition's conformation, the reasons for the different levels of complexity from party to party can be understood. For if systems of electoral control discourage complexity, *different levels of efficiency of electoral control must correspond to different levels of organizational complexity*. The question is then what makes electoral control more efficient. The answer is that electoral control is more efficient when there are elites vying for power (and thus where people can choose among them).[67] Electoral control is more efficient when the dominant coalitions are *divided* and less efficient when they are *cohesive*. Superior levels of complexity should then be more generally associated with cohesive dominant coalitions (having less efficient electoral control) than with divided ones. This partially explains why the PCI, PCF, and SPD are (or were) more "complex" than the SFIO and PSI.

Electoral systems

The former considerations force us to consider those important "rules of the game" – the electoral systems in operation in the parties and their relation to intra-organizational conflicts. Political scientists are divided over this point. On the one hand, there is the thesis that the electoral system influences the party's internal power relations (e.g. factions proliferate in proportional electoral systems but not majoritarian ones).[68] Others maintain, however, that the type of electoral system in use is a *reflection* of power relations between internal groups, not their *cause*.[69] These theses are both, in our opinion, partially true. A party's power relations, i.e. its internal distribution of power, are what determine the choice of one or another type of electoral system. But once such a choice has been made, the adopted electoral system affects the power relations among the groups. If the dominant coalition is composed of many factions, it tends to adopt a proportional system which safeguards each faction's power. Once adopted, the proportional system reinforces factionalism and sometimes encourages the proliferation of new factions and/or allows for their organizational reinforcement. In both the DC and the PSI, the choice of a proportional electoral system in the sixties was the product (not the cause) of factionalization due to an increased control of internal groups over public resources. This in turn encouraged a further proliferation of factions. The reciprocal influence of the type of electoral system and power distribution was clarified in a study on the DC[70] when (in the fifties and early sixties) its electoral system was majoritarian, though corrected by *panachage* (the option to vote for candidates on more than one list). The functionality (i.e. its contribution to the reduction of internal conflict) of this electoral system depended on the nature of the party's divisions. When they were rigid, the existing system weakened conflict; when they were fluid, the system weakened conflict to the point of encouraging transformism.

The *same* electoral system could thus manifest quite different effects in accordance with the type of conflict among the groups.

Conclusion

In this chapter we have discussed the possible effects of a series of technical factors – organizational size, sub-unit size, division of labor, electoral system – on party functioning. The problem of power constantly cropped up in our discussion. An organization's technical problems are always related to underlying political problems, and thus to its internal distribution of power resources. Technical solutions are thus a function of power equilibria. Contrary to Michels' contention, size seems to have no important independent effect on organizational dynamics, except in exceptional cases. It is rather the relationship between the organization and its external environment (a problem not discussed by Michels), which plays the important role here. We shall discuss this relationship in the next chapter.

11

Organization and environment

Throughout our analysis we have referred to two different aspects of the organization–environment relation: the effects of pressures and environmental changes on the organization; and the importance of its hunting ground, i.e. the part of the environment targeted by the organization's ideology, which the organization must control if it is to maintain its identity. We have also seen that the degree of adaptation to the environment depends on two factors:

(1) Environmental characteristics. Certain environments demand adaptation, while others allow for manipulation.
(2) The level of institutionalization. The greater the institutionalization, the less the party tends to passively adapt itself to the environment, and the more it is able to dominate it; and vice-versa: the weaker the institutionalization, the greater its passive adaptation tends to be.

It follows that organization–environment relations must be considered relations of interdependency. In this chapter we shall attempt to systematically explore these relations. As in the preceding chapter, our analysis shall be more theoretical than empirical.

Environmental characteristics

Organizations' *degrees of uncertainty* concerning their environments is one of the most systematically explored problems in organizational theory. In chapter 3 we equated control over this form of uncertainty with one of the fundamental trump cards of organizational power. Environmental uncertainty is, however, a variable: some environments are quite predictable while others are completely unpredictable. And the same environment can shift from one to the other.

The literature on this subject usually invokes three dimensions of unpredictability: complexity/simplicity; stability/instability; liberality/hostility.

Environmental complexity. In the last chapter we saw that many authors follow Michels in maintaining that organizational complexity is essentially a function of size. Others assert, however, that environmental complexity is the cause of organizational complexity. With size held constant, the more diversified and heterogeneous (complex) the organization's environment, the greater the organization's complexity.[1]

This premise of this theory is essentially that the more complex the environment the less predictable it is. Unpredictability pushes the organization towards internal specialization, i.e. to the multiplication of specialized roles in dealing with different aspects of the environment, in the hope of dominating it. This increases the number of organizational "relays"[2] (or "boundary personnel"),[3] that is the number of actors with privileged relations with the different parts of the environment. The more numerous the "boundary personnel," the more pronounced are the organization's internal tensions, for control over environmental uncertainty is more dispersed within the organization.

This theory thus views environmental complexity as creating pressures which increase organizational complexity and, consequently, tension within the organization.

Environmental stability. A second aspect of environmental uncertainty is its stability/instability. According to one hypothesis, the less stable the environment (i.e. the more it oscillates and changes) the less predictable it is. A well-known theory states that, in highly unstable environments, only organizations with highly decentralized decision-making structures can function, while more centralized organizations function better in stable environments.[4]

Different degrees of stability/instability are conceivable. Environments can be differentiated by using a typology which locates them on a continuum from placid (very stable) to turbulent (very unstable).[5] The hypothesis here is that environmental instability increases uncertainty and produces diversification among the internal groups; this leads to greater conflict over differences in political strategies.

A turbulent environment increases the relative uncertainty of organizational decision-making processes. . . . Lacking exact knowledge about what to provide increases the necessity of feedback from boundary personnel. . . . The increase of feedback coordination likewise promotes a diffusion of decision-making processes throughout the organization, thus making centralized and hierarchical authority structures less viable.[6]

This theory, adapted to the case of parties, tells us that the more its environment is unstable, the more uncertainty is experienced by the party. Deep internal conflicts are to be expected because: (1) "turbulence" encourages the diffusion of decision-making power within the party. (2) The number of actors believing they can cope with environmental uncertainty thus grows, multiplying the number of political solutions proposed. When the environment is turbulent, the party's dominant coalition thus tends to be divided and unstable.

Environmental hostility. Some organizations operate in hostile environments in which their very survival is brought into question. As we have already seen, the "survival threshold" may not be crossed by new-born organizations encountering formidable environmental barriers. The same environment can be very hostile to certain organizations and liberal to others. The environment's tolerance level towards an organization can vary widely. A generally accepted hypothesis is that the greater the environmental hostility, the more internally cohesive the organization.[7] This agrees with the idea that external threats tend to increase group cohesion.[8] The SPD's cohesion while institutionalizing can *also*, as we have already seen, be explained by the intensity of the external challenge, i.e. the threat the anti-socialist laws posed to the party's survival. According to this hypothesis, environmental hostility produces environmental uncertainty, and uncertainty encourages organizational cohesion. It should be observed that the uncertainty provoked by hostility has effects diametrically opposed to those which result from uncertainty due to environmental complexity or instability. This apparent incongruency is insufficiently explained in the organizational literature. To understand it we must take into account the difference between complexity and instability, on the one hand, and environmental hostility on the other. The former (below certain thresholds, as we shall see) threaten *only* organizational stability, i.e. they throw authority channels into question. They represent a threat to organizational *order*. Hostility is a threat to the organization's very *survival*. This fundamental difference explains their different effects.

Complexity, instability and hostility are interrelated. Complex environments are usually also unstable. Beyond a certain threshold, a very complex and unstable environment becomes (or is perceived by the organization's members as being) hostile; it threatens not only the organization's order but its survival. Environmental hostility can, of course, be caused by factors unrelated to complexity or instability (for example: state repression). More often, however, a clear tie exists.

This allows us to postulate the existence of a curvilinear relationship between environmental uncertainty and organizational stability. We can hypothesize that organizations tend towards internal cohesion under tranquil environmental conditions (simple and/or stable environments), are more internally divided under conditions of uncertainty (complex and/or unstable environments), and only tend once again towards cohesion under extremely uncertain conditions (very complex and/or unstable environments), i.e. under hostile conditions.

Before taking a closer look at party–environment relations through the optic of these concepts, we should clarify a point. The literature on contingency theory treats organizational order as a dependent variable of environmental characteristics. But this agrees only partially with our analysis for: (1) Organizations not only adapt to but also have their own autonomous effect on the environment: they can thus ward off the blows of environmental changes and pressures, to some extent. (2) Variations in party physiognomy are not merely the effect of variations in complexity (i.e. in environmental stability and tolerance) but are also, in our view, the effect of the different conformations of their dominant coalitions. (3) A crucial aspect of party-environment relations (neglected by contingency theory) concerns the conquest/defense of the "domain" from which a party gets its identity. Environmental complexity is, in our perspective, related to this problem.

Party environments: arenas

Environments directly influencing parties – which are in their turn structured by institutional constrictions[9] – can be conceived as arenas in which relations between parties and other organizations take place. They are like gambling tables at which the party plays and obtains – in accordance with its performance – the resources it needs to function. In some arenas the party exchanges resources with other organizations. This exchange can be mutual, favor the party or favor the other organization. In other arenas the party competes with other organizations for resources.

Party arenas are interdependent and can be conceived as a network of "relevant" environments. Resources obtained in one arena are spent in another, and success at one gambling table – the exchange of resources under favorable conditions – often affects the extent of one's success at other tables. The money a party gets from an interest group in exchange for favorable governmental measures is, for example, spent in stealing votes from other parties; electoral success, helps, in turn, to attract more financing. The legitimation Western communist parties obtained in the thirties from the Comintern in exchange for their subordination to its directives was spent in the electoral arena to increase party following among the working class. These electoral successes were, in turn, "recycled" by communist leaders to improve their positions in the hierarchy of international communism.

The exchanges and bargaining between parties and other organizations define the external areas of organizational uncertainty. They are areas of uncertainty because environments are, by definition, potentially variable. At any moment, the terms of exchange can deteriorate in one arena and, thereby affect – due to the interdependency of arenas – all the others, including the electoral and parliamentary arenas. Each party has many arenas (e.g. the party exchanges resources with the bureaucracy, with interest groups, etc.). Party arenas can never be completely isolated *a priori*. They vary over time, and their number and structure must be determined empirically. The international environment may not be relevant, for example, in times of stability for certain parties, but an international crisis can transform it into a crucial arena.

Whatever the other arenas may be, the two which are always "relevant environments" are the electoral and the parliamentary arenas. The physiognomy of these two produce some of the most important effects on party organizations.

Among the many possible aspects we could consider, we shall discuss two, both of which are correlated to environmental uncertainty: (1) the effects of different degrees of control by the party of the electoral arena, and (2) the effects of the different manifestations of the interdependence between electoral and parliamentary arenas.

The electoral arena

Party competition for votes develops in the electoral arena which can have differing degrees of stability and complexity. These, in turn, influence the environment's degree of hostility/liberality towards the organization. When the electoral arena is relatively stable, i.e. there are no big shifts in power relations among parties and in vote distribution from election to election (as was true for a long time in most European political systems),[10] we can expect greater cohesion and stability in the parties' dominant coalitions (or at least in those parties which operate under conditions of environmental stability). When the electoral arena is "turbulent" i.e. is characterized by electoral fluidity and by serious shifts in party power relations, predictability is impaired and the dominant coalition is likely to have more difficulty keeping environmental uncertainty under control, and serious internal tensions.

We must qualify these considerations with two observations: a party's level of institutionalization is a decisive variable, intervening between environment and organization. The more institutionalized a party (i.e. the more autonomous from its environment), the less disruptive the impact of environmental uncertainty: strong institutionalization reduces environmental uncertainty. Secondly, environmental uncertainty is largely dependent on party institutionalization. A turbulent arena is thus one in which the "belonging" vote has been reduced and the "opinion" vote is greater (i.e. one votes on the basis of issues and/or candidates). The opposite holds true for the "semi-placid" (stable) arena. This is because the greater the proportion of opinion over "belonging" voting, the greater the (potential) electoral fluidity and thus the greater the degree of environmental uncertainty. European electoral arenas have for a long time been semi-placid, because the quantity of "belonging" vote has been considerable (i.e. electoral attitudes have been dictated by loyalty and identification due to tradition and/or associative ties). A substantial percentage of this kind of vote is not accidental: it is the product of strong political mass organizations with branching vertical ties to the electorate (i.e. with strong political sub-cultures) capable of "freezing" electoral divisions, even from one generation to the next.[11] In many cases an electoral arena is semi-placid only if it is highly controlled by the parties. Control presupposes a highly structured party system, i.e. that the parties (or sponsoring organizations in the case of externally legitimated parties) operating in this arena are strong. A counter-example is the French Fourth Republic: a system with a turbulent electoral arena while electoral stability prevailed in other European countries.[12] The turbulence was mainly due to the fact that the institutionalization of French parties (with the exception of the PCF) and the degree of structuration of the party system as a whole were very low.

It is true that the degree of uncertainty due to the stability/instability of the electoral arena influences parties, but it is also true that parties, if they are strong institutions, can control the electoral arena to a certain extent and thus reduce its instability. A party's degree of control depends on its level of institutionalization, but *also* on the arena's complexity. The latter involves many factors, but most importantly the presence of party competitors, i.e. other parties or groups (collective movements, terrorist organizations, etc.) that hunt in the same hunting ground and/or aim for the same electoral resources. A party can find itself in a position of opposition to or competition with other parties.[13] Opposition without competition exists when the two parties' hunting grounds do not overlap. This doesn't necessarily mean that there is no overlapping of electorate, but simply that the domain (i.e. the party's share of the electoral base upon which its identity depends) cannot be usurped by the opposing party. This could be the case, for example, in a two-party system composed of a "popular-Catholic" party appealing to Catholic workers and a "liberal-Protestant" party appealing to the Protestant bourgeoisie. The two parties could be fierce opponents but never compete for votes. On the other hand, two parties might cooperate and yet compete for the same hunting ground – e.g. in the case of an electoral alliance between two parties which both claim to represent the working class. (We will take a more in-depth look at the effects of competition and opposition further on.) The electoral arena's degree of complexity depends (in descending order of importance) on the *existence of competitors*, their *attraction* to the party's hunting ground, and their *number*.

An extremely simple (from a particular party's point of view) electoral arena will have only oppositional parties. A complex arena will have, in addition to oppositional parties, at least one competitive party. The arena's degree of complexity increases with the number of competitors each party has and with their attraction to its "hunting ground."

Environmental complexity (in terms of competitors, their number and attraction) increases environmental uncertainty because it, like instability, affects the perception of the situation by the elites and the other organizational members. A complex environment, like an unstable one, maximizes uncertainty and increases internal organizational tension because there are many internal actors proposing their own political strategies for dealing with the complexity. A simple environment involves low levels of environmental unpredictability.

Let us examine the case of the SPD during the period of the anti-socialist laws. Despite the extreme illiberality of the political system (which contributed, however, to the party's cohesion) the electoral arena was a relatively simple environment. The SPD's power grew with every election because it was the only organization that could credibly claim to be the working-class party (workers representing the overwhelming majority of its electorate). Problems of competition (essentially with leftist liberals) were minimal and decreased with every election.

The SPD's only concern was to continue its electoral expansion among the workers, and that required further organizational effort. No one really threatened its hunting ground or, thus, its identity. It had no credible competitors: its environment was relatively simple.

This was also true for the British Labour and Conservative parties in the early fifties: the two parties were opponents but not competitors. The Conservatives had a stable but limited hold on the workers (a third of their electorate) and couldn't hope to increase it. Labour had a stable but just as limited hold on the upper-middle classes (a third of their electorate) and little hope for expansion. The two parties certainly competed for the fluctuating electorate, but their hunting grounds were always well protected. And the majoritarian electoral system itself represented a barrier (the specific institutional constraint of the English electoral arena) which gave both considerable security against the emergence of competitors (the communists for Labour and an extreme right-wing party for the Conservatives).

Inversely, the electoral environment of a party with many competitors – often as many to its right as to its left, as occurs in multi-party systems – is highly complex and thus highly unpredictable. The PSI after World War II was a classic case of a party operating in a highly complex electoral arena, due to the presence of a competitor (the PCI) with an enormous attraction for its working-class electorate. This complexity increased after the PSDI's schism (1947), the latter becoming a rightist competitor able to appeal to the urban and rural socialist petit bourgeoisie (the second genetic hunting ground of the Socialist Party, the workers constituting its first). It should be noted that while the PSI had formidable competitors both to its left and to its right, the PCI's electoral arena was much simpler; it had only one competitor to the right (the PSI) and this competitor was organizationally weaker.

The aforementioned theory sustains that environmental complexity acts on the level of unpredictability, making the organization more complex and thus destabilizing it (through the increase of boundary personnel). In adapting this theory to a different perspective, we must admit that this is only one perhaps marginal aspect of the problem. Environmental complexity – defined in terms of number and competitor attraction capacity – doesn't destabilize the organization much by increasing its internal complexity. Instead it directly threatens its identity (which depends on the control exercized over its hunting ground). If a confessional party loses part of its religious electorate to a new religious party, the result is more than an electoral defeat because the party's very identity is at stake. The party can bear the loss of a portion of its secular electorate better than that of a smaller part of its religious electorate. The first loss only calls into question electoral strategy; the second throws the organization's identity into question. Analogously, a workers party can more easily stand a loss in its bourgeois electorate than in its worker electorate.

The competitor's attack on the party's identity destabilizes the organization because it impairs its ability to distribute collective incentives and thus raises doubts about the leadership's credibility (i.e. legitimacy). Environmental uncertainty due to complexity favors divisions and instability in the dominant coalition, providing ammunition to the internal minorities.

When complexity (of the environment) is very high the environment destabilizes the organization creating political in-fighting among the various internal groups; loss of identity reduces the dominant coalition's control over the distribution of collective incentives.

Complexity and instability of the electoral arena therefore produce divisions within the party. Crossing certain thresholds, however, opposite effects may be produced – the party may become more unified. If the electoral arena becomes very complex (many competitors attractive to the same voters) or the environment becomes excessively turbulent (considerable instability due to extreme electoral fluidity), the arena automatically becomes hostile to the organization; members are then likely to stick closely to the leaders, eliminating internal minority maneuverability. This hypothesis is supported by various studies of the strong cohesion at work in very competitive electoral arenas.[14] We can therefore postulate the existence of a curvilinear relation between environmental uncertainty and organizational stability. A simple and/or semi-placid environment shouldn't put much pressure on the organization; this facilitates its stability and allows its dominant coalition to significantly control the party's internal division. Destabilizing pressures become stronger as the environment becomes more complex and/or unstable. Beyond a certain threshold, extreme complexity and instability translate into hostility (threat to survival); this leads to a new party stabilization and increased cohesion of its dominant coalition.

An interesting example is the German Liberal Party (FDP) when – divided into a moderate and a progressive faction in the fifties and sixties – it faced serious challenges: exclusion from government after the formation of the Great Coalition (1966–9) and a progressive loss of electoral consensus which brought it dangerously close to the electoral cut-off point of 5 per cent. Faced with an extreme environmental hostility threatening its survival, the party reacted with a radical turnover of its leadership (involving the victory of the internal left), an increase in cohesion and stability of the dominant coalition, and a considerable strengthening of the organization.[15]

We shall conclude here with two observations. Firstly, the distinction between simple/complex and stable/unstable environments is only analytical. It functions to distinguish complementary facets of the same problem; although different possible combinations are always possible, the most probable ones are those we have just stated. The presence or absence of competitors affects the electoral fluidity which, in turn, increases the probability of competitors emerging.

Secondly, the role of the level of institutionalization should never be forgotten in a discussion of the effects of environmental pressure on organizations. As we have maintained, the more highly institution-

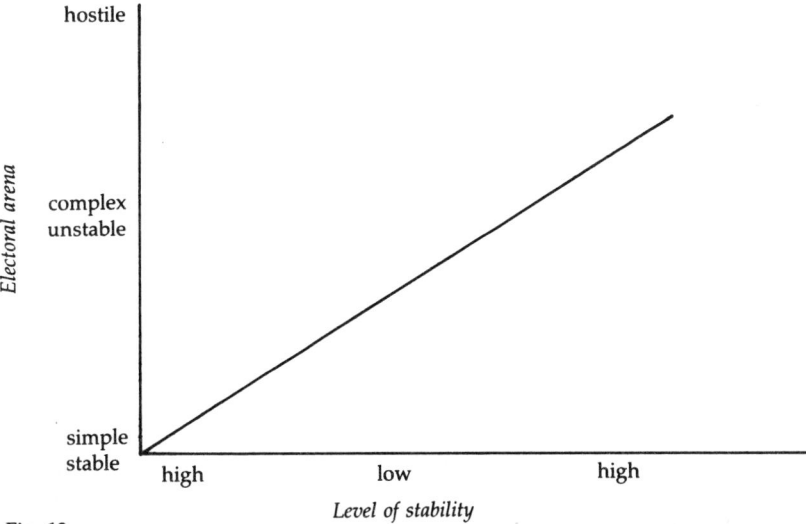

Fig. 12

```
           hostile  |
                    |
                    |
                    |                              /
   Electoral arena  |                         /
          complex   |                    /
          unstable  |               /
                    |          /
                    |      /
                    |   /
           simple   |/
           stable   |_____
                     high          low          high
                            Level of stability
```

alized a party, the fewer the effects of environmental pressure. Strong institutionalization functions, within certain limits, to reduce uncertainty. The stronger the institutionalization, the more the party is able to control the electoral arena, both by increasing stability (e.g. through the creation of a vast "belonging" electorate by means of a political sub-culture) and reducing complexity (strong institutionalization discourages the emergence of competitors). One could thus jump to the conclusion that a system of parties which are strong institutions *must* correspond to a simple or semi-placid electoral arena, and vice-versa. In other words, one could conclude that it is *only* level of institutionalization which determines the characteristics of the electoral arena. This would probably be the case if party arenas were not numerous and interdependent.[16] The electoral arena is influenced by and influences many other party arenas. This interdependence among arenas is the main source of environmental change; changes in interest group physiognomy or in state bureaucracy, for example, and consequent changes in the terms of exchange in these or other party arenas, affect all other arenas, including the electoral one. Even strong institutions can only control their own environments up to a certain point. Latent imperialism, i.e. the aggressive strategy of environmental colonization, therefore only protects a strong institution up to a certain point. Not only because this strategy elicits aggressive reactions from organizations which feel threatened, but also because the interdependence among arenas (and their high number) makes the environment uncontrollable even for a strong institution.[17]

These observations remind us that it would be a grave error to examine *only* electoral arena characteristics when discussing party–environment relations. Parties operate in many arenas, and their enumeration requires *ad hoc* investigation. Effects of a complex and unstable electoral arena can thus always be neutralized by or combined with pressures from different arenas.

Electoral and parliamentary arenas: interdependence

The parliamentary arena is an autonomous source of environmental pressure. Institutional constraints structuring the arena (e.g. the parliament's level of institutionalization, parliamentary regulations, etc.), the distribution of power among the various parliamentary groups, and the type of party represented are all factors affecting the exchange processes each party establishes in this arena with other parties. We shall limit ourselves to considering only one aspect: the way interdependence between electoral and parliamentary arenas affect internal party order. Generally speaking, we can examine both (1) a party's relations in each of the two arenas in terms of exchange with other organizations, and (2) the interdependence between the two arenas: exchanges in one arena condition and are conditioned by exchanges in the other.[18] It is obvious that there is an interdependence between the electoral and the parliamentary arenas: whatever the mediation of the type of electoral system (and its possible over-representative or under-representative effects on the parties),[19] the number of parliamentary seats controlled depends on the number of votes attained. The number of seats affects the relations among parties (i.e. governmental options, practicable strategies, etc.). An oppositional party, for example, that acquires enough seats to form a parliamentary group has an incomparably higher choice of action than one that does not.

In the preceding chapter we mentioned that electoral size can affect party organizations. We can now say that it *indirectly* influences the relation between the organization and its environment. We must distinguish here between parties with "coalition" or "blackmail" potential and those without.[20] If the party's electoral size is too small to condition other parties, parliamentary tactics and strategies, the party will be politically irrelevant. This probably has negative effects on its organizational size as well. Since it is politically irrelevant and remains so for a long time, the initial enthusiasm dies down, many active members leave, size drops or stagnates, and the chance to cross the "survival threshold" (which would permit institutionalization) disappears. We can thus hypothesize that failure to develop "coalition potential" because of insufficient electoral size, reinforces the vicious cycle of sectarianism typical of parties below the survival threshold.

The triangular relation among electoral size, party relations with the environment (first and foremost within the parliamentary arena), and organizational consequences, is complex and largely unexplored. We shall analyze only one important aspect. One might suggest that variations in electoral size (producing variations in parliamentary power relations and thus affecting the available political options), affect the cohesion and stability of the party's dominant coalition. In particular, the *number* of political options a party has in any legislature is *also* a function of its electoral size. Our hypothesis is that the greater the number of possible parliamentary alliances, the greater the choice of styles of opposition ("hard," "soft," etc.),[21] and the greater the party's internal tension. If there are many parliamentary alternatives, there are likely to be just as many groups within the party proposing different political strategies. The party's parliamentary arena is complex, putting a destabilizing pressure on the party. On the contrary, when a party – due to a small electoral size – has few practicable parliamentary alternatives, its parliamentary arena is "simple" and exerts little or no destabilizing pressure. This happens, for instance, when a party has no alternative to "total opposition to the system," other than that of accepting, on conditions entirely dictated by its partners, participation in a coalition government. We shall illustrate this with an example from the SPD's history during the Imperial period.

Until 1884, *Fraktion*, the SPD's parliamentary group, was quite marginalized in the Reichstag, i.e. could not influence parliamentary games. It limited itself to using parliament as a tribune for its socialist propaganda. In 1884 it gained a significant electoral success (9.7 per cent of the vote as opposed to 6.1 per cent in 1881) and put twenty-four deputies in parliament:

The election stands as a turning point, not only for election increases, but also for the policies of the party in a deeper sense. The quantitative changes implied some qualitative changes. For the first time, in the twenty-year life of the political labor movement, the party's deputies were in a position where they could possibly affect the outcome of Reichstag voting. This was true, not merely because of their twenty-four seats, but because the parties on which Bismarck could rely had again failed to achieve an absolute majority. The possibility emerged therefore that the Social Democrats could become a factor in the parliamentary bargaining for votes, especially when Bismarck's opposition needed support on close issues. In addition, with twenty-four deputies, the party leaders sensed a responsibility to their own electorate, to consider to what extent they were obligated to pursue a positive policy in the Reichstag rather than their usual intransigent opposition.[22]

The 1884 electoral success thus allowed the SPD to leap qualitatively from a sect to a party, acquiring "blackmailing" and "coalition" potentials. Its prior situation, permitting only one strategy (uncompromising opposition) gave way to one which offered many options: uncompromising opposition, limited cooperation with bourgeois parties, and so on. This cooperational strategy was spear-headed by the "moderates" (parliamentarians) whose number had grown because of the elections. At the same time, there was a new openness towards the SPD in the country. State repression through the antisocialist laws then in vigor temporarily diminished, leading to a decrease in environmental hostility. On the one hand, the parliamentary arena had become more complex: before 1884 there was only a single practicable strategy (intransigent opposition), afterwards there were numerous choices. The radicals proposed to continue the "no compromise" strategy, the moderates a positive strategy of cooperation, and Bebel eventually adopted a more ambiguous strategy, neither frontal opposition nor open collaboration. On the other hand, the environmental hostility had diminished. The combination of the two ushered in a phase of very severe intra-organizational conflict. A crisis exploded in 1884 when Bismarck proposed state financing for steam navigation. It split the Social Democrats because the strengthening of the merchant marine was perceived as a further step of German colonialism. *Fraktion*'s more moderate fringe supported the measure because it foresaw possible advantages for employment. The radicals violently opposed it because they considered it an attempt to reinforce Germany's imperialistic tendencies. The conflict within *Fraktion* was fierce, and discipline threatened to break down. Radicals and moderates adopted opposing stances. Its deputy, Ignazio Auer stated that:

The Socialist Workers Party is not a sect in which the members are sworn to the letter, but a political party in which there is room, as there must be, for different opinions on subordinate points. . . . That touched the fundamental issue of the whole crisis, involving more than the steamship subsidy itself. Were the Social Democrats willing to recognize the full implications of the fact that their movement was changing from a single minded protest movement to a modern parliamentary political party? Auer and the other moderates were prepared to follow these implications. For the radicals, however, it was a painful transformation, because they could not overcome their ambivalent attitude toward parliamentarism.[23]

The crisis was resolved through a compromise, but conflict between radicals and moderates continued (the next crisis exploded over the problem of political control of the "Sozialdemokrat," the party's clandestine organ) until the St Gall Congress (1887) after the disastrous electoral results. In this period (1884–7), Bebel tried to discourage a flight-to-the-right by moderate parliamentarians, but at the same time adopted reformist strategies, and bargained with bourgeois parties to obtain concessions for the working class. The radicals' polemic against Bebel was particularly violent at that time.

After 1886, the political situation changed again. The anti-socialist laws were stiffly applied by Bismarck (e.g. Bebel, Auer and Vollmar were arrested that year). The environment once again became very hostile for the SPD. In the 1887 elections the SPD won a still higher percentage of the vote (from 9.7 per cent to 10.1 per cent), but suffered a decisive loss of seats (from 24 to 11). The party's coalition and blackmail potentials were drastically reduced: the parliamentary arena once again became relatively simple as there were very few parliamentary options available. This – combined with the renewal of repression – "solidified" the organization, increasing the cohesion and the stability of its dominant coalition (Bebel definitively consolidated his power at this time). In the new parliamentary situation:

The small delegation posed some disadvantages but this did not disappoint Bebel. A large delegation, as the preceding years had shown, was difficult to control. If the Social Democrats had won thirty seats, then Bebel thought, they would have had at least "20 little Statesmen" with which to contend. With a small group, Bebel could look forward to his own control of the Fraktion as soon as he had completed his prison term.[24]

Opposition and competition: the politics of alliance

An environment with competitors is complex and therefore unpredictable. A party's leaders tend to take on an even more hostile and aggressive stance towards competitors than they do towards their official opposition. The history of the relationship between socialists and communists in different countries is a long sequence of fierce polemics ("class betrayal," "social-fascism," "totalitarianism," etc.) interrupted by brief moments of reconciliation. This is not accidental; it corresponds, rather, to the parties fundamental needs for stability. The competitor in laying claim to another party's hunting ground, threatens the latter's identity and destabilizes it; its dominant coalition's only defense is to be hostile. It must deny the competitor's claim to the hunting ground in order to preserve its identity (both in reference to the hunting ground itself – the party's social base – and to the party members). Consequently, an alliance between two competing parties is likely to threaten both parties' identities. The paradoxical effect – contradicting a well-known theory on coalitions[25] – is that the most stable alliances take place among *opponents* (ideologically distant) while the least stable take place among *competitors* (ideologically similar).

Another consequence is that, level of institutionalization held constant, a dominant coalition's stability and cohesion is greater if the party operates against all other competing parties (whether in government or in the opposition), than if it operates in a coalition with competitors. The party can only stem the destabilizing pressure of competitors by avoiding coalitions with them. This in part explains the traditional instability of the DC's dominant coalition which constantly governs with different partial competitors.[26] It can also explain why serious tensions shook the Labour Party during the government experiment (with external support from a competitor party, the Liberals) from 1929–31, whereas during the Attlee government (having an absolute Labour majority) its cohesion was not impaired.[27] Other examples are how the SFIO's dominant coalition – the Blum–Faure axis which had carried the party for fifteen years – dissolved when the SFIO entered government with the Popular Front and the support of its competitor, the PCF; the serious conflicts in the British Conservative Party during its coalition with the Liberals (1915–21);[28] and the conflicts which arose in the SPD at the 1912 elections due to the shared ballot with the Liberals.[29]

In summary, a party's stability depends on its ability to defend its own identity. Identity is, however, threatened by the existence of competitors; and it is even more endangered if an alliance is made with them. Alliances between competing parties threaten both parties' stability, and thus increase environmental unpredictability. This, in turn, makes the alliance all the more precarious. In order for two ideologically similar parties to maintain a stable alliance at least one of the following conditions must be satisfied:

(1) The two parties are only competitors in appearance: though their symbol systems (i.e. the ideological goals defining their domains) are similar, they appeal to electorates which are sociologically and politically distinct. An example of this could be that of an alliance between a socialist party (whose hunting ground is working class and white collar) and a "new left" party (whose hunting ground is students and intellectuals of radical orientation).

(2) One of the partners in the alliance is too weak and thus incapable of attracting the other's hunting ground. In this case, the stronger party's identity is not threatened: its environment is relatively simple and environmental uncertainty is minimal and easily controlled. The weak party, due to its extreme vulnerability, finds itself in a very hostile environment (maximum complexity and instability). The curvilinear relationship between environmental uncertainty and

organizational stability insures that its dominant coalition will tend to be cohesive and stable. Neither partner being threatened (though for opposite reasons), the alliance will remain stable. This was in part true of the "unity of action pact" between communists and socialists in Italy during the Cold War. The PSI's weakness wasn't so much a numerical problem (i.e. due to electoral weakness), as a more general condition of competition with the PCI: in times of acute polarization during the Cold War, the latter was the authentic representative of "the home of socialism" (the Soviet Union) and the PSI had no choice but to accept a subordinate position. Its environment was for the same reasons so hostile that it stabilized its dominant coalition (the Nenni–Morandi alliance).[30]

This reasoning explains the traditional difficulties in alliances and the recurrent conflicts between European socialist and communist parties.

It also explains why the most stable governmental coalitions occur traditionally in consociative democracies,[31] i.e. in "segmented" societies in which the parties have non-overlapping electoral followings (Verzuiling, Pillars). These parties may be opponents but not competitors. The government coalitions are stable because while the opponents are obliged to cohabit, competition among them is structurally impossible.[32] The end of the consociative alliance's stability comes when (as happened in Holland) segments (or political subcultures) erode and electoral fluidity grows, permitting parties to become competitors.[33]

We should, however, recall that the level of institutionalization of allied competitive parties is an important intervening variable. A strongly institutionalized party can defend its stability better than a weakly institutionalized party despite an alliance with a competitor. Thus an alliance between competitors who are both strongly institutionalized can be stable. This corresponds to the case described by Wilson of the coalition of two organizations, both of which are autonomous and dispose of substantial resources.[34] It is, however, very rare for two equally institutionalized organizations to ally. Alliances thus inevitably destabilize the less institutionalized organizations by putting additional de-institutionalizing pressures on them (thus increasing their internal tension) and dividing their dominant coalitions. The pressure at that point to break up the alliance in order to safeguard party stability becomes irresistible.

As opposed to temporary *ad hoc* convergences, stable alliances are very rare in politics. The main reason for this is not "bad faith" on the part of leaders, but is rather the environmental pressures brought to bear on the organizations.

12
Political and bureaucratic professionalism

In the course of this book we have referred to party bureaucracy and level of bureaucratization, meaning by the former the set of salaried bureaucrats, and by the latter the number of bureaucrats out of the organization's total number of members. Discussing the case of charismatic parties (in chapter 8), we pointed out that a rather clear division of labor, formally defined spheres of competence, and recognizable hierarchies are proper to bureaucracies.

This brief definition has, nonetheless, enabled us to focus on important aspects of differences between parties. Differences in level of bureaucratization (i.e. in number of bureaucrats) served – though combined with other factors – as the backbone of our distinction between strong and weak institutions. A highly institutionalized party, possessing an extensive central (national) bureaucracy (in addition to its other characteristics), can achieve autonomy from its environment as well as high internal structural coherence. Autonomy is correlated with level of bureaucratization, as it is one of the properties of bureaucratic structures to attempt to "eliminate or control all extraorganizational influences on the behavior of its members. Bureaucratic characteristics are designed to close off the organization from unwanted influences, insofar as this is possible."[1] Structural coherence (i.e. the level of systemness) is, in turn, correlated with level of bureaucratization because of the centralizing tendencies inherent in bureaucratic development: in a strong bureaucracy the "center" possesses a very efficient tool with which to control the organizational periphery.

The role of bureaucracy is thus central to the analytic framework developed here. The brief definition used up until now sufficed for the goals we had set ourselves. Once we examine the concept more stringently, we encounter intricate problems which are very confused in the existing literature. Ostrogorski, Weber, and Michels aside, bureaucracy is surely the most neglected theme in studies on parties. Little (and no comparative) research has been done on party bureaucracy (e.g. on relations between different hierarchical levels, attitudes of bureaucrats, etc.), and the very number of paid bureaucrats in most parties is unknown – partly because of the reticence of party leaders to furnish information on the make-up of the bureaucratic apparati. This is due to the generally negative connotation attributed to the term bureaucracy[2] as well as to the public's bad image of the professional politician (of which the bureaucrat is but a particularly significant sub-species). The following analyses aim, on the one hand, at a conceptual clarification of the phenomenon, and at a framing of the problem of party bureaucracy within a typology of political professionalism, on the other. As in the preceding chapters (on size, complexity, and environmental influence), the hypotheses and generalizations formulated cannot be, for the reasons already explained, corroborated by sufficient empirical data.

Political and bureaucratic professionalism

Full time bureaucrats usually conform to the prototype of the "political professional," he who "lives politics," according to the Weberian definition.[3] Political "bureaucrat" and "professional politician" are generally used synonymously. But the bureaucrat – a full-time administrator stably employed in a political organization – is only one possible incarnation of political professionalism. A political professional is simply one who dedicates most, if not all of his work activity to politics and finds there his main source of sustenance. A party leader, for example, is a political professional (his political commitment certainly does not leave room for substantial extra-political work activity), but is rarely a bureaucrat. He should rather be seen as an entrepreneur (according to the view of political leadership laid out in this book). The distinction between these two types of political professionals – bureaucrats and entrepreneurs – is but one of the many we can provide.

A second distinction must be made between bureaucrats and experts, between administrators specialized in the functioning of the party "machine," and "professionals" (in accordance with the technical use of this term by the sociology of professions) – people who have special extra-political and extra-party skills. Eliassen and Pedersen,[4] in their examination of the professionalization of parliamentarians after the success of mass parties, point out the ambiguous and multi-valent usage of the expression "political professionalism" in the literature. Such expressions often indicate two rather different things, for example two different types of "professionalization." One type is that of the replacement of the "cadre" party's notables by the mass party's bureaucrats, and political professionalism is taken here to be synonymous with party bureaucracy. But professionalization is just as often used to indicate a very different process: the progressive replacement of parliamentary personnel from aristocratic and entrepreneurial backgrounds (in liberal and conservative parties) and from working-class backgrounds (in socialist parties) by new highly-educated personnel of upper-middle class extraction; people who are mainly employed in typical jobs of the upcoming classes created by expansion due to state intervention (e.g. teachers, public managers, etc.). This phenomenon is generally explained as the effect of increasingly technical nature of political decisions which require "expert" skills far more than in the past. In this second sense, professionalization actually signifies an increase of the parliamentary–technical component with an intensive educational background in all sectors in which the state intervenes. Guttsmann,[5] for example, in his discussion of the transformations in the social composition of the British parliament, uses the term "professionalization," but it is clear that, in a system in which neither the Labour parliamentarians nor the Conservatives are party bureaucrats (for in both parties bureaucrats are prohibited from running for public office), the author is using the term in the second sense. Eliassen and Pedersen correctly observe that, to avoid confusion, we must distinguish between two processes which have changed the composition of parliaments in this century: a political professionalization (i.e. the parliamentarization of party bureaucrats) due to mass party mobilization, and an intellectual professionalization (i.e. the parliamentarization of the experts) due to the growing differentiation, complexity and technicality of political decisions. We have brought up this theory in order to show how complex the problem of political professionalism is. The party bureaucrat already appears as only one of the many possible figures within the realm of political professionalism. To draw further distinctions we must now better define the concept of bureaucracy, and, more specifically, that of party bureaucracy.

Party bureaucracy: definitions

Like so many other concepts frequently used in the social sciences, bureaucracy is defined in various ways.[6] Among all the possible meanings attributed to this term only three[7] seem useful – though to differing degrees – in describing bureaucratic phenomena in parties:

(1) The bureaucracy as *administrative component*, the proportion of bureaucrats responsible for the maintenance of the organization to the total membership.[8]
(2) Bureaucracy as an organization whose characteristics are defined by the Weberian ideal-type.
(3) Bureaucracy as the "domination of the bureaucrats."

The first is basically the definition we have used so far to distinguish between strong and weak institutions. We have made some use of the second meaning as well: bureaucracies (e.g. the Conservative Central Office) are characterized by hierarchy, division of labor, standardization of roles, procedures, and at times competency and impartiality. As in Weber's own methodology, some but not all of an ideal-type's components *must* be found in a concrete case (especially hierarchy and division of labor). For a first approximation, a manageable and useful definition of party bureaucracy seems to be that of a body of administrators dedicated to the maintenance of the machine which has at least some features of the Weberian ideal-type. The fact that they are paid bureaucrats with routine administrative functions explains such bureaucratic traits as ritualistic attitudes, risk avoidance, and attachment to the machine itself.[9]

The third definition is less useful. It presupposes that a bureaucratic organization is controlled by its bureaucrats. As we have seen, however, bureaucratic organizations – and even parties – are almost never controlled by bureaucrats but rather by entrepreneurs and managers. Contrary to Michels' contention, policy is shaped more by politicians rather than by bureaucrats even in parties with the highest proportions of bureaucrats.[10] This criticism also mirrors Ostragorski's and Weber's position; they saw bureaucracy as a central factor in modern political parties, but maintained that political leadership could not, nonetheless, be reduced to bureaucracy. Weber admitted that in certain rare cases bureaucrats could run the party, undermining the politicians: Ebert's replacing of Bebel in the second half of the first decade of this century marks the shift – according to Weber – from domination by politicians to domination by bureaucrats in the SPD.[11] In certain cases, the bureaucrats acquire such a dominant role that they become indistinguishable, at the top, from pure politicians. The organizational leadership is usually, in such cases, made up of managers (more oriented towards risk-taking and "profit") and bureaucrats (more concerned with routine, with the maintenance of the machine). But even in these cases, we should distinguish between managers of bureaucratic origin and those of other origins, rather than hypothesize a situation of "domination by bureaucrats." We shall thus retain our previously formulated definition, that of bureaucracy as a body of full-time administrators, dedicated to the maintenance of the organization, which exhibits some (but not necessarily all) features of the Weberian ideal-type. It is, nonetheless, clear that we do not yet have the proper tools at our disposal to understand the dynamic of party organizations' "bureaucratic phenomena."

It is part and parcel of the preceding definition that bureaucrats are *designated*, chosen by the managers and/or by formal examinations, to carry out certain tasks. They must, moreover, concern themselves *exclusively* with administrative activity, with the maintenance of the machine. This is not, however, always true in the case of party bureaucracy.

In certain parties, the bureaucracy actually does fit the definition, for example, in the British Conservative Party and the Labour Party, the bureaucrats are appointed by those at the top, are rigorously excluded from public political activity, and must devote themselves entirely to administrative tasks. In many other parties, however – especially in mass socialist and communist parties – bureaucrats are hired and assigned their different tasks by the leaders, but their designation generally requires further ratification in the form of *election* by the rank and file. They do not dedicate themselves exclusively to administrative activity but also – and sometimes especially – to public activity; they are political leaders who participate in electoral campaigns and in all of the party's internal and external political activities.

There are thus two different types of party bureaucracies – we will call them *executive* and *representative* bureaucracies.[12] The representative character of many parties' bureaucracies depends on the fact that a party is, in a certain sense, a hybrid which combines features of bureaucratic organizations (and thus a system of interests) with those of voluntary associations (and thus a solidarity system). It depends, more specifically, on the fact that selection of leaders at various levels involves two different requisites: that of *functionality* and that of *legitimation*. As has been observed:

It should be emphasized that the process of leadership selection through political parties is considerably complicated in modern industrial societies. In contrast to bureaucratic organizations, where personnel recruitment can be oriented nearly exclusively on the functional requirements of positions and offices to be filled, the political party as a voluntary association has in addition to secure the democratic legitimacy of leadership selection, mainly through the competitive electoral process.[13]

There are therefore two types of bureaucracy. The one corresponds in large measure to the administrative component of other organizations (the executive bureaucracy) while the other is typical and exclusive of parties and trade unions (the representative bureaucracy).

The difference between the two can be interpreted as the difference in the systems of control the bureaucracy has to undergo. In the case of the executive bureaucracy the system of control (as in the Weberian ideal type) is unique: the hierarchy. The executive bureaucrats are designated their tasks by the political leaders. They fully correspond to the figure of the administrator. The representative bureaucracy simultaneously undergoes two control structures: hierarchy and (afterwards) electoral control. This results from the fact that the representative bureaucrat is not only an administrator, but a political leader as well. The placement of the representative bureaucrat is therefore ambiguous, and indicative of the more general ambiguity (from the organizational standpoint) of parties. He must respond to his superiors for his actions and decisions, but is also periodically judged by the rank and file. The role of this second control system (namely electoral) must not, of course, be exaggerated. The use of representative bureaucracy always coincides with clear predomination of the leadership (e.g. in the SPD, PCI, and PCF), i.e. with situations in which the nomination of bureaucrats ensures the dominant coalition's control over the party, while their "representativeness" (electoral investiture) has the function of legitimating their role.[14] In such parties, bureaucrats are far more docile tools of the "top" than representatives of the "base." Electoral investiture (easily manipulated by a cohesive dominant coalition) only reinforces the leaders' positions *vis-à-vis* the rank and file activists. In the PCI, for example, the representative bureaucracy runs the overwhelming majority of the federal executive organs,[15] and its delegates form a majority in the national congresses.[16] In other words, the bureaucrat who owes his career perspectives to his superiors' decisions (i.e. the national leaders), also guides the federations and is "chosen" by the rank and file to judge these same superiors at the congresses.

The importance of electoral control must thus not be over-estimated, but not under-estimated either. For the same mechanism stops the (designated) bureaucrat from "snubbing" electoral ratification. Excessive difficulties on these occasions could seriously hurt his reputation *vis-à-vis* his superior by demonstrating his inability to establish a relation of trust with rank and file activists. A solid relation of trust, on the other hand, strengthens his control over a zone of organizational uncertainty (the leaders must take into account his success among the activists).

A favorable position in vertical exchange relations (with rank and file activists), in other words, helps him in subsequent exchanges with the leaders. It is this same mechanism which – because of its ambiguity – pushes the representative bureaucrats to do everything in their power to keep the two superimposed control systems (the hierarchical and electoral) from colliding, and concretely motivates them to gain the base's consensus around the political strategy (decided by their superiors).

We conclude this discussion with the remark that while there are conspicuous differences between executive and representative bureaucracies, they should not be overestimated. The distinction between the two types of bureaucracy, like that between politics and administration, is fuzzy, and the dividing line between them constantly shifts.

This is firstly because even the representative bureaucrat – albeit a politician as well – must dedicate a good deal of his activity to administration, to the maintenance of the organizational machine. The representative bureaucrat often internalizes values and attitudes which are more consistent with the role of an administrator engaged in routine activity than with that of a leader engaged in managerial activity.

Secondly, even executive bureaucrats sometimes take an active part (though limited to the party's internal life) in political debates, and cannot permit themselves (if they are to work efficiently) conflictual relations with volunteer activists.[17] Finally, aside from these pure forms of bureaucracy – namely, executive and representative – there are also many mixed forms: e.g. the CDU's bureaucracy which unites political bosses and simple employees.[18] Both executive and representative bureaucracies are *tools* in the hands of the party's dominant coalition. From the point of view of degree of institutionalization, it thus makes little difference whether we are dealing with one or the other. Electoral control systems aside, there is practically no difference between conservative regional agents and upper-level bureaucrats of communist federations.

Bureaucracy and political attitudes

Strong bureaucracy leads to the centralization of decision-making. But it has also been said (in chapter 10) that a strong bureaucracy implies many hierarchical levels and thus leads to a decentralization of administrative decisions (or of routine). A highly bureaucratized party combines high centralization of governmental (political) decision-making with just as high a decentralization of administrative decision-making. What might not appear entirely clear is why delegation of authority in the administrative domain does not exert pressure towards decentralization in the political domain as well (especially since the dividing line between the two is hazy).

It would, in fact, seem logical that someone with a good deal of decisional autonomy in a certain domain could easily use this autonomy to acquire decisional power in others. But this only rarely happens because of a phenomenon already discussed (in chapter 2): the bureaucrat's usually highly disadvantageous position in exchange relations with the national leaders. To become a party bureaucrat is generally an irreversible, definitive choice. Such a bureaucrat cannot easily find an equivalent job on the external market; the relative unsubstitutability of the selective incentives he enjoys renders him highly susceptible to leaders' pressures: job security plays a decisive role here.[19] Bureaucrats can only make their careers within an organization; this explains their conformity, their subordination to their leaders' decisions, and by consequence, the highly centralized authority which always accompanies high levels of bureaucratization, and the centripetal character of the "opportunity structures." A strong bureaucratic apparatus also explains the generally stable and cohesive nature of highly bureaucratized parties' dominant coalitions. As selective incentives are rather unsubstitutable, the dominant coalition has an advantageous position in vertical exchanges with bureaucrats; and its position is all the more advantageous in horizontal power relations, for example, *vis-à-vis* minority elites. Controlling a strong bureaucratic apparatus gives the dominant coalition an advantage analogous to that enjoyed by governing parties in their relations with opposition parties: having a series of resources at its disposal that its opponents lack.[20] But the relative unsubstitutability of selective incentives is not the only factor which explains why party bureaucracy is a docile tool in the leaders' hands, for the bureaucrat is himself a "believer" (the distinction between believers and careerists is, as we have seen, only analytic), i.e. he too benefits from identity incentives. In highly institutionalized parties, a bureaucratic career often requires a long apprenticeship. Among the communist bureaucrats interviewed by Hellman, the majority came from the ranks of the youth federations, and 70 per cent had gone to communist party schools.[21] Many studies have shown that organizational loyalty depends as much on the time spent within the organization as on the difficulty of career advancement.[22]

Secondly, bureaucrats in all parties have, at least until recently, been recruited from the less well-to-do classes. The increased status mobility of communist and socialist bureaucrats – in and thanks to their respective parties – usually increases their gratitude and loyalty to the party. Analogously, the psychological identification of lower-class British Conservative agents – at the beginning of the century – with the upper classes explains their fidelity to the organizational leadership.[23]

It is the combination of selective and identity incentives which cannot easily be found on the external market which explains why even a representative bureaucrat who carries out political functions may be unable to create favorable power relations with the leaders and to block the centralization of decisional authority. It also explains why he often tends to be *de facto* more of an administrator than a politician. It explains, for example, bureaucrats' tendencies – detected in the PCI's strong federations by Hellman – to translate political problems into administrative ones.[24] It even explains the markedly apolitical character of medium and low-level bureaucrats' behavior in the SPD after 1905. In the SPD:

> The men who were selected to serve as secretaries would have to enjoy a reputation for neutrality, for being above the intra-party struggles. This qualification could only reinforce the "unpolitical" character which the secretary's regular tasks might impose in the first instance. When almost every new issue in political life unleashed a factional struggle within the party, the bureaucracy tended to recoil from "politics." The principle positive task of the bureaucracy, to build up the party for electoral victories, necessarily involved a negative attitude toward any pressure for a change in tactic which would either divide the party or alienate the non-socialist voter. What the party functionary wanted above all else was peace and unity in the organization.[25]

The centralization of authority in highly bureaucratized parties thus depends on the low substitutability of the selective and identity incentives enjoyed by bureaucrats. But changes in market conditions can at least partly modify this situation. The recent increase in highly educated bureaucrats of middle-class extraction and decrease in bureaucrats of working-class extraction[26] in the PCI seems to destroy the apparatus' solidity, unity and docility, and not simply because this change creates problematic relations between the new type of bureaucrats and the old activist rank and file, but also because this change significantly modifies bureaucracy–national leader relations. Although alternative possibilities decrease as more and more time is invested in making one's career, young high school graduates with networks of personal connections due to their middle-class family origins succumb much less than the old bureaucrats of working-class extraction to pressure to conform; and not having acquired mobility the former are also less "grateful" to the party. This turn-over in bureaucratic structure thus favors organizational de-institutionalization and loss of cohesion and stability in the dominant coalition: because, for the individual bureaucrat at this point loyalty to one of the internal competing groups may become more important than loyalty to the party.[27]

Experts and hidden professionals

Having identified the party bureaucrat, we must now differentiate his role from that of other professionals and in particular from that of the "expert," the professional in the strict sense. But even here we must reckon with the persistently ambiguous jargon used in social science, for example, the failure to distinguish between the different types of political professionalism, and the unclear and equivocal distinction in organizational literature between bureaucrats and professionals. According to the textbooks bureaucrats and professionals fill occupational roles which have at least one thing in common: they both require specialized knowledge (though of different types) but the professional's training generally takes longer than that of the bureaucrat. What is, however, important here is the different *control systems* to which bureaucrats and professionals are submitted. The bureaucrat's control system is hierarchy, i.e. subordination to superiors; the professional's takes the form of "peer judgement" with well-defined evaluation criteria (professional ethics).[28]

It is clear, however, that this distinction concerns bureaucrats who work (by definition) within the organization, on the one hand, and independent professionals (lawyers, notaries, engineers, architects, etc.) – i.e. those working in the liberal professions – on the other. The distinction becomes more complicated when we want to separate out bureaucrats and professionals in organizations; in such cases, the dividing line is usually between *line* roles (bureaucrats) and *staff* roles (professionals). But what really differentiates the two are still the control systems. Executive and representative bureaucracies differ in that while the former is subject to hierarchical control, the latter is subject both to hierarchical and electoral control. Similarly, the professional – the expert possessing specialized knowledge – is subject to a dual control system composed of hierarchy and peer judgement (especially of independent peers).

In the case of representative bureaucracy, the bureaucrat's main problem is to keep the two control systems from working against each other. In the same way, professionals are subject to dilemmas and pressures due to the dual control systems which take the form of role conflicts, problems of "cross-cutting loyalties," etc., and which make their professional position intrinsically unstable.

Let's now apply this reasoning to parties. Take the case of a full-time paid economist in a party research office. It is probable that he will experience role conflicts and dilemmas related to the dual control system. In so far as he is an employee of the organization, he will have to restrain himself from publicly criticizing his party's political–economic positions. But in so far as he is a professional, he cannot afford to lose face *vis-à-vis* his peers, namely, independent economists (since, for example, an eventual teaching position at a university could be more attractive and prestigious than working for the party).

The difference between bureaucrats and (staff) professionals should not, of course, be exaggerated. Abstractly speaking, the difference between the economist and a bureaucrat is clearly a difference between *staff* and *line* roles. But the analogy between parties and firms only holds up to a certain point. In a firm the staff offices and line offices are quite recognizable, but in a party this is not always the case. For example, in many cases a party journalist is not a professional, i.e. is not subject to a dual control system; he is often a bureaucrat – his working for the party's paper is just a step in his bureaucratic career. If the "research office" economist is politically talented and lucky he may be elected to parliament. Though he will probably continue to work primarily on economic problems, line–staff distinctions become problematic.

The distinction between bureaucrats and professionals is often unclear in other types of organizations as well. The rigid distinctions (which I have accepted up until now) between them correspond to "idealized models" of the two organizational components:

> the empirical studies which decompose the Weberian model into its constituent dimensions . . . tend to treat professionalism as a constellation of variables with attitudinal referents, some of which can be sealed. The evidence at which these studies arrive challenges the notion of a *global* conflict between professionalization and bureaucratization . . . These predictable findings indirectly confirm the large common historical origins of both modes of work organization; they reinforce, that is, Stincheombe's hypothesis that bureaucracy and professionalism are two sub-types of a larger category – that of rational administration . . .[29]

Empirical research thus seems to indicate only partial incompatibility between bureaucratic and professional roles; more often we find balance and mutual support: many bureaucrats acquire professional attitudes and many professionals acquire bureaucratic attitudes.[30] The intrinsic instability of professional roles within the organization depend on their ambiguous character:

> For a large category of professionals whose concept of career is *inseparable* from technobureaucratic advancement, "professionalism" represents an ambiguous alternative: a "professional career" *within* the organization is *a sign of career immobility*. It can be perceived as such, or not. Professionals like engineers and accountants *already* have a stable status in the wider society:

their credentials and degrees, guaranteed by professional institutions, in theory give them relative assurance of their "status continuity in a labor market." What they expect to *gain* in the organizational context is, precisely, technobureaucratic power: the "professional ladder," however, provides neither control of resources nor participation in central decision-making.[31]

These observations can also explain why professional roles are intrinsically unstable in parties: to make his career in the organization, a professional *must* become a bureaucrat (or a party representative in a public elected office), shifting from a staff to a line role – otherwise he will sooner or later be forced to look for a better job outside the party. Another factor complicating the picture and obscuring the distinction between bureaucrats and professionals is the consistent quota – especially in government parties dedicated to patronage and colonization of the public apparatus – of hidden or clandestine political professionalism. We are dealing with a type of *sui generis* professional politician which is widespread in the Italian DC,[32] and the Austrian Social Democratic Party,[33] and in many other parties. Many activists appear in the party's official roll as administrators who serve in public or semi-public organs. Often they are part of the party's hidden professionalism. Many activists obtain external jobs, usually in public (government run) organisms, thanks to the party's help. Often these jobs are "sinecures," which leave the activists free to work almost full-time for the party without weighing down the party's budget. The fact that the growth of state intervention has led to a great deal of hidden professionalism explains many of the difficulties encountered in empirical analyses of political professionalism.

Bureaucratization and professionalism

Although the grey area around the distinction between bureaucrats and (staff) professionals needs to be articulated, they do constitute, however, different professional figures. It is thus not equivalent to say that a party is undergoing bureaucratization or professionalization. Bureaucratization implies a growth of a specific type of political professionals, i.e. administrators who are devoted to the organization's maintenance and are in a highly disadvantageous position in relations with national leaders because of the relative unsubstitutability of the selective and identity incentives they enjoy. Professionalization on the other hand, involves the increase in the number of experts employed in the organization (or recruited with short-term contracts). Professionalization is the distinguishing feature of the organizational change political parties are currently undergoing; it implies the decreasing importance of the old bureaucracy and the increasing importance of the staff. Accentuated professionalization processes can lead to conspicuous alterations (many of which have already come about in American parties)[34] in power relations within parties. As opposed to bureaucratic organizations, professional organizations (or those in which the professional component is very important) tend to be decentralized.[35] Decentralization is due to the fact that the organizational leaders have a harder time controlling specialists than administrators. Staff professionals, unlike bureaucrats, can find work on the external market, and are thus much less easily bought off. The tendential replacement of bureaucrats by professionals should thus reduce centralization of authority and lead to fragmentation of dominant coalitions. Professionalization can, however, also have somewhat different effects. Since the professional tends to be a specialist in a "pure" work relation with the party, i.e. a technician who exchanges professional services with his own political/party clientel, he has less need for more traditional identity incentives. Professionalization can, like other factors, increase the leaders' freedom of movement, by sparing them the onus of identity incentive distribution (and thus from problems of political strategy coherence). In any case, professionalism inevitably encourages – along with the decline of the traditional bureaucratic apparatus – a decrease in party institutionalization.

Executives and professionals: a classification

In the course of this chapter we have discussed many organizational roles which fall under the rubric of political professionalism. And we have seen that the bureaucrat is just one of the many types of political professionals. Party leadership is made up of many different professional types, and Weber's simple distinction between professionals and dilettantes is thus insufficient.[36] There are many different types of professionals, and there are many limit cases between professionals and dilettantes. We can isolate seven fundamental types of political executives, distinguishable on the basis of resources, political style, and degree of professionalness:

(A)   Managers (or political entrepreneurs)
(B)   Notables
(C)   Representative bureaucrats
(D)   Executive bureaucrats
(E)   Staff professionals
(F)   Hidden professionals
(G)   Semi-professionals

(A) Managers

Managers make their appearance with the emergence of modern political parties (in their original form as "cadre" parties). National leaders all have managerial roles, but so do many other professional figures, e.g. the bosses of the former electoral machines in the United States. Of course many types of managers, with many different styles, can emerge. The three most important are leaders with notabilary origins, leaders with bureaucratic-party origins, and charismatic leaders emerging outside of traditional recruitment channels.

(B) Notables

Notables are the typical political "dilettantes" who live off extra-political resources and convert a socio-economic centrality into political power. They were the backbone of the old "cadre" party. Weber's (and Duverger's) prediction that the notables were destined to disappear with the emergence of the mass party was only partly borne out by history. Notables continue to coexist in contemporary parties with political professionalism in its many forms.

(C) Representative bureaucrats

While notables were the figures most tied to "cadre" parties, representative bureaucrats are the prototype of political professionals in the golden age of mass parties. Professionalization processes are bound to lead to the reorganization of their role; although they won't easily eliminate them altogether. They rather create tension between staff professionals and representative bureaucrats, and power struggles between leaders tied to the bureaucracy and leaders who use professional structures.

(D) Executive bureaucrats

Executive bureaucrats, unlike the figures heretofore mentioned, have no managing or leadership position. Professionalization does not create special problems for them – this is evidenced by British parties in which professionalization is already quite advanced.[37] It jeopardizes representative bureaucrats' positions in a more significant way than those of the executive bureaucrats (because even with a high quotient of professionalization, administrative activity dedicated to the maintenance of the organization must be carried out).

(E) Staff professionals

Staff professionals are specialists, technicians, whose role grows in importance as decisions become increasingly technical, education becomes more widespread, and – last but not least – interparty competition changes due to the mass-media (the expert has the task of convincing the public of the "technical" advantages of the party's chosen solutions to various problems). Professionalization involves a growth in the role of the staff, but its effects are more far-reaching. The intrinsic instability of professional roles pushes experts, after a certain time, to abandon professional politics (though not necessarily the party) for more prestigious jobs outside of the organization or to try to attain leadership roles within the party. Professionalization means that elective (and especially public) offices progressively come to be filled by experts in different sectors – Eliasen and Pederson refer to this as "intellectual" professionalization. The "technicians" do not, naturally, supplant the "politicians" (as the technocratic utopians maintain), and the extent of the conflict between bureaucrats and experts must not be exaggerated. The experts simply become political leaders (executives). But their different training, their greater political independence, and the fact that they are executives – who, unlike bureaucrats, do not come from the bottom ranks and have not risen through the ranks of a bureaucratic career – make them quite different from their predecessors.

(F) Hidden professionals

Hidden professionals are inextricably tied to the expansion of intervention by the state and to its colonization on the part of the parties. Hidden professionals – those who nominally work in public or semi-public organizations (at least partly controlled by the party) but who are actually engaged in party politics on a full-time basis – are the most ambiguous of the professionals. They are "pure" politicians dedicated to their political careers, but also have a *sui generis* place within the organization (being neither volunteer activists nor party bureaucrats), and thus experience less pressure to interiorize party values. Their loyalty is primarily *personal* (in relation to single leaders or groups); they are often "pure" careerists without strong identificatory ties with the organization. In certain parties – especially those holding the governmental reins for a long time – they represent a very important percentage of the political personnel.

(G) Semi-professionals

Semi-professionals are also only partly definable, situated as they are between notables and experts.[38] They have always represented a considerable proportion of many parties' parliamentary and local elected personnel, but can be found at other levels and in other organizational areas as well. They are economically independent as they dispose of extra-political incomes and a good deal of free time. Lawyers,[39] university professors, and journalists (as Weber pointed out) must be situated somewhere between professionals and dilettantes. In time, they tend to become professionals.[40] As is the case with experts, i.e. staff professionals, the semi-professional is an intrinsically unstable political role.

To recapitulate, quite a number of different political figures can be found in important and powerful positions in party organizations. A typology of parties' ruling classes going beyond a simple enumeration of professional figures would have to take all of the possible combinations into account.[41] Limiting ourselves to but a few considerations, we can observe that a prevalence of managers (A) and notables (B) corresponds to the (pure) case of weak institutions, while a combination of managers and representative bureaucrats (C) corresponds to the (pure) case of strong institutions. But no party completely coincides with either model, and the different ruling classes thus include many other professional figures, for example, semi-professionals (G), hidden professionals (F), experts (E), etc. If Kirchheimer's theory about the transformation of mass parties into catch-all parties is correct,[42] the evolution of modern political parties would be essentially the result of modification in the ruling classes from A–B combinations (weakly institutionalized, "cadre" parties) to A–C or A–D combinations (highly institutionalized, mass parties) to A–E–G or A–E–F combinations (weakly institutionalized, "catch-all" parties).

Part IV
Organizational change

13
Environmental challenges and elite circulation

We can pose three questions in analyzing the process of organizational change. The first refers to the direction of the change and revolves around its *necessary* or *contingent* character. The second deals with its *degree of intentionality*, and the third with its *origin* – i.e. the exogenous or endogenous nature of its causes.

Evolutionism versus "political development"

In utilizing the classical sociological theory of social change,[1] researchers have usually adopted interpretive schemas according to which organizational "development" follows laws determinable *a priori*. Organizations pass, in this perspective, through definable development phases similar to those of biological organisms (birth, growth, decay, etc.). A typical feature of the evolutionist perspective, for instance, is the idea that organizations tend to increase in size, and thus in internal complexity. This growth leads to a constant increase in the division of labor (differentiation), which in turn increases the need for further coordination (i.e. expanded hierarchy and increased formalization).

Michels' theory of party development is, for instance, evolutionistic. An even more subtle form of evolutionism holds that organizations, pushed by entrepreneurial logic, grow to reinforce their leaders' power and prestige in the widest social context.[2] We have thrown the supposed necessity of this type of evolution into question in the course of this book, demonstrating the existence of organizations without expansive tendencies.

A different perspective can be found in the so-called theories of political development.[3] They take organizational change as the effect of changes in alliances among organizational actors,[4] not as stemming from an organization's necessary development. The directions and modalities of change cannot be established *a priori*, as they are "contingent," not necessary. It follows that: (1) an organization can change in various ways in accordance with alliances formed within it; (2) organizations can undergo different changes. There is no obligatory path to organizational change in this perspective.

Our historical–comparative reconstruction (part II), and the differences we found between the development of specific parties and the ideal-type of organizational evolution (chapters 1 and 9), demonstrate that the notion of political development is far more realistic and persuasive than the evolutionistic perspective. There are many paths to change; the way the organization forms and consolidates (its type of genetic model and modes of institutionalization), the type of environmental pressures, and the way these pressures affect internal power relations determine the path. We do not completely disregard the evolutionary theory, however; the notion that any organization must institutionalize to stay alive (and the essential differences are those of degree of institutionalization) still has certain common points with it.

Intentionality and non-intentionality

The second focus on the dispute about organizational change concerns its degree of intentionality. *Management* theories see the change as the effect of deliberate and conscious choices, while more recent theories maintain that change is the arbitrary result of the organizational dynamic.[5] The managerial formulations have always had an interest in claiming change to be intentional; for only if it is does it make sense to ask what the best means are to arrive at the desired ends. On the contrary, it makes little sense to discuss possible choices if organizational change is the product of uncontrollable factors. The strong point of the thesis of intentionality lies in the empirical observation that many organizational actors have a certain "freedom of action", and that they regularly use it to make choices that affect organizations, modifying some of their characteristics.[6] The thesis of non-intentionality of change is also plausible: above all the observation that the "disfunctions" (or at least what are perceived as such by the organizational actors) produce reactions and choices and they lead to change *only when* they are exceptionally serious, in situations of acute organizational crisis.[7] The leaders, in fact, immediately perceive the need for change, but, given the potential costs (in terms of internal conflict) that organizational change could bring about, they often do nothing.[8] When a crisis finally explodes, their freedom of choice is drastically reduced. This phenomenon (perception of the problem, inaction, and then action with limited maneuverability when the situation has become critical) is the effect of a so-called "resistance to change" manifested by many organizational actors because "any change is dangerous, in that it inevitably throws the [actor's] conditions of the game, his sources of power and his freedom of action into question, modifying or eliminating the zones of uncertainty he controls."[9] Whether organizational change be deliberate or arbitrary, it always has the effect of altering the distribution of resources among different internal groups. Resistance to change is also the main reason why, once institutionalized, an organization tends to perpetuate itself.

The existence of pressure opposing innovative choices (i.e. resistance to change) challenges the credibility of the thesis that change is entirely due to such choices. Any attempt to introduce an innovation usually leads to an effect which is not that specific innovation: it is rather the result of two opposing pressures, i.e. the attempt to innovate, and the resistance to change. The greater the resistance to change, the less the innovation introduced will correspond to its initiator's intentions. The problem of "counter-intuitive effects" is to be added here: each choice, being effected in a complex context, produces a plethora of effects unforeseen by its authors.[10] Since an organization is, moreover, a system of interdependent parts, change in one part leads to changes in the entire organization;[11] this virtually excludes the possibility of entirely deliberate and controlled change – for the actors themselves have only "bounded rationality"[12] and cannot foresee everything.

But while change involves the entire organization, the velocity and intensity with which change in one part affects all the other parts depends on the organization's degree of institutionalization: if its structural coherence is high, interdependence is high, and so thus are the speed and intensity of the change's "propagation".[13]

The hypotheses of intentionality and non-intentionality correspond to the "rational" and the "natural systems" models. It only makes sense to think of change as the effect of deliberate choices (geared at maximizing efficiency in attaining goals) if the organization is an instrument for realizing specific goals. It only makes sense to conceive of change as the effect of more impersonal organizational dynamics if the organization is a natural system dominated by survival imperatives and by the mediation of particular demands. Organizations, however, manifest both of these characteristics: pressures coexist within them pushing them in both directions, and the maintenance of organizational stability depends on the balancing of these two forces. Neither of the two schools is, thus, entirely wrong: organizational change is the fruit of both choices and, because of the actor's bounded rationality and the multiplicity of organizational pressures, unforeseeable effects. Change is the result of deliberate choices (made within the dominant coalition) influenced by bounded rationality and anonymous pressures (e.g. resistance to change, environmental changes, technological changes, etc.) which interact with the choices to produce both desired innovations and counter-intuitive effects.

Exogenous versus endogenous origins

There are two schools of thought concerning this question. According to the first, essentially identifiable with contingency theory, change has an exogenous origin,[14] i.e. it is externally induced. The organization is forced to adapt to environmental changes (although in the non-predictable fashion discussed above) in order to survive.

The second school sees organizational change as having essentially endogenous origins, i.e. as being mainly due to changes in the organization's internal distribution of power. In its pure form, this school defends the notion of "political development" formerly discussed. Neither of the theories is sufficient alone. The thesis of externally-induced change is insufficient because it postulates a simple stimulus–response schema (environmental and/or technological change leading to organizational innovation) and because organizational adjustment to environmental change is often slow and at times non-existent.[15] The thesis of endogenous change, on the other hand, leaves unexplained what produced change in the power structure in the first place. One of the theses most frequently cited by historians and political scientists, according to which change in party power structure is the product of generational changes, is unconvincing.

The most persuasive hypothesis, in our opinion, is that organizational change is, in most cases, the effect of an external stimulus (environmental and/or technological) which joins forces with internal factors which were themselves undermining the power structure (even, for example, generational changes). The external stimulus acts as a catalyzer accelerating power structure transformation (e.g. of resource distribution among different groups) where the internal preconditions of this transformation already existed. And change in the power structure (according to the theory of political development) stimulates organizational innovation. When neither environmental challenges nor internal preconditions are present, organizational change cannot take place.

Change in political parties

Until now we have investigated organizational change in general. At this point we can evaluate more closely how and why changes in political parties take place.

It is necessary first to define organizational change. Strictly speaking, any alteration can be considered a change. Every organization undergoes continual changes. But not all of these changes interest us here. We are interested in fundamental changes, which change the organization's authority structure, i.e. its *organizational order*. Such changes imply alterations serious enough to modify relations among the organization's various components. The biggest empirical problem is thus how to distinguish real changes in the organizational order from the many small changes continually present which do not affect the organizational order (though together they may constitute the precondition for later fundamental change). In a like manner, the main empirical problem in analyzing political regimes is to distinguish between their incessant changes and changes of political regime.[16] A change in organizational order is a change in the conformation of the party's dominant coalition. It modifies relations among the organization's internal groups, altering the distribution of control over incentives and restructuring vertical power games (the elite–follower exchanges), and thus horizontal power games (the elite–elite exchanges) as well. As we have seen in chapter 9, a dominant coalition's conformation changes in accordance with variations in: (1) The coalition's degree of cohesion, i.e. the degree of organization in its internal groups. (2) The coalition's degree of stability, i.e. the ability of its components to effectuate satisfactory compromises. (3) The organizational map of power understood as: (a) organogram: relations of power/subordination among the different offices and (b) inter-organizational relations. If the conformation of the dominant coalition changes in one register, it is likely to change in one or more of the other registers as well.

Change in organizational order can be broken down, for purely analytical purposes, into three phases:

The first is introduced by an organizational crisis unleashed by strong environmental pressure.[17] Electoral defeat and deterioration in terms of exchange in the electoral arena are classic types of external challenges which exert very strong pressure on the party. They catalyze organizational crises where internal preconditions already exist (such as generational turnover pushing new potential leaders to the fore, decreasing organizational performance, organizational rigidity, etc.).

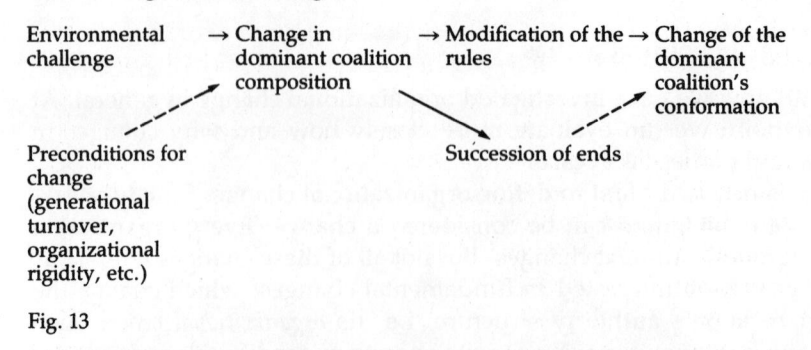

Organizational change

```
Environmental    → Change in           → Modification of the → Change of the
challenge           dominant coalition      rules                 dominant
                    composition                                   coalition's
                                                                  conformation

Preconditions for                           Succession of ends
change
(generational
turnover,
organizational
rigidity, etc.)
```

Fig. 13

The second phase sees the discrediting of the old coalition which was unable to handle the crisis, the formation of new alliances, and the replacement of the leading group.

The third phase is that of organizational restructuring, i.e. change in the organization's physiognomy involving two central organizational "areas." In the first place, certain rules of the game – namely, rules of internal competition – are changed (and are sometimes ratified by statutory revisions), because the new leaders must support their newly acquired control of the party with organizational innovations (above all to avoid possible position reversals instigated by the dethroned groups which are still influential in certain sectors of the party). Rules of the electoral system are often changed. The organogram is restructured: certain offices (i.e. those controlled by former leaders or their supporters) decline in importance and are reorganized, while new ones grow in importance thereby changing the modes of coordination, etc. Resource distribution among the internal groups is altered, the changes are ratified and fixed into the organizational fabric, and its physiognomy is thereby at least partly modified.[18]

Secondly, the organization's official goals are redefined; this legitimizes the new group in power. It is necessary because it must show the organization's members that the change of leadership was effected for profound and noble reasons related to the destiny of the organization itself (not because of banal rivalry or personal ambition). We see a *succession of ends* (i.e. a substitution of new official goals for older official goals).[19] At times "ultimate ends" are changed and the organization's identity and hunting ground are radically altered (as, for instance, when a socialist party declares that it no longer takes socialism as an objective). But more often than not, it is the party's strategy which is changed.

At this point the cycle is complete and the crisis has been resolved through restructuring of the organizational order. The change in *composition* of the dominant coalition (disintegration of the old alliance and birth of a new alliance) provoking transformations in the organizational physiognomy (rules of the game, goals) ends in a change in the *conformation* of the dominant coalition. At the end of the cycle the entire system of intra-organizational exchanges has been modified. Changes are evident in the party's degree of cohesion, its degree of stability, and its map of organizational power. The organogram undergoes considerable alteration; or, inter-organizational relations change as elites from other organizations enter the dominant coalition or are expelled (or their role grows or shrinks).

The innovations can, of course, have counter-intuitive (unforeseen) effects and create conditions which facilitate new organizational crises when new external challenges arise. Changes in the organizational order can also affect institutionalization, i.e. they may affect the party's degree of autonomy *vis-à-vis* the environment and its systematicity.

Change in a party's organizational order – and thus in its political strategy, manifested in the succession of ends – will naturally alter its behavior and its political activity.

Two aspects of the change cycle require specification: (1) Why does the organization respond to external challenge with changes in the composition of its dominant coalition? And (2) why does the cycle lead to a succession of ends and thus result in a restructuring of organizational identity? These two questions are closely linked and require contextual examination. With the articulation of ends, the necessity to maintain manifest goals (upon which organizational identity depends) and to pursue the other organizational needs, have undergone a process of mutual adjustment. The latter allows the dominant coalition to balance contradictory needs: that of distributing collective identity incentives to the believers (in accordance with the rational model), and selective status and/or material incentives to the careerists (in accordance with the natural systems model). Party behavior in the political arenas is the product of this adaptation.

Behavior, organizational ends, and organizational physiognomy make up an *equilibrium system* which is more the result of the dominant coalition's efforts to combine these three factors in such a way as to ensure organizational stability (and, thereby, party control) than the result of an "invisible hand" or of a generic tendency of systems towards points of equilibrium. The dominant coalition does not have, however, an infinite number of possible combinations at its disposal. Its legitimacy is tied to specific manifest objectives, and the organization has been adapted to them. As long as the system is in equilibrium – i.e. as long as the dominant coalition is able to balance the distribution of identity and selective incentives – minority elites and groups excluded from the dominant coalition cannot easily restructure internal alliances in their favor, given that the power "trumps" (financing, technical expertise, recruitment, relation to the environment, control over communication and control over the interpretation of rules) are almost completely concentrated in the hands of the dominant coalition. It is the breakdown of equilibrium – due to external challenges – which opens the way for them. Environmental challenge suddenly demonstrates to the organization's members that the dominant coalition is no longer able to control the organizational zones of uncertainty, and that in consequence the incentive system is challenged, and symbolic and material remunerations are compromised. Believers and careerists are willing (though for different reasons) to transfer their support to minority elites who have been preaching change in the party's political strategy in order to legitimize their position with respect to the dominant coalition. External challenge, in shaking up the organization, demonstrates that the old strategies of adaptation to or predominance over the environment (i.e. the party's behavior) no longer reduce or control environmental uncertainty. This uncontrollability sets off an organizational crisis which is really an *identity crisis*. The dominant coalition's control over other zones of uncertainty also vacillates, communication among the organization's members disoriented by the crisis increases, and this communication flow cannot be controlled by the dominant coalition.[20] The dominant coalition's ability to distribute collective identity incentives to its following decreases. As the organizational identity vacillates, the full support given by the believers in exchange for symbolic remuneration (namely, the tutelage of the collective identity) is withdrawn. The specific consensus the careerists gave in return for material remuneration and/or status is also withdrawn. The dominant coalition proves to be insolvent, panic spreads, and the bank's clients put their savings in a safer bank, i.e. they shift their support to the minority elites who, having been excluded from decision-making, are not held responsible for the crisis and have their own recipe for resolving it. Their proposals had previously been rejected by the organization's active members because the collective (symbolic), and material incentives had not been jeopardized. But when an indentity crisis takes place, trust in the dominant coalition begins to break down.[21] The minority elites represent an "adventure," a move towards the unknown, a restructuring of environmental relations, and thus an, at least partial, modification of the organization's identity. This is why their proposals were systematically refused. But in a crisis situation, the worst choice is to do nothing, to avoid confronting the new and unknown. With the changing of the guard, i.e. the change in the dominant coalition's composition, succession of ends takes place. The crisis is overcome, and organizational stability is restored when the equilibrium of (new) ends, (new) organizational physiognomy, and behavior is reconstituted on a new basis.

Two further observations should be made here: (1) the phases isolated (change of dominant coalition composition, and restructuring of organizational physiognomy) refer to *logical* sequences; in reality the two processes working to change organizational order intertwine and are indistinguishable; (2) our model implies that the greater the change in coalition composition, i.e. the more important the turnover of leading party elites, the more profound the restructuring of the organizational order.

Extent of change: amalgamation and circulation

Our model exposes itself to the criticism of being overly mechanistic. Like all models, however, it does not pretend to exhaustively describe change, but simply to explain certain recurrent factors and their relations. Change in organizational order necessarily varies from case to case in accordance with each organization's particularities and the different environmental challenges. We will nevertheless attempt to demonstrate with some examples that our model describes aspects of a recurrent process. The only variant is the *extent* of the change (the relation between its different elements does not vary).

One essentially empirical problem is the existence of an exception to the rule that changes in the dominant coalition's *composition* imply changes in its *conformation*, i.e. a restructuring of the organizational order. The exception is the case of renewal of the dominant coalition's composition as a result of *cooptation*. Empirical analysis often finds changes in the composition[22] of parties' ruling groups which are not accompanied by significant alterations in organizational physiognomy (rules of the game and organizational ends) or by consequence, of organizational order. This is because much of the turnover in the party is not due to changes in power relations among internal groups, but rather to normal cooptative processes. Cooptation, regulating generational physiological turnover, does not necessarily alter the equilibrium among the groups. Only people not representing an alternative to the dominant coalition, are, in fact, coopted. The fact that most parties' leading organs tend (as we saw in chapter 10) to progressively expand, is often an empirical indicator of cooptative processes which do not alter power relations among the different groups. Cooptation produces a molecular change in dominant coalition composition, but it does not change internal group power relations and thus does not produce a change in the organizational order. It is rather difficult in practice to distinguish between renewal due to cooptation and that due to alterations in the internal power structure. *Both* components can simultaneously be present in varying degrees. We can generally hypothesize a prevalence of cooptation under normal circumstances (i.e. in the absence of organizational crisis) at the two extremes of the scale of institutionalization (very weak and very strong institutions). In communist parties, examples of strong institutionalization, regular renewals of parliamentary groups,[23] and leaders at other levels (accompanied by long periods without renewal of key positions) have often been noted.[24] Here renewal is due to deliberate decisions of very cohesive dominant coalitions; it is a kind of cooptation whose task is to maintain the organization's "muscular tonus" through careful doses of selective incentives. At the other extreme, we have weak institutions supported by divided and (tendentially) unstable coalitions such as the Italian DC and the PSI at certain moments of their history. In these cases, turnover and change in dominant coalition composition are due to choices of different factional leaders that had to remunerate their followers while producing few alterations in the balance of power among the internal components.

Another apparent difficulty with our model is that change is at times not seen as restructuring the organizational order − because the changes in political strategy and the rules of the game, etc., are accompanied by leadership continuity, or, at least, relative stability in the most visible leadership. This would appear to throw into question the causal relationship between ruling group turnover and political and organizational innovation. But a dominant coalition can change even if some of its most visible national leaders (leader-symbols) retain their positions. Organizations are *always* guided by coalitions (even in charismatic parties, where the leader's predominance does not mean the absence of a dominant coalition). Change in dominant coalition composition does not necessarily imply the replacement of the most visible leader. The change often is precisely due to a shift in the alliance guided by the most visible leader who abandons the alliance with the old groups and builds a new alliance. This was precisely what happened in the PCI's important restructuring in 1956 (as we shall see).

The model's third apparent difficulty is that change and goal redefinition often take place cautiously and slowly. To speak of a succession of ends might thus seem an exaggeration, for official goals are rarely entirely replaced. This objection, however, does not invalidate the model: it merely demonstrates that organizational change may be more or less thoroughgoing. Change in organizational order depends, in fact, on how much renewal has occurred in the dominant coalition (excluding renewal through cooptation). The fact that organizational change in parties is often small, is due to the circumstance that changes in the composition of the dominant coalitions are often small as well. As Michels observed, only rarely do changes at the head of a party take the form of a "circulation of elites," i.e. of a brusque and radical replacement of one leading group by another. In the majority of cases, we see an "amalgamation" rather than a "circulation:"[25] the shift in power relations between different competing groups translates into gradual and at times hardly perceptible compromises.

"Amalgamation" is more common than "circulation" as an organization's members more easily accept identity redefinitions (produced by the former) than simple substitutions of one identity with another (which would be the result of the latter). We can thus place potential renewal levels of dominant coalition composition along a continuum. At one extreme we have "circulation of elites" – the very rare phenomenon of a total changeover of the dominant coalition; and at the other we have a situation of "stability" – the just as rare phenomenon of turnover due exclusively to cooptation. All intermediary points represent varying degrees of amalgamation:

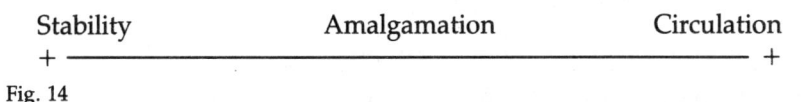

Stability   Amalgamation   Circulation
+ ─── +

Fig. 14

The further one moves from left (stability) to right (circulation), the deeper the change in the party's organizational order (and the greater the alterations in the rules and official goals) as a result of a greater dominant coalition turnover. Both stability and circulation are limit-cases; parties most often renew their leading groups through varying degrees of amalgamation. Michels thought that renewal happens in small steps, and therefore with degrees of amalgamation closer to the left end of the continuum. If this were the case, deep restructuring of organizational order would never take place. Michels based his observations on the internal workings of the SPD at the beginning of the century. The SPD, however, was a strong institution, and the maneuverability of minority elites was very limited. A frontal attack on the dominant coalition would have been hazardous even under conditions of great uncertainty. In a strong institution, the dominant coalition's renewal will most often occur through (weak) amalgamation, unless an absolutely devastating challenge arises, and the change in organizational order will thus not be very profound.

Relatively high degrees of amalgamation do, however, occasionally occur. It is possible to hypothesize that it is more likely to take place in weakly institutionalized parties. Under considerable stress, weak institutions may undergo significant dominant coalition renewal and thus thoroughgoing restructuring of the organizational order. Hellman's investigation of PCI federations seems to support this claim: leadership turnover was generally higher in weak federations (such as that of Padova) than in strong ones (such as in Bologna). Turnover assumed the character of a circulation of elites, in the strong federation of Florence at the time of the Eighth Congress in 1956, because of a serious challenge (local electoral defeat coupled with national party crisis).[26] Comparing renewal levels in the PCF, SFIO, and French Radical Socialist Party, Duverger isolated two alternative models: one defined by slow and circumspect renewal with continuity over time, the second characterized by sudden "regeneration" and by extensive renewals which followed long periods of immobility and organizational and political sclerosis.[27] Duverger saw both of these cases as involving circulation of elites. In our terms, however, his first model corresponds to stability and renewal by cooptation, his second to circulation of elites in conjunction with the two opposite extremes of institutionalization.

Organizational change: some examples

Throughout its history, the British Conservative Party changed according to the causal chain described above. On each occasion, organizational change was related to an elite turnover catalyzed by unresolved environmental challenges. The organizational change always – except in 1906 and 1975 – strengthened party institutionalization. The 1906 electoral débâcle brought about a modification of the dominant coalition (Balfour, the old leader, lost power to Chamberlain); the result was a temporary reorganization which de-institutionalized the party, taking power from the Central Office (then controlled by Balfour) and giving it to the National Union (then controlled by Chamberlain). The dominant coalition became extremely divided and unstable. The defeat in 1910 brought Bonar Law and a new generation of leaders to power, leading to significant organizational restructuring (with Steel–Maitland at the head of the Central Office). The party's political strategy *vis-à-vis* its main competitor, the Liberal Party, became very aggressive. A new restructuring (involving a good deal of bureaucratization) accompanied Baldwin's ascent and the redefinition of conservative identity, which acquired the name of "new conservatism"[28] (an attempt to compete in a populist way with Labour for working-class votes). The next most important reform took place in

1948 under the impact of the renewal imposed by the 1945 defeat.[29]

The internal movement for organizational reform regained vitality after the 1964 electoral defeat.[30] The crisis set off by that defeat (which put Edward Heath in Douglas Home's seat) resulted in an innovation which was to have a serious influence on the party's later evolution, namely, modification of the parliamentary leader selection system. Up until then the new leader had been chosen through an informal meeting of party notables. Afterwards the leader was *elected* by the parliamentary group, and ballots were used if no candidate obtained an absolute majority in the first round.[31]

In 1975, after another electoral defeat, criteria for the election of the leader were once again modified. Two new clauses were introduced: the local party associations had to be consulted before electing a leader, and the parliamentarians gained the right to propose a vote of no confidence for the leader in office.[32] These signified a "democratization" of the party which was imposed by the organization's rightist tendencies; it resulted in deep restructuring of the organizational order and drastic modification of the leader's position *vis-à-vis* the parliamentary group. From being an almost absolute monarch, able to govern with the support of but a small entourage, the leader became a hostage of the Conservative parliamentarians. It was this organizational change which explains the "Thatcher phenomenon," i.e. the shift to the right in the party's politics. As a result of these changes the leader is now much more conditioned by Conservative parliamentarians' preferences and by the attitude of the local party associations.[33]

The change in the dominant coalition composition and the victory of the rightist tendencies brought about a deep restructuring of organizational physiognomy: an alteration of the rules of internal competition, and a "succession of ends," i.e. a radical redefinition of the Conservative identity around Thatcher-type "neo-liberalism." This significant change in organizational order brought about the de-institutionalization of the organization (as did the change in 1906). The dominant coalition's loss in traditional cohesion is attested to by the Thatcher government's difficulties after the 1979 victory, due to increasing party factionalism.

Various elements of the model are visible in the PCI's organizational change of 1956. That year's crisis was set off by Khrushchev's revelation of Stalin's crimes at the Twentieth Congress of the PCUS. This identity crisis, brought on by an external change, was not like a bolt from the blue hitting a strong and flourishing organization. The party had already been in serious trouble for several years: membership had stagnated after 1951 and fallen significantly in 1955,[34] the traditional incentive system could not maintain high internal participation,[35] and turnover at the different levels was blocked because – although a new generation of potential local, intermediary and national leaders crowded into waiting rooms – positions were filled by old guard Stalinists.[36] Moreover, the Italian (like the international) political situation had been changing quite a bit. Fanfani was revitalizing the DC in the wake of centrism, and signs of a future turn to the center–left governments of the sixties were visible. All the internal preconditions for change were in the air.

In general, the main characteristic of the PCI in the 1951–6 period seems to be substantial stability of organized power and structural order. As time went on, however, the "closure" which typified the PCI in the early fifties was not sufficient to hold off the gradual erosion of its acquired positions. Its organizational apparatus, no longer sustained by the impetus which had characterized its constitution, and lacking salient goals of heroic occasions, ended by closing itself off in self-propelling routine, only entering a phase of renewal in response to the shock of events in the communist world.[37]

The weary organization in which many conditions for renewal had accumulated over time, was hit by the crisis of de-Stalinization. It set off an extensive revamping of dominant coalition composition. The lynchpin of the operation was the same party secretary who, in an interview with *Nuovi Argomenti* (formulating the theory of polycentrism),[38] had implicitly preannounced the restructuring of the internal alliance. The Eighth Congress ushered in the greatest turnover ever undergone by the party's ruling class. By the end of the Congress, 56.4 per cent of the Central Committee members had been newly elected (as opposed to 25 per cent in 1948, 12.5 per cent in 1951, 39.8 per cent in 1960, and 26.4 per cent in 1962). It was thus a serious amalgamation (but not a circulation of elites, for only 22 per cent of the *Direzione* – the executive committee – was newly elected):[39] part of the old dominant coalition followed Togliatti and allied itself to new sectors which had until then been excluded from power. The changes at the top were only the tip of the iceberg of the confrontation between "innovators" (sustaining the new Togliattian political strategy, the "Italian road to socialism") and "conservatives" (the old Stalinist guard) throughout the party. Acute conflicts arose in many federations between these two tendencies. The new generation of peripheral leaders (already supported by Rome) was able to overthrow the old ruling class.[40] More generally, the turn in 1956 led to extensive generational turnover in the organization's entire bureaucratic structure.[41]

The de-Stalinization crisis thus acted as a detonator, allowing a new generation of leaders to come into the limelight (Togliatti vouching for the more "docile" sectors of the old guard) at all levels of the party. The change in dominant coalition composition was accompanied by significant restructuring of the organizational order. At the Congress, the so-called "theory of polycentrism" (i.e. the affirmation of the right to build socialism in a way independent of Moscow) – introduced with the slogan "the Italian road to socialism" – became the new official party doctrine. Change in dominant coalition composition was thus accompanied by a partial succession of ends which redefined party identity and inaugurated significant changes in political strategy and daily behavior. The rules were also changed: significant statutory changes were made at the Eighth Congress (the most substantial since World War II)[42] which created important preconditions for the party's political–organizational comeback. The choice to forcefully favor territorial sections over cells (the former already existed in embryonic form in the "New Party" after the war) distanced the PCI from its original Leninist model.[43] The electoral system was changed (the new system allowed for open lists and secret ballots, if requested by one-fifth of the voters)[44] – and this is a crucial sign of change in power relations among internal groups. All of these changes brought about a restructuring of the organizational order, and a modification of the dominant coalition. It was an immediate change less in the degree of cohesion and stability of the dominant coalition than in the map of organizational power: the intervention in the organizational physiognomy – following the change in dominant coalition composition – partly modified the organogram,[45] i.e. there was a restructuring of relations between different organization offices. The groundwork was laid down, furthermore, for reduction in party institutionalization. The Eighth Congress, allowing the PCI to better establish itself in Italian society, reduced party autonomy *vis-à-vis* the environment (and increased pressure for a political stance more independent from the Soviet Union). De-institutionalizing pressure, in turn, made the cohesion of the dominant coalition somewhat less (setting the stage for the internal conflicts of the sixties).[46]

Bad Godesberg: the succession of ends

The SPD's transformation in Bad Godesberg is a good example (all elements of the transformation being clearly visible) of the validity of our model of change, and merits closer examination.

Change was catalyzed by the 1957 elections. The result, although better than that of 1953 (31.8 per cent vs. 28.8 per cent), confirmed the SPD's inability to get off the ground. It had disastrous effects on party morale because, for the first time, the CDU/CSU obtained an absolute majority (moving from 45.2 per cent to 50.2 per cent) and won 270 seats (as opposed to the SPD's 169). The demoralization sparked off a revolt, first in the parliamentary group and then at the Stuttgart Congress, against the party's old dominant coalition. The 1957 elections catalyzed a turnover and a regeneration which ended two years later in the adoption of a new program at Bad Godesberg. But they were no more than a catalyst: this external challenge arose in a long-term situation of diffuse crisis. Until the day of reckoning in 1958, the dominant coalition whose leaders were Kurt Schumacher and then Erich Ollenhauer,[47] comprised party bureaucrats. Its configuration was the same as in Ebert's time: there were a few leaders with long experience as party bureaucrats who controlled the bureaucratic apparatus and had long been faithful to the traditional party's organizational principles (e.g. subordination of the parliamentary group to the leadership, and centralization of power at the party's vertex).

In 1944–6, under the emerging leadership of Schumacher, the bureaucracy resumed its former privileged role. Of the 25 members in the executive committee in 1946, 23 were elderly party bureaucrats (already active within the organization before the war).[48] This generation of bureaucrats, legitimated by political party traditions, continued to dominate even after Schumacher's death in 1952 and the ushering in of Ollenhauer (from the same group). The organizational principles remained unchanged: the 1950 statutes, replacing the provisional ones made in 1946, merely reactivated the statutory norms of the Weimar period.[49]

After World War II, however, the bureaucratic apparatus no longer had the same chance of party control as it had had before. Above all, it could no longer count on syndical support: the trade union leaders in dealing with the CDU/CSU (the governmental parties), proclaimed their political neutrality, moving to the right in order to negotiate more freely with the government.[50] The apparatus was no longer as large or unified as it had once been. During the Weimar period, the SPD's bureaucratic structure had already weakened,[51] its golden age (i.e. the age of Ebert) having passed. Opposition tendencies then assumed a greater position of force. The "traditionalists" were attacked on two fronts: from the left by the "radicals," and from the right by the "new socialists" (the pragmatists). The radicals controlled about 10 per cent of the party in the fifties, and aimed at reform which would undermine the traditionalist bureaucracy while maintaining party control over its deputies and other public representatives. The radicals (mainly young intellectuals) used the typical symbols of the revolutionary–socialist tradition.[52] The pragmatists, or new socialists, were the social–democrats of the new generation. They were thirty to forty years old, well-educated, and of higher class extraction than the traditionalists.[53] They had won public offices in the parliament, the Länder, and the large cities during the fifties without passing through the apparatus, i.e. without work experience in the organization. They aimed at reform which would grant more power to the parliamentary group and to the other party representatives, on the one hand, and to the peripheral party organizations (at the National Party Center's expense) on the other. They used symbols of party modernization: liquidation of old myths from the 1800s (i.e. Marxism), and professionalization by opening up to experts in various sectors of political intervention.[54]

In the course of the fifties the new socialists (Brandt, Schmidt, and many others) grew stronger. The trade unions' break with traditional social–democratic ideology worked in their favor. So did the fact that the SPD succeeded electorally in the Länder and in the cities (where it always did better than the CDU). By the mid-fifties the new socialists came to control many national and local party organizations through their public offices and as a result of the central bureaucratic apparatus' declining control over the periphery. Activists began to compare the new socialists' local success with the old leadership's failures in the federal elections.[55]

The alarm bell sounded for the traditionalists at the 1954 congress. The SPD had suffered an electoral defeat in 1953 (from 29.7 per cent of the vote to 28.8 per cent), and its most prestigious leader, Schumacher, had died two years earlier. Membership had fallen from 875,000 in 1947 to 600,000 in 1954,[56] and the party membership was conspicuously aging: which meant that the increased internal divisions pushed the dominant coalition to choose organizational stasis. Resentment towards the bureaucrats grew. Both radicals and new socialists contributed to spreading malcontent. In 1954, the traditionalists managed to remain in power, but their margin of success was slight:

The entire paid membership of the executive was re-elected, but with substantially fewer votes than in 1952 (the only exception was Alfred Nan, party treasurer, who was apparently considered capable and politically neutral). Elections of the unpaid membership suggested a desire for "new blood." . . . Von Knoeringen, generally first, was reduced to second of those elected, by Herbert Wehner, who received 302 of 366 votes. Among the new members were Max Brauer and Willi Birkelbach. Both Fritz Erler and Willi Brandt, while not elected, received substantial support.[57]

The two-pronged attack of the radicals and new socialists had its effects. Ollenhauer was forced to accept a revision of the party's program. A commission (controlled by the traditionalists) was nominated to prepare and present the program at the following congress. The traditionalists, confident of their power, prepared a substantially non-innovative document. But it never became the party's new program.

256   Organizational change

The Stuttgart Congress took place after the 1957 elections. By that time the rebellion had already exploded. It started immediately after the elections, being provoked by the parliamentary group in the Bundestag when, in October 1957, the majority of the deputies adopted a resolution contrary to Ollenhauer's will:

> Rejecting the official proposal to re-elect the existing delegation leadership, or to add a third vice-chairman, the deputies agreed to elect three new vice-chairmen. The rebels proposed three candidates: Carlo Schmid, Herbert Wehner, and Fritz Erler. Ollenhauer was re-elected chairman by 132 votes over 3 opposition votes and 16 abstentions. His influence was diminished, however, by the success of the rebellion.[58]

Schmid and Erler were new socialists; Wehner was a radical. But the dissidents were now the majority within the parliamentary group. The revolution erupted at the congress. A very significant turnover took place at the party's vertex: the traditionalists suffered a heavy loss (partly due to the fact that the new socialists controlled many peripheral organizations, and thus occupied a good number of the delegate seats). Ollenhauer was re-elected president, but with only 319 of the 380 votes (a loss of 49 votes with respect to the preceding congress), and the few traditionalists not mowed down lost a great deal of their popularity. The new guard burst onto the scene: "Of the twenty-nine elected to the executive on the general ballot, fourteen were chosen for the first time (only six had been replaced in 1956, about the average turn-over)."[59] Willy Brandt, then mayor of Berlin, was victorious over his rival Franz Neumann, the old traditionalist bureaucrat.[60]

The change of guard was preceded by a conflict over the statute. The pressure to drastically reduce the bureaucrats' political clout was very great, and the resolutions passed at the congress all aimed at strengthening the non-salaried leaders.[61] Against Ollenhauer's will, for example, the decision was made to hold elections for the bureaucrats and non-salaried members of the executive committee together (they had always been chosen in separate lists before). By the end of the congress, the traditionalists' defeat was total:

> Ollenhauer's declaration of 7 July 1959 that he would not accept any office in a future SPD-led government, and the announcement of the formation of a committee constituted largely of members of the party's pragmatic–reformist wing (George-August Zirm, Max Brauer, Brandt, Deist, Schmid, Erler, but also Mehner) to plan an electoral strategy for 1961 signified the decline of the party traditionalists as the determining intra-party tactical and ideological force.[62]

The dominant coalition's conformation had changed (even if its final arrangement took place after the 1961 elections). The SPD's map of organizational power had been redefined: the executive committee suffered cuts favoring both the parliamentary group and peripheral organizations – and the central apparatus weakened. The new dominant coalition was the fruit of an "amalgamation" of new socialists (the majority), sectors of the old guard, and members from the ranks of the radicals (especially Wehner who gave up his initial leftist position). The cycle closed in the extraordinary Bad Godesberg conference in November 1959. The new program was approved with only sixteen dissenting votes. Marxist ideology – which had dominated the party as far back as Erfurt (1881) – was abandoned, and the redefinition of organizational identity was very far-reaching.[63]

Brandt, who had so skilfully used Berlin as a national arena, was nominated as the candidate to the Chancellery in 1960 by the Executive Committee. The SPD's new look was launched. At the 1960 Congress, the team which was to serve as "shadow government" – and to be the governmental nucleus in the event of victory – was presented. The members were all new socialists of the "pure politician" and "expert" types; this completed the party's new image of political–managerial competence.[64]

Brandt conducted his 1961 electoral campaign in a "Kennedian" way, using mass-media (a technique totally unknown to the traditionalists). The election confirmed the choice of party reform: the SPD moved from 31.8 percent of the vote to 36.2 percent. It was once again on the up and up: the choices made turned out to be the right ones and the dominant coalition was able to pass its road test. Brandt became the party's vice-president at the 1962 Congress. The road to power was now wide open.

The CDU: from electoral party to mass organization

In chapter 8 we left off our discussion of the CDU at the point at which the party had consolidated under Adenauer's guidance as an organization dominated by the Chancellor and intermediary leaders. It was an organization with a non-existent extra-parliamentary center and no bureaucratic apparatus; it was permeated by external interest groups; it could be considered an agglomeration of semi-autonomous organizations held together only by shared advantages of power and by Adenauer's personality. It had no push towards expansion, a membership of about 200,000 at the end of the Adenauer era, and little if any internal participation.

At the end of the seventies the CDU is a mass party with 700,000 members, significant internal participation, and a relatively strong and highly professional central bureaucracy. It has made the transition from being a weak institution to being a strong one. Many of its former features have obviously not disappeared (a certain autonomy of the intermediary organizations, the presence of external interest groups in party life, etc.) in spite of the profundity of the change.

Expulsion from central power was the chief catalyst of change. Though the party was still essentially the same in 1969 as in Adenauer's time, many preconditions for change had accumulated. After Adenauer's withdrawal from the Chancellery, the dominant coalition grew very unstable under the weak and indecisive Chancellors who followed (namely, Erhard and Kiesinger).[65] From 1963 to 1965, the party was torn by conflict over foreign policy (precisely the issue around which the CDU in the Adenauer era found greatest internal unity). The opposition between "Atlantists," led by Chancellor Erhard, and the so-called "Gaullists," led by Strauss and Adenauer himself (the latter occupied the office of party president from 1963 to 1965), divided the organization into two large "factions." Meanwhile, a new generation of leaders was emerging and preparing for the battle of succession. In 1964 a beginner, Rainer Barzel, leader of the organization in North-Rhine Westphalia, was elected president of *Fraktion* because of "renewal" pressures; other young leaders – Helmut Kohl in particular (the organization's leader in Rheinland–Palatinate) – tried to make their way onto the national scene: their battle cry was party reform. Their thesis was that the party structures were inadequate for competition with the post Bad Godesberg SPD. The dominant coalition was extremely divided and unstable in this phase, and there seemed to be little room for internal compromise. The choice to form the Great Coalition was a choice against Erhard (who was tied to the traditional policy of alliance with the Liberals).[66] Kiesinger was elected party president and then arrived at the Chancellery thanks to the party's innovative wing lead by Kohl. Kiesinger's election was more due to the heterogeneous coalition's attempt to stop Barzel (who had, from his position of strength in *Fraktion*, announced his candidature) than to his specific capabilities. The rivalry between Kohl and Barzel for party control led to skirmishes in this period. Pressure for "reform" was very strong, but the reform never took place: the dominant coalition was too divided and unstable, and its various components blocked each other.

The year 1969 was one of defeat and expulsion from power. Although the shock was very strong, the predominant thesis within the party was that the electorate would "come to its senses" and correct its "error" in the next elections. Barzel who had acquired prestige as president of *Fraktion* extended his authority and political weight. Having lost the Chancellery, the *Fraktion* (along with Barzel) became the party's ruling organ. Kohl, although not deputy, entered the national executive committee after the defeat and reproposed party reform to reinforce the extra-parliamentary organization. He encountered the usual resistance of the leaders of the Landesverbande, weakened but still vocal within the party, but it was above all Barzel who blocked the way to reform. Reinforcing the extra-parliamentary organization would have favored Kohl, a party man, and not Barzel whose authority depended almost exclusively on the *Fraktion*'s new preeminence in the CDU's map of organizational power. At the Saarbrucken Congress (October 1971) Barzel obtained the office of party president, beating Kohl with 344 votes against 174.[67] The relation between the extra-parliamentary organization and the *Fraktion* thus remained unchanged.

The confirmation of the party's exclusion from power came in 1972, provoking an organizational crisis. Barzel was discredited. Moreover, many newly elected delegates did not owe their election to him. The changing of the guard came in the spring of 1973. Kohl was elected party president while Carstens (a Kohl supporter) replaced Barzel at the head of the *Fraktion*. The power equilibrium between the extra-parliamentary organization and the *Fraktion* had changed. Kohl consolidated his position with a vast organizational reform carried out by the new secretary of the central headquarters (*Bundesgeschaftsstelle*) Biedenkopf, and with a more aggressive political strategy towards the SPD. The secretary of the BGS had up till then been a lightweight administrative position. With Biedenkopf (1973–7) it became a political role of primary importance. The Kohl–Biedenkopf tandem resembled the Disraeli–Gorst team which transformed the British Conservatives into a modern party. Biedenkopf ushered in an expansion and a strong centralization of the party's central organization. He:

> lent full support to the training of officials, a new development in the CDU from the early 1970s which was facilitated by a more active party membership. Personnel planning became the new "in" word in party organization, and was illustrated by the creation of a personnel data bank at the BGS in 1972 and the general work of the personnel planning department there.[68]

Alongside courses of cadre formation, research centers which furnish information on political problems and have the task of promoting internal communication, were instituted after 1975. The impulse to increase membership grew to a peak. The move from 300,000 to 650,000 members from 1969–77 upset all internal party relations. While the extra-parliamentary "center" expanded and became more professional, it also received new funding through increased revenues from membership dues.[69] The federal party reinforced its position with respect to the *Fraktion* and to the Landesverbande, whose loss of organizational and political weight was continual and constant. The original imprint, however, was never totally removed. Centralization still has that "soft" semblance of coordination (resembling the relations between the Central Office and the local Conservative Party associations) and has to leave at least some of the old prerogatives to the Landesverbande. By the end of the seventies, however, the CDU had "become much more a mass-organized party, with the extra-parliamentary organization having greater political weight, a growing professional attitude to party activities and the increasingly active involvement of the membership in party affairs."[70]

Conclusion

There are essentially two theses which historians and political scientists advance concerning party changes. The first maintains that organizational change is to be understood as the effect, intentional and predictable, of the ruling group's decisions to improve the organization's performance. The second maintains that change is the effect of generational factors. Whereas neither thesis is entirely false, neither is completely satisfactory either. The first omits the notion of power and power conflicts, forgetting that organizational innovation is never politically neutral (i.e. that every change alters the distribution of resources among groups, modifies their ability to control zones of organizational uncertainty, and thus alters the exchange system upon which organization power is based). The second, while not underestimating the role of conflict, looks for its cause in generational turnover. The latter is rarely, however, a precondition for change. If turnover is controlled by cooptation, conflict never appears, organizational stability is not threatened, and there is no organizational change. If dominant coalition conformation allows for regular and continuous cooptation processes, potential for generational conflicts dissipates. It was the blocking of new blood in the UNR's dominant coalition (composed exclusively of "Gaullists de toujours") which led to the conflict between old and new Gaullists, when the crisis of Gaullism broke out bringing about its first electoral defeat. This was the cause of the restructuring of the party's organizational order at the Lille Congress in 1967.

The external challenge produces more or less pronounced effects on the organization in relation to:

(1) The *seriousness* of the challenge: the graver the challenge, the more extensive the restructuring.

(2) The degree of development of the internal preconditions for change.
(3) The level of party institutionalization. Given equal conditions for (1) and (2), change is more extensive the weaker the institutionalization.

Restructuring of organizational order and change in dominant coalition composition can give rise to alterations in organizational institutionalization level. The 1956 crisis, which laid the way for reinforced PCI involvement in Italian society, also laid the way for its (relative) de-institutionalization (i.e. less autonomy from the national political scene in conjunction with some minimal signals of distancing from the Soviet Union). Analogously, the organizational change undergone by the SPD at Bad Godsberg sanctioned a (relative) decrease in institutionalization (indicated by the weakening of the bureaucratic apparatus and by the new predominance of the parliamentarians over internal party leaders). The transformations undergone by the CDU after 1969 transformed a traditionally weak institution into a highly institutionalized one.

No institution can, however, entirely escape from its past. No matter how extensive the renewal of leadership, change in the organization, or "succession of ends" may be, many traces of the organization's "genetic model" remain visible.[71]

14

Parties and democracy: transformation and crisis

Current transformations of Western parties may be examined in two different ways. We can consider the level of vitality still existing in old organizational forms, look for signs of their decline, and evaluate the modalities and directions of possible transformation; or we can shift our interest to the activities traditionally carried out by parties in different political systems and examine their possible changes and crises. The first would provide a specific enough field to permit individual analyses of single party organizations; the second provides a wider field, more difficult to grasp, in which to study the operation and transformation of democratic political regimes (which hinge upon parties).

The two problems are implicitly connected in this work. There is a strict connection between parties' activities and their internal organization. A change in organizational physiognomy implies change in party activity and behavior. A consideration of the organizational changes taking place in Western parties can therefore be a starting point for reflection on broader political processes.[1]

Mass bureaucratic parties and electoral–professional parties

At the beginning of the fifties, Maurice Duverger pointed out how the mass party was becoming the dominant form of political organization in democratic regimes; his work may, to a certain extent, be interpreted as a "hymn" to the mass party's political virtues. The "deviant" cases, the American electoral parties – he maintained – were clearly cases of organizational backwardness, with respect to the old continent's mass parties whose development had been so different.

Fifteen years later, Otto Kirchheimer rejected, in his catch-all theory, Duverger's thesis: the mass party was for him but a step – which had already been (or was in the process of being) surpassed – in the organizational development which was transforming class and religious "integration" parties (mass parties by definition) into electoral agencies more and more similar to American parties.²

Contrary to widespread opinion, Kirchheimer's catch-all party was not an organization whose electoral following was so heterogeneous as to represent the whole social spectrum and whose connection with its original *classe gardée* had completely disappeared. Kirchheimer was well aware that no party could ever maintain such a position (since no party could ever afford to completely lose its identity *vis-à-vis* competing organizations), and yet, that the old mass parties had never organized their *class gardée* alone: since their hunting grounds, i.e. their *classe gardée*, upon which their identities depended, were never sufficient – parties always had to seek wider electoral followings including other social strata.

The transformation of the mass party into catch-all party was, according to Kirchheimer, less striking; ties with the old *classe gardée* loosened and weakened; the party simply opened its doors to different social groups. In our terms, this implies a change in the hunting ground, and therefore a new definition of organizational identity (as happened to the SPD at Bad Godesberg), but *not* a wide-open social representation. The party concentrated on categories "without clear conflicts of interest" and was always bound in its action by political traditions and the social stratification system.³

The exaggerated attention given to the more sociological implications of the catch-all party theory (i.e. to the changes in the social composition of different parties' electorates) has often overshadowed aspects which were more important to Kirchheimer:

(1) The de-ideologization process, i.e. the reduction of the party's "ideological baggage," and the concentration of its propaganda on *valence issues*,⁴ i.e. on general issues concerning which large sectors of the electorate were in agreement: economic development, the maintenance of public order, etc.

(2) The increased party dependence on interest group influence, and the transformation of collateral, religious, trade-union organizations, etc., into interest groups with weaker and less regular party ties.

(3) The members' loss of political weight, and the significant decline in the role of rank and file political activism.

(4) The strengthening of the leaders' organizational power, and their greater reliance on external interest groups than on members in financing the organization and in keeping close contact with the electorate.⁵

(5) Weaker and more discontinuous party–electorate relations, no longer linked to strong social settlements and to solid and unified political sub-cultures.

Kirchheimer's analysis, however, only treats implicitly a problem which we consider to be of the utmost importance: the increasing *professionalization* of party organizations. In the mass party described by Weber, Michels, and Duverger, a crucial role is played by the apparatus, the party bureaucracy: the "representative bureaucracy" (in our terms) is used by the mass party leaders to maintain close ties with the members, and, through the members, with the *class gardée*. In the new type of party a much more important role is played by professionals (the so-called experts, technicians with special knowledge), they being more useful to the organization than the traditional party bureaucrats, as the party's gravitational center shifts from the members to the electorate. Professionalization comports, in its turn, a number of organizational consequences about which we advanced some hypotheses in chapter 12.

The distinction between bureaucrats and professionals can help us isolate two ideal types of parties: the mass bureaucratic party and the electoral–professional party.[6] They differ as follows:

Mass bureaucratic parties	Electoral–professional parties
(a) central role of the bureaucracy (political-administrative tasks)	central role of the professionals (specialized tasks)
(b) *membership* party, strong vertical organizational ties, appeal to the "electorate of belonging"	electoral party, weak vertical ties, appeal to the "opinion electorate"
(c) pre-eminence of internal leaders, collegial leadership	pre-eminence of the public representatives, personalized leadership
(d) financing through membership and collateral activities (party cooperatives, trade unions etc.)	financing through interest groups and public funds
(e) stress on ideology, central role of the believers within the organization	stress on issues and leadership, central role of the careerists and representatives of interest groups within the organization

These differences need no particular comment; they summarize the organizational changes, in part discussed by Kirchheimer, in part derived from the analysis made in the preceding chapters, and in part described in the literature on recent changes in Western parties. They are ideal types. No party ever completely fits the "mass bureaucratic" type and no party completely fits the "electoral–professional" type. Parties have different organizational histories which produce different results. The electoral–professional ideal type (like the mass bureaucratic one) is above all useful for looking at some general trends; the differences from one organization to another are yet to be explained. Moreover, "new" and "old" features tend to overlap and coexist (and to cause internal tensions and conflicts) in every organization. Transformations vary widely from party to party, and from society to society.

There seem, however, to be two main variables which most influence speed and intensity of transformation:

The first variable is institutionalization. Transformation is faster the lower the degree of institutionalization *before* transformation begins. The higher the degree of institutionalization, the more the party can resist transformatory pressures; e.g. the PCF, a very strong institution, resists change far more than other French parties, and the Italian DC and PSI change, at least in certain respects, more than the PCI, etc.[7]

The second variable is mentioned by Kirchheimer and consists in the level of fragmentation of the party system. Kirchheimer states that big parties (electorally speaking) experience the greatest pressure to transform. The less fragmented the party system, the more it is controlled by a few large organizations; change will thus begin sooner and takes place more quickly. Excessive fragmentation of the party system tends to delay transformation.

The main causes of the affirmation of the electoral–professional party are to be found in the party environment. Organizational change is spurred on by external challenge, by environmental change (which acts on parties in the ways discussed in chapter 13). There are two main types of environmental change in Western society which seem to be behind this kind of transformation.[8]

The first type of change, which is the main subject of sociological research, is related to social stratification systems, and to changes in importance of various employment groups (e.g. the decreasing laborforce in industry, the expansion of the tertiary sector, etc.) and above all in the peculiarities and cultural attitudes of each group. Analyses describing the social composition of the electorate and party membership tend to ignore this latter factor. To observe, for example, that a communist or socialist party's electorate includes more or less the same percentage of "workers" as in the past, means little given that working-class physiognomy has greatly changed in the meantime, i.e. while in the past the principle working-class divisions had taken place between skilled and unskilled workers, nowadays it is between the "central" industrial workers (politically and syndically represented) and "peripheral" marginal workers.[9] This transformation modifies the political nature of the electorate of these parties, because it affects the composition of the political interests.

Similarly, it is useless to measure middle-class membership levels in various parties without considering the structural changes in those classes. Once again, measuring the "quantity" of denominational parties' supporters is futile unless consideration is given to the changes that both secularization and diffusion of education have brought about in relations between believers, religious institutions, and parties.

Social structural transformation – which contemporary sociological theory tries to understand in different ways and with a variety of categories (e.g. complex society, post-industrial society, late-capitalist society, etc.)[10] – influences parties, modifying their hunting grounds and political arenas. Electorates, for instance, have become more socially and culturally heterogeneous, and less controllable by parties. All of these factors encourage organizational change.

The second type of change is technological and consists in restructuring the political communication systems under the impact of the mass media, and particularly of television (the symbolic date here is 1960, the year of the American presidential elections). As television became central in political competition, it began to affect party organization.[11] Changes in communication techniques is causing an earthquake in party organizations: old bureaucratic roles becoming obsolete in the organization of consensus; new professional roles are gaining ground.[12] Changing the terms of political communication in favor of a more heterogeneous and educated public, mass-media are driving parties towards personalized campaigns, candidate-centered as well as issue-oriented i.e. centered on specific subjects with a high technical content, involving expert preparation.

Television and interest groups become far more important links (though precarious by definition) between parties and electorates than the traditional collateral organizations, the bureaucracy and party members. Bureaucrats and activists are still necessary, but their roles are now less important. Maps of organizational power have thus changed. Members and party bureaucrats have less weight both financially speaking and as links with voters; internal leaders are thus losing some of their political clout (based as it was on unequal exchange with members and bureaucrats) while public representatives appointed through election are correspondingly gaining in importance.

Changes in social structure and in political communication work together to erode traditional political sub-cultures, frozen for so long because of strong organizational settlements typical of mass bureaucratic parties. The "electorate of belonging" shrinks, and party identification – which had formerly assured electoral stability in most European countries – declines.[13] The electorate becomes more independent from the party, and social integration "from the cradle to the grave" is now almost everywhere limited to declining minorities. Electoral arenas have thus become more turbulent and unstable, forcing parties toward the electoral–professional model through imitative and reciprocal adjustment processes.

Mass bureaucratic parties were strong institutions. Electoral–professional parties are weak ones. The transition from one to the other thus involves de-institutionalization. The party's independence from the environment decreases as voter autonomy and interest groups' political role increase. Structural coherence decreases as parties tend to be incorporated within the state, the bureaucratic apparatuses become less important and the political weight of experts and appointed representatives increases. The strong political subcultures which stabilized the electoral arena and ensured the autonomy of many parties from the environment and structural consistency are disappearing. The historical epoch of strong parties/strong institutions (the mass parties analyzed by Weber and Duverger) seems to be drawing to a close.

Party crisis

Although Kirchheimer wrote in an era marked by economic development and political stability – keeping the debate over the end of ideology as a reference point – he was quite aware that the success of the catch-all party posed serious risks for democracy. His analysis ended with these words:

Will this limited participation which the catch-all party offers the population at large, this call to rational and dispassionate participation in the political process via officially sanctioned channels, work? The instrument, the catch-all party, cannot be much more rational than its nominal master, the individual voter. No longer subject to the discipline of the party of integration – or, as in the United States, never subject to this discipline – the voters may, by their shifting moods and their apathy, transform the sensitive instrument of the catch-all party into something too blunt to serve as a link with the functional powerholders of society. Then we may yet come to regret the passing – even if it was inevitable – of the class–mass party and the denominational party, as we already regret the passing of other features in yesterday's stage of Western civilization.[14]

By now most of his predictions have come true, and terms such as "ungovernability" and "legitimation crisis" are in vogue in Western social science. Kirchheimer's projections were thus well-grounded. The electoral–professional party's success coincides with the "crisis of parties" – one of the topics most discussed by those who wonder about the future of Western democracy. But to discuss a real or supposed party crisis in specific terms, we must shift our attention to the activities traditionally carried out by these organizations in democratic regimes: if there is a crisis, it will definitely appear as a crisis in these activities.[15] Following Kirchheimer once again, three "functions"[16] may be seen as traditionally peculiar to parties.

(1) An "integrative" or "expressive" function. Parties organize general requests for defence/transformation of the social and political order.[17] (They, of course, never transmit/organize general requests alone, they always make specific group and sectorial requests as well.)[18] The most important aspect of this function is the creation and preservation of collective identities through ideology. In that ideology serves as a means of deferring benefits to the future (sacrifice today is accepted in the hopes of a better society tomorrow),[19] it is possible to understand why the integrative/expressive function has often played a decisive role in political system stabilization; even so-called anti-system parties have often contributed to political system stabilization, acting as institutionalized channels for social protest.[20]

(2) A function of the selection of candidates to elective office. Also in varying proportions from country to country the appointment of managers and administrators to different state positions.

(3) A function of participating in forging public policy, i.e. taking part in binding collective decisions.

None of these functions has ever been monopolized by parties. The integrative/expressive function is carried out by other social institutions (e.g. family, school, religious institutions) too. The selection of elites is always influenced by interest groups. And state decisions are always made through negotiations among parties, "private" interest groups,[21] and institutional power centers (high-level bureaucracy, military elites, etc.). If we consider crisis with regard to the functions traditionally carried out by parties, we must not consider it as the loss of a (never existent) monopoly, but rather as a process of marginalization. This takes place with the emergence of the electoral–professional party. This type of party, as opposed to the old mass bureaucratic party, does not in fact organize stable collective identities. The erosion of political sub-cultures kept together by ideology, means the virtual end of activities related to the integrative/expressive function. This crisis, in turn, affects the other functions. The gap in collective identity caused by the professional–electoral party's emergence has two effects: it leads to the diffusion of "unconventional" political behavior (we shall see this aspect further on); and – more pertinent to us here – it makes the setting off of the multiplication and fragmentation of interest representation structures easier.[22] The party's ability to independently select elites – where such independence existed – is impaired: interest groups break into the political arena even more forcefully than in the past, directly sponsoring their own political representatives (while just nominally belonging to the party). The party's ability to influence state policy is also compromised, as it is hampered by interest groups, the autonomization of political–administrative systems,[23] and the multiplication and competition of single-issue associations. Being less and less an organizer of collective identities, it is compelled to compete directly with interest groups in the transmission/fulfilment of "specific requests" (so fragmenting and weakening the decision-making process).[24] In other words, the power relation between parties and other organizations in different political arenas favors the parties when they can use their ability to organize/represent collective interests. When this trump card is no longer exploitable, their position is weakened in every arena.

Changes in political cleavages

In his portrayal of European party systems, Stein Rokkan depicted four main structural cleavages which explain the uniformities and differences of different political systems' physiognomies: the center–periphery cleavage, the church–state cleavage, the city–country cleavage (i.e. the conflict between landowners and urban bourgeoisie) and class cleavage (employers–employees). Each of these cleavages led to political divisions and conflicts on specific issues. The church–state cleavage, for example, caused conflicts about education in the 1800s, the city–country cleavage led to tariff conflicts, etc. There were numerous differences in conflict intensity and timing, and not every cleavage always gave rise to a specific party. The class cleavage was, however, the exception:

> Conflicts in the *labor* market proved much more uniformly divisive. Working-class parties emerged in every country of Europe in the wake of the early waves of industrialization. The rising masses of wage earners, whether in large-scale farming, in forestry, or in industry, resented their conditions of work and the insecurity of their contracts, and many of them felt socially and culturally alienated from the owners and employers. The result was the formation of a variety of labor unions and the development of nationwide socialist parties.[25]

The class cleavage was at the root of the crucial political division between socialist and non-socialist parties. The issues related to this division headed the "hierarchy" of political problems in most European countries.[26]

We can thus understand why the political space of electoral competition became permanently *one-dimensional*: the right–left continuum became dominant almost everywhere as the "cognitive map" through which party identification was organized and attitudes towards politics were shaped.[27] The right–left continuum, at least in Europe, centered mainly around socio-economic problems related to class cleavage; in the age of welfare politics, state intervention in economics was the main political issue allowing voters and parties to be placed along this continuum.[28]

Are transformations taking place now which can change the physiognomy of competition's political space? We think so, for the connection between structural cleavages and political issues is changing everywhere. This connection has become stable and durable through parties and the political sub-cultures they organized. But the latter have been fading away as the electoral–professional party gains currency. The terms of the political divisions are also changing. In the past the main political division concerned the *quantum* of state intervention in the economy: increased intervention meant "socialist" policies, decreased intervention "capitalist" policies. Class divisions – groups favored or hurt by various choices – were recognizable (culturally recognizable through the more or less distorting lens of the political sub-cultures) in the conflicts around the economic policy. Since the late seventies, the problems have indeed changed: the unemployment/inflation alternative, for instance, does not divide social groups within definite limits. Unemployment includes intellectual unemployment; inflation divides workers into groups protected by trade unions that enjoy welfare benefits and non-protected marginal groups, simultaneously dividing the middle class, seizing labor revenues, damaging industrial power, favoring industrial debt, and encouraging financial-speculative groups and factions.[29] Cultural divisions (subordinate versus privileged classes, collective versus individual mobilization, collectivization of the means of production versus free market, etc.) that gave meaning as well as substance to the right–left "cognitive map," become fuzzy when it is no longer evident which social group is damaged and which is favored by a given choice.

In the conflicts related to so-called "anti-politics,"[30] the short circuit of traditional right–left divisions became even clearer. The opposition to "Big Government" (United States), to the "party state" (Germany), and to the "partitocrazia" (Italy) may result from forces with opposing political motivations (e.g. libertarian protest against state bureaucratic oppression or conservative revenge against state expansion).[31] Ecological issues gather radical youth consensus along with that of people who, living in the countryside, are directly menaced by nuclear installations. The women's liberation movements of the seventies deeply divided the traditional political sub-cultures. The revival of ethnic-linguistic conflicts of the late seventies cannot be understood on the basis of traditional right–left divisions. The "alternative" electoral lists (ecological) in France and Germany, unlike the more traditional ones of the New Left in the sixties, are supported in some cases by traditional middle–right voters, etc.

In this way political space is becoming multi-dimensional; the traditional right–left continuum is still a crucial political dimension, but a new dimension is emerging. In his examination of the political consequences of the emergence of post-materialist values, Ronald Inglehart speaks about an *establishment/anti-establishment* division different from the classical right–left division.[32] It is a division between ruling-groups (both right *and* left, i.e. conservative *and* socialist parties, industrial organizations *and* big trade unions) and large citizen groupings. There are many signs (in several European countries) that this division may last and perhaps even deepen: it first appeared in the collective movements of the sixties and seventies, and is now evident in a variety of unconventional political attitudes – from protest votes to electoral abstention, from the more or less transitory support of "alternative" lists to the total detachment from politics.[33] This cleavage does not ensure the emergence of any new political organization (just as the cleavages examined by Rokkan did not always lead to the creation of new parties). Political space is, however, changing, becoming an at least two-dimensional one: along with the traditional right–left dimension tied to party identification and conventional political attitudes, there is a new permanent dimension at the root of unconventional attitudes.[34]

The following objection is often raised to this thesis: the only political divisions that count, at least in the long run, are those related to "structural cleavages" (à la Rokkan), cleavages which divide society either into clear and distinct groups or, as in church–state conflicts, institutions. This objection may be met in three different ways:

First of all, we still know too little about the relation between transformations of social stratification systems and political conflicts to categorically reject the existence of a connection between an establishment/anti-establishment division and (new) structural cleavages. Changes in working and middle-class composition (which could, for instance, foreshadow alliances between highly educated people in the tertiary sector and the marginal proletariat)[35] induced by state intervention might be found to be the source of this division.

Secondly, Rokkan's theory (like other similar theories) was developed to explain the *birth* and *consolidation* of present European political regimes. Hence we cannot really expect it to shed light on the stages to follow, i.e. on the changes political regimes are currently undergoing. More specifically, the analytical framework distinguishing between structural cleavages and their political manifestation (recalling, not by chance, the Marxian distinction between structure and superstructure) was erected to explain the formation of political regimes in the age of competitive capitalism, in other words, when the state was not yet the main agent of reproduction/transformation of the social system. It is doubtful that this framework can be employed without modification to explain current conflicts and political divisions.

Thirdly, not even in the past did structural cleavages alone affect politics. Some time ago, Hans Daalder stressed how two kinds of divisions ("nationality" and "constitutional regime"), which had no necessary or immediately recognizable connection with structural cleavages, played central roles in the formation of modern Europe's political systems.[36] These divisions marked the passage from pre-industrial to industrial society. It wouldn't be impossible to hypothesize that the establishment/anti-establishment cleavage may very well turn out to be a main source of conflict in the political transition from industrial to post-industrial society. Of course the terms and intensity by which this cleavage could manifest political effects will depend upon how the political leaders currently emerging react within their different national contexts.[37]

The transformation of political space into a multi-dimensional one is related to the success of the electoral–professional party and to its accompanying political tensions. The establishment/anti-establishment division helps speed up party transformation and weaken traditional political sub-cultures. The success of the professional–electoral party, in its turn, destroys collective identities, deepening the political system's legitimation crisis, and thus exacerbating the establishment/anti-establishment division. This cleavage contributes to the ungovernability of political systems.[38] One-dimensional political space, allowing the voters to economize on information (the general "image" of the party counting more than a knowledge of its programs and policies), makes electoral choices easier, stabilizes attitudes and expectations, and offers political actors (voters and leaders) unequivocal standards of evaluation and choice.[39] In multi-party systems in which voters have difficulty telling one party from another,[40] one-dimensional political space is indispensable in making exchange on the electoral market more stable. The shift to multi-dimensional space annuls this advantage, disorients the political actors, makes competition more chaotic, and accentuates the "turbulence," instability, and unpredictability of the political arena.

Conclusion

In light of a classic paradigm of social change theory, the passage from "total" participation of the integration (mass bureaucratic) party, to the limited participation of the electoral–professional party may be viewed as one of the many effects of a more general tendency of big social aggregates. Some of the parties' former functions are taken over by other organizations; for example, the "private" welfare systems organized by socialist and denominational parties in the late 1800s and early 1900s, gave way to "public" welfare systems. New state agencies take over party functions. Political socialization no longer depends upon party organization, but rather upon mass-media and the interpersonal contact facilitated by increased horizontal mobility. Parties are driven to specialize even more, and the passage from the "cradle to the grave" participation to partial and limited participation is but one of the consequences. There is however risk in this interpretation: the sociological tradition I have referred to considers all increases in differentiation and specialization in social systems as evidence of progress, but it underestimates the disfunctional and destabilizing aspects of over-specialization. The emergence of the electoral–professional party, in fact, creates more problems than it solves. It is the result of modernization, increase in education, improvement in the living conditions of certain groups, classes and class segments that were previously socially and politically under-privileged. Such transformation often coincides with a type of participation which is far less respectful and subordinate to political elites than had been the case in the mass bureaucratic party. But the electoral–professional party also creates a vacuum at the level of collective identities. The voter becomes more independent and autonomous, less controlled and blackmailed by the oligarchies described by Michels. He also becomes, however, more isolated and puzzled. The social malaise appearing in the establishment/anti-establishment division, in the turbulence of electoral arenas, and in the effervescence of collective movements, is also due to the decadence, and the loss of credibility and attractiveness, of the old communitarian (both political and pre-political) structures.[41] In time, the electoral–professional party may turn out to be but a transitory and comparatively short-lived phenomenon.

Though the situation varies from country to country, three lines of possible developments (separately or jointly) seem to be more likely than others.

The first is that the electoral–professional party will turn out to be an intrinsically unstable institution, foretelling the *dissolution of parties* as organizations.[42] The parties completely lose their own organizational identity and appear to be only convenient tags for independent political entrepreneurs. This has, according to many authors, already happened in the United States. It is, however, improbable (at least in its extreme form) where parties began and consolidated as strong institutions. At any rate, the crisis of democratic political regimes seems destined to worsen (according to this scenario).

The second possibility is that an ideological backlash will take place, i.e. an attempt by the existing parties to resume their traditional expressive functions and former identities, returning to the extremism (leftist or rightist) of their far-off origins.[43] Such political innovation (which would, in fact, be a re-introduction of old politics under changed conditions) starts *from the heart* of the political system and is led by the old organizations reacting to environmental challenges. But it is not clear whether stable collective identities can be re-established in this way, nor with which political–organizational solutions they would be associated.

The third possibility is real political innovation (whose terms are, of course, unforeseeable). But innovation is unlikely to originate from within the political system or manifest itself through already dominant organizations.[44] More often it enters from the *outside* and is brought into the system by new organizations and political leaders who enter into competition with organizations already in power. This assumption is in agreement with Weber's theory whereby innovation – instead of coming from institutionalized organization – presupposes outbursts of "real revolutionary forces," i.e. charismatic movements. The collective identity vacuum created by the decline of parties' integrative/expressive function (along with other factors), could at least facilitate the creation of political movements quite different from the organizations which have been dominant up until now. In the years to come we may see an entrance onto the political scene of actors trying to create new and stable collective identities, to redefine and revamp those Western societies most plagued by social malaise. The organizational characteristics to be assumed by future political movements will help us understand whether the more pessimistic predictions concerning democracy's destiny are founded; whether an unheralded authoritarianism is destined to become dominant after sweeping away our fragile liberal constitutionalism;[45] or whether democractic regimes will be nourished by adjustments and/or transformations introduced by new political entrepreneurs.

Notes

Preface

1 C. Perrow, *Complex Organizations. A Critical Essay*, Glenview, Scott, Foresman and Co., 1972, p. 14.

2 C. Tilly, "Reflections on the History of European State-making," in Tilly (ed.), *The Formation of National States in Western Europe*, Princeton, Princeton University Press, 1975, p. 3.

3 On the comparative-historical method in sociology see T. Skocpol, M. Somers, "The Uses of Comparative History in Macrosocial Inquiry," *Comparative Studies in Society and History*, XXII (1980), pp. 174–97.

4 On the uniformity and the differences in the processes of political modernization of European countries the most important reference is Stein Rokkan; see the collection of important essays in *Citizens, Elections, Parties. Approaches to the Study of the Processes of Development*, Oslo, Universitesforlaget, 1970.

5 On the role of analysis by "geo-political" areas as an instrument for reducing the operative variables, see amongst others, A. Lijhart, *Il metodo della comparazione, rivista Italiana di Scienza Politica*, 1 (1971), pp. 79ff.

6 On the differences between the mono- and multi party systems see G. Sartori, *Parties and Party Systems. A Framework for Analysis*, Cambridge, Cambridge University Press, 1976.

7 R. Bendix, *Nation-Building and Citizenship*, New York, Wiley and Sons, 1964, p. 79. See also, S. M. Lipset, *The First New Nation*, New York, Anchor Books, 1967.

8 See the analysis on the "first" and successive systems of American parties in W. N. Chambers (ed.), *The First Party System: Federalists and Republicans*, New York, Wiley and Sons, 1972 and W. N. Chambers, W. D. Burnham (eds.), *The American Party System, Stages of Political Development*, New York, Oxford University Press, 1967.

9 B. Moore Jr, *Social Origins of Democracy and Dictatorship*, Boston, Beacon Press, 1966, p. 121.

1 Organizational dilemmas

1 W. Crotty, "A Perspective for the Comparative Analysis of Political Parties," *Comparative Political Studies*, III (1970), p. 281.

2 R. Michels, *Zur Soziologie des Parteiwesens in der Modernen Demokratic*, Leipzig, Klinkhardt, 1911; English trans., *Political Parties*, New York, The Free Press, 1962.

3 M. Duverger, *Les Parties politiques*, Paris, Armand Colin, 1951, English trans., *Political Parties*, New York, Wiley and Sons, 1963.

4 A typical manifestation of sociological prejudice can be found in a very influential

work written in the sixties by S. Eldersveld, entitled *Political Parties: A Behavioral Analysis*, Chicago, Rand McNally Co., 1964. Eldersveld, explicitly contrasting Michels theory, maintains that a diffuse power structure exists at many "levels of command" in a party, and that, in consequence, power is not simply concentrated in an oligarchy. These "levels of command" are the direct expression of internal "sub-coalitions," each representing socio-economic interests and/or particular socio-cultural interests (economic interest groups, ethnic minorities, etc.). In the case of the Democratic and Republican parties in Detroit (examined by Eldersveld), this was probably true. Eldersveld was mistaken, however, in taking the conclusions of his research as valid for the majority of parties. As we shall see, in the majority of cases the external social interests are filtered through barriers and structures of organizational mediation (even if they are of varying force and intensity according to the level of party institutionalization). See chapter 4 on this point.

5 This is the more or less implicit hypothesis behind analyses of party social composition, of sociological profiles of members, ruling groups, leaders, parliamentary groups, etc. It is a sort of *correspondence theory* postulating that, for instance, if the leader is of working-class origin, he will be representative of worker–electorate attitudes. This is a theory, to be generous, of dubious validity. Michels realized the problem seventy years ago in his remarks on the phenomenon of "embourgeoisment" among party bureaucrats coming from the working class. Sociographic studies comprise the better part of party literature. They can furnish, if used carefully, useful *additive* information within a different theoretical reference, but do not by themselves contribute much to the understanding of party functioning. The correspondence theory justifying sociographic party analyses goes hand in hand with the theory according to which the state bureaucracy is "representative" and receptive to the needs of its clients if there is some correspondence between the social origin of the bureaucrats and the social composition of the clients. For a confutation of this theory, see P. Sheriff, "Sociology of Public Bureaucracy," *Current Sociology*, IV (1976), pp. 73ff.

6 And in fact, as we shall see further on, parties with different sociological electorates sometimes have similar organizational structures, and parties with similar sociological electorates often have different structures.

7 In accordance with the Weberian distinction between different arenas of social action (that were for Weber related to class, status, and party), arenas which are certainly interdependent but never totally overlapping. See also G. Sartori, "Alla ricerca della sociologia politica," in *Rassegna Italiana di Sociologia*, IV (1968), pp. 597–639.

8 K. L. Shell, *The Transformation of Austrian Socialism*, New York, State University of New York, 1962, p. 4.

9 F. Gross, "Sociological Analysis of a Political Party," in *Il Politico*, XXXII (1967), p. 702.

10 Of this type are, for example, the analyses of communist parties that take Marxist–Leninist ideology as their primary explanatory variable in trying to understand their organizational physiognomy: see for example, J. Monnerot, *Sociologie du communisme*, Paris, Gallimard, 1949, and P. Selznick, *The Organizational Weapon: a Study of Bolshevik Strategy and Tactics*, New York, McGraw-Hill, 1952, two works already outdated, but which continue to have followers. For a critical analysis of this tradition, and, more generally, of any approach that explains organizations on the basis of their ideology rather than considering the reciprocal interactions of the organization and ideology, see A. Panebianco, "Imperative organizzativi, conflitti interni e ideologia nei partiti communisti," *Rivista Italiana di Scienza Politica*, III (1979) pp. 511–36.

11 A. Downs, *An Economic Theory of Democracy*, New York, Harper and Row, 1967, p. 28.

12 "Electoral victory," as a single attribute or in combination with others, is indicated as the party's fundamental goal in the majority of "minimal" party definitions given by political scientists: see amongst others J. Schlesinger, "Political Party Organization," in C. March, ed., *Handbook of Organizations*, Chicago, Rand McNally, 1965, pp. 767ff, L. D. Epstein, "Political Parties" in F. I. Greenstein, N. W. Polsby, eds., *Handbook of Political*

Science, Nongovernmental Politics, vol. IV, Reding Addison Welsley, 1975, pp. 229ff.

13 R. Michels, "Some Reflections on the Sociological Character of Political Parties," *American Political Science Review*, XXI (1927), pp. 753–71.

14 The extreme form of the thesis that parties pursue "electoral victory" is that for which the party's goal is to "maximize" votes. This, as is known, is Anthony Downs' theory in *An Economic Theory of Democracy*. For convincing objections, see J. Schlesinger, "The Primary Goals of Political Parties: a Clarification of Positive Theory," *American Political Science Review*, LXIX (1975), pp. 840–9, for whom the strategy of votes maximization is only one possible electoral strategy. Just as convincing is the objection in David Robertson's *A Theory of Party Competition*, London, Wiley, 1976. According to Robertson, parties cannot move freely along the left–right continuum in search of the optimal position for consensus maximization, as Downs' theory would suggest. Parties are hindered from this by activists who can exert a "veto" power with respect to changes in the party's political orientation belying their ideological orientation. For a similar discussion, in some ways, to Robertson's, see further on in this chapter; for a more theoretical discussion see chapter 2.

15 It is thus no accident that Duverger provides no definition of parties and that he limits himself to saying that "a party is a community with a particular structure," *Political Parties*, p. xv. As opposed to the authors mentioned before, Duverger was probably aware that any "common sense" definition (the likes of which I analyse here), would compromise the kind of organizational analysis that he proposed to make.

16 The specific activity of a certain organization does not define its goal, unless in a circular and tautological way: it doesn't make much sense to say that the goal of a firm that produces automobiles is automobile production. More generally on this point, but only on this point, I am in agreement with Fred Riggs when he maintains that the criteria for party analysis and classification must be *structural* and not functional or based on "motives," "goals," and the like: see F. Riggs, "Criteri di classificazione dei partiti," in D. Fisichella, ed., *Partiti e gruppi di pressione*, Bologna, Il Mulino, 1972, pp. 122–5.

17 A somewhat different perspective can be expressed in Alain Touraine's words: we can speak of the co-presence of a series of "oppositional couples" (determining ineliminable tensions in all organizational systems) from whose partial and precarious conciliation is derived the system's equilibrium. See A. Touraine, *La Production de la societé*, Paris, Editions du Seuil, 1973.

18 For this perspective see the influential article by Talcott Parsons, "Suggestions for a Sociological Approach to the Theory of Organization," *Administrative Science Quarterly*, I (1956), pp. 63–85.

19 P. Georgiou, "The Goal Paradigm and Notes towards A Counter Paradigm," *Administrative Science Quarterly*, XVIII (1973) pp. 291–310.

20 M. Shubik, "Approaches to the Study of Decision Making Relevant to the Firm," *Journal of Business*, XXXIV (1961), pp. 101–18.

21 B. Abrahamsson, *Bureaucracy or Participation: The Logic of Organization*, London, Sage Publications, 1977, p. 118.

22 *Ibid.*, p. 118.

23 *Ibid.*, p. 124.

24 See the distinction between "official goals" and "operative goals" proposed by C. Perrow, "The Analysis of Goals in Complex Organizations," *American Sociological Review*, V (1961), pp. 854–66.

25 See M. Crozier, E. Friedberg, *L'Acteur et le système: les constraintes de l'action collective*, Paris, Editions du Seuil, 1977.

26 This is, for example, the perspective adopted by A. Downs, *Inside Bureaucracy*, Boston, Little, Brown and Co., 1967, pp. 272ff. See also P. Selznick, *Leadership in Administration: A Sociological Interpretation*, New York, Harper and Row, 1957, that defines in these terms the passage from "organization" to "institution."

27 On ideologies, symbols, and myths, and on their relation to power the following classic remains fundamental: H. Lasswell, A. Kaplan, *Power and Society*, New Haven and London, Yale University Press, 1950. On the relation between "official" goals and power

in organizations, see S. Clegg, D. Dunkerley, "Il carattere ideologico e legittimante dei fini organizzativi," *Studi Organizzativi*, XI (1979), pp. 119–34.

28 See P. Lange "La teoria degli incentivi e l'analisi dei partiti politici," *Rassegna Italiana di Sociologia*, XVIII (1977), pp. 501–26, for a persuasive demonstration of the validity of an approach to the study of parties that combines the perspective of the "rational model" and that of the "natural systems model."

29 One can find many more organizational "dilemmas" in the specialized literature than the few considered here. Among the most important are the centralization/decentralization dilemma, and the efficiency/democracy dilemma. The first is a classic theme of organizational theory. I have preferred to consider this problem in relation to institutionalization (in chapter 4). On the efficiency/democracy dilemma see footnote 56.

30 On the theory of voluntary associations see D. Sills' classic, *The Volunteers*, Glencoe, The Free Press, 1957.

31 The theory of incentives owes its first formulation to C. Barnard, *The Functions of Executive*, Cambridge, Mass., Harvard University Press, 1938. Its most refined formulation can be found in J. Q. Wilson's *Political Organizations*, New York, Basic Books, 1973.

32 Peter Lange utilizes a reelaborated version of the theory of collective incentives in the work cited in note 28: the incentives of "solidarity," "identity," and "purpose" are incentives that the organization distributes to everyone in the same way.

33 For a convincing discussion of the problem of selective incentives, see D. Gaxie, "Economie des partis et retributions du militantisme," *Revue Française de Science Politique*, XVII (1977), pp. 123–54.

34 M. Olson, *The Logic of Collective Action: Public Goods and the Theory of Groups*, Cambridge, Harvard University Press, 1965. Naturally the distinction between collective and selective incentives is relative in the sense that a certain incentive can be either collective or selective according to different actors' positions. For example, the incentives of "solidarity" are collective incentives if we take the party activists' point of view (because they all profit from them equally) but are selective incentives reserved only to activists from the voters' point of view.

35 B. Barry, *Sociologists, Economists and Democracy*, Chicago, The University of Chicago Press, 1978.

36 For a further look at parties' bureaucratic dimension, see chapter 12.

37 See J. A. Schlesinger, *Ambition and Politics*, Chicago, Rand McNally, 1966.

38 The "electorate of belonging" is that portion of the party electorate integrated in the party's subculture. This type of voter is virtually a "born" supporter. In the majority of cases his family and friends support the same party as well. His loyalty and identification with the party are so strong that he votes for his party independently of the party's strategy. See A. Parisi and G. Pasquino, "Relazioni partiti-elettori e tipi di voto," in A. Parisi and G. Pasquino, eds., *Continuita' e mutamento elettorale in Italia*, Bologna, Il Mulino, 1977, pp. 215–49.

(*Translator's note*: The expression "elettorato di appartenenza" has been rendered here as "electorate of belonging" because the two aforementioned authors who coined the term, are also responsible for its initial translation in English in this way. Other, perhaps more metaphoric renditions of the term such as "all-weather electorate" or "thick and thin electorate" might have been used, but they have the tendency of conveying an overly active sense to the voter's allegiance.)

39 This does not mean, naturally, that the selective incentives cannot also favor – under certain conditions – the formation of "loyalty." At any rate, the strongest organizational loyalties are always tied to processes of identification that, at least partly, ignore the daily *do ut des*, the "rational choices" related to the distribution of selective incentives. For a different point of view closely relating party loyalty to selective incentives, see E. Spencer Wellhofer, T. Hennessy, "Models of Political Party Organization and Strategy: Some Analytical Approaches to Oligarchy," in I. Crewe ed., *British Political Sociology Yearbook, Elites in Western Democracies*, vol. 1, London, Croom Helm, 1974.

40 On the "dissimulation function" of ideology, see Gaxie, "Economie des partis." This point is taken up again in chapter 2.

41 The most important current of organizational theory, oriented towards the interpretation of organizational–environmental relations in terms of "adaptation," is the "contingency theory." On this theory, and for an attempt to apply it to the case of parties, see Part 3, and especially chapter 11.

42 For this statement see, among others, K. McNeil, "Understanding Organizational Power: Building on the Weberian Legacy," *Administrative Science Quarterly*, XXIII (1978), pp. 65–90, J. Bonis, "L'Organisation et l'environment," *Sociologie du Travail*, XIII (1971), pp. 225–48, C. Perrow, *Complex Organizations*.

43 I use the expression coined by Sartori, *Parties and Party Systems*, p. 327.

44 J. Blondel, *Political Parties: A Genuine Case for Discontent*, London, Wildwood House, 1978, pp. 22ff, distinguishes, in a somewhat analogous way, between "representative parties," those that reflect political demands, and "parties of mobilization" that organize these demands.

45 For a recent exposition of the Leninist and Gramscian doctrine of the political party, see L. Gruppi, *La teoria del partito rivoluzionario*, Rome, Editori Riuniti, 1980.

46 In political science the tendency is often to consider the electoral arena above all as a party's relevant environment. Although a *distinctive* arena (together with the parliamentary arena) of this particular type of organization, the electoral arena is instead only *one* of the party's environments. The entire society is every organization's environment, and it is only for analytical reasons that it makes any sense to distinguish those environments that more continually and directly influence organizations from others. For an exhaustive summary of the state of knowledge about organizational–environmental relations, see A. Anfossi, "L'organizzazione come sistema sociale aperto," in P. Bontadini, ed., *Manuale di Organizzazione*, Milan, ISEDI, 1978, pp. 1–38.

47 On the "social integration" party see S. Neumann, "Toward a Comparative Study of Political Parties," in S. Neumann, ed., *Modern Political Parties*, Chicago, University of Chicago Press, 1956. It constitutes a reelaboration of the "mass party" model of Duverger and Weber, but from the perspective of the network of vertical ties by which the organization integrates its own electoral following in a "society within the society."

48 It is the process implied by the concept of "negative integration" utilized by G. Roth, *The Social-Democrats in Imperial Germany*, Totowa, The Bedminster Press, 1963.

49 Bonis, "L'Organisation et l'environment," p. 234.

50 On the importance of the organization's "domain" or "reserved" territory, see J. Thompson, *Organizations in Action*, New York, McGraw-Hill, 1967. On the functions of the organizational goals in relation to the "domain," see P. E. White *et al.*, "Exchange as a Conceptual Framework for Understanding Interorganizational Relationship: Application to Nonprofit Organizations," in A. R. Negandhi, ed., *Interorganizational Theory*, Kent, The Kent State University Press, 1975, pp. 182–95.

51 The distinction adaptation/domination is, naturally, an analytic distinction: the relations between an organization and its environment always imply adaptation (of the organization to the environment) and domination (transformation of the environment by the organization), but it is still possible to distinguish between those relations in which an adaptation by the organization is *prevalent*, and those in which a deliberate strategy of environmental transformation is *prevalent*.

52 For a now classic analysis which emphasizes the autonomous role of organizational leaders, see Selznick, *Leadership in Administration*. See also J. Child, "Organization, Structure, Environment and Performance: The Role of Strategic Choice," *Sociology*, VI (1972), pp. 1–22.

53 See the criticism of Child's article in the above footnote by H. E. Haldrich, *Organization and Environment*, Englewood Cliffs, Prentice-Hall, 1979, pp. 138ff.

54 See R. Mayntz, "Conceptual Models of Organizational Decision-making and their Applications to the Policy Process," in G. Hofstede, M. Sami Kassen, eds., *European Contributions to Organizational Theory*, Amsterdam, Van Gorculum, 1976, pp. 114–25. The decision-making process is therefore strongly influenced by the negotiations and conflicts between the "informal associations" existing within the organization, i.e. has to do with the phenomenon of "clique:" see M. Dalton, *Men Who Manage*, New York, Wiley and Sons, 1959. At least in part, the "cliques" that Dalton refers to correspond to those

subgroups that make up "factions" and "tendencies" in parties. On the question of factions and tendencies, see chapter 3.

55 For a discussion of organizational "strategic games," see Crozier and Friedberg, *L'Acteur et le systeme*.

56 It is with respect to the leader's margins of maneuverability *vis-à-vis* other organizational members that the classical theme of "party democracy" must be considered. It is a theme which has been widely discussed in the literature, but mostly with reference to Michels' "iron law of oligarchy," or rather with the intention of providing examples for and against Michels' thesis concerning the impossibility of democracy in parties. But the theme has often been dealt with ideologically and using interpretative tools of dubious value. The best works on the subject have dealt with trade unions, instead of parties, as their subject: see the classic by S. M. Lipset, M. A. Trow, J. S. Coleman, *Union Democracy*, New York, The Free Press, 1956, and more recently J. D. Edelstein, M. Warner, *Comparative Union Democracy*, London, Allen and Unwin, 1975. On the basis of some of Peter Blau's intuitions, it is perhaps possible to speak of the existence of an efficiency/democracy dilemma, affecting, above all, voluntary associations, but that may be found as well, albeit in a more attenuated form, in other organizations. It is related to the dilemmas that I have here considered as primary. As much as the organization is an instrument for the pursuit of its "official goals," it has a problem of efficiency, of selection of the most suitable means for realizing its prescribed ends. Qua natural system pursuing the satisfaction of particular and diversified demands, the organization has a problem of "democracy," of choices which can guarantee the satisfaction of interests according to a priority scale (as well as of legitimate procedures that allow for the establishment of priorities in a way acceptable to the majority of the organization's members). Depending on the type of actor and his organizational position (in particular, whether he is part of the leadership or not), he will be more concerned with efficiency or with "democracy." This gives rise to conflicts and tensions, as the choices tending to maximize efficiency often conflict with the procedures aimed at establishing priorities. In parties, the demand for greater "democracy" is the typical political tool used by internal minorities to gain consensus against the majority. On the dilemma efficiency/democracy, see P. Blau, M. W. Meyer, *Bureaucracy in Modern Society*, New York, Random House, 1956.

57 On the "succession of ends," see chapter 13.

58 T. J. Lowi, *The Politics of Disorder*, New York, Norton Co., 1971, p. 49. As we shall see in chapter 3, the articulation of ends is concretely determined through the mediation of a "political strategy."

59 On the distinction between "latent ideology" and "manifest ideology," see P. Lange, "La teoria degli incentivi e l'analisi dei partiti politici."

60 Reechoing the definition used by the Austrian socialist reformer, Karl Renner, at the beginning of the century to define the ambiguities of his party, *die Politik der radikalen Phrase* (the politics of radical phraseology), we can define this particular kind of articulation of ends with the expression "politics of verbal radicalism." The politics of verbal radicalism has characterized many socialist and communist parties in different phases of their history. It is a programmed policy made up of "incoherencies" built around a stable dissociation between affirmations of principles and behaviors. Its characteristic is the co-presence of an "anti-system" revolutionary ideological appeal and of a practical behavior which negates the revolutionary symbols evoked either through a policy of passivity or through a pragmatic and reformist praxis (even if hidden through under-the-table bargaining with governmental parties). The Italian socialist Maximalism of the years preceding fascism, the PCF, the PCI in the fifties and sixties and the SPD of Kautsky and Bebel are all examples of this. The politics of verbal radicalism in party–environment relations leads to that "negative integration" phenomenon described by Roth, *Social Democrats*.

61 For a balanced evaluation of the advantages and the limits of the Weberian method, see N. S. Smelser, *Comparative Methods in the Social Sciences*, Englewood Cliffs, Prentice-Hall, 1976, pp. 114–50.

62 A. Pizzorno, "Introduzione allo studio della partecipazione politica," *Quaderni di Sociologia*, XV (1966), pp. 235–87.
63 *Ibid.*, p. 252.
64 *Ibid.*, pp. 256ff.
65 But later on, however, it will become necessary: see chapter 4.
66 The tendency towards the reduction of the leaders' freedom of movement after the party's institutionalization does not preclude the eventual development of an oligarchy. Often the oligarchies are capable of successfully resisting pressures from the base which aim at supplanting the leaders, but are at the same time incapable of guiding the party, i.e. of choosing political strategies appropriate to the circumstances, and thus become "prisoners" of the organization's needs. On oligarchy as a particular type of leadership, and for an interesting typology of oligarchical systems within trade union organizations, see Edelstein and Warner, *Comparative Union Democracy*, pp. 31ff.

2 Power, incentives, participation

1 This theme is dealt with both in studies on Michels and in many empirical analyses of parties (which classify a party as democratic or un-democratic according to how its decisions are made and how candidates for its public-elective positions are chosen). For the first type of study, see C. W. Cassinelli, "The Law of Oligarchy," *American Political Science Review*, XLVII (1953) pp. 773–84; G. Hans, "Roberto Michels and the Study of Political Parties," *British Journal of Political Science*, I (1971) pp. 55–172; D. W. Medding, "A Framework for the Analysis of Power in Political Parties," *Political Studies*, XVIII (1970), pp. 1–17; E. J. Cook, "Roberto Michels: Political Parties in Perspective," *The Journal of Politics*, XIII (1971) pp. 773–96. For the second type of study see, e.g. J. Obler, "Intra-party Democracy and a Selection of Parliamentary Candidates: The Belgian Case," *British Journal of Political Science*, IV (1974), pp. 163–85.

2 On exchange theory, see P. Blau, *Exchange and Power in Social Life*, New York, Wiley, 1964.

3 M. Crozier, E. Friedberg, *L'Acteur et le système*, p. 59.

4 This naturally has very important (but often neglected) implications for the problem of "party democracy." It also has implications for the problem of "authority," i.e. of the "legitimacy" of organizational power, which we shall discuss in chapter 3.

5 D. Gaxie, "Economie des partis," p. 151.

6 M. Duverger, *Political Parties*, pp. 90ff.

7 A. Parisi, G. Pasquino, *Relazioni partiti-elettori e tipi di voto*, who distinguish between the vote of those who "belong to the party," opinion vote, and (clientelistic) exchange vote. The vote of those belonging to the party is a direct expression of the existence of political subcultures that tie parties to the electorate. On political subcultures, see chapter 4. On relations between extension of *appartenenza* vote, stability in the electoral arena, and functioning of party organizations, see chapter 11.

8 As many empirical studies demonstrate: see for example, S. H. Barnes, *Party Democracy: Politics in an Italian Socialist Federation*, New Haven, Yale University Press, 1967, G. Poggi, ed., *L'organizzazione partitica del PCI e della DC*, Bologna, Il Mulino, 1968.

9 Maurice Duverger, after having compared electoral trends and trends in party membership, observes that between the "electoral community" and the "community of members." "It is just as if the latter group constituted, by comparison with the former, a closed circle, an exclusive world of which the reactions and the general behavior obeyed its own laws, different from those which determine the changes amongst electors, that is the variations in public opinion." M. Duverger, *Political Parties*, p. 101.

Their "own laws" are related, in my view, to the different combinations of incentives that the two communities utilize. We would naturally have to consider the fact that each party's electorate is not a homogeneous body, but can be broken down into the "belonging to the party" electorate, electorate of opinion, and client-type electorate, and that therefore, the incentives that tie the various portions of the electorate to the party are of different types.

10 For empirical analyses of the discontinuity of political activism, see S. Eldersveld, *Political Parties: A Behavioral Analysis*, pp. 140ff, and in the case of Canadian parties, A. Kornberg et al., *Semi-Careers in Political Work: The Dilemma of Party Organizations*, Sage Professional Paper in Comparative Politics, Series Number 01-008, vol. 1, 1970.

11 But only in part, as I will attempt to demonstrate in chapter 10.

12 On the relation between structural differentiation and need for social control see D. Rueschemeyer, "Structural Differentiation, Efficiency, and Power," *American Journal of Sociology*, LXXXIII (1977), pp. 1–25.

13 D. Gaxie, "Economie des partis," p. 131.

14 *Ibid.*, p. 134.

15 Which helps to explain the usually very high turnover within the members' universe, not to mention the discontinuities in participation at the lower levels of the party hierarchy. On the PCF's significant membership fluctuations, see N. McInnes, *The Communist Parties of Western Europe*, London, Oxford University Press, 1975, pp. 5ff.

16 D. Gaxie, "Economie des partis," p. 138.

17 The line–staff distinction is essential to the analysis of organizational systems. There are usually three classical schemas: the *hierarchical* organization (line), the *functional* organization (staff), and the *hierarchical–functional* organization (line–staff). Starting from these three basic models, the possible variants are innumerable, and organizational theory has elaborated more complex "secondary" models: see A. Fabris, "Gli schemi organizzativi fondamentali," in P. Bontadini, ed., *Manuale de organizzazione*, pp. 1–43. In this book I have essentially focused on the *processes* of exchange between actors rather than on the *structures* within which the exchange takes place. This is because it is only through empirical research (which is today more or less nonexistent) on parties' actual divisions of labor (and *not* those that appear in their statutes) that it would be possible to approach party organizations using models elaborated in studying other types of organizations.

18 See, for instance, the analyses of the Italian communist and christian-democratic activists in F. Alberoni, ed., *L'attivista di partito*, Bologna, Il Mulino, 1967.

19 In his research on the Italian Socialist Party, Samuel Barnes found that about 60 per cent of the members did not identify with either of the two factions then fighting for party control, and that identification with either one or the other increased as the levels of education and participation in party affairs increased. See S. Barnes, *Party Democracy: Politics in an Italian Socialist Federation*, pp. 105ff. Among the christian-democratic activists interviewed in the research cited in the preceding footnote, a very high percentage only partly identified with any one specific current, and, what's more, only in terms of "ideal reference" points (*L'attivista di partito*, pp. 323ff). This is a problem related to the incentive system: if selective incentives prevail (which happens when a latent ideology intervenes with a large availability of material public resources), it is probable that the believer–careerist ratio swings in favor of the second. The Italian Christian-Democrats are often represented by their adversaries in these terms. The case of the Christian-Democrats is discussed in chapter 7.

20 As long as a close connection exists between the level of education, mobility aspirations, and real mobility opportunities, we can understand parties' "natural" tendencies to maintain – at the medium to high levels of the organization – a clear overabundance of personnel of high social extraction. This explains why only the constraining and explicit measures, often adopted, for instance, by communist parties, can check this natural tendency by creating "reserved positions" (for activists of worker or peasant extraction, for women, etc.).

21 On splits as phenomena due to internal defeats of leaders and activists in the competition for party positions, see E. Spencer Wellhofer, T. M. Hennessey, "Political Party Development, Institutionalization, Leadership, Recruitment and Behavior," *American Journal of Political Science*, XVIII (1974), pp. 135–65.

22 See the observations of A. Stinchcombe, "Social Structure and Organizations," in March, *Handbook of Organizations*, p. 181.

23 M. Zald, D. Jacobs, "Compliance/Incentive Classifications of Organizations: Underlying Dimensions," *Administration and Society*, IX (1977), p. 409.
24 On party bureaucracies, see chapter 12.

3 Dominant coalition and organizational stability

1 The thesis according to which "coping with uncertainty," i.e. controlling the zones of uncertainty, is the principal resource of organizational power, elaborated by Michel Crozier in the works cited in the following footnote, has been further developed by, amongst others, D. J. Hickson *et al.*, "A Strategic Contingencies' Theory of Intraorganizational Power," *Administrative Science Quarterly*, XVI (1971), pp. 216–29.

2 I've taken this classification, with few variations from Crozier, Friedberg, *Attore, sociale e sistema*, pp. 55ff, adding, however, financing and recruitment which they did not treat. Crozier discusses the concept of uncertainty in a restricted way in his classic, *Le Phénomène bureaucratique*, Paris, Editions du Seuil, 1963.

3 *Ibid.*

4 Downs, *Inside Bureaucracy*, p. 62.

5 Gianfranco Poggi's observation, in the preface of the research on the PCI and the DC as organizations, is worth noting: "We are not simply dealing, let us reiterate, with interpretation of the typical material of legal investigation – in particular the successive versions of the party's statutes and regulations – i.e. those problems regarding jurists; we are also, and above all, dealing with a critical meditation upon a body of information (more or less pertinent to organizational problems) which is much more extensive and varied than the party's juridical 'cards'." *L'organizzazione partitica del PCI e della DC*, pp. 15–16.

6 On the tendency of the different power resources to accumulate in the same hands through a process defined as "agglutination," see H. Lasswell, A. Kaplan, *Power and Society*, New Haven, Yale University Press, 1950.

7 On phenomena of informal communication within organizations and their effects upon hierarchical relations, see P. Blau and W. R. Scott, *Formal Organization: A Comparative Approach*, San Francisco, Chandler Publishing Co., 1962.

8 David Wilson, author of an excellent study of the bureaucratic structure of British parties, describes an exception to the rule of the iron control of Central Office (the general headquarters of the Conservative Party) over local agents, hired to coordinate the party's activities in their own zones of competency for the center: the case of the agent for West Midlands, J. Galloway, who maintained throughout his entire career an almost total independence from the central bureaucracy, thanks to an autonomous control of his financial sources. Galloway was the only agent capable of eluding the eight-year rotation rule, that of periodic movement from one area to another through which Central Office can guarantee its control over its agents, hindering them from developing overly close ties with the party sectors to which they are assigned. See D. J. Wilson, *Power and Party Bureaucracy in Britain*, Lexington, Lexington Books, 1975, p. 52.

9 On this point, my analysis differs substantially from that of Crozier and Friedberg (in their *L'Acteur et le système*) who seem to underestimate the importance of "organizational history" in limiting the actors' freedom of action.

10 R. M. Cyert, J. G. March, *A Behavioral Theory of the Firm*, New York, Prentice-Hall, 1963, and T. Barr Greenfield, "Organizations as Social Inventions: Rethinking Assumptions about Change," *The Journal of Applied Behavioral Science*, IX (1973), pp. 551–74.

11 The analysis of all the cases cited here is developed in Part II.

12 The distinction between factions and tendencies comes from R. Rose, *The Problem of Party Government*, Harmondsworth, Penguin Books, 1976, pp. 312–28. On factionism see F. P. Belloni, D. C. Beller, eds., *Faction Politics: Political Parties in Comparative Perspective*, Santa Barbara, ABC-Clio, 1978.

13 This term comes from Eldersveld, *Political Parties: A Behavioral Analysis*, but I use it in a different way to indicate a group within the party with a local base of power within the organization – even if in certain cases it can control one or more leaders on the national level. As opposed to Eldersveld's sub-coalitions, ours are not necessarily representatives of "specific" socio-economic or socio-cultural interests (even if they sometimes are).

14 On various organized formations within parties as aggregations of smaller groups, see Duverger, *Political Parties*, pp. 151ff.

15 A more in-depth discussion of the concepts discussed above is taken up in chapter 9 (where, after having examined a certain number of concrete parties, we will elaborate a typology of dominant coalitions) and in chapter 13 (where the problem of change within dominant coalitions will be examined).

16 For a discussion of the leader as political entrepreneur, see N. Frohlich *et al.*, *Political Leadership and Collective Goods*, Princeton, Princeton University Press, 1971.

17 Cautiously, because "legitimation" is one of the most ambiguous concepts in modern power theory. On the many problems linked to the concept of legitimation in Max Weber, see J. Bensman, "Max Weber's Concept of Legitimacy: An Evaluation," in A. J. Vidich, R. M. Glassman, eds., *Conflict and Control: Challenge to Legitimacy of Modern Government*, London, Sage Publications, 1979, pp. 17–48. For an attempt to relate the distribution of individual benefits to the problem of legitimacy in the framework of a utilitarian theory, see R. Rogoswki, *Rational Legitimacy*, Princeton, Princeton University Press, 1970.

18 In this perspective, the leadership's *authority* (legitimate power) is a function of the satisfaction derived from the exchange by the other actors, and is maintained and continually invigorated by the exchange. A fundamental difference, however, exists between exchanges centered on selective incentives, and those centered on collective incentives: in the second type of exchange the actors that benefit from the incentives are *not* conscious of negotiating, and this type of exchange thus cannot be interpreted in a utilitarian way. It is through the leader's mediation and his "political strategy" that the "believers" renew their faith in the organization, and continually find confirmation of their identity as part of a collective subject.

19 On the fact that participation, in order to be activated, requires the hope that the collective action is valid and efficient, see the interesting examination by S. Berglund, *The Paradox of Participation: An Empirical Study of the Swedish Party*, paper presented at the ECPR workshop on Political Organizations, Grenoble, 1978.

20 I am obviously aware that the expression "political strategy," extracted from the daily political lexicon, is very vague. But, in reality, what is actually vague is that to which the expression refers, its empirical referent: a political strategy, in fact, is but a series of affirmations formulated by the leaders about the party's intermediate objectives and how to realize them (alliance policies, etc.). These affirmations are often ambiguous, and are usually utilized at different organizational levels as generic criteria for daily action. In my perspective, a political strategy is principally an instrument for the maintenance of party identity, and only secondarily a guide for action.

21 Naturally, the means (the political strategy) is only analytically distinguishable from ends (the official goals dictated by organizational ideology). When changes in political strategy take place, even the organizational ideology is, at least in part, redesigned. We will speak in such cases of a "succession of ends;" on this point see chapter 13. A political strategy, in our sense, is such only if it is openly announced by the leaders – for its primary function is that of lending credibility to the official goals, and of preserving in this way organizational identity. A political strategy, however, obviously has effects (forseen or not) upon the relation between the party and its environment. On the concept of "strategy" in the sociology of firms, see A. Chandler, *Strategy and Structure*, Cambridge, MIT Press, 1962.

22 "Aspiring leaders who have a low probability of victory in the competition for the leadership position are likely, on the other hand, to have a higher probability of remaining opposition leaders. Under the circumstances, an opposition leader with a low probability of acquiring the leadership position may concentrate on obtaining donations for actions taken in terms of the opponent's role instead of (or in addition to) activities aimed at the acquisition of the leadership position. Such an individual might find it

advantageous to provide a variety of services in exchange for the contributions required to make it profitable to continue to occupy the role of opposition leader."

23 See the model of organizational change elaborated in chapter 13.

24 In fact, the more selective incentives prevail over collective incentives, the more organizational ideology remains latent (with vague and contradictory objectives) and the less important the political strategy's role in the distribution of incentives.

25 This redefinition of Michels' thesis suggests that the oligarchy's objectives are as much geared to the conservation of the organization, as to the defence of its own preeminent position within the organization.

26 For a refutation of Michels' thesis on this point, see among others, Wilson, *Political Organizations*, p. 208.

27 The best formulation of this theory is to be found in Stinchcombe, *Social Structure and Organizations*. For the case of political parties, the theory is taken up by E. Spencer Wellhofer, "Political Parties as 'Communities of Fate:' Tests with Argentina Party Elites," *American Journal of Political Science*, XVIII (1974), pp. 347–69.

28 On the relation between size and political cohesion, see chapter 10.

29 I treat these problems, in the framework of an analysis of the relations between party organizations and the environment, in chapter 11.

30 See, on the organization of the DC, chapter 7.

31 R. A. Day, J. V. Day, "A Review of the Current State of Negotiated Order Theory: an Appreciation and a Critique," *Sociological Quarterly*, XVIII (1977), pp. 126–42.

4 Institutionalization

1 Cf. D. Silverman, *Sociology of Organizations*, London, Heinemann Educational Books, 1970, on the concept of "genetic model."

2 Duverger, *Political Parties*.

3 On the historical origins of parties and for an original interpretation, see P. Pombeni, "Il problema del partito politico come soggetto storico: sull'origine del 'partito moderno,' Premesse ad una ricerca," in F. Piro, P. Pombeni, eds., *Movimento operaio e società industriale in Europa 1870–1970*, Padova, Marsilio, 1981, pp. 48–72. See also A. Colombo, *La dinamica storica dei partiti politici*, Milan, Istituo Editoriale Cisalpino, 1970.

4 K. Eliassen, L. Svaasand, "The Formation of Mass Political Organizations: An Analytical Framework," *Scandinavian Political Studies*, X (1975), pp. 95–120.

5 *Ibid.*, p. 116.

6 J. Elklit, "The Formation of Mass Political Parties in the Late 19th Century: The Three Models of the Danish Case," and L. Svaasand, "On the Formation of Political Parties: Conditions, Cause, Patterns of Development," papers presented at the ECPR workshop on political organizations, Grenoble, 1978.

7 This problem is touched upon by L. Svaasand in the paper quoted in the preceding footnote; he distinguishes between "monocephalic" and "polycephalic" parties.

8 On situations of the *statu nascenti*, with a different emphasis, see F. Alberoni, *Movimento e istituzione*, Bologna, Il Mulino, 1977, and Touraine, *La production de la societe*, A. Melucci, ed., *Movimenti di rivolta*, Milan, Etas Libri, 1976. For a more in-depth discussion of the literature on charismatic leadership, see chapter 8.

9 R. Tucker, "The Theory of Charismatic Leadership," in D. Rustow, ed., *Philosophers and Kings: Studies in Leadership*, New York, Braziller, 1970, pp. 81–2.

10 See chapter 8 for details on this point.

11 Selznick, *Leadership in Administration*.

12 *Ibid.*

13 *Ibid.*

14 On institutionalization as a modality of stabilization for both intra-organizational and organizational–environmental exchanges, see S. N. Eisenstadt, *Social Differentiation and Stratification*, Glenview, Scott, Foresman and Co., 1965, p. 39ff. See also, in the same vein, Blau, *Exchange and Power in Social Life*, pp. 211ff.

15 A. Pizzorno, "Interests and Parties in Pluralism," in S. Berger, ed., *Organizing Interests in Western Europe*, New York, Cambridge University Press, 1981, pp. 247–84.

16 The difference between "loyalty" and "interests," in the way we use them here, largely corresponds to Easton's distinction between "diffuse support" – the consensus which is given to the system as such, regardless of immediate compensations – and "specific support" – consensus given to leaders in exchange for immediate advantages: see D. Easton, *A Systems Analysis of Political Life*, Chicago, University of Chicago Press, 1979, p. 267ff. Naturally even specific consensus, when satisfied, generates "loyalty," but it is more likely to be an *ad personam* loyalty (i.e. a loyalty to the leader or leaders who satisfy the particular requests) than to the institution as such, as in the case of diffuse consensus.

17 I have chosen these and only these "parameters" of institutionalization, because it is through the autonomy *vis-à-vis* the environment and the level of systemness that, in my view, organizations tend to move in the same direction. In other words, and as I shall try to demonstrate in this and in the following chapters with concrete examples, the greater the autonomy *vis-à-vis* the environment, the greater the systemicity will tend to be; and correlatively, the less the autonomy, the less the systemness. The well known criteria, adopted by Samuel Huntington, to measure institutionalization – autonomy, coherence, complexity, and flexibility – don't seem very useful in empirical analysis. Nothing seems to guarantee that an increase in autonomy *also* increases complexity, coherence, and flexibility: see S. Huntington, *Political Order in Changing Societies*, New Haven and London, Yale University Press, 1968.

18 Bonis, *L'Organization et l'environment*.

19 See M. Cotta, *Classe politica e parlamento in Italia 1946–1976*, Bologna, Il Mulino, 1979, on the interaction between parliamentary institution and party structure.

20 A. Gouldner, *For Sociology*, Harmondsworth, Penguin Books, 1975; J. A. Van Doorn, "Conflict in Formal Organizations," in A. Renck, *Conflict in Society*, Boston, Little Brown and Co., 1966, p. 1.

21 Haldrich, *Organizations and Environment*, pp. 77ff.

22 For E. Spencer Wellhofer, "Dimensions of Party Development: A Study in Organizational Dynamics," *The Journal of Politics*, XXXIV (1972), pp. 153–69, both "bureaucratization" *and* "formalization" (the production of written norms and regulations) are constitutive elements of institutionalization. While I agree with the first point, I do not agree with the second: as we shall see, various signs seem to indicate that formalization can be present even where organizational institutionalization is weak.

23 On the concept of "opportunity structure," see J. A. Schlesinger, *Ambition and Politics*, Chicago, Rand McNally, 1966.

24 Huntington, *Political Order and Social Change*, pp. 21ff.

25 See the typology proposed by Pizzorno, *Introduzione allo studio della participazione politica*.

26 On the discontinuity of careers in weakly organized parties, see Eldersveld, *Political Parties*, pp. 140ff, Kornberg *et al.*, *Semi-Careers in Political Work*.

27 See Spencer Wellhofer, *Political Parties as "Communities of Fate."*

28 On these concepts see R. S. Robins, *Political Institutionalization and Integration of Elites*, London, Sage Publications, 1976.

29 On the differences in elite recruitment between the "guild system" (which requires a long apprenticeship within the organization) and "lateral entrances," see R. Putnam, *The Comparative Study of Political Elites*, Prentice-Hall, 1976, p. 47ff.

30 In certain cases, the presence of a strong subculture is related to situations of "organizational encapsulement:" see G. Sartori, "European Political Parties: The Case of Polarized Pluralism," in R. A. Dahl, D. E. Neubauer, eds., *Readings in Modern Political Analysis*, New York, Prentice-Hall, 1968, pp. 115–49.

31 This fact explains the tendency of the more institutionalized parties, which organize popular classes, to internally reproduce (within certain limits), social inequalities – in particular, by over-representing bourgeois groups in the middle-high level. For empirical evidence see D. Gaxie, "Les Logiques recruitment du politique," *Revue Française de Science Politique*, XXX (1980), pp. 5–45. Social inequalities, however, are *always* reflected with more immediacy in weak rather than strong institutions. The fact, as Michels noted, that there were more intellectuals in the PSI and SFIO's national elites than in the SPD's (where the worker component was much stronger) should be attributed to a difference in degree of institutionalization; see R. Michels, *Proletariato e Bourghesia nel movimento Socialista italiano*, Torino, Bocca, 1908.

32 Duverger distinguishes, in *Political Parties*, between "strongly articulated" and "weakly articulated" parties. This distinction partly corresponds to our distinction between low and high degrees of systemness, of internal structural coherence, which depends on the existence of strong central coordination (or lack thereof). In this sense, the distinctions – crucial to Duverger's organizational theory – between cell party, militia, branch, and caucus correspond, in my perspective, to differences in degree of systemness: an organization whose basic unit is the cell or militia normally has (but *not*, as we shall see, if it is a charismatic party) a greater internal structural coherence than an organization based on territorial section; the latter, in its turn, has a greater structural coherence than an organization based on committees.

33 Elklit, "Formation of Mass Political Parties," and Svaasand, "Formation of Political Parties." On the inability of Italian liberals to organize a modern party see G. Galli, *I partiti politici*, Turin, UTET, 1974.

34 For an explanation of why we do not consider the CDU to be an externally legitimated party, as opposed to the other confessional parties, see chapter 7.

35 It is naturally possible to hypothesize that an external organization can produce the same effects as those produced by charisma, i.e. the absence of institutionalization accompanying a dominant coalition's strong cohesion; this is likely when the external organization is so cohesive as to impose an analogous cohesion upon the sponsoring party. This was probably formerly the case of the CGP (Clean Government Party) in Japan, a political emanation of a very cohesive and compact religious organization, the *Soka Gakkai*; see T. Tsutani, *Political Change in Japan*, New York, McKay, 1977, p. 151ff. But organizations are rarely so cohesive; the most "normal" outcome is that of a weakly institutionalized party with a divided dominant coalition.

36 Many factors can be very important. The institutional characteristics of the political regime are among the most important (e.g. the type of state bureaucracy); the elapsed time between the party's birth and its accession to national government is also quite important. (A party which undergoes organizational consolidation while in power – instead of while in opposition – is not very likely to become a strong institution). The intensity of the environmental threats experienced in the formative phase is also an important factor here, e.g. in the case of fusion between two or more organizations (a variant of territorial diffusion): as we shall see in the next chapter, a combination of state repression and fusion between two relatively centralized organizations can help explain why the SPD became a strong institution.

5 Oppositional parties

1 I would like at this point to make three comments to the reader: (1) the analysis that follows in this and in the three succeeding chapters, is an attempt to test the typology of relations between the genetic model and institutionalization developed in chapter 4. The analysis will consequently be limited to as brief an examination as possible of the formative phase of different parties. When particular historical situations have forced me to touch upon subsequent events, I have made brief and sometimes superficial reference to them. Furthermore, in particular in chapter 13 where I treat the problem of organizational change, I have spoken of more recent developments. (2) This analysis has involved a re-reading (summary but touching upon all essential points) of the history of some parties in the light of the theoretical schema laid out in the first part of this book. One must keep this schema in mind in order to grasp the "sense" of the comparisons which follow. To increase readability, I have preferred to keep the schema in the background, to avoid (when possible) introducing concepts which would submerge the historical narration of sociological jargon. (3) For partly the same reason, I have chosen to describe comparatively the formation of the different parties without gathering data and/or giving minute descriptions of the physiognomy and functioning of various party organs. I have preferred instead to regularly refer the reader to the texts mentioned in the footnotes which contain this data. This is so as not to weigh down the text, but also to demonstrate that organizational analysis, contrary to a widespread opinion, need not involve a flat and boring assemblage of data and minute and pedantic statutory descriptions. It can rather be construed as an attempt to interpret the "logic" of an organization's functioning, an attempt to understand its "syntax."

2 L. Longinotti, "Friedrich Engels e la 'Rivoluzione di Maggioranza'," *Studi storici*, XV, 1974, pp. 769–827.

3 J. P. Nettle, "The German Social Democratic Party 1890–1914 as a Political Model," *Past and Present*, LXXIV, 1965, pp. 65–95.

4 The importance of the SPD is such that the party's general histories have not exhausted it. Among so many works, one can profitably consult the classic study by F. Mehring (a protagonist of the Social Democratic venture in the imperial period), *Geschichte der Deutschen Sozialdemokratie*, Berlin, 1960. D. A. Chalmers, *The Social Democratic Party of Germany: From Working-Class Movement to Modern Political Party*, New Haven and London, Yale University Press, 1964, and I. Rovan's *Histoire de la social–democratie allemande*, Paris, Editions du Seuil, 1978.

5 On the formation and organization of the two parties, see R. Morgan, *The German Social Democrats and the First International, 1864–1892*, London, Cambridge University Press, 1965.

6 V. L. Lidtke, *The Outlawed Party: Social Democracy, 1878–1890*, Princeton, Princeton University Press, 1966, pp. 39ff.

7 *Ibid.*, p. 43.

8 U. Mittrmarm, "Tesi sullo sviluppo organizzativo di partito della socialdemocrazia tedesca durante l'impero," in L. Valiani, A. Wandruszka, eds., *Il movimento operaio e socialista in Italia e in Germania dal 1870 al 1920*, Bologna, Il Mulino, 1978, pp. 69–70.

9 Lidtke, *The Outlawed Party*, p. 54.

10 *Ibid.*, p. 54.

11 Mittrmarm, "Tesi sullo sviluppo organizzativo," p. 73.

12 Lidtke, *The Outlawed Party*, p. 98.

13 *Ibid.*, pp. 82ff.

14 On Kautsky's role and, more generally, on ideological conflicts in the SPD, see H. J. Steinberg, *Sozialismus und Deutsche Sozialdemokratie*, Bonn–Bad Godesberg, Verlag, 1976. See also M. Salvadori, *Kautsky e la rivoluzione socialista, 1880–1938*, Milan, Feltrinelli, 1976.

15 The Bavarian parliamentarians (whose most energetic and representative leader was Georg Vollmar) sided with the right wing, and their electorate consisted mainly of peasants. Their rightist "deviationism" can be explained by a difference in "electoral constituency." Eduard Bernstein, after distancing from Kautsky and the *Neue Zeit* group, became their ideological spokesman (playing, in relation to Vollman, the same role that Kautsky played in relation to Bebel). In the SPD both the dominant coalition and the oppositional tendencies distributed collective identity incentives to their followers (and fought each other in the horizontal power games) through ideologues of great intellectual persuasion. The leftist tendency had a certain following in the party schools and in the study groups led by Luxemburg and other "revolutionary intellectuals." See C. E. Schorske, *German Social Democracy, 1905–1917*, Cambridge, Harvard University Press, 1955, pp. 111ff.

16 G. Roth, *Social Democrats*.

17 K. Egon Lonne, "Il dibattito sul revisionismo nella social democrazia tedesca," in Valiani and Wandruszka, *Il movimento operaio e socialista*, pp. 121ff.

18 Schorske, *German Social Democracy*, p. 251.

19 *Ibid.*, p. 252.

20 *Ibid.*, pp. 118ff, for an accurate analysis of the organizational changes following the Jena Congress. Bureaucratization was so rapid that a few short years later, in 1910, the

SPD had 3,000 permanent staff members, i.e. one bureaucrat for every 250 members. See Duverger, *Political Parties*, p. 206.

21 Schorske, *German Social Democracy*, pp. 12–13.

22 On Bebel's victory and, more generally, on the results of the Jena Congress, see the impassioned *resumé* by Michels (then a Social Democratic militant) "Le socialisme allemand et le congrès d'Jena," *Mouvement Socialiste*, 1905, pp. 283–307.

23 See K. Kautsky, *Der Weg zur Macht*, Berlin, Buchhandlung Vorwarts, 1909, for a hard-lined defense of the primacy of the party over the union.

24 On the SPD–SFIO conflict, see C. Pinzani, *Jaurès, l'Internazionale e la guerra*, Bari, Laterza, 1970.

25 See A. J. Beralu, *The German Social Democratic Party, 1914–1921*, New York, Octagon Books, 1970, and L. Steurer, "La socialdemocrazia tedesca e la prima guerra mondiale," in Valiani and Wandruszka, *Il movimento operaio e socialista*, pp. 281–318.

26 See W. Abendroth, *Sozialgeschichte der Europaischen Arbeiter Arbeiterbewegung*, Frankfurt am Main, Suhrkamp Verlag, 1965. See also F. Andreucci, "La Seconda Internazionale," in L. Bonanate, ed., *Politica Internazionale*, Florence, La Nuova Italia, 1979, pp. 178–94 and the ample bibliography he provides.

27 See A. Agosti, ed., *La terza internazionale: storia documentaria*, Rome, Editori Riuniti, 4 vols., 1976. For a more general discussion of the formation of the communist parties, see A. Lindemann, *The "Red Years": European Socialism versus Bolshevism, 1919–1921*, Los Angeles–Berkeley, University of California Press, 1974.

28 On the role of size in organizational dynamics, see chapter 10.

29 See J. Fauvet, *Histoire du Parti Communist français, 1920–1976*, Paris, Fayard, 1977, and, on its genetic phase, A. Kriegel, *Aux origines du communisme français*, Paris, Mouton, 1964. See also R. Wohl, *French Communism in the Making, 1914–1924*, Stanford, Stanford University Press, 1964.

30 R. Tiersky, *Le Mouvement communiste en France, 1920–1972*, Paris, Fayard, 1973, p. 351.

31 See on this point A. Downs, *An Economic Theory of Democracy*, p. 92ff, and for an attempt to relate the speed of leaders' careers to the party's levels of organizational development, E. S. Wellhofer, T. M. Hennessey, "Political Party Development, Institutionalization, Leadership, Recruitment, and Behavior," *American Journal of Political Science*, VIII (1974), pp. 135–65.

32 On this question see F. Claudin, *La Crisis del Movimiento Communista. De la Komintern al Kominform*, Paris, Ruedo Iberico, 1970.

33 On the PCF decision to reduce its membership in connection with the adoption of sectarian policies, see N. McInnes, *The Communist Parties of Western Europe*, London, Oxford University Press, 1975, p. 5ff. On the organizational boundaries "contraction" and "expansion" policies, see chapter 10.

34 On this period, see G. Dupeux, *Le Front Populaire et les élections de 1936*, Paris, Colin, 1959, and N. Racine, L. Bodin, *Le Parti communiste français pendant l'entre-deux-guerres*, Paris, Colin, 1972.

35 R. Tiersky, *Le Mouvement communiste en France*, p. 269.

36 A. Kriegel, *Les Communistes français*, Paris, Editions du Seuil, 1970, pp. 117ff.

37 *Ibid.*, pp. 126ff.

38 See S. Tarrow, "Communism in Italy and France: Adaptation and Transformation," in D. L. M. Blackmer, S. Tarrow, eds., *Communism in Italy and France*, Princeton, Princeton University Press, 1975.

39 On these issues see J. Humbert-Droz, *Mémoire de Jules Humbert-Droz*, 3 vols., Neuchâtel, Editions de la Baconnière, 1969.

40 P. Spriano, *Storia del Partito Comunista Italiano, Da Bordiga a Gramsci*, Turin, Einaudi, 1967, and G. Galli, *Storia del Partito Comunista Italiano*, Milan, Il Formichiere, 1976, and the pro-Bordiga interpretation by L. Cortesi, *Le origini del PCI*, Bari, Laterza, 1971.

41 On the crisis of 1956, see chapter 13.

42 L. Paggi, "La formazione del partito comunista di mass," *Studi Storici*, XII (1971), pp. 339–55.

43 See S. Bertelli, *Il gruppo*, Milan, Rizzoli, 1980.

44 The best analysis of the local, intermediate and central structures of the PCI remains that found in G. Poggi, ed., *L'organizzazione del PCI e della DC*, Bologna, Il Mulino, pp. 27–196. See also G. Sivini, "Le Parti communiste: structure et fonctionnement," in AA.VV. *Sociologie du communisme en Italie*, Paris, Presses de la Fondation Nationale des Sciences Politiques, 1974, pp. 55–141, and G. Are, *Radiografia di un partito*, Milan, Rizzoli, 1980.

45 See the empirical analyses in Blackmer and Tarrow, *Communism in Italy and France*.

46 Poggi, *L'organizzazione del PCI e della DC*, and Tarrow, *Peasant Communism in Southern Italy*, New Haven and London, Yale University, 1967.

47 On the PCI's organizational tensions in the fifties, see Poggi, *L'organizzazione del PCI e della DC*, p. 167ff.

48 See G. Pasquino, "The PCI: a Party with a Governmental Vocation" (Occasional Paper), Johns Hopkins University, Bologna Center, 1978, and P. Lange, "La politica della alleanze del PCI e del PCF," *Il Mulino*, XXIV (1975), pp. 499–527. On the events of the sixties, see P. Allum, *The Italian Communist Party since 1945: Grandeurs and Servitudes of a European Socialist Strategy*, Reading, University of Reading, 1970, and G. Mammarella, *Il partito comunista italiano, 1945–1975. Dalla liberazione al compromesso storico*, Florence, Vallecchi, 1976.

49 On organizational change, see chapters 13 and 14.

50 On the PCI's susceptibility to environmental influence, and in particular to pressure from the collective movements, see M. Barbagli, P. Corbetta, "Base sociale del PCI e movimenti collettivi," in A. Martinelli and G. Pasquino, eds., *La politica nell'Italia che cambia*, Milan, Feltrinelli, 1978, pp. 144–70.

51 See F. Alberoni, ed., *L'attivista di partito*, Bologna, Il Mulino, 1967, and on the French communists attitudes towards collateral associations, J. Lagroye, G. Lord, "Trois féderations des partis politiques: esquisse de typologie," in *Revue Française de Science Politique*, XVI (1974), pp. 559–95.

52 On the decline of the unions in Italy in the seventies, see B. Manghi, *Declinare crescendo*, Bologna, Il Mulino, 1977.

53 See chapter 13.

54 On the organization of the Austrian Social Democratic Party, see M. A. Sully, "The Socialist Party of Austria," in W. E. Paterson and A. H. Thomas, eds., *Social Democratic Parties in Western Europe*, London, Croom Helm, 1977, pp. 213–33.

55 On the ideological and organizational components of the Leninist model, see A. G. Meyer's unsurpassed *Leninism*, Cambridge, Mass., Harvard University Press, 1957. On party bureaucracy and, more generally, political professionalism, see chapter 12.

56 A. O. Hirschman, *Exit, Voice, and Loyalty*, Cambridge, Mass., Harvard University Press, 1970.

57 "The internal opposition's pulverization, fragmentation, and lack of institutional mechanisms favor the rise of leaders individually, rather than the turnover taking place in groups or in blocks, related to the prevalence (as demonstrated by electoral results) of one particular orientation within the party. The turnover, thus – which at certain times can be held to a minimum – happens more gradually." Poggi, *L'organizzazione del PCI e della DC*, p. 195.

6 Oppositional parties

1 On the origins of British Socialism, see H. Pelling, *Origins of the Labour Party*, London, Oxford University Press, 1965. On Hardie, see K. O. Morgan, *Keir Hardie: Radical and Socialist*, London, Weidenfeld and Nicolson, 1975. Also very useful is D. Marquand's *Ramsay MacDonald*, London, Cape, 1977. On party formation and British parties in general, see A. R. Ball, *British Political Parties*, London, Macmillan Press, 1981.

2 See R. Moore, *The Emergence of the Labour Party, 1880–1925*, London, Hodder and Stoughton, 1979, p. 75ff. See also C. F. Hoover, *The British Labour Party: A Short History*,

Stanford, Hoover Institution Press, 1974. On syndicalism see H. Pelling, *A History of British Trade Unionists*, Harmondsworth, Penguin Books, 1976.

3 Moore, *Emergence of the Labour Party*, pp. 75ff.
4 *Ibid.*, p. 98.
5 *Ibid.*, p. 99.
6 *Ibid.*, pp. 111–13.
7 R. T. McKenzie, *British Political Parties*, London, Heinemann, 1963, pp. 300ff.
8 R. Moore, *Emergence of the Labour Party*, p. 156. On the "peripheral" organizational evolution of Labour see D. J. Wilson, *Power and Party Bureaucracy*, p. 31ff.
9 On the reform and, in particular, its effects on the intermediate organization, see D. J. Wilson, *Power and Party Bureaucracy*, and R. McKibbin, *The Evolution of the Labour Party, 1910–1924*, Oxford University Press, 1974.
10 Excellent analyses of the Labour Party's statutary organs can be found in R. Rose, *The Problem of Party Government*, Harmondsworth, Penguin Books, 1969, and S. E. Finer, *The Changing British Party System, 1945–1979*, Washington, American Enterprise Institute, 1980.
11 Rose, *Problem of Party Government*, pp. 226ff.
12 B. Simpson, *Labour: The Unions and the Party. A Study of the Trade Unions and the British Labour Movement*, London, Allen and Unwin, 1973, p. 226.
13 For a comparative analysis which underlies these differences, see D. J. Wilson, "Party Bureaucracy in Britain: Regional and Area Organization," *British Journal of Political Science*, II (1972) pp. 373–81, and *Power and Party Bureaucracy*.
14 For example, in 1970 the Conservatives had 357 electoral agents for their 537 local associations, and Labour had 141 agents for their 618 associations: Rose, *Problem of Party Government*, pp. 152–3.
15 See M. Rush, *The Selection of Parliamentary Candidates*, London, Nelson and Sons, 1969, p. 131ff. Also see W. L. Guttsman, "Elite Recruitment and Political Leadership in Britain and Germany since 1950: A Comparative Study of MPs and Cabinets," in I. Crewe, ed., *British Political Sociology Yearbook*, vol. 1, pp. 89–125.
16 Rush, *Selection of Parliamentary Candidates*, pp. 153–4.
17 The analysis of the unions' organizational development is thus obviously of major concern. In addition to the works cited in the previous footnotes, see T. Forester, *The Labour Party and the Working Class*, London, Heinemann Educational Books, 1976. The dispersal of organizational resources among the party's inner groups is due to the particular type of syndical structure prevalent in England: it is more decentralized than that found in other European countries, and is organized by job rather than by firm to such an extent that: "the workers of the same firm may be represented by up to 15 or 20 different unions which at times disagree over their respective areas of jurisdiction," Pizzorno, *I soggetti del Pluralismo*, p. 221.
18 The pact between trade union and parliamentary leaders may also break down due to the pressure of rank and file union delegates when the party is in opposition: e.g. the conflict between the Labour leader Gaitskell and the party in 1960–1 over the famous problem of the abolition of the fourth clause of the statute (on the socialization of the means of production). See L. D. Epstein, "Who Makes Party Policy: British Labour, 1960–61," *Midwest Journal of Political Science*, VI (1962), pp. 165–82.
19 On the conflicts between the Labour government and the unions after the war, see L. Minkin, P. Seyd, "The British Labour Party," in Paterson and Thomas, *Social Democratic Parties in Western Europe*, p. 113ff.
20 On the more recent organizational transformation of the Labour Party, see Finer, *Changing British Party System*.
21 See J. J. Fietchter, *Le Socialisme français: de l'affaire Dreyfuss à la grande guerre*, Geneva, Librairie Drotz, 1965, P. Luis, *Histoire du socialisme en France*, Paris, Librairie Marcel Rivière, and J. Touchard, *La Gauche en France depuis 1900*, Paris, Editions du Seuil, 1977.
22 C. Willard, *Les Guesdistes: le mouvement socialiste en France (1893– 1905)*, Paris, Editions Sociales, 1965.
23 *Ibid.*, pp. 108ff.

24 Ibid., p. 355ff.
25 J. Touchard, *La Gauche en France*, p. 64ff.
26 M. Perrot, A. Kriegel, *Le Socialisme français et le pouvoir*, Paris, EDI, 1966, p. 88.
27 Ibid., p. 85. An interesting analysis of the period is provided by M. Reberioux, "La classe operaia francese e le sue organizzazioni di fronte alla nascita della società industriale agli inizi del XX secolo," in Piro and Pombeni, eds., *Movimento operaio e societa*, pp. 145–65.
28 See C. Hurtig, *De la SFIO au Nouveau parti socialiste*, Paris, Colin, 1970, and F. L. Wilson, *The French Democratic Left, 1963–69*, Stanford, Stanford University Press, 1971. On the PSF see B. Criddle, "The French Parti Socialiste," in Paterson and Thomas, *Social Democratic Parties*, pp. 25–57.
29 For a description of the functioning of the statutory organs and, in particular, of the executive organ – the CAP (Commission Administrative Permanente) – see Touchard, *La Gauche en France*, p. 142ff, and G. A. Codding, W. Safran, *Ideology and Politics: The Socialist Party of France*, Bouldner, Westview Press, 1979, pp. 60ff.
30 This explains the party's *movimentista* character under Jaurès, i.e. the impossibility of substituting selective material incentives related to the bureaucratic processes for collective identity incentives. The confrontation between Babel and Jaurès in the International was a conflict between a heavily bureaucratized organization – which had to adopt cautious policies (on the crucial problems of rearmament and militarism) to preserve itself – and a flexible organization, which had not yet articulated its ends with respect to its organizational needs, and which thus *had* to consistently (and vehemently) pursue its own manifest ideological objectives. See C. Pinzani, Jaurè's *L'Internazionale e la guerra*.
31 See T. Judt, *La Reconstruction du Parti Socialiste, 1921–1926*, Paris, Presses de la Fondation Nationale des Sciences Politiques, 1976.
32 Ibid., pp. 31–2.
33 Ibid., pp. 50ff.
34 On the SFIO's internal conflicts during this period, see N. Greene, *Crisis and Decline: the French Socialist Party in the Popular Front Era*, Ithaca, Cornell University Press, 1969.
35 Ibid., pp. 208ff.
36 See R. Quillot, *La SFIO et l'exercise du pouvoir, 1944–58*, Paris, Fayard, 1972.
37 Ibid., pp. 239ff.
38 See E. Ragionieri, *Socialdemocrazia tedesca e socialisti italiani*, Milan, Feltrinelli, 1976.
39 G. Arfé, *Storia del socialismo italiano (1892–1926)*, Turin, Einaudi, 1965, p. 31. See also L. Valiani, *Questioni di storia del socialismo*, Turin, Einaudi, 1958. A good guide to the history of Italian socialism is I. Granata, *Il socialismo italiano nella storiografia del secondo dopoguerra*, Bari, Laterza, 1981.
40 Arfé, *Socialisme italiano*, p. 31. On Turati's positions on the party and its strategic positions in relation to European socialist currents, see L. Strik Lievers, "Turati, la politica delle alleanze e una celebre lettera di Engels," *Nuova Rivista Storica*, LVII (1973), pp. 129–60.
41 L. Valiani, "Il Movimento operaio e socialista in Italia e in Germania del 1870 al 1920," in Valiani and Wandruszka, eds., *Il movimento operaio e socialista*, p. 22.
42 Ibid., p. 18.
43 H. Hesse, "Il gruppo parlamentare del Partito Socialista Italiano: la sua composizione e la sua funzione negli anni della crisi del parlamentarismo italiano," in Valiani and Wandruszka, *Il movimento operaio e socialista*, p. 210.
44 Ibid., p. 211.
45 On "municipal socialism" and, more generally, on the socialist "subculture," see G. Sivini, "Socialisti e cattolici in Italia dalla società allo Stato," in Sivini, ed., *Sociologica dei partiti politici*, Bologna, Il Mulino, 1971, especially pp. 79ff.
46 On the relations between parties and state bureaucracy at that time, see M. Minghetti's classic, *I partiti politici e la ingerenza loro nella Giustizia e nell'Amministrazione*, Bologna, Zanichelli, 1881.

47 On unions see I. Bardadoro, *Storia del sindacalismo italiano. Dalla nascita al fascismo*, 2 vols., Florence, La Nuova Italia, 1973.
48 On the relations between the two leaders, see B. Vigezzi, *Giolitti e Turati. Un incontro mancato*, 2 vols., Milan–Naples, Ricciardi, 1976. "Giolittism" – after Giovanni Giolitti, the dominant figure in several Italian governments over the first two decades of the twentieth century – is the term now used by historians to define an era of compromise and cooperation between the liberal bourgeoisie (represented by Giolitti) and the socialist movement (led by Turati).
49 H. Hesse, "Il gruppo parlementare," p. 211.
50 See R. Michels, *Political Parties*, which speaks of the bourgeois and intellectual character of the PSI's leadership in relation to that of the SPD; see, in particular, p. 76ff, as well as p. 106ff. At the beginning of the century, 87.8 percent of the socialist parliamentarians were university graduates, as opposed to 16 percent of the SPD's. See also Hesse, "Il gruppo parlementare," p. 213ff.
51 Hesse, "Il gruppo parlementare," p. 211.
52 Arfé, *Storia del socialismo italiano*, pp. 111ff.
53 *Ibid.*, pp. 163ff.
54 M. Degl'Innocenti, *Il socialismo italiano e la guerra di Libia*, Rome, Editori Riuniti, 1976.
55 Arfé, *Storia del socialismo italiano*, p. 156.
56 *Ibid.*, p. 156.
57 The expression comes from Arfé, *Storia del socialismo italiano*.
58 Hesse, "Il gruppo parlementare," p. 204.
59 Valiani, "Il movimento operaio e socialista," p. 22.
60 Hesse, "Il gruppo parlementare," p. 219.
61 See C. Vallauri, *I partiti in Italia dal 1943 al 1975*, Rome, Bulzoni, pp. 105ff.
62 F. Cazzola, *Carisma e democrazia nel socialismo italiano*, Rome, Edizioni Sturzo, 1967, p. 30.
63 See C. Vallauri, "Morandi e l'organizzazione di partito," *Citta e Regione*, no. 6 (1978), pp. 38–56; on Morandi's political activity, see A. Agosti, *Rodolfo Morandi. Il pensiero e l'azione politica*, Bari, Laterza, 1971.
64 R. Zarinski, "The Italian Socialist Party: A Case Study in Factional Conflict," *American Political Science Review*, LVI (1962), p. 389. On the characteristics of the PSI's bureaucratization under Morandi, see S. H. Barnes, *Party Democracy: Politics in an Italian Socialist Federation*, New Haven, Yale University Press, 1967, pp. 138–9.
65 See Cazzola, *Carisma e democrazia*. On socialist organization after World War II, Cazzola, *Studio di un caso: il PSI*, Rome, Edizioni del Tritone, 1970.
66 On factionistic dynamics at that time, see Barnes, *Party Democracy*.
67 On the post-1976 changes, see A. Panebianco, "Analisi di una sconfitta: il declino del PSI," in A. Parisi, G. Pasquino, eds., *Continuità e mutamento elettorale in Italia*, Bologna, Il Mulino, 1977, pp. 145–84.

7 Governmental parties

1 On the role of the *Zentrum* during the Weimar Republic, see G. E. Rusconi, *La crisi di Weimar*, Turin, Einaudi, 1977.
2 On the formation of the political system of the Federal Republic see T. Burkett, *Parties and Elections in West Germany, The Search of Stability*, London, Hurst and Co., 1975 and K. W. Deutsch, E. A. Nordlinger, "The German Federal Republic," in R. C. Macridis, R. E. Wards, eds., *Modern Political Systems: Europe*, Englewood Cliffs, Prentice-Hall, 1968, pp. 301–450.
3 An important aspect of the Church–CDU relationship comes from the fact that the Protestants are divided into two groups, Lutherans and Calvinists: the former are of a more conservative orientation and will sustain Adenauer in alliance with the Catholics. The latter group will frequently represent a source of tension in the CDU on account of a political orientation more open to leftist ideologies.

4 The existence of occupational zones, making communication difficult, is certainly the immediate cause explaining the autonomous developments of the CDU's peripheral organizations. It should however be remembered that this factor operates within a national context which has historically been characterized by very strong socio-cultural regional differences which tend to get "incorporated" in the organizations from the outset, which thus reflect these differences internally (with "automizing" effects of the organized peripheries amongst themselves and in relation to the national "center"). This phenomenon naturally appears within the SPD as well, but it is counterbalanced by the presence of a strong central apparatus.

5 I have essentially based my reconstruction on A. J. Heidenheimer, *Adenauer and the CDU. The Rise of the Leader and the Integration of the Party*, The Hague, Martinus Nijhoff, 1960, and G. Pridham, *Christian Democracy in Western Germany. The CDU/CSU in Government and Opposition, 1945–1976*, London, Croom Helm, 1977.

6 On this point see D. Childs, *From Schumacher to Brandt. The Story of German Socialism, 1945–1965*, Oxford, Pergamon Press, 1966.

7 A. J. Heidenheimer, *Adenauer and the CDU*, pp. 152ff.

8 *Ibid.*, p. 187.

9 *Ibid.*, p. 190.

10 Pridham, *Christian Democracy*, p. 97ff for a detailed analysis of the party's organizational system. On its financial system see U. Schleth, M. Pinto-Duschinsky, "Why Public Studies Have Become the Major Source of Party Funds in West Germany but Not in Great Britain," in A. J. Heidenheimer, ed., *Comparative Political Finance*, Lexington, Heath and Co., 1970, pp. 23–49. These analyses show that, in the fifties, more than 400 out of 500 bureaucrats employed, worked in the peripheral organizations, and the remaining were distributed between the party's headquarters, the *Fraktion*, and the party's collateral organizations.

11 W. L. Guttsman, "Elite Recruitment and Political Leadership in Britain and Germany since 1950: A Comparative Study of MPs and Cabinets," in Crewe, ed., *British Political Sociology Yearbook*, pp. 93ff.

12 Pridham, *Christian Democracy*, p. 270.

13 See Schlecht and Pinto-Duschinsky, "Public Subsidies."

14 See D. Herzog, "Carriera parlamentare e professionismo politico," *Rivista Italiana di Scienza Politica*, I (1971), pp. 515–44.

15 G. Pridham, *Christian Democracy*, pp. 79–80. It is also because the CDU parliamentary group is united to the Bavarian Christian Social Union, the CSU. So as not to complicate things, I did not make an analysis of this party, although it is undoubtedly the case that the CSU leadership, at times in conflict and at times in cooperation, comprised part of the dominant coalition, and the relations between the two parties are based on a system of complex interorganizational exchanges. On the CSU see A. Mintzel, "The Christian Social Union in Bavaria: Analytical Notes on its Development, Role, and Political Success" in M. Kaase, K. Von Beyme, eds., *Elections and Parties. German Political Studies*, vol. 3, London and Beverly Hills, 1978, pp. 191–225.

16 Heidenheimer, *Adenauer and the CDU*, p. 204.

17 On the changes the CDU experienced after its passage into the opposition see chap. 13.

18 G. Poggi, "La chiesa nella politica italiana dal 1945 al 1950," in S. J. Wolf, *Italia 1943/ 50. La ricostruzione*, Bari, Laterza, 1975, p. 271ff. See also Poggi's analysis of the role of "Azione Cattolica," *Il clero di riserva*, Milan, Feltrinelli, 1963. See also A. Giovagnoli, "Le organizzazioni di massa dell'Azione Cattolica," in R. Ruffilli, ed., *Cultura politica e partiti nell'eta' della costituente*, vol. I, Bologna, Il Mulino, 1979, pp. 263–362.

19 See P. Pombeni, *Il gruppo dossettiano e la fondazione della democrazia italiana (1938–1948)*, Bologna, Il Mulino, 1979, and R. Moro, *La formazione della classe dirigente cattolica (1929–1937)*, Bologna, Il Mulino, 1979. On the political nature of the Christian Democratic leadership group in relation to the debate on the constitutional order, see R. Ruffilli, ed., *Costituente e lotta politica. La stampa e le scelte costituzionali*, Florence, Vallecchi, 1978, pp. 141–67 and more in general, on the relation between the DC and the state

before the centre–left government, see R. Ruffilli, "La DC e i problemi dello Stato democratico (1943–1960), *Il Mulino*, XXV (1976), pp. 835–53.

20 On De Gasperi's role see P. Scoppola, *La proposta politica di De Gasperi*, Bologna, Il Mulino, 1977.

21 On the "partito popolare" see G. De Rosa, *Il partito popolare italiano*, Bari, Laterza, 1969.

22 On these matters I used G. Poggi, ed., *L'organizzazione partica del PCI e della DC*, J. P. Chasseriand, *Le parti democratie Chretien en Italie*, Paris, Colin, 1965; G. Baget Bozzo, *Il partito cristiano al potere. La DC di De Gasperi e di Dossetti, 1945–1954*, 2 vols., Florence, Vallecchi, 1974; G. Galli, *Storia della DC*, Bari, Laterza, 1978.

23 A. Cavazzani, "Organizzazione, iscritti ed elettori della Democrazia Cristiana," in G. Sivini, ed., *Partiti e partecipazione politica in Italia*, Milan, Giuffre', 1972, p. 172.

24 G. Poggi, ed., *L'organizzazione del partitica del PCI e della DC*, p. 201.

25 *Ibid.*, p. 206.

26 *Ibid.*, p. 206.

27 Sociological–historical analyses of this movement are developed by Sivini, *Socialisti e cattolici*, and by Galli, *I partiti politici*, pp. 101ff.

28 For a global evaluation of the organizational system of the party around 1965 see G. Poggi, ed., *L'organizzazione del partitica del PCI e della DC*, pp. 295–308.

29 See A. Manoukian, ed., *La presenza sociale del PCI e della DC*, Bologna, Il Mulino, 1968.

30 G. Miccoli, "Chiesa, partito cattolico e societa' civile," in AA.VV., *L'Italia contemporanea. 1945–1975*, Turin, Einaudi, 1976, p. 227.

31 *Ibid.*, p. 238ff.

32 The premonitory signs of the successive development were already present during the De Gasperi era, when the enactment of many constitutional laws were postponed and the ability/possibility for parliamentary control on governmental acts was sacrificed: "This strategy corresponded to the needs of a party of recent formation, appearing on the Italian scene without a consolidated political base, and without preferential channels of access within the public apparatus; it was thus necessary, on the one hand, not to offer space to the leftist forces and, on the other, to construct bases of autonomous power able to reduce the party's dependence on the Church and on big moneyed interests, avoiding even the ministerial bureaucracy, which in being of pre-fascist and fascist origin, didn't offer adequate guarantees of loyalty (there was, at any rate, to be an intense colonization on the part of the party of the ministerial bureaucracy)", F. Ferraresi, *Burocrazia e politica in Italia*, Bologna, Il Mulino, 1980, p. 63.

A significant role is to be attributed to the lack of agreement over the "rules of the game" and to the mental reserve the different political actors participating in the "constituting" negotiating of the new political regime had, which could not have its effects on all the institutions, beginning with parliament: see G. Di Palma, *Surviving without Governing*, Berkeley, University of California Press, 1977.

33 On these matters, see, among others, R. E. Irving, *The Christian Democratic Parties of Western Europe*, London, Allen and Unwin, 1979, pp. 77–82.

34 On this process and its effects on the party see G. Pasquino, "Crisi della DC e evoluzione del sistema politico," *Rivista Italiana di Scienza Politica*, V (1975), esp. p. 453ff; A. Zuckerman, *Political Clienteles in Power: Party Factions and Cabinet Coalitions in Italy*, Beverly Hills, Prentice-Hall, 1975 and F. Cazzola, ed., *Anatomia del potere DC*, Bari, De Donato, 1979.

35 See the essays contained in G. Sartori, ed., *Correnti, frazioni e fazioni nei partiti italiani*, Bologna, Il Mulino, 1973 and A. Zuckerman, *The Politics of Faction. Christian Democratic Rule in Italy*, New Haven and London, Yale University Press, 1979.

36 J. La Palombara, *Interest Groups in Italian Politics*, Princeton, Princeton University Press, 1964.

37 On the transformation of clientelism in Italy see L. Graziano, *Clientelismo e sistema politico. Il caso dell'Italia*, Milan, Franco Angeli, 1980. For a more in depth analysis of a case

see M. Caciagli, *Democrazia Cristiana e potere nel Mezzogiorno*, Florence, Guaraldi, 1977. The "Cassa del Mezogiorno" is the special public organism which has been dealing with the industrial underdevelopment of Southern Italy, from the end of World War II.

38 G. Poggi, ed., *L'organizzazione del partitica del PCI e della DC*, p. 500.

39 F. Alberoni, ed., *L'attivista di partito*, p. 312ff and p. 391ff. In this sense the DC's "organizational emancipation" from the Church, a sub-species transference of activists' loyalties from the external organization to the party, is almost complete by the end of the seventies: see P. Ignazi, A. Panebianco, "Laici e conservatori. I valori politici della base democristiana," in A. Parisi, ed., *Democristiani*, Bologna, Il Mulino, 1980, pp. 153–74.

40 See Zuckerman, *Political Clienteles*, pp. 102–3. On the characteristics of the Italian bureaucratic system which, after World War II, was filled by members of governmental parties, for historical reasons of weakness and inefficiency of its apparatus with respect to other European bureaucracies, see Ferraresi, *Burocrazia e politica in Italia* and S. Cassese, *La formazione dello stato amministrativo*, Milan, Giuffre', 1974.

41 See G. Pasquino, "La Democrazia Cristiana: trasformazioni partitiche e mediazione politica," in Martinelli and Pasquino, ed., *La politica nell'Italia che cambia*, pp. 124–43.

42 See A. Cavazzani, "Organizzazione," p. 182, and M. Rossi, "Un partito di anime morte? Il tesseramento democristiano fra mito e realta'," in Parisi, ed., *Democristiani*, pp. 13–59.

43 See Elklit, *The Formation of Mass Political Parties*, and L. Svaasand, *Organizing the Conservatives: A Study in the Diffusion of Party Organizations in Norway*.

44 McKenzie, *British Political Parties*.

45 On recent transformations see chap. 13.

46 McKenzie, *British Political Parties*, pp. 54ff.

47 On the party's formation see R. Blake, *The Conservative Party from Peel to Churchill*, London, Eyre & Spottiswoode, 1970, and C. L. Butler, ed., *The Conservatives. A History from Origins to 1945*, London, Allen and Unwin, 1977.

48 Eliassen and Svaasand, *Formation of Mass Political Organizations*.

49 See H. Parris, *Constitutional Bureaucracy*, London, Allen and Unwin, 1969.

50 E. J. Feuchtwanger, "J. E. Gorst and the Central Organization of the Conservative Party, 1870–1882," *Bulletin of Historical Research*, XXII (1959), p. 199.

51 *Ibid.*, p. 208.

52 Wilson, *Power and Party Bureaucracy*, p. 17.

53 J. Ramsden, *The Age of Balfour and Baldwin, 1902–1940*, London and New York, Longman, 1978, p. 26.

54 Wilson, *Power and Party Bureaucracy*, pp. 19–20.

55 *Ibid.*, p. 19.

56 Ramsden, *Age of Balfour and Baldwin*, p. 68.

57 *Ibid.*, p. 68.

58 *Ibid.*, p. 69.

59 *Ibid.*, pp. 71ff.

60 *Ibid.*, p. 72.

61 *Ibid.*, p. 231.

62 *Ibid.*, p. 236.

63 Wilson, *Power and Party Bureaucracy*, p. 23.

64 *Ibid.*, p. 23.

65 Schleth and Pinto-Duschinsky, "Public Subsidies," pp. 47–48. On that occasion a prohibition was established forbidding interest groups to finance single candidates' campaigns: see Rush, *Selection of Parliamentary Candidates*, p. 31.

66 D. J. Wilson, *Power and Party Bureaucracy*, and also Rose, *The Problem of Party Government*, p. 162ff. In 1970 the Conservative Party employed, in addition to the Central Office and its intermediary bureaucrats, 399 electoral agents in local associations as opposed to the 144 employed by the Labour Party.

67 Schleth and Pinto-Duschinsky, "Public Subsidies."

68 *Ibid.*, p. 38.

69 Rose, *Problem of Party Government*, pp. 312–28.

70 On the "Monday Club," Conservative group of the extreme right, and organized in part as a national faction, see P. Seyd, "Factionalism within the Conservative Party: the Monday Club," *Government and Opposition*, VII (1972), pp. 464–87. On certain moments of acute factionalism in the pre-war period, see G. Peele, M. Hall. "Dissent, Faction and Ideology in the Conservative Party: Some Reflections on the Inter-War Period," paper presented to the ECPR workshop on conservatism, Brussels, 1979.

71 See Rush, *Selection of Parliamentary Candidates*, p. 13ff. See also Guttsman, *Elite Recruitment and Political Leadership in Britain and Germany since 1950*.

72 In an analysis of political carriers in five countries (USA, Canada, England, Australia and France during the Fourth Republic) the Conservative parliamentary group proved to be the youngest of all those parliamentary groups considered, with 75 percent of their deputies being under forty-five years of age: see J. A. Schlesinger, "Political Careers and Party Leadership," in L. J. Edinger, ed., *Political Leadership in Industrialized Societies*, New York and London, Wiley and Sons, 1967, pp. 266–93.

73 D. J. Wilson, *Power and Party Bureaucracy*.

74 Rush, *Selection of Parliamentary Candidates*, p. 19.

75 L. Epstein, *Political Parties in Western Democracies*, p. 219.

76 Rush, *Selection of Parliamentary Candidates*, p. 100.

77 *Ibid.*, p. 100. See also L. Epstein, "British MPs and their Local Parties: The Suez Case," *American Political Science Review*, LIV (1960), pp. 374–90.

78 The comparison of the DC and the LDP, which is legitimate if not pushed beyond a certain point, should not make us forget certain fundamental differences between the two organizations: (1) the LDP has uninterruptedly held the absolute majority of seats since its foundation: in Giovanni Sartori's terms it is a dominant party. This helps explain its more stable dominant coalition. (2) The LDP was born through the fusion of two preexisting parties, the Democratic Party and the Liberal Party, which, in their turn, were very factionalized organizations. (3) The imperial Japanese bureaucracy is traditionally a strong and efficient institution, rich in autonomous resources. The relation between the party and the bureaucracy is not thus homogeneous with the Italian case. (4) The LDP's factions are autonomous organizations, with their own local electoral machines (the "koenkai") which include around 900,000 "clients" (according to reliable estimates), whereas the party organization, until just a few years ago, was almost nonexistent as on a national level. In my opinion the crucial difference between the two cases is that the DC was (predominantly) born as a solidarity system and becomes an interest system at the moment of institutionalization, while the LDP was born with relatively pure characteristics of the interests system. On the LDP, see R. A. Scalapino, J. Masuky, *Parties and Politics in Contemporary Japan*, Berkeley and Los Angeles, University of California Press, 1967, N. Thayer, *How Conservatives Rule Japan*, Princeton, Princeton University Press, 1969.

79 "the DC confirms . . . its impossibility in completely being a 'bourgeois' party as those exemplified for Germany and Japan. The DC's profound nature as a permanent government party legitimated by 'Eusebian' political theology impedes an evolution of this type. It is for this same reason that the problem of the party's laicization can only be the object of an academic debate. The DC is a moderate party in as far as its explicit program and its electoral base is concerned, and is different from the large liberal–bourgeois mass parties in that it draws its theoretical inspiration from the Church, and maintains its hold on the society from its management – without alternative – of political power." Galli, *Storia della DC*, p. 378.

Along with "Gelasian," "Agostinian" models, the "Eusebian" model is one of three models of political theology that have historically defined the relation between Church and political power, according to Baget Bozzo. See (in addition to that already indicated), *Il partito cristiano e l'apertura a sinistra. La DC di Fanfani e di Moro, 1954–1962*, Vallecchi, 1977.

80 On the organizational problems related to the governmental alliance with competing parties, see also chap. 11.

8 Charismatic parties

1 See, for example, C. J. Friedrich, "Political Leadership and the Problem of Charismatic Power," *Journal of Politics*, XX (1971), pp. 299–305, and H. Wolpe, "A Critical Analysis of Some Aspects of Charisma," *The Sociological Review*, XVI (1968), pp. 305–18.

2 M. Weber, *Economy and Society*, Berkeley, University of California Press, 1978.

3 See R. Bendix, G. Roth, *Scholarship and Partisanship: Essays on Max Weber*, Berkeley, University of California Press, 1971. Also see L. Cavalli, "Il carisma come potenza rivoluzionaria" in AA.VV., *Max Weber e l'analisi del mondo moderno*, Turin, Einaudi, 1981, pp. 161–88.

4 On the nascent state see Alberoni, *Movimento e istituzione*.

5 On "official charisma" and, more specifically, on the phenomenon of "charismatic bureaucracy" in regimes and communist parties, see V. Belohradsky, "Burocrazia carismatica. Ratio e carisma nella società di massa," in L. Pellicani, ed., *Sociologia delle rivoluzioni*, Naples, Guida, 1976, pp. 181–231. The problem, however, not sufficiently developed in Belohradsky, is that to move towards "charismatic bureaucracy" (as the Russian Bolshevik party did) one must *first* objectify a personal charisma (e.g. Lenin).

6 There is a good deal of literature on the Fifth Republic. For an analysis of the institutional and political evolution of contemporary France, see R. C. Macridis, "France," in R. C. Macridis and R. E. Ward, eds., *Modern Political Systems: Europe*, Englewood Cliffs, Prentice-Hall, 1968, pp. 153–298 and the original and suggestive interpretation by S. Hoffmann, *Sur la France*, Paris, Editions du Seuil, 1976. Focusing on the Fifth Republic, see S. Bartolini, *Riforma istituzionale e sistema politico*, Bologna, Il Mulino, 1981; and on the Gaullist constitution, see M. Volpi, *La democrazia autoritaria*, Bologna, Il Mulino, 1979. For a Weberian interpretation of the transition from the Fourth to the Fifth Republic, see M. Dogan, "Charisma and the Breakdown of Traditional Alignments," in Dogan and Rose, eds., *European Politics: A Reader*, London, The Macmillan Press, 1971, pp. 413–26. On the "Rassemblement du Peuple Français," see R. Barillon, "La Rassemblement du Peuple Français," in M. Duverger, ed., *Partis Politiques et Classes Sociales*, Paris, Colin, 1955, pp. 277–90.

7 M. Crozier, *I partiti francesi*, Turin, Quaderni della Fondazione G. Agnelli, 1980, pp. 10ff.

8 The frequent name changes were related to the party's charismatic origin. The movement's "refoundations" (Jacques Chirac's last act in 1976) remind us that an organization has not value in and of itself, but is valued because of the original doctrine of its founding leader. At the moment of refoundation, the party's original "nascent state" was more or less recreated.

9 On the Gaullist doctrine and De Gaulle's personality, see J. Touchard, *Le Gaullisme. 1940–1969*, Paris, Editions du Seuil, 1978.

10 J. Charlot, *L'UNR Etude du pouvoir au sein d'un parti politique (UNR)*, Paris, Colin, 1967, and his *Le Phénomène gaulliste (PG)*, Paris, Favard, 1970.

11 Charlot, *UNR*, p. 41.
12 *Ibid.*, p. 43.
13 *Ibid.*, p. 40.
14 *Ibid.*, p. 106.
15 *Ibid.*, p. 47.
16 *Ibid.*, p. 50.
17 *Ibid.*, p. 50.
18 *Ibid.*, p. 139.

19 Charlot, *PG*, pp. 130ff. There were innumerable Gaullist organizations, and many of them were not collateral organizations in the strict sense but rather autonomous political organizations guided by their own leaders and only linked to the "movement" by their loyalty to De Gaulle. In 1963 one of these organizations, the Union Démocratique du Travail – representing Gaullism's leftist tendency – associated with the UNR. But many Gaullists remained unaffiliated with the "central" organization, leading to a myriad of associations identifying with the "movement" but not with the party.

20 Also, because the party was locally organized by districts, which made it into an

efficient electoral machine for the national elections, but did not encourage active grass roots participation.

21 S. Tarrow, *Partisanship and Political Exchange in French and Italian Local Politics: A Contribution to the Typology of Party Systems*, London, Sage Publications, Contemporary Political Sociology Series, Vol. 1, N. 06-004. On this peculiarity of the French right, also see M. Anderson, *Conservative Politics in France*, London, Allen and Unwin, 1974, pp. 231–68.

22 See Bartolini, *Riforma istituzionale*, pp. 85ff.

23 Ibid., p. 90.

24 Ibid., p. 57, and Charlot, PG. On the relationship between organizational size and power structure in parties, see chapter 10.

25 Cited by M. Volpi, *La democrazia autoritaria*, p. 200.

26 Charlot, UNR.

27 Charlot, PG.

28 On the Gaullist constitution, see Volpi, *La democrazia autoritaria*.

29 See chapter 7.

30 F. L. Wilson, R. Wiste, "Party Cohesion in the French National Assembly: 1958–1973," in *Legislative Studies Quarterly*, XII (1979), pp. 82–103.

31 S. Bartolini, *Riforma istituzionale*, pp. 249ff.

32 Charlot, UNR, pp. 216ff.

33 Charlot, PG, pp. 133–5.

34 Ibid., pp. 134–5.

35 See P. Lecomte, "Rassemblement pour la République et Parti Republicain. Eléments d'analyse comparative," paper presented at the CERP workshop on "conservative politics," Brussels, 1979, unpublished manuscript; and C. Crisal, *La Machine RPR*, Paris, Fayolle, 1977.

36 I have naturally limited myself to considering only the Weimar period, given that the only types of party that interest us here are those operating in a competitive democracy.

37 The heterogeneity of the Nazi ideological tendencies is documented by B. Miller Lane, L. J. Rupp, eds., *Nazi Ideology Before 1933. A Documentation*, Manchester, Manchester University Press, 1978.

38 M. Duverger, *Political Parties*, pp. 36ff.

39 See K. D. Bracher, *Die Deutsche Diktatur. Entstehung Struktur folgen des Nationalsozialismus*, Cologne, Berlin, Kiepenheur Witsh, 1969. Also see D. Orlow, *The History of the Nazi Party: 1919–1933*, Pittsburgh, University of Pittsburgh Press, 1969.

40 Bracher, *Diktatur*. On the *Führerprinzip*, W. Horn, *Führeideologie und Parteiorganisation in der NSDAP (1919–1933)*, Dusseldorf, Droste, 1972.

41 J. Nyomarkay, *Charisma and Factionalism in the Nazi Party*, Minneapolis, University of Minnesota Press, 1967, p. 78.

42 Bracher, *Diktatur*.

43 Ibid., p. 225.

44 Up until 1931, the Hitler Youth maintained a good deal of maneuverability independent of the NSDAP and the SA. It had its own "interpretation" of National Socialism in a socialist vein. See P. D. Stachura, *Nazi Youth in the Weimar Republic*, California, Clio Books, 1975, p. 43ff.

45 Bracher, *La dittatura tedesca* (translated from the Italian version) p. 187.

46 Nyomarkay, *Charisma*, p. 27. In the Nazi party, "party members who were commissioned by Hitler became part of an "inner circle". Because Hitler's favor was the sole determining factor for placement in this "circle", the way to gain entrance was to conform righteously to his position and flatter him. Once included in the "circle", each lieutenant had to guard persistently against the loss of Hitler's favor and confidence." J. V. Downton, Jr, *Rebel Leadership. Commitment and Charisma in the Revolutionary Process*, New York, The Free Press, p. 49.

47 Nyomarkay, *Charisma*, p. 28.

48 Ibid., p. 31.

49 Ibid., p. 31. On the Nazi elite, see D. Lerner et al., "The Nazi Elite," in Lasswell and

Lerner, eds., *World Revolutionary Elites. Studies in Coercive Ideological Movements*, Cambridge, Mass., The MIT Press, 1967, pp. 194–318. On social composition, see H. Gerth, "The Nazi Party: Its Leadership and Composition," *American Journal of Sociology*, XLV (1940), pp. 517ff.

50 Charlot, *Les Partis politiques*, Paris, Colin, 1971, pp. 55ff.

51 See A. Ulam, *Lenin and the Bolsheviks*, Glasgow, Collins, Fontana, 1969; and E. H. Carr, *The Bolshevik Revolution, 1917–1923*, 3 vols., London, Macmillan, 1950–3.

52 R. De Felice, *Mussolini il rivoluzionario, 1883–1920*, and *Mussolini il fascista. La conquista del potere, 1921–1925*, Turin, Einaudi, 1965 and 1966. On the organization of the fascist paty, see A. Lyttelton, *La conquista del potere. Il fascismo dal 1919 al 1920*, Bari, Laterza, 1974, pp. 67–122.

53 See S. Hoffman, *Le Mouvement Poujade*, Paris, Colin, 1956.

54 The more important difference obviously is between totalitarian or authoritarian oriented charismatic parties and democratically oriented ones. The latter can not internally incorporate formal organizational principles which would subordinate them to the leadership. Such parties are thus likely to be characterized by ineluctable tensions between the charismatic organizational pole and the democratic–legal organizational pole (involving the election of leaders and the ratification of decisions by the base, etc.), which lead to much greater internal conflict.

55 See Lecomte, "Rassemblement."

9 Organizational order: a typology

1 Poggi, ed., *L'organizzazione partitica del PCI e della DC*.

2 Eldersveld, *Political Parties*.

3 Nor should other analogous attempts be forgotten: for example, Duverger's distinction in *Political Parties*, between "highly articulated" and "weakly articulated" parties or Crotty's distinction between parties with a "hierarchical role" and those with a "diffused role" (*A Perspective for the Comparative Analysis of Political Parties*). See also the models of "mechanical solidarity" and those of "organic solidarity" used by T. Burns, G. M. Stalker, *The Management of Innovation*, London, Tavistock, 1961, or even the distinction between "sect" and "coalition" organizations employed by Van Doorn, *Conflict in Formal Organizations*.

4 This could be the case for certain parties – above all regional parties representing ethnic or linguistic minorities, or the Scandinavian agrarian parties, which represent particular political phenomena of the historical development of the small Scandinavian democracies – not mentioned in this study.

5 M. Barbagli, P. G. Corbetta, "Una tattica e due strategie. Inchiesta sulla base del PCT," *Il Mulino*, XXVII (1978), pp. 922–67.

6 See data found in Rose, *The Problem of Party Government*, pp. 165ff.

7 On hidden professionalism, see chap. 12.

8 The advantage of having a wide range of cases is that they increase the probability that other cases (not considered) resemble one of those examined and that still different cases may be the sum of some of the characteristics already delineated, allowing for a more immediate deciphering of their organizational "logic."

9 It could be objected that leaders like Jaurès, Blum or Adenauer were strong "centers" and that the "situational charisma" is precisely the effect and/or the cause of this situation. This, however, is not the case: Jaurès, Blum and Adenauer divided control of the zones of uncertainty with a number of less visible leaders. They were undoubtedly the collectors of a vast part of the party's electoral loyalty, but whole sectors of the organization evaded their control. A real "center" must hold control over all or almost all of the principle zones of organizational uncertainty.

10 This was the case for the better part of the history of the Japanese Liberal Democratic Party.

11 On the problem of organizational thresholds, see chap. 10.

12 As we have instead seen, charismatic parties (cohesion of the dominant coalition in the absence of institutionalization) can behave in different and not entirely comprehensible ways with respect to our knowledge of the functioning of this type of party. In certain cases they will be expansive and will maintain high levels of internal participation (like the Nazis), while in others the leader's fear of reaching a premature objectivization of charisma might dissuade him (as in the Gaullist case) from exercising expansive policies. The latter case seems most likely, especially for democratic charismatic parties, in which a formal tie exists to the respect for internal democratic–electoral procedures, and in which the risks of internal contestation of the leadership are greater.

13 These are concepts which tend to obfuscate exchange and bargaining as crucial dimensions of power relations.

14 W. R. Schonfeld, "La Stabilite des dirigeants des partis politiques: la theorie de l'oligarchie de Robert Michels," *Revue Française de Science Politique*, XXX (1980), p. 858.

15 *Ibid.*, p. 858.

16 See R. A. Dahl, *Polyarchy. Participation and Opposition*, New Haven and London, Yale University Press, 1971. For a discussion which contrasts polyarchy and monocracy, see H. Eckstein, T. R. Gurr, *Patterns of Authority, A Structural Basis for Political Inquiry*, New York, Wiley and Sons, 1975, pp. 121ff.

17 Duverger, *Political Parties*, pp. 182ff.

18 "The general characteristics of stratarchy are the proliferation of the ruling group and the diffusion of power prerogatives and power exercise. Rather than centralized 'unity of command' or a general dilution of power throughout the structure, 'strata comands' exist which operate with a varying, but considerable degree of independence." Eldersveld, *Political Parties*, p. 9.

19 See White *et al.*, *Exchange as a Conceptual Framework*.

20 A. Anfossi, "Le interazioni fra organizzazioni," *Studi Organizzativi*, XI (1979), pp. 86ff.

10 Size and organizational complexity

1 C. Perrow, *Organizational Analysis: A Sociological View*, Belmott, Wadsworth, 1970.

2 G. Gasparini, *Tecnologia, ambiente e struttura*, Milan, Franco Angeli, 1978.

3 Child, *Organization, Structure, Environment and Performance: The Role of Strategic Choice*.

4 Crozier and Friedberg, *Social Actors and System*, pp. 89ff.

5 Michels, *Sociology of Political Parties*, p. 71.

6 On this point see C. W. Cassinelli, "The Law of Oligarchy," *American Political Science Review*, XLVII (1953), p. 783.

7 Michels, *Sociology of Political Parties*, p. 65.

8 *Ibid.*, p. 188ff.

9 Cassinelli, "Law of Oligarchy"; also see the critical discussion by J. Linz in the introduction to the Italian translation of Michels, Bologna, Il Mulino, 1966, pp. vii–cxix.

10 We follow here the interpretation of Abrahamsson, *Bureaucracy or Participation*, p. 57ff.

11 Weber's essential disagreement with Michels concerned the importance of the "environment's" influence on the organization, as the following quotation demonstrates: "It is probably impossible to make useful generalizations. The party's internal technical dynamics and the economic and social conditions of each individual case, are always too closely interconnected," cited by J. Linz in his introduction to the Italian translation of Michels', (p. LIII). Thus even Weber generalized, but (unlike Michels) he did so with great attention to the interaction between organizational dynamics and socio-economic and political environments. See Weber, *Economy and Society*, vol. 2, pp. 1443ff. For a critique which asserts that Michels didn't take into account political and social conditions in Germany and their influence on the SPD, see Roth, *The Social-Democrats in Imperial Germany*, pp. 243ff.

12 See, among others, D. S. Pugh *et al.*, "Dimensions of Organizational Structure,"

Administrative Science Quarterly, XIII (1968), pp. 65–105; J. Child, R. Mansfield, "Technology, Size and Organization Structure," *Sociology*, VI (1972), pp. 369–93; P. Blau, R. A. Schoenherr, *The Structure of Organizations*, New York, Basic Books, 1971.

13 Duverger, *Political Parties*, p. 107.

14 On this point see the next chapter.

15 Other criteria should, in fact, also be taken into account, e.g. the percentage of actual voluntary activists out of all the members, the number and the organizational consistency of the party's possible collateral associations, etc.

16 See L. Coser, *Greedy Institutions: Patterns of Undivided Commitment*, New York, The Free Press, 1974; R. O'Toole, *The Precipitous Path: Studies in Political Sects*, Toronto, Peter Martin Associates, 1977; Van Doorn, *Conflict in Formal Organizations*.

17 G. Sjoblom, *Party Strategies in a Multiparty System*, Lund, Berlingska Boktryekekeriet, 1970, p. 185.

18 O. Kirchheimer, *Politics, Law and Social Change*, New York and London, Columbia University Press, 1969, p. 250.

19 S. L. Fisher, *The Minor Parties of the Federal Republic of Germany*, The Hague, Martinus Nijhoff, 1974.

20 Maintaining naturally, the organization's age as a constant.

21 Abrahamsson, *Bureaucracy or Participation*, p. 204; and J. Child, "Participation, Organization, and Social Cohesion," *Human Relations*, XXIX (1976), pp. 429–51.

22 Poggi, ed., *L'organizzazione partitica del PCI e della DC*.

23 S. Hellman, "Organization and Ideology in Four Communist Italian Federations," Ph.D. dissertation, Yale University, 1973, p. 162.

24 Olson, *The Logic of Collective Action*.

25 Blau and Meyer, *Bureaucracy in Modern Society*.

26 Blau, "A Formal Theory of Differentiation in Organizations," *American Sociological Review*, XXXV (1970), pp. 20, 201–18; Blau and Schoenherr, *Structure of Organizations*.

27 P. Blau, *On the Nature of Organizations*, New York, Wiley and Sons, 1974, pp. 330ff.

28 Poggi, ed., *L'organizzazione partitica del PCI e della DC*.

29 *Ibid.*, p. 42.

30 Wellhofer and Hennessey, "Political Party Development."

31 For example, the number of sections between 1954 and 1965 remained invariable despite the decrease in size; and at the Eighth Congress – in the middle of a phase of declining membership – new internal coordinating organs were formed in the federations (the "decentralized organs"). See Poggi, *L'organizzazione partitica del PCI e della DC*; Sivini, "Socialisti e cattolici," p. 98ff; Hellman, "Organization and Ideology," p. 145.

32 W. D. Gray, *The German Left since 1945: Socialism and Social Democracy*, Cambridge, The Oleauder Press, 1976, p. 107.

33 H. Haldrich, "Organizational Boundaries and Interorganizational Conflict," in F. Baker, ed., *Organizational Systems*, Homewood, Irving-Dorsey, 1973, pp. 379–93, and Haldrich, *op. cit.*

34 *Ibid.*, p. 244.

35 *Ibid.*, p. 245.

36 For this data see M. Barbagli, P. G. Corbetta, "L'elettorato, l'organizzazione del PCI e movimenti," *Il Mulino*, XXIX (1980), pp. 467–90. The "historical compromise" was the official PCI strategy of the seventies aimed at establishing a stable and longlasting alliance with the Catholic world and the DC.

37 On the policy of incorporation of new social groups associated with an alliance strategy to the DC known as the historical compromise, see P. Lange, "Il PCI e i possibili esiti della crisi italiana," in L. Graziano, S. Tarrow, eds., *La crisi Italiana*, Turin, Einaudi, 1979, vol. 2, pp. 157–718.

38 For an analysis of the PCI's internal problems in that phase see M. Fedele, *Classe e partiti negli anni '70*, Rome, Editori Riuniti, 1979, pp. 169ff.

39 R. Tiersky, Il partito comunista francese, In H. Timmermann, eds., *I partiti communisti dell'Europa mediterranea*, Bologna, Il Mulino, 1981, p. 81.

40 Another scenario is also possible: other groups mobilized by collective movements, can enter the organization with the scope of discouraging an accommodating strategy. It is during the phase in which the PCI developed its consociative strategy that it absorbed the loose ends of the students' and workers' movements of 1968–69: See Barbagli, Corbetta, *Base sociale del PCI e movimenti collettivi*. What the authors demonstrate in a subsequent work is the existence of a negative correlation between the PCI's organizational force in the different zones and its capacity to absorb collective movements (Barbagli, Corbetta, "L'elettorato, l'organizzazione del PCI e i movimenti," p. 481), which is perfectly congruent with the theory of institutionalization we have attempted to sketch out for parties: where the PCI is a strong institution, it has a greater autonomy from its environment and is thus less "permeable" by movements. Where it is a weaker institution, its dependence on the environment is greater and therefore so is its permeability.

41 See Panebianco, *Imperativi organizzativi*.

42 The existence, for example, of a public financing system for parties represented in parliament can offer crucial resources towards institutionalization, even for a very small party, if it is able to attain a few seats.

43 Downs, *Inside Bureaucracy*, p. 158.

44 See, in the case of the PCI, for example, Poggi, ed., *op. cit.*, and Hellman, "Organization and Ideology." The observation can in effect cover all political parties.

45 See G. Sartori, "Techniche decisionali e sistema dei comitati," *Rivista Italiana di Scienza Politica*, IV (1974), pp. 5–42.

46 R. D'Alimonte, "Regola di maggioranza, stabilità e equidistribuzione," *Rivista Italiana di Scienza Politica*, IV (1974), pp. 43–105.

47 On the function of secrecy in bureaucratic organizations, see Crozier, *Les Phénomènes bureaucratique*.

48 Rush, *The Selection of Parliamentary Candidates*, p. 51.

49 *Ibid.*, p. 51.

50 Heidenheimer, *Adenauer and the CDU*, p. 202.

51 G. Sani, "Alcuni dati sul ricambio della dirigenza partitica nazionale in Italia," *Rassegna Italiana di Sociologia*, VIII (1967), p. 135.

52 W. R. Schonfeld, "La Stabilité des Dirigeants des Partis Politiques," *Revue Française de Science Politique*, XXX (1980), pp. 477–504.

53 Sani, "Alcuni dati sul ricambio della dirigenza partitica nazionale in Italia," pp. 135–6.

54 See among others concerning this thesis, Downs, *Inside Bureaucracy*.

55 R. Cayrol, "Les votes des Fédérations dans les Congrès et Conseil Nationaux du Parti Socialiste, (1958–1970)," *Revue Française di Science Politique*, XXI (1971), p. 65.

56 Olson, *The Logic of Collective Action*.

57 For B. Barry's objections to Olson's theory, *Sociologists, Economists and Democracy*, pp. 23–39. The principal limit to Olson's position is that it doesn't take into consideration that participation, beyond selective incentives, can depend on the distribution of collective identity incentives. This point is formulated and elaborated by Pizzorno, *Interest and Parties in Pluralism*.

58 Gaxie, *Economie des partis et retributions du militantisme*, p. 139.

59 The list includes as much the criteria used by Blau as "Aston's indexes," used in several empirical studies on private firms by the so called "Aston Group" under D. S. Pugh's direction. Some of these studies are cited in note 12.

60 See Pugh *et al.*, "Dimensions of Organizational Structure."

61 Numerous studies highlight this aspect: for example, Selznich, *op. cit.*, Crozier, *I partiti francesi*, Perrow, *Organizational Analysis*. More specifically, on the distinction between governmental decisions – routine decisions, see Haldrich, "Organizational boundaries," p. 11.

62 P. Blau, "Decentralization in Bureaucracy," in M. N. Zald, ed., *Power in Organizations*, Nashville, Vanderbilt University Press, 1970, pp. 97–143.

63 On the high formalization of distribution procedures of funds among the LDP's national factions and on the importance of adhering to the "rules" to avoid acute conflicts, see Thayer, *How the Conservatives Rule Japan*, pp. 277ff.

64 L. Donaldson, M. Warner, "Struttura burocratica e struttura democratica in un

gruppo di sindacati e associazioni professionali in Gran Bretagna, in G. Gasparini," ed., *Sindacato e organizzazione*, Milan, Franco Angeli, 1978, p. 238.

65 "indirect representation is an admirable means of banishing democracy, while pretending to apply it," Duverger, *Political Parties* p. 140.

66 Donaldson and Warner, "Struttura burocratica."

67 On "open" intra-organizational competition among elites as a *sine qua non* condition for efficient electoral control of the rank and file, see Lipset, Trow, Coleman, *Union Democracy*. For the case of parties see Barnes, *Party Democracy*. Alongside open competition among elites in the presence of an equilibrium of force, the existence of a solid local autonomous organization is indicated as a factor which facilitates electoral control by Edelstein, Warner, *Comparative Union Decocracy*, pp. 70ff.

68 Sartori, "Tecniche decisionali e sistema dei comitati," pp. 96ff.

69 See the contribution of G. Pasquino and G. Zincone, in *Correnti, frazioni e fazioni nei partiti politici italiani*, Bologna, Il Mulino, 1973.

70 Poggi, ed., *L'organizzazione partitica del PCI e della DC*, p. 248.

11 Organization and environment

1 J. Gabarro, "Organizational Adaptation to Environmental Change," in Baker, ed., *Organizational System*, pp. 196–215.

2 The expression comes from Crozier and Friedberg, *L'Acteur et le système*, p. 112.

3 P. E. White, "Intra and Interorganizational Studies: Do they Require Separate Conceptualizations?," *Administration and Society*, VI (1974), pp. 107–52.

4 P. R. Lawrence, J. Lorsch, *Organization and Environment: Managing Differentiation and Integration*, Cambridge, Harvard University Press, 1967.

5 See F. E. Emery and E. L. Trist, *Toward a Social Ecology*, London, Plenum Press, 1973, and by the same authors, "The Causal Texture of Organizational Environments", in Baker, *Organizational System*, pp. 165–77.

6 D. S. Mileti and D. F. Gillespie, "An Integrated Formalization of Organization–Environment Interdependencies," *Human Relations*, XXIX (1976), p. 91.

7 Cf. S. M. Shortell, "The Role of Environment in a Configurational Theory of Organizations," *Human Relations*, XXX (1977), pp. 275–302, and P. N. Khandwalla, *Environment and the Organization Structure of Firms*, Montreal, McGill University Press, 1970.

8 L. Coser, *The Functions of Social Conflict*, New York, The Free Press, 1956.

9 By *institutional constraints* I understand those relatively stable factors which structure party arenas and consequently influence their organizations. In this respect, many observations advanced over thirty years by Duverger are still valuable today, e.g. on the role of the electoral systems and of the configuration (centralized or decentralized) of statal apparatuses. Proportional electoral systems tend to favor higher centralization of power within parties than majoritarian electoral systems. An analogous effect is favored by high administrative centralization of the state. It is a type of influence that can be annulled by the workings of other factors (e.g. genetic model and institutionalization); and, in fact, there often coexist, within the same electoral system and/or statal organization configuration, parties with different levels of power centralization. Aside from the institutional constraints which have a certain importance, we should also mention legislation concerning parties' internal lives (West Germany) as well as the laws concerning public financing of the parties. On this latter point, see H. E. Alexander, ed., *Political Finance*, London, Sage Publications, 1979.

10 See R. Rose, ed., *Electoral Behavior: A Comparative Handbook*, New York, The Free Press, 1974.

11 Rokkan, *Citizens, Elections, Parties*.

12 F. L. Wilson, *The Revitalization of French Parties*.

13 Developed on the basis of a distinction made by J. Q. Wilson in *Political Organizations*, p. 262ff. See also Eliassen and Svaasand, *The Formation of Mass Political Organizations*, p. 103.

14 See among others D. S. Catlin, "Toward a Functionalist Theory of Political Parties:

Inter-Party Competition in North Carolina," pp. 217–45, and W. J. Crotty, "The Party Organization and its Activities," in W. J. Crotty, ed., *Approaches to the Study of Political Organizations*, Allyn and Bacon, 1968, pp. 247–306. J. A. Schlesinger, *Ambition and Politics*, p. 130.

15 On this event see G. E. Roberts, "Organization, Identity and Survival: The Free Democratic Party in West Germany," paper presented at the ECPR workshop on political organizations, Grenoble, 1978, mimeographed.

16 Social changes can, of course, intervene which seriously affect the party's social base, its hunting ground: such structural modifications are traditionally studied by sociologists. I do not, as opposed to those who adopt a so to speak "pure" sociological approach – perhaps it would be more appropriate to say "reductive" (i.e. reducing sociology to a study of the social classes alone) – believe that a "purely" sociological explanation of party evolution (for the reasons amply enumerated in this book) is sufficient (though certainly necessary) to understand the evolution and changes in organizations.

17 This also has to do with the "unintended consequences" of social action in multiple, complex and interdependent systems: see R. Boudon, *Effets pervers et ordre social*, Paris, Presses Universitaire de France, 1977.

18 For a preliminary exploration of some effects of interdependence, see T. M. Hennessey, J. Martin, "Exchange Theory and Parliamentary Instability," in Kornberg, ed., *Legislature in Comparative Perspective*, pp. 182–202.

19 Fisichella, *Sviluppo politico e sistemi elettorali*.

20 Sartori, *Parties and Party Systems*, pp. 121–5.

21 On the various types of parliamentary opposition, see Kirchheimer, *Politics, Law and Social Change*, p. 295ff. See also M. N. Franklin, "Patterns of Opposition Behavior in Modern Legislatures," in Kornberg, ed., *Legislatures in Comparative Perspective*, pp. 421–46.

22 Lidtke, *The Outlawed Party*, p. 185.

23 *Ibid.*, pp. 198–9.

24 *Ibid.*, p. 260. This observation of a subtle historian is, incidentally, the best response to those who believe that a party's "goal" is always the "maximization" of votes. The complexity of organizational phenomena is such that an electoral defeat can, at times, be viewed – by certain actors, occupying particular roles – as an event more welcome than victory.

25 See M. Leiserson, "Factions and Coalitions in One-Party Japan," *American Political Science Review*, LXII (1968), pp. 770–87, and R. Axelrod, *Conflict of Interest*, Chicago, Markham Publishing Co., 1970.

26 Partial competitors because with De Gasperi, starting in 1948, the DC's hunting ground included as much the Catholic world as – with the notables as intermediaries – sectors of the secular middle class. The PRI, PSDI, and PLI – the DC's traditional governmental partners – were (and remain) competitors precisely in relation to these latter sectors.

27 See Minkin and Seyd, *The British Labour Party*.

28 Ramsden, *The Age of Balfour and Baldwin*, pp. 147ff.

29 Schorske, *German Social Democracy*, pp. 191ff.

30 The end of the Cold War determined, on the one hand, the dissolution of the alliance between the two parties, and on the other, a growth in the instability of the PSI's dominant coalition – both events explainable, in the light of our hypothesis, in terms of a reduction of environmental hostility.

31 On the case of the Netherlands, see A. Lijphart, *The Politics of Accommodation*, Berkeley, University of California Press, 1975. In the period from 1918 to 1965, stable coalition governments were the rule in Holland (as opposed to the other small European democracies): see H. Daalder, "Governi e sistemi di partito in dieci piccole democrazie europee," *Rivista Italiana di Scienza Politica*, I (1971), p. 278.

32 The leaders' firm "oligarchical" control over the respective party organizations is the rule in "consociative" type coalition governments: see Lijphart, *Politics of Accommodation*, p. 141ff.

33 On the growth in electoral instability as bringing about the end of consociative democracy, see A. Pappalardo, "Le condizioni della democrazia consociativa. Una critica logica e empirica," *Rivista Italiana di Scienza Politica*, IX (1979), pp. 367–445.

34 See J. Q. Wilson, *Political Organizations*, p. 263ff. The difficulties encountered by the parties in forming coalitions are still greater in the cases of attempted fusion. After having maintained that the power of the parties depended on the quality of their bureaucracies, Max Weber observed that: "The mutual hostility of party machines much more than programmatic differences accounts for the difficulties of merging parties," *Economy and Society*, p. 1399. In fact, a fusion implies an identity restructuring in which it is not at all clear at the outset – unless there is a clear power imbalance (which itself, however, makes the fusion still less likely) – which groups will turn out to be victorious in the struggle for control of the new organization.

12 Political and bureaucratic professionalism

1 Haldrich, *Organizations and Environment*, p. 13.

2 See F. Ferraresi and A. Spreafico, eds., *La burocrazia*, Bologna, Il Mulino, 1975 (especially the introduction, pp. 13–56), and M. Albrow, *Bureaucracy*, London, Pall Mall, 1970.

3 Weber, "Politik als Beruf" in *Gesammelte Politische Schriften*, Tübingen Mohr, 1958.

4 K. A. Eliassen and M. N. Pedersen, "Professionalization of Legislatures: Long-term Change in Political Recruitment in Denmark and Norway," *Comparative Studies in Society and History*, XX (1978), pp. 286–318.

5 Guttsmann, *Elite Recruitment*. See also R. W. Johnston, "The British Political Elite, 1955–1972," *Archives Européennes de Sociologie*, XIV (1973), pp. 35–77.

6 Fred Riggs has recently isolated twelve different significations attributed to the term "bureaucracy" in the literature: see his "Introduction: Shifting Meanings of the Term "Bureaucracy"", *International Social Science Journal*, XXXI (1979), pp. 563–84.

7 Albrow, *Bureaucracy*, enumerates, aside from these three, four other possible meanings of the concept: bureaucracy as "organizational inefficiency," as "public administration," as a synonym of "organization," and as "modern society."

8 This is essentially the definition of bureaucracy adopted by P. Blau in his studies, e.g. Blau and Meyer, *Bureaucracy in Modern Society*. For an analogous definition, see Abrahamsson, *Bureaucracy or Participation*.

9 R. K. Merton, *Social Theory and Social Structure*, New York, The Free Press, 1968. There is little literature on political professionalism: among the few studies on the subject, see G. S. Black, "A Theory of Professionalization in Politics," *American Political Science Review*, LXIV (1970), pp. 865–78, C. E. Schultz, "Bureaucratic Party Organization Through Professional Political Staffing," *Midwest Journal of Political Science*, VIII (1964), pp. 127–42. On parliamentary political professionalism see D. Herzog, *Carriera parlamentare e professionismo politico*, pp. 515–44. Also see G. Sani, "La professionalizzazione dei dirigenti di partito italiani," *Rivista Italiana di Scienza Politica*, II (1972), pp. 303–33.

10 G. Sartori, "Democrazia, burocrazia e oligarchia nei partiti," *Rassegna Italiana di sociologia*, I (1960), pp. 119–36.

11 Weber, *Economy and Society*. To Duverger, it was also possible, in certain circumstances, for the party bureaucracy to become dominant: see his *Political Parties*.

12 In this case, representative bureaucracy is qualified by the existence of an electoral control and thus differs from the "representative bureaucracy" (as opposed to the "punitive bureaucracy") discussed by A. Gouldner in *Patterns of Industrial Bureaucracy*, Glencoe, The Free Press, 1954. For Gouldner, the distinctive characteristic is "competence."

13 D. Herzog, "Political Parties and Political Leadership Selection," in O. Stammer, ed., *Party Systems, Party Organizations and the Politics of New Masses*, Berlin, Babelsberger, 1969, p. 164.

14 In this regard we should point out that the norms regulating the PC's "democratic

centralism" could not, by themselves, guarantee the traditional unity and discipline if they were not sustained by a bureaucratic structure which extends from the top to the periphery, by a body of bureaucrats which guarantees it. On democratic centralism, see Pasquino, *Organizational Models of Southern Communist Parties.*

15 The high level of professionalization among the federation leaders is noted by Hellman (among others) in his *Organization and Ideology.* He observes that, at the time of the research (the late seventies), both the directive committees of the two "strong" federations (in Bologna and Florence) were entirely composed of bureaucrats, while in the two "weak" federations (in Padova and Lucca), the percentages of bureaucrats in the city committees were 47 per cent and 57 per cent respectively. The same image of high political professionalization in federations is given by F. Lanchester, "La dirigenza di partito: il caso del PCI," *Il Politico,* XVI (1976), pp. 690–718.

16 Account being taken of the rate of professionalization of the PCI's leaders, at all levels, the thesis is easily demonstratable by the fact that the national regional and federal leaders made up 71 percent of the delegates at the Eighth Congress, 78.8 percent at the Ninth, 79.8 percent at the Tenth, 80.4 percent at the Eleventh, and 80 percent at the Twelfth: see Sivini, *Le Parti Communiste,* p. 123.

17 As can be seen in the empirical research on local and regional bureaucrats in British parties done by, for example, R. Frasure and A. Kornberg, "Constituency Agents and British Party Politics," *British Journal of Political Science,* 5 (1975), pp. 459–76.

18 This was true, however, in the period preceding the professionalization of the seventies (see chapter 13); see U. Schleth, M. Pinto-Duschinsky, "Public Subsidies," pp. 32–3.

19 S. Barnes, "Party Democracy and the Logic of collective Action," in Crotty, *Approaches to the Study of Party Organizations,* p. 132, observes that in the PSI: "The leaders acknowledged that paid party workers were constrained in their behavior. They were under substantial pressure to emerge on the winning side of intraparty disputes: a miscalculation could mean loss of office." On the contrary, the "semi-professionals" were clearly favored: "Non-party positions such as lawyer or schoolteacher alleviated some of the financial insecurity associated with factional politics. Leaders of either working-class backgrounds or those in the middle class who had never finished their education, becoming politically active at an early age, were in a more tenuous position. They had nowhere else to turn."

20 Barnes, *Party Democracy,* pp. 84–6.

21 Hellman, *Organization and Ideology,* p. 390. Aside from the links with the young electorate, the youth organizations are very important to party leaders, both in bureaucratic parties and in factional parties. A long activism initiated at a very young age in these organisms is the best guarantee of both real internalization of party (or faction) values and of the formation of solid personal ties.

22 Spencer Wellohofer, Hennessey, *Political Party Development.*

23 Ramsden, *The Age of Balfour and Baldwin,* p. 46.

24 Hellman, *Organization and Ideology,* p. 354.

25 Schorske, *German Social Democracy,* p. 127.

26 Lanchester, "La dirigenza di partito."

27 There is also the problem of "cross-cutting" loyalties of the "decentered" bureaucrats, i.e. of those bureaucrats assigned to collateral organizations: on the one hand, their excessive identification with the collateral organization would give rise to an undesired independence of the collateral organization; but, on the other hand, their exclusive identification with the party could mean a lack of vitality in the collateral organization which would diminish its political utility. In the PCI of the fifties, many problems in the relationship between the party and civil society depended on the inability of the collateral associations to develop autonomous activity within the orbit of the party's political line: the bureaucrats in the unions, feminist organizations, etc. considered themselves to be, first and foremost, communist, and were not inclined to act independently of the party; the collateral organizations (a very important axis in the Togliattian "new party" hypothesis) were unable to carry out their functions with vitality: see Poggi, ed., *L'organizzazione partitica del PCI e della DC,* pp. 171ff.

28 See J. A. Jackson, ed., *Professions and Professionalization*, Cambridge, Cambridge University Press, 1970.
29 M. Sarfaty Larson, *The Rise of Professionalism: A Sociological Analysis*, Berkeley, University of California Press, 1977, p. 191. See also the work of A. L. Stinchcombe "Bureaucratic and Craft Administration of Production," *Administrative Science Quarterly*, IV (1959), pp. 168–87.
30 Sarfarty Larson, *The Rise of Professionalism*, pp. 191ff.
31 *Ibid.*, p. 193.
32 Zuckerman, *The Politics of Faction*, pp. 105ff.
33 Shell, *The Transformation of Austrian Socialism*, p. 110.
34 I will come back to this point in chapter 14.
35 Blau, *On the Nature of Organizations*, pp. 229–30.
36 As D. Herzog has noted (among others) in his "Carriera parlamentare e professionismo politico."
37 Rose, *The Problem of Party Government*. I will come back to this point in chapter 14.
38 On "semi-professionalism," see G. Sartori, *Il parlamento italiano*, Naples, ESI, 1963. Also see Cotta, *Classe politica e parlamento in Italia, 1946–1963*, and J. Fishel, "Parliamentary Candidates and Party Professionalism in Western Germany," *Western Political Quarterly*, XXV (1972), pp. 64–80.
39 On the peculiar role of lawyers in politics, see H. Eulau and J. Sprague, *Lawyers in Politics: a Study in Professional Convergence*, Indianapolis, Bobbs-Merril, 1961.
40 Sartori, *Il parlamento italiano*.
41 A preliminary attempt to construct a map of the roles within the Italian political class is presented in P. Farneti's "Problemi di ricerca e di analisi della classe politica italiana," *Rassegna Italiana di Sociologia*, XIII (1972), pp. 79–116.
42 On the "catch-all" party, see chapter 14.

13 Environmental challenges and elite circulation

1 R. Nisbet, *Social Change and History*, Oxford, Oxford University Press, 1969.
2 Stinchcombe, *Social Structure and Organizations*, Downs, *Inside Bureaucracy*.
3 W. M. Teulings, "Modeles de Croissance et de Development des Organisations," *Revue Française de Sociologie*, XIV (1973), pp. 352–71.
4 Simplifying somewhat, a perspective of this sort is offered by Crozier and Friedberg, *L'Acteur et le système*.
5 See F. Butera, "Per una ridefinizione del concetto di cambiamento organizzativo," *Studi Organizzativi*, IX (1977), pp. 43–78.
6 See G. Zalman *et al.*, *Innovations and Organizations*, New York, Wiley and Sons, 1973, and G. Dalton *et al.*, *The Distribution of Authority in Formal Organizations*, Cambridge, Mass., The MIT Press, 1968.
7 Crozier, *Le Phénomène bureaucratique*, pp. 257ff.
8 R. P. Lynton, "Linking an Innovative Subsystem into the System," in Baker, ed., *Organizational Systems*, p. 316.
9 Crozier and Friedberg, *L'Acteur et le système*, p. 334.
10 See Boudon, *Effets pervers et ordre socials*, and Crozier and Friedberg, *L'Acteur et le système*, p. 157.
11 Crozier, *Phénomène bureaucratique*.
12 On the theory of "bounded rationality," see J. G. March, H. A. Simon, *Organizations*, New York, Wiley and Sons, 1958.
13 Using the concept of "loose coupling" to indicate the relative reciprocal autonomy of the organizational subsystem, Haldrich, *Organizations and Environment*, pp. 76ff., maintains a largely analogous thesis.
14 See literature cited in chapter 11.
15 Lynton, "Innovative Subsystem."
16 On these problems see L. Morlino, *Come cambiano i regimi politici*, Milan, Franco Angeli, 1980.

17 The environmental challenge as catalyzer of organizational change is a theme treated by sociological literature: for example, on the transformations the industrial firm under external pressure, see L. Gallino, *Indagini di sociologia economica e industriale*, Milan, Communita', esp. pp. 45–61.

18 The tight connection between the reforms in United States party organizations from the nineteenth century to today and the struggles for power among the different factions is brought out by A. Ranney, *Curing the Mischiefs of Faction: Party Reform in America*, Berkeley, University of California Press, 1975.

19 A useful discussion on the differences between "substitution of ends" and "succession of ends" can be found in Blau, and Scott, *Formal Organizations. A Comparative Approach*, p. 285ff. My opinion remains that the alternative is not between substitution and succession, but rather between "articulation of ends" and "succession of ends."

20 The internal debates on "party democracy" acquire more vitality in these moments of crisis. As long as the dominant coalition is able to rule the organization securely, the party's collective identity is safeguarded and the rewards of status and material are guaranteed; the problem of *how* and *who* is to make the decisions only interests a small minority. In crisis the problem attracts the attention of more actors (and it is not by chance that the theme "internal democracy" is a classical battle cry of minority elites in their attack against the majority). The increase in attention on procedural decisions and in debate can thus be seen in many cases as an indicator of organizational crisis.

21 The crucial difference between economic exchange and the more general social exchange is that the "payments" in the latter type are not accurately quantifiable and therefore the "trust" among the contracting parties plays an even more important role: see Blau, *On the Nature of Organizations*, pp. 205–9.

22 See Sani, *Alcuni dati sul ricambio della dirigenza*, and Schonfeld, *La Stabilite des Partis Politiques*.

23 Duverger, *Political Parties*, pp. 163ff., Schonfeld, *La Stabilité des partis politiques*, and G. Pasquino, "Ricambio parlamentare e rendimento politico," *Politica del Diritto*, VII (1976), pp. 543–65.

24 Schonfeld, *La Stabilite des partis politique*, and Poggi, ed., *L'organizzazione partitica del PCI e della DC*, pp. 549ff.

25 Michels, *Political Parties*, pp. 256–8. Michels later believed he could extend the "amalgamation of elites" law (from the political party to political regimes) opposing it to Pareto's "circulation of elites" law: see R. Michels, *Corso di sociologia politica*, Milan, Instituto Editoriale Scientifico, 1972, Id., *Studi sulla democrazia e sull'autorita'*, Firenze, La Nouva Italia, 1935, Id., *Nuovi studi sulla classe politica. Saggio sugli spostamenti sociali e intellettuali del dopoguerra*, Milan, Dante Alighieri, 1936.

26 Hellman, *Organization and Ideology*, p. 309.

27 Duverger, *Political Parties*, pp. 157–68.

28 Ramsden, *The Age of Balfour and Baldwin*, pp. 213ff.

29 D. J. Wilson, *Power and Party Bureaucracy*, pp. 24ff.

30 See P. Seyd, "Democracy within the Conservative Party?," *Government and Opposition*, X (1975), pp. 219–37.

31 Rose, *The Problem of Party Government*, p. 130.

32 Finer, *The Changing British Party System*, p. 79.

33 Peele and Hall, *Dissent, Faction and Ideology in the Conservative Party: Some Reflections on the Inter-War Period*.

34 Poggi, ed., *L'organizzazione partitica del PCI e della DC*, p. 72.

35 On the crises and transformation of the PCI's incentive system and more generally on the dynamics connected to the 1956 crisis, see P. Lange, "Change and Choice in the Italian Communist Party: Strategy and Organization in the Postwar Period," Ph.D. Dissertation, M.I.T., 1974, pp. 120ff.

36 On "generational pressure" in the federations before 1956 see Lange, *ibid.*, p. 120ff.

37 Poggi, ed., *L'organizzazione partitica del PCI e della DC*, p. 76.

38 On these questions see G. Galli, "Il PCI rivisitato," *Il Mulino*, XX (1971), pp. 25–52.

39 For data on this question see Poggi, ed., p. 550.

40 Hellman, *Organization and Ideology*.

41 Lanchester, *La dirigenza di partito: il caso del PCI*, p. 692. See also, by the same author, "Continuita' e cambiamenti nella dirigenza comunista," *Il Mulino*, XXVII (1978), p. 457.
42 Sivini, *Le Parti Communiste*, pp. 83ff.
43 See P. Lange, "La politica della alleanze del PCI e del PCF," *Il Mulino*, XXIV (1975), pp. 499–527.
44 Sivini, *Le Parti Communiste*, p. 83.
45 In this sense the most important innovations regard the reinforcement of control and advisory organs to the detriment of the bureaucratic apparatus that dominated the ruling organisms (even if there was a partial reevaluation of the apparatus after 1958). Furthermore, the number of sections remains unchanged, although, as a result of the reduction in members, their size decreases (a measure which tends to stimulate base participation). Finally, after 1956 the deterioration of the cells was rapid: there were 45,000 before the Eighth Congress and only 35,000 in 1959. For this data see, Sivini, *Le Parti Communiste*, pp. 85, 98, 113.
46 On the conflicts of the 1960s following Togliatti's death and the publication of the "Yalta memorial," see Galli, "Il PCI rivisitato," pp. 38ff.
47 See Childs, *From Schumacher to Brandt. The Story of German Socialism, 1945–1965*. On Schumacher see L. J. Edinger, *Kurt Schumacher. A Study in Personality and Political Behavior*, London, Oxford University Press, 1965.
48 H. K. Shellenger Jr, *The SPD in the Bonn Republic: A Socialist Party Modernizes*, The Hague, Nijhoff, 1968, p. 94. Schellenger's text gives the best description of the process of transformation that led up to Bad Godesberg, and I have thus kept essentially to this account. See also, however, Rovan, *Histoire de la Social-Democratie Allemande*, esp. pp. 258ff.
49 Schellenger Jr, *The SPD in the Bonn Republic*, p. 59.
50 See Gray, *The German Left Since 1945*, pp. 117ff.
51 Schellenger Jr, *The SPD in the Bonn Republic*, p. 62. The Social Democratic bureaucracy, however, even if in a state of deterioration with respect to the imperial period, was still very powerful during Weimar, as is demonstrated by R. Hunt, *German Social Democracy, 1918–1933*, New Haven and London, Yale University Press, 1964, pp. 56ff.
52 Gray, *The German Left Since 1945*, pp. 159ff.
53 *Ibid.*, p. 150.
54 *Ibid.*, pp. 150ff.
55 Schellenger Jr, *The SPD in the Bonn Republic*, p. 162. The combined influx of local electoral victories which had brought many "new socialists" to local government and thus to a position from which they could control the peripheric organization of the party, with the weakening of the bureaucracy, had made the Länder organizations and the federations (*Bezirke*) more independent of central bureaucratic power in comparison to the pre-war period.
56 Gray, *The German Left Since 1945*, p. 141.
57 Schellenger Jr, *The SPD in the Bonn Republic*, p. 79.
58 *Ibid.*, p. 156.
59 *Ibid.*, p. 158.
60 On the conflict for control of Berlin between the "new socialist" Brandt and the old bureaucrat Neumann see *ibid.*, pp. 117ff.
61 *Ibid.*, p. 156.
62 Gray, *The German Left Since 1945*, p. 189.
33 See G. E. Rusconi, "Bad Godesberg e' un modello?," *Il Mulino*, XXVIII (1979), pp. 920–42.
64 Schellenger Jr, *The SPD in the Bonn Republic*, pp. 173ff.
65 My description on these matters was drawn from Pridham, *Christian Democracy in Western Germany*.
66 *Ibid.*, pp. 164ff.
67 *Ibid.*, p. 196.
68 *Ibid.*, pp. 265–6.
69 *Ibid.*, p. 266. Naturally, in the financial reinforcement of the central extraparliamen-

tary organization, public financing under the form of electoral reimbursements after 1967 played an important role. See the comparative analysis on the effects of financing by D. Leonard, "Contrasts in Selected Western Democracies: Germany, Sweden, Britain," in Alexander, ed., *Political Finance*, pp. 41–73.

70 Pridham, *Christian Democracy in Western Germany*, p. 267.

71 I didn't treat the case of the passage of the SFIO to the PSF because it is more a refounding, than a restructuring of the organizational order. Even if, however, the PSF is incontestibly a new party, it should be noted that many elements of the old SFIO are incorporated in the organization (in the first place, the central role of the federations). See, on this process of transition, Hurtig, *De la S.F.I.O. au Nouveau Parti Socialiste*.

14 Parties and democracy: transformation and crisis

1 On these questions, with particular regard to the Italian case, see Pasquino, *Crisi dei partiti e ingovernabilita'*. A different elaboration, which however was also influential in this book, above all on the crucial problem of the decline of collective identity, has been developed by Pizzorno, *Interest and Parties in Pluralism*.

2 O. Kirchheimer, "The Transformation of the Western European Party Systems," in La Palombara and Weiner, eds., *Political Parties and Political Development*, pp. 177–200.

3 *Ibid.*, p. 252.

4 On the distinction between "valence" and "positional" problems, see D. Stokes, "Spatial Models of Party Competition," *American Political Science Review*, LVII (1963).

5 Membership recruitment as an instrument of organizational financing loses importance, not only as a result of the intervention of interest groups, but by recourse to public financing, whose generalized introduction wasn't foreseeable at the beginning of the sixties when Kirchheimer wrote. It should, however, be noted that financing both by the public and by interest groups, although converging to diminish the members' organizational weight, seem to exert contradictory effects on the organization: while public financing (with variations from party to party and according to the different national legislations) has an effect of "power concentration," or putting in the leaders' hands monetary resources superior to those at the disposition of their internal adversaries, interest group financing acted in the opposite way, provoking "fragmentation" of organizational power: sponsorship of individual "personal" candidates in different parties on the part of interest groups, not to mention financial intermediation by the politicians themselves, place financial resources which are convertible in political resources (and exploitable in the internal competition), in the hands of a tendentially elevated number of leaders.

6 The mass bureaucratic party and the professional–electoral party are nothing other than ideal types referred to in the works of Duverger and Kirchheimer, respectively. I have preferred using the term professional–electoral party rather than that of the catch-all party not only to accentuate the aspect of professionalization, but to underline that the crucial dimension is the organizational one. With some differences and with certain reserves, the typology which comes closest to that presented here has been elaborated by Wright, *Comparative Party Models*.

7 Seen from another point of view, however, the Italian case leaves wide margins of uncertainty: the PCI is a party in which professionalization is a very advanced process and in which aspects of both types have interacted and overlapped (giving way to internal tensions) for several years.

8 We are dealing, moreover, with different challenges. The external challenge which acts as "catalyst" of organizational change is a "conjunctural" challenge (an electoral defeat, etc.). The challenges we are now considering are instead of a "structural" type. They emerge after long-term transformations in the parties' environments. Naturally, there is a relation between conjunctural and structural challenges, in the sense that the second type must be "activated" by the first type, in order to produce transformations in the parties.

9 See Pizzorno, *I soggetti del pluralismo*, p. 209. With respect to the Italian case, labour

market studies have widely explored these aspects: see *AA.VV., Mutamento e classi sociali in Italia*, Naples, Liguori, 1981.

10 On post-industrial society the key reference is to two works from different scientific and political positions, which have brilliantly dealt with the theme: D. Bell, *The Coming of Post-Industrial Society*, New York, Basic Books, 1973 and A. Touraine, *La Societe Post-Industrielle*, Paris, Editions Denoel, 1969. For a critical analysis of the literature see K. Kumar, *Prophecy and Progress*, Harmondsworth, Penguin Books, 1978.

11 See L. Maisel, ed., *Changing Campaign Techniques*, London, Sage Publications, 1977. For the case of the United States see A. Rawley Saldich, *Electronic Democracy*, New York, Praeger, 1979.

12 Two types of professionals emerge under the pressure of the transformations in the political communications system: one includes communications technicians, i.e. the poll-taking experts, the specialists in mass media, etc.; the other includes the specialists of the party's various sectors of intervention (economists, urban planners, etc.) because campaigning on the "issues" requires a growing technical knowhow around the content of political messages. On the highly professionalized character of electoral campaigns in the United States, useful data is available in R. K. Scott, R. J. Hrebenar, *Parties in Crisis. Party Politics in America*, New York, Wiley and Sons, 1979, esp. p. 155ff. On the professionalization reached by British parties (with temporary contracts given to specialists in publicity), see Rose, *The Problem of Party Government*, pp. 60–89. On the CDU, see E. K. Schench, R. Wildermann, "The Professionalization of Party Campaigning," in Dogan and Rose, eds., *European Politics: A Reader*, pp. 413–26.

13 See the electoral developments examined by S. B. Wolinetz, "*Stabilità e mutamento nei sistemi partitici dell 'Europa occidentale*," Rivista Italiana di Scienza Politica, III (1978), pp. 3–55. See also the analysis contained in P. H. Merkl, ed., *Western European Party Systems*, New York, The Free Press, 1980. The phenomenon of the decline in party identification, before becoming evident in Europe, had already happened in the United States: see N. H. Nie, S. Verba, J. R. Petrocik, *The Changing American Voter*, Cambridge, Harvard University Press, 1976, and on the connections between the decline in party identification, mass media and changes in the social structure, E. C. Ladd Jr, C. D. Hadley, *Transformations of the American Party System*, New York, Norton Co., 1978.

14 Kirchheimer, *The Transformation of Western European Party Systems*, p. 200.

15 The problem of the transformation/crisis of parties with reference to its effects on the political process has been widely approached in recent years: see, among others, L. Maisel, P. M. Sacks, eds., *The Future of Political Parties*, London, Sage Publications, 1975, L. Maisel, J. Cooper, eds., *Political Parties: Development and Decay*, London, Sage Publications, 1978.

16 Kirchheimer, *Transformation of Western European Party Systems*, p. 188. Here (as in Kirchheimer) "function" means "relevant activity for the political system." I preferred maintaining the established term although sharing the objections lodged by Pizzorno (*I soggetti del pluralismo*, p. 11ff) concerning the functionalist theories of the political party. It should, moreover, be clear that the examination of the functions in my perspective only makes sense if the analysis is geared to the political system, while I consider it completely out of place if the object of the study is the single party considered in its organizational dimension. I am now introducing this question because it is only in this chapter that our analysis shifts from parties to the political system.

17 Which does not at all mean that parties "follow objectives" of the defense/transformation of the social and political order, as the teleological perspectives would like to believe.

18 See Pizzorno, *I soggetti del pluralismo*, pp. 19ff.

19 *Ibid.*, pp. 130ff.

20 See G. Lavoni, "The PCF, the State, and the Revolution: An Analysis of Party Policies, Communications and Popular Culture," in Blackmer and Tarrow, eds., *Communism in Italy and France*, pp. 59–99.

21 On the role of firms in the decision-making process of polyarchies, see C. Lindblom, *Politics and Market*, New York, Basic Books, 1977.

22 This implies the crisis of neo-corporative regimes, or at least makes the neo-

corporative strategies vascillate where they had once been strong. The neo-corporate orders are in fact able to maintain stability if a restricted number of organizations exist which represent hierarchically ordered interests: on neo-corporativism see P. C. Schmitter, G. Lehmbruch, eds., *Trends toward Corporatist Intermediation*, London, Sage Publications, 1979.

23 It is the theme developed by N. Luhmann, *Politische Planung*, Opladen, Westdeutscher Verlag, 1971.

24 In Stein Rokkan's terms, the "ingovernability" can be considered the result of a tension between the "electoral-territorial" channel controlled by parties and the "functional-corporative" channel controlled by interest groups. This tension tends today to increase as a result of two contradictory processes: on the one hand, increased international interdependence which favors the "transnationalization" of interest groups and reduces decisional capabilities of national states: on the other hand, the complete mobilization of the "peripheries" of European countries within the different national arenas which reinforces "territoriality" and blocks the possibility of supra-national political solutions (federalist, etc.) to the crisis of the nation-state: see S. Rokkan, "I voti contano, le risorse decidono," *Rivista Italiana di Scienza Politica*, V (1975), pp. 167–76.

25 S. Lipset, S. Rokkan, "Cleavage, Structure, Party Systems and Voter Alignments: An Introduction," in Lipset and Rokkan, eds., *Party Systems and Voter Alignments*, New York, The Free Press, 1967, p. 21.

26 The political problems, in European countries, were almost always hierarchically ordered on the basis of their "saliency." This depended on the fact that the voter was not usually called to express his opinion on single problems, but rather on packages. *Ibid.*, pp. 2, 6.

27 See Sartori, *Parties and Party Systems*, pp. 324–56. For an empirical confirmation of the role of left/right dimension in European electoral competitions, see W. R. Inglehart, H. D. Klingemann, "Party Identification, Ideological Preference and the Left–Right Dimension among Western Mass Publics," in I. Budge et al., eds., *Party Identification and Beyond*, New York, Wiley and Sons, 1976, pp. 243–73.

28 It was not by chance that the idea of a left/right one-dimensional political space had been developed by Downs in reference to the different party' positions on the problem of state intervention in the economy: see Downs, *An Economic Theory of Democracy*.

29 See F. Hirsch, I. Goldthorpe, eds., *The Political Economy of Inflation*, London, 1978.

30 S. Berger, "Politics and Antipolitics in Western Europe in the Seventies," *Daedalus*, Winter (1979), pp. 27–50, and J. Clayton Thomas, "The Changing Nature of Divisions in the West: Trends in Domestic Policy Orientation in Ten Party Systems," *European Journal of Political Research*, VII (1979), pp. 397–413.

31 Moreover, the intertwining between state and parties (in Europe, not in the United States) often makes anti-party revolts indistinguishable from anti-welfare revolts. On these problems see M. D. Hancock, G. Sjoberg, eds., *Politics in the Post-Welfare State*, New York and London, Columbia University Press, 1972.

32 R. Inglehart, "Political Action. The Impact of Values, Cognitive Level and Social Background," in S. H. Barnes, M. Kaase, eds., *Political Action. Mass Participation in Five Western Democracies*, London, Sage Publications, 1979, p. 353. The existence of an establishment/anti-establishment division in the Italian case is empirically documented by A. Marradi, "Dimensioni dello spazio politico in Italia," *Revista Italiana di Scienza Politica*, IX (1979), pp. 263–96.

33 On non-conventional political behavior, see Barnes and Kaase, eds., *Political Action*. The protagonists are predominantly young and women. The generational and sexual differences do not however explain everything. In the "establishment/anti-establishment" division, as I intend it here, a plurality of attitudes and behaviors enter the scene (including the sympathy for political terrorism and fiscal backlash movements) whose only common denominator is opposition to the existing ruling class.

34 Naturally a clear division doesn't always exist between conventional political behavior (tied to the notion of left/right) and non-conventional political behavior. Many protagonists and sympathizers of "anti-political" movements have ideological reference points on the "right" or on the "left" as well.

The outcomes of these processes are obviously unforseeable. It is always possible that an eventual development of the "establishment/anti-establishment" division ends by creating, in certain countries, masses destined to become instruments of new subversive organizations (with respect to the democratic regimes), either of the "extreme-right" or of the "extreme left." Thus, the one-dimensionality of political space would be reconstructed, opening up, however, as in the twenties and thirties, grave risks for the democratic regimes.

35 For a brilliant exploration of the possible conflicts and alliances among upwardly and downwardly mobile social classes in post-industrial and developed societies, see S. P. Huntington, "La politica nella societa' postindustriale," *Rivista Italiana di Scienza Politica*, IV (1974), pp. 489–525.

36 H. Daalder, "Parties, Elites and Political Development in Western Europe," in La Palombara and Weiner, eds., *Political Parties and Political Development*, pp. 43–77.

37 On the active role played by the elites in the formation and deepening of political divisions, see A. Zuckerman, "Political Cleavage: a Conceptual and Theoretical Analysis," *British Journal of Political Science*, V (1975), pp. 243ff.

38 See L. Thurow, *The Zero-Sum Society*, New York, Basic Books, 1980.

39 Sartori, *Parties and Party Systems*, pp. 324ff.

40 *Ibid.*, p. 341.

41 The crisis of traditional solidarity is, for certain authors, tied to the erosion of the "prescribed nucleus," that agreement about the "foundations" without which no social or political order is possible. In this interpretation ingovernability is nothing other than the political manifestation of a deeper process: the erosion of communitary rules, in turn the extreme consequence of modernization. See G. Germani, "Democrazia e autoritarismo nella societa' moderna," *Storia Contemporanea*, 11 (1980), pp. 177–217 and D. Bell, *The Cultural Contradictions of Capitalism*, New York, Basic Books, 1976.

42 This is the hypothesis put forth by Pizzorno in "Interest and Parties in Pluralism." The thesis of an already accomplished decomposition of political parties in the United States has above all been put forward by W. D. Burnham: see "American Politics in the 1970s: Beyond Party?," in Maisel and Sacks, eds., *The Future of Political Parties*, pp. 238–77. See also A. Ranney, "The Political Parties: Reform and Decline," in A. King, ed., *The New American Political System*, Washington, Enterprise Institute, 1978, pp. 213–47.

43 Conservative neo-liberalism and Labour's neo-socialism in Great Britain from the end of the seventies are cases in point. Analogous tendencies have occurred in other European countries as well.

44 There is naturally the French example of "Mitterrandism." It is best to suspend judgement here in that we have tried to construct our hypotheses on history, on solid terrain rather than on hearsay. Accepting the peculiarities of the French case (strong executive, only postwar experience of a succession from a democratic regime to another democratic regime, etc.), only one hypothesis – and this with caution – can be advanced: first with Gaullism and then with Mitterrandism, France could effectively represent a model. "Democratic Bonapartism" – the "plebiscitarian democracy" guided by the type of head Max Weber wrote about – and of which the French Fifth Republic is a rather faithful example, could show itself in the emerging post-industrial society, to be the form of government most suited to safeguarding democracy, and guaranteeing political expression to the continual eruptions of the social system.

45 This is the pessimistic thesis implicit in the essay by Germani, "Democrazia e autoritarismo nella societa' moderna."

Index

Adenauer C., 37, 52, 99, 116–23, 169, 171–2, 257–9
Allemand J., 95
amalgamation vs. circulation of elites, 247–50
Arnold K., 122
Attlee C., 95, 218
Auer I., 216
Australian Social Democratic Party, 231
Australian Socialist Party (SPÖ), 59, 83, 86
autonomy and systemness, 55–8
Azione Cattolica, 123, 127

Bad Godesberg, 70, 86, 116, 123
Baldwin S., 136, 250
Balfour A., 133–4, 250
Barbé H., 81
Barnes S., 91
Barry B., 9
Bartley G. C. T., 133
Barzel R., 259
Bebel A., 70–7, 217
Belgian Christian Democratic Party (DCB), 65
believers and careerists, 25–30
Bernstein E., 74
Bismarck O., 71, 217
Blain H., 136–7
Blanquists, 95
Blau P., 189
Blum L., 37, 80, 100, 169, 218
Bolsheviks 100, 161
Bolshevism, 65, 78, 81–7
Boraston J., 135
Bordiga A., 82
Bouhler P., 157
Brandt W., 256
Brauer M., 255

British Conservative Party, 58–9, 65, 92, 130–42, 147, 149, 150–1, 165, 187, 210–11, 218, 222, 224, 250–1
British Labour Party, 37, 52, 55, 58, 65, 86, 88, 92–4, 104, 110–11, 166–8, 176, 210–11, 218, 222
British Liberal Party, 250
Brousse P., 95
bureaucracy, 220–8.

catch-all party, 262–4
Célor P., 81
Central Office, 132–40, 165
CGIL, 85, 178
Chaban-Delmas J., 149
Chamberlain N., 133–4, 136, 250
charisma, 52–3, 65–7, 143–7
Charlot J., 160
Chirac J., 172
Churchill W., 52
CGL, 104–5, 107
CGT, 59, 81, 85–6, 96
Conservative Workers Organization, 138
Comintern, 78, 80
Crozier M., 147

Daalder H., 272
De Felice R., 161
De Gasperi A., 52, 117, 124–8, 145, 154, 168–9
De Gaulle C., 52, 148–55, 167
Delbecque L., 149
Disraeli B., 131–4, 259
dominant coalition, 37–40: composition 39–40, 247; conformation 39–40, 247
Doriot J., 81
Dorpinghans B., 118
Dossetti G., 127, 145
Downs A., 5, 11, 27, 35, 195
Drexler A., 156

315

Duverger M., xi, xii, 3, 37, 50, 55–6, 65, 98, 160–1, 163, 173, 186, 191, 250, 262, 264, 267

Ebert, F., 75, 223, 254
Eldersveld S., 163
electoral arena, 208–14
electoral–professional party, 262–7
Eliassen K., 51, 221–2, 234
Engels, F., 71
Erhard L., 258
Erler F., 256
evolutionism and "political development," 239–42
experts, 229–32
external "sponsor" institution, 51–2

Fabian society, 89, 92
factions, 38–9, 92
Fanfani A., 108, 125, 127–8, 167, 174
Faure P., 37, 80, 97, 100, 166
Fourcade M.-M., 149
Fraktion, 72, 120, 122
Fraser M., 135
French Communist Party (PCP), 6, 37, 59, 70, 78–86, 92, 100–2, 110–12, 139–40, 165, 172–5, 191–2, 200, 202, 209, 218, 225, 250, 265
French Radical Socialist Party, 250
French Socialist Party (SFIO), 37, 44, 51–2, 59, 65, 79, 88, 95–100, 104–7, 110–12, 120, 129, 131, 136, 145, 148, 150, 166, 169, 171–2, 202, 218, 250
French Socialist Party (PSF) (after 1969), 97, 172
French Workers' Party (POF), 95–7
Frey R., 149

Gaullist Party, 52, 147, 149, 161, 167, 260
Gaxi A., 25
Gedda L., 126
General L., 126
General German Worker's Association (ADAV), 70–1
Gerke G., 119
German Christian Democratic Party (CDU), 37, 44, 52, 59, 65, 99, 114, 115–23, 126, 131, 136, 138–9, 141–2, 148, 150, 152, 154, 167, 169, 171–7, 186, 197, 226, 253–5, 257–61
Gernan Communist Party, 156
German Liberal Party, 212
German National Socialist Party (NSDAP), 155–62
German Social Democratic Party (SPD), 12, 31, 51–2, 58–9, 65, 71–8, 83–6, 88, 92, 96–100, 106, 110, 112, 117–18, 121, 130, 139, 140, 151, 165, 172–5, 178, 186, 190, 200, 202, 206, 210, 215–18, 223, 225, 228, 249, 253–60, 263
German Workers Party, 156
Giolitti G., 104
Gorst J. E., 132–4, 259
Gramsci A., 81–2
Grayson V., 91
Gronchi G., 145
Guesde J., 95–7
Guttsmann W. L., 222

Haldrich H., 190
Hardie J., 52, 88–91, 145
Hasselman W., 71
Heath E., 251
Hellman S., 228
Henderson A., 90–2
Hermes A., 116
hidden professionals, 231
Hilpert W., 119
Hitler A., 52, 156–62
Hilter Youth, 156, 158
Home D., 251

incentives, collective and selective, 9–11, 24–5, 30–2
Independent Labour Party, 52, 88–90
Italian Christian Democratic Party (DC), 43, 52, 65, 86, 92, 108–9, 114, 123–31, 141–2, 146, 148, 150, 163, 166–8, 171, 202, 218, 231, 248, 252, 261, 265
Italian Communist Party (PCI), 37, 59, 70, 78, 82–6, 92, 107–12, 130, 139–40, 163–6, 172–5, 178, 187–91, 200–2, 211, 219, 225, 228, 248, 250–3, 265
Italian Fascist Party, 52
Italian Labour Party, 124
Italian Popular Party, 65
Italian Social Democratic Party (PSDI), 211
Italian Socialist Party (PSI), 59, 65, 88, 97, 102–12, 122, 129, 131, 136, 148, 166, 169, 171, 178, 202, 219, 248, 265

Japanese Liberal Democratic Party (LDP), 86, 142
Japanese Socialist Party, 65
Jaurès, J., 52, 77, 95–8, 100, 122, 145, 169, 172
Jenkins W., 135

Kaiser J., 118–23
Kautsky K., 73–4
Khrushchev N., 251
Kirchheimer O., 262–4, 268
Kohl H., 259

Index

Lafargue P., 95
Länder, 118–23
Lasalle F., 70–1, 74
legitimation, internal vs. external, 51–2, 67
Lenin V., 79, 82–3, 99, 146
Lib–Lab Alliance, 88–9
Liebknecht W., 70–3
Löns J., 117
Loriot F., 79
Lowi T., 16
Luxemburg R., 73, 75

MacDonald R., 89–92, 145
Marceuet A., 149
Marnes G., 88
Marx K., 71
mass bureaucratic party, 262–7
Matteotti G., 82
Maximalists, 166
McKenzie R., 130
Mehring F., 75
Michels R., xi, xii, xiii, 3, 7–8, 16–17, 23, 27, 30, 32, 37, 43–4, 73, 163, 188, 201, 203, 221, 223, 239, 249, 264, 273
Middleton R.W.E., 133
Milan Workers Party, 102
Millerand A., 95
Mitterand F., 155
Mollet G., 44, 99, 101–2, 172
monocracy, 171–3
Moore B., xv
Morandi R., 103, 108, 166, 219
Mosca G., xiii
Mussolini B., 52, 82, 106–7, 166

National Economic Council (NEC), 92–4
National Socialist Party, 52, 147
natural system model, 6–9
Nenni P., 108–9, 219
Neue Zeit, 73
Neumann F., 256

oligarchy, 171–3
Ollenhauer E., 254–6
Olson M., 9, 199
opposition and competition, 217–19
organizational power map, 38, 173–9
organizational evolution, 17–20, 164–8
organizational thresholds, 193–5
organograms, 174–6
Ostrogorski M., xi, 37, 221, 223

Pareto V., xiii
parliamentary arena, 214–17
party size, 185–95
Pizzorno A., 18

political cleavage, 269–73
polyarchy, 171–3
Popular Front, 101
Poujadists, 161

Rassemblement du Peuple Français (RPF), 151–2, 161
rational model, 6–9
recruitment, centripetal vs. centrifugal, 60–1
Rokkan S., 272
Röhm E., 157
Roosevelt F. D., 52
Rose R., 139
Roth G., 74
RPR, 172
Russian Communist Party (PCUS), 84, 165, 251

SA, 156, 158
Schmid C., 256
Schumacher K., 117, 254
Schumpeter J., 40
Selznick P., 53
Shackleton D., 91
Social Democratic Federation, 89
Social Democratic Workers' Party (SDAP), 70–1
Soustelle J., 149–50, 153, 160
Spofforth M., 132
SS, 157
Stalin J., 79, 81, 83, 146
Steel-Maitland, 134–5, 250
sub-coalitions, 38–9
sub-unit size, 195–9
succession and articulation of ends, 15–17, 243–6
Svaasand L., 51

Tarrow S., 152
territorial diffusion, 50–1
territorial penetration, 50–1
Thatcher M., 251
Thorez M., 37, 79–81
Tillet B., 91
Togliatti P., 37, 80, 82, 252
Trade Union Congress (TUC), 59, 88–9, 92
Tucker R., 52
Turati F., 102, 104–5, 107, 126, 129, 145, 169, 171, 173, 176, 178

unequal exchange, 22–5, 30–2, 177–9
Union for the New Republic, 147–60, 167–8

Valliant E., 95

Verzuiling, 219
Veyssières J., 149
Vollmar G., 74, 216
Von Doorn J., 187
Von Schweitzer J. B., 71

Weber M., xi, xii, xiii, 17, 37, 40, 52, 66, 143–45, 147, 161, 221–5, 232, 235, 264, 267

Wehner H., 256
West German Communist Party (KDP), 190
World War I, 103, 107
World War II, 103, 107

Zentrum, 115, 123
zones of uncertainty, 33–6